The Transformation of Work in Welfare State Organizations

How has New Public Management influenced social policy reform in different developed welfare states? New managerialism is conceptualized as a paradigm, which not only shapes the decision-making process in bureaucratic organizations but also affects the practice of individuals (citizens).

Public administrations have been expected to transform from traditional bureaucratic organizations into modern managerial service providers by adopting a business model that requires the efficient and effective use of resources. The introduction of managerial practices, controlling and accounting systems, management by objectives, computerization, service orientation, increased outsourcing, competitive structures and decentralized responsibility are typical of efforts to increase efficiency. These developments have been accompanied by the abolition of civil service systems and fewer secure jobs in public administrations.

This book provides a sociological understanding of how public administrations deal with this transformation, how people's role as public servants is affected, and what kind of strategies emerge either to meet these new organizational requirements or to circumvent them. It shows how hybrid arrangements of public services are created between the public and the private sphere that lead to conflicts of interest between private strategies and public tasks as well as to increasingly homogeneous social welfare provision across Europe.

Frank Sowa is a Professor of sociology at University of Applied Sciences Georg Simon Ohm in Nuremberg, Germany. He received his PhD degree from the University Erlangen-Nuremberg and worked as senior researcher at the Institute for Employment Research (IAB). He is a sociologist specialized in qualitative and ethnographic methods. His past experiences have drawn his interest in organizational ethnography of public employment services, trends of globalisation of social policy, New Public Management as well as identity politics of the Greenlandic Inuit.

Ronald Staples is a post-doctoral researcher at the Institute of Sociology at the University of Erlangen-Nuremberg, Germany. Before taking up his studies of Sociology and Theatre- and Mediastudies he was a professional theatre actor. Main research focus is on Organizations, Bureaucracy, Innovation and Digitization. He published recently a book on the relationship of Innovation and Organisations: "Doing Innovation" (2017), Springer VS and coedited a volume dealing with interaction and digitization: "Leib und Netz" (2018), Springer VS.

Stefan Zapfel studied sociology and political sciences at the University of Vienna. He is a researcher and assistant managing director at the Institute for Empirical Sociology at the University of Erlangen-Nuremberg. His work especially focuses on labour market research, social security systems, vocational rehabilitation, and inclusion of people with disabilities.

The Transformation of Work in Welfare State Organizations

New Public Management and the Institutional Diffusion of Ideas

Edited by Frank Sowa, Ronald Staples and Stefan Zapfel

LONDON AND NEW YORK

First published 2018
by Routledge
2 Park Square, Milton Park, Abingdon, Oxon OX14 4RN

and by Routledge
711 Third Avenue, New York, NY 10017

Routledge is an imprint of the Taylor & Francis Group, an informa business

© 2018 selection and editorial matter, Frank Sowa, Ronald Staples and Stefan Zapfel; individual chapters, the contributors

The right of Frank Sowa, Ronald Staples and Stefan Zapfel to be identified as the authors of the editorial material, and of the authors for their individual chapters, has been asserted in accordance with sections 77 and 78 of the Copyright, Designs and Patents Act 1988.

All rights reserved. No part of this book may be reprinted or reproduced or utilised in any form or by any electronic, mechanical, or other means, now known or hereafter invented, including photocopying and recording, or in any information storage or retrieval system, without permission in writing from the publishers.

Trademark notice: Product or corporate names may be trademarks or registered trademarks, and are used only for identification and explanation without intent to infringe.

British Library Cataloguing in Publication Data
A catalogue record for this book is available from the British Library

Library of Congress Cataloging in Publication Data
A catalog record for this book has been requested

ISBN: 978-1-138-08456-8 (hbk)
ISBN: 978-1-315-11174-2 (ebk)

Typeset in Bembo
by codeMantra

Contents

List of figures   vii
List of tables   ix
List of contributors   xi
Acknowledgements   xv

Introduction: The transformation of work in welfare state organisations   1
FRANK SOWA, RONALD STAPLES AND STEFAN ZAPFEL

1 Managerial control of public sector IT professionals via IT systems   13
CLIVE TRUSSON

2 Performance targets as negotiation devices – accounting management in French job centres   35
JEAN-MARIE PILLON

3 Labour market experts and their professional practices technologies of self-control of job placement professionals   54
FRANK SOWA AND RONALD STAPLES

4 Managerial doctors: Professionalism, managerialism and health reforms in Portugal   74
HELENA SERRA

5 Accountability requirements for social work professionals: Ensuring the quality of discretionary practice   92
JORUNN THERESIA JESSEN

6 Critical perspectives on accounting, audit and accountability in public services: a study of performance management in UK local museums 107
WHYEDA GILL-McLURE

7 Doing meaning in work under conditions of new public management? Findings from the medical care sector and social work 128
MASCHA WILL-ZOCHOLL AND FRIEDERICKE HARDERING

8 Marketing without moralising: Service orientation and employer relations in the Swiss disability insurance 147
EVA NADAI

9 Collective mobilization among welfare professionals in Sweden – the politicisation of caring 164
ANNA RYAN BENGTSSON

10 Street level bureaucracy under pressure: Job insecurity, business logic and challenging users 182
MICOL BRONZINI AND DIEGO COLETTO

11 New managerialism as an organisational form of neoliberalism 203
KATHLEEN LYNCH AND BERNIE GRUMMELL

12 Framing work injury/sickness in a changing welfare state – naming and blaming 223
ANTOINETTE HETZLER

13 Comply or defy? Managing the inclusion of disabled people in the Netherlands 242
LIESKE VAN DER TORRE AND MENNO FENGER

Index 259

List of figures

1.1	ICT-enabled 'Managed Professionalism' Model for Public Sector IT professionals	25
1.2	Application of ICT-enabled 'Managed Professionalism' Model to study of mobile policing (Lindsay et al. (2014))	29
1.3	Application of ICT-enabled 'Managed Professionalism' Model to studies of nursing (Russell, 2012; Petrakaki & Kornelakis, 2016)	30
5.1	Mechanisms to improve the discretionary decision-making of social work professionals. ($N = 626$.) Mean	102
6.1	Scotcity, two tier structure 1975–1996	116
6.2	Scotcity East and West museum districts 2010–present	120
13.1	The 'work ladder' for disabled people	246

List of tables

1.1	Descriptions of the three Midshire County Council teams visited	17
1.2	Data collected at the three Midshire County Council teams visited	18
5.1	Directions and mechanisms of accountability	96
5.2	The experiences of managerial and occupational control ($N = 620-626$). Per cent	101
6.1	Performance management technologies	113
6.2	Museum staffing pre and post restructure 1996–2014	121
12.1	Population percentages 2012–2015: Age, sick leave and gender	228
12.2	Naming others as involved in the process. Percentages for the year 2012 and 2015	232
13.1	Four implementation modalities of the SWA for municipalities	245
13.2	Explanation of compliance and defiance	251
13.3	Impact of the ideational changes and managerial changes	255

List of contributors

Anna Ryan Bengtsson is a PhD candidate at the Department of Social Work, Gothenburg University, Sweden. With a background in public policy and administration, her interest lies on welfare political changes and effects of New Public Management. Her current research is focused on collective mobilisation among welfare professional groups involved with care work in Sweden.

Micol Bronzini is Assistant Professor of economic sociology at the Department of Economics and Social Sciences, Università Politecnica delle Marche, Italy. She received her PhD degree from the University of Brescia (Italy) and worked as a post-doc researcher at the Università Politecnica delle Marche. She is an economic sociologist specialized in qualitative methods. Her main interests are: welfare policies, in particular healthcare and housing policies, the sociology of organizations.

Diego Coletto is Associate Professor of economic sociology at the Department of Sociology and Social Research, University of Milano-Bicocca, Milan, Italy. He received his PhD degree from the University of Brescia, Italy, and worked as a post-doc researcher at the University of Milano and as an assistant professor at the University of Milano-Bicocca. He is an economic sociologist specialised in qualitative and ethnographic methods. His main interests are: the informal economy, street-level bureaucracy, urban ethnography and employment relations.

Menno Fenger is endowed Professor 'Governance of modern welfare states' at Erasmus University Rotterdam, the Netherlands. He obtained his PhD at Twente University. His research focuses on processes of long-term policy change in the welfare state. He is also co-dean at the Netherlands School of Public Administration (NSOB).

Whyeda Gill-McLure is Senior Lecturer in Employment Relations at the University of Wolverhampton, UK. Her research focuses on the political economy of public service and public administration reform and its impact on employment relations (UK, Europe, US). She is on the editorial board of Capital & Class.

Bernie Grummell is a Senior Lecturer in the Departments of Education and Adult & Community Education, Maynooth University, Ireland, in the areas of education and social justice, research methods, and transformative community development. She previously worked with the School of Sociology and the Equality Studies Centre in University College Dublin. She is currently a member of the Social Science research Subcommittee in Maynooth University, as well as actively engaging in education, community and civil society groups. Her research explores the complex landscape, processes and experiences of equality and transformation across different sectors of education and society.

Friedericke Hardering is a post-doctoral researcher at the Institute of Sociology at Goethe-University Frankfurt, Germany. She received her doctorate at the RWTH Aachen. Since 2014, she leads the research project "Societal conceptions about what makes work meaningful and individuals' experiences of meaningfulness at work" that is funded by the German Research Foundation (DFG). Her fields of research are Sociology of Work, Economic Sociology and Sociology of Organisations. Her work especially focuses on meaningful work, identity work, the future of work, entrepreneurship and qualitative analysis.

Antoinette Hetzler is Professor of sociology with emphasis on social policy at Lund University, Sweden. She received her PhD degree from the University of California, Santa Barbara and has been assistant professor at New York University before accepting a position as associate professor at the Department of the Sociology of Law, Lund University. She is a visiting fellow 2017, at the Weatherhead Center, Harvard University. Her research interests are the changing welfare state, transformation of work in the public sector, neoinstitutionalism and policy implementation.

Jorunn Theresia Jessen is a Senior Researcher at NOVA – Norwegian Social Research, Oslo Metropolitan University, Norway. She is a sociologist with a PhD in Social Work and Health Science. Her main areas of research is social policy, public welfare services and the studies of organisations and professions.

Kathleen Lynch is the UCD Professor of Equality Studies, an Irish Research Council Advanced Research Scholar for 2014–2017. She is a founder of the Equality Studies Centre and the School of Social Justice in UCD, and is currently a member of the UCD School of Education. An academic and an activist, she is guided by the belief that the purpose of scholarship and research is not just to understand the world but to change it for the good of all humanity. She has published and campaigned widely on equality issues, both nationally and internationally.

Eva Nadai is Sociologist and Professor at the School of Social Work of the University of Applied Sciences Northwestern Switzerland. Her mostly ethnographic research focuses social policy "on the ground", i.e. how local practices in street-level bureaucracies transform policy programmes and regulations in the field of unemployment and welfare. She is currently directing a research project, which analyses the constitution of the employability of unskilled workers as a practical accomplishment between employers, labour market intermediaries and workers/jobseekers.

Jean-Marie Pillon is Lecturer in sociology at Paris-Dauphine University, France. He received his PhD degree from Nanterre University. His work focuses on quantification devices in public services, new public management programs, and on the transformation of work in street level bureaucracies. His major fieldwork dealt with a sociology of unemployment policies and its steering in the French job centre (Pôle emploi).

Helena Serra is Associated Professor of Sociology at NOVA School of Social Sciences and Humanities, Universidade NOVA de Lisboa, Portugal. She has published on healthcare research, organisations and professions and given several keynote presentations at international conferences. She was member of the ESA Executive Committee until August 2017 and is President of the ISA RC52 'Sociology of Professional Groups'.

Frank Sowa is professor of sociology at University of Applied Sciences Georg Simon Ohm in Nuremberg, Germany. He received his PhD degree from the University Erlangen-Nuremberg and worked as senior researcher at the Institute for Employment Research (IAB). He is a sociologist specialized in qualitative and ethnographic methods. His past experiences have drawn his interest in organizational ethnography of public employment services, trends of globalisation of social policy, New Public Management as well as identity politics of the Greenlandic Inuit.

Ronald Staples is post-doctoral researcher at the Institute of Sociology at the University of Erlangen-Nuremberg, Germany. Before taking up his studies of Sociology and Theatre- and Mediastudies he was a professional theatre actor. Main research focus is on Organisations, Bureaucracy, Innovation and Digitisation.

Clive Trusson is Lecturer in Human Resource Management and Organisational Behaviour at the School of Business and Economics, Loughborough University, UK. After a career working in the IT profession (for the UK Government and large companies), he studied for a PhD degree at Loughborough. His research interests are broadly in the areas of IT work, knowledge work and service work.

Lieske van der Torre is Assistant Professor at the Utrecht School of Governance (USG), the Netherlands. She received her PhD from the Erasmus University Rotterdam. Her dissertation discussed the strategies and results of sheltered work companies. Her current research focuses on successful local governance.

Mascha Will-Zocholl is an Assistant Professor of social sciences at University of Applied Sciences, Hessian University of Police and Administration (HfPV) in Wiesbaden, Germany. She got her doctoral degree from Technische Universität Darmstadt and worked as a Post-Doc at the Goethe-University Frankfurt and as a temporary professor at University of Applied Sciences, Darmstadt. With a Sociology background, she focusses on relations between work, technology and organisation. Her main areas of research are: digitisation in the world of work, trust and cooperation and social perceptions of meaningful work, with special emphasis on engineering, social and public administration work.

Stefan Zapfel studied sociology and political sciences at the University of Vienna, Austria. He is a researcher and assistant managing director at the Institute for Empirical Sociology at the University of Erlangen-Nuremberg, Germany. His work especially focuses on labour market research, social security systems, vocational rehabilitation, and inclusion of people with disabilities.

Acknowledgements

First, the editors would like to thank our authors, who made these comprehensive contributions and therefore the book itself possible. We also owe Routledge debt of gratitude for accepting our proposal and finally publishing the book. They accompanied the whole publication process straightforwardly and professionally. Finally, we would like to thank especially our research assistant Lea Lewitzki, who carefully read the whole manuscript and kept an eye on the consistency of formatting.

Introduction

The transformation of work in welfare state organisations

Frank Sowa, Ronald Staples and Stefan Zapfel

New frame conditions in welfare state organisations[1]

Over the past two decades, welfare state organisations in western industrialised countries have been restructured extensively. The responsibility for this lay not least with the change in the labour markets, which became increasingly dynamic. At the end of the 20th century, the advanced welfare states in Europe were confronted with an increased unemployment rate, which has failed to achieve the ideal of full employment ever since.[2] Politically speaking, it was not only economic and structural changes resulting in financing shortages in different socio-political service types that were deemed responsible (Lessenich, 2012), but also particularly deficiencies in the adjustment of certain players to the labour markets – primarily employees and welfare state institutions (Wren, 2001; Foucault, 2008). In the course of this, welfare state organisations, their organisational practices and the direction commonly taken by social policy until the 1980s or 1990s increasingly ended in the crosshairs of criticism that was primarily inspired by neo-liberal thinking (Urban, 1995; Butterwegge, 1999; Jessop, 2002; Offe, 2008). Through the Europeanisation of social and labour market policy (Weishaupt & Lack, 2011) and the "diffusion of ideas" (Kocyba, 2004; Crouch, 2004; Sahlin-Andersson, 2001), which was not least sparked by the convergence of European social democracy with liberal ideas regarding the economy, a widespread reform in the western industrial states took place, whose approaches were largely aligned (Mohr, 2008). Thus, the welfare structures of welfare states that had traditionally diverged began to converge step-by-step (Esping-Andersen, 1990).

The criticism of the welfare state and its organisational sections gradually led to the privatisation and commercialisation of public duties (Crouch, 2004; Newman & Clarke, 2009), whereby the contact between citizens and the authorities was designed in a way that was both more personal and more individualised (Boltanski & Ciapello, 2005). As the political effect of this criticism gradually grew, it reduced the circle of people entitled to welfare benefits. This rendered the drawing of benefits more conditional (Opielka,

2008; Bäcker et al., 2010), contributed to a drop in the level of benefits (Gilbert, 2005) and required particularly of the unemployed that they put in their own effort, take responsibility for themselves and be prepared to take the initiative to a greater degree (Olk, 2000; Lessenich, 2013). It increasingly transformed those receiving welfare benefits (Castel, 2011) into co-producers of socio-political pension and support benefits (Osborne et al., 2010), thereby ensuring a fundamentally new direction in both national social policy and the administrative organisations concerned with it (Sowa & Zapfel, 2015). This resulted in the forming of new institutions and new contextual conditions that (initially) created new realities and required action on the polity level (Lessenich, 2012).

This left its mark on the operational structures of public administrative departments, which were to be organised so that they were more effective and efficient, following the model of private enterprises. Furthermore, it was intended to include actors in their operations and strategies that had been outside of the public sector up to that point (Crouch, 2004; Nassehi, 2014). Thus, hybrid organisational arrangements emerged between the public and private sectors concerning the provision of welfare state benefits, under the buzz words "New Public Management" (NPM) (Newman & Clarke, 2009). Conflicts of interest between the two sectors that accompanied this were accepted, some of them consciously, some as side effects (Greve & Hodge, 2010).

The goal of NPM is to transform the public administrative departments of traditional, bureaucratic organisations into modern service companies (Sowa & Staples, 2016). However, they still remain public authorities with corresponding duties and bureaucratic structures, but now have to follow economic, management-based operational patterns, use their resources effectively and efficiently, counteract (foreseeable) undesirable developments and, keeping up with the neo-liberal telos of constant progress, do better in reaching welfare state target dimensions (Rose, 1996; Osborne, 2010). The introduction of management techniques from the private sector, the application of systematic controlling, the support of digital registration systems, results-orientated operations (Ruiner & Wilkesmann, 2016), forced outsourcing, the implementation of synthetic competitive structures (Crouch, 2011) and the decentralisation of administrative organisations (Jessop, 1992, 2002) are some of the essential characteristics of this welfare state transformation (Reichard & Röber, 2001).

This process was accompanied by the diversification of atypical employment (not only) within the scope of welfare state organizations and by an increase in employment contracts that were less protected and less protective. The fact of the public sector becoming precarious (Crouch, 2011) became a phenomenon that was no longer unusual or limited to low-qualified activities. As a result of this, the relationship changed between the staff employed in public administrative departments, between them and their work and between them and the clients they supervised. As with possible manifestations of "secondary adjustments" (Goffman, 1961) as a reaction of the operative staff to conflicting behaviour guidelines, there have been few repercussions to speak of in the socio-scientific literature with regard to the relationship of NPM and its concrete implementation at the social micro-level. This includes unintentional consequences of actions and possible conflicts concerning targets and actions arising from the discrepancy between new management specifications and the supervision and work requirements occurring in the interaction with the citizens. To date, organisational aspects connected to historically divergent welfare regimes have also only been highlighted at best rudimentarily from a socio-scientific perspective. So far, the only findings that exist are of neo-institutionalist origin, mostly showing isomorphisms from the perspective of organisational theory (Meyer & Rowan, 1977). In this respect, regarding institutionalised welfare states, similar NPM strategies can be identified in different welfare states that are to be interpreted as (political) legitimation strategies in the dominant neo-liberal discourse. These also lead to window-dressing and decoupling phenomena in the well-known fashion of classical organisational theory. Here, the introduction of target and management systems in bureaucratic welfare organisations in order to deal with resources more effectively and efficiently can be given as an example.

It is unquestionable that the governing techniques that can be subsumed under NPM or, in the more recent debate, as New Governance, have changed the actions of the welfare state, both at the level of political decisions (who is entitled to what) and at the administrative level. In the administrative departments, the different kinds of discourse intersect and become concrete in the administrative files and in the interactions between the members of the administration and the citizens asking for benefits. The relationships between the administrative departments as organisations, their members and their environment (the citizens) change due to the NPM discourse. With the instruments of indirect management, the administrative organisations gain different ways to access their positions and no longer have to rely on their "Beamtenethos", the ethos of the public servant (Weber, 1978; Hood, 2005). However, this characterised the culture of these organisations for a long time and cannot simply be exchanged for an ethos characterised by competitive relationships. For the members, this means a new, more dynamic relationship between the post they began with and possible hopes of promotion, as other assessment criteria are established for fulfilling duties – although the promotion sequences are still characterised by appreciation rather than admiration (Voswinkel, 2011). The relationships between citizens and members of the administrative department also change visibly, which becomes evident when citizens are addressed as customers. For the citizens, administrative departments become visibly more efficient, and echoes of organisational elements from the private – service – sector can be found. However, the price for this is that citizens are explicitly required to participate in the service production themselves and to be 'active' indicating a trend towards recommodification (Sowa, Reims & Theuer, 2015). In welfare state institutions, these different expectations, which are produced by means of the structural reforms driven by NPM, are shown in diverse, often contradictory ways in practice. However, this ambivalent diversity cannot be explained sufficiently by classical approaches, such as a decoupling from the steering strategies of an organisation and its concrete activities. This would systematically underestimate the fact that the members of administrative welfare state organisations mostly endeavour to structure their activities in a way that is congruent with the goals of the organisation, which entails a considerable effort spent on sensemaking practices (Weick, Sutcliffe & Obstfeld, 2005).

Perspectives of this edited volume

What has been lacking so far, however, are empirical analyses that correlate the four aspects of social policy, welfare state authorities, their members and citizens/clients with each other and attempt to comprehend the interdependencies between these relationships and the irritations accompanying the implementation of new methodologies and are bound to arise. In this edited volume, we wish to contribute to filling in some of the above-mentioned gaps in the body of knowledge. For this purpose, we have compiled several examples of the outlined transformation process of welfare state organisations in different European countries. A total of 13 articles from eight countries (Germany, Ireland, France, Italy, Portugal, Switzerland, Sweden and The Netherlands) treat the subject matter from different perspectives and, in this context, deal with various state organisations active in different public domains.

The volume consists of three parts: *Accountability and Control* (Part I), *Acting and Coping Strategies* (Part II) and *Organizational Culture and Daily Working Life* (Part III). The first part, *Accountability and Control*, presents studies concerned with the precarious relationship of 'what is attributable' and its instrumentalisation for disciplinary purposes. The indirect management of organisations using parameters is an effective strategy implemented by companies to switch from hierarchical to results management without ultimately handing over the controls. In authorities, these management practices pose serious challenges to those involved: Which parameters can be used to provide direction if the driving refinancing problem of companies has been at least partly suspended in this case? How can degrees of freedom be guaranteed both at the organisational level and for the members affected in order to be able to integrate variation in the organisation?

Parameter management has consequences for the actions of the members of the authorities. Traditional action strategies are challenged by the changed management premises and thus put pressure on the relationships between the organisation and its members and their clients. How these new operational frictions are dealt with is the subject of the second part, *Acting and Coping Strategies*. It is not only the members of the organisation who, if the goals of the organisation have changed, for example, develop operational variations in order to be able to pursue tasks that are closer to the ethos of the public servant (Weber, 1978), or the professional ethos. The organisation itself must also vary its decision programmes to be able to address new goals.

If the structure of organisations changes – the way it refers to goals to be met and the way decisions should be met – it is obvious that the culture of the respective organisation and the informal cooperation (or social relationships) are exposed to a certain pressure to adapt. This describes phenomena that are already well established in the sociological debate pertaining to labour, with buzz words like "work intensification" and "blurring of boundaries" regarding work being used. However, so far they have not been subject to much attention in the context of welfare state organisations. The third part, *Organizational Culture and Daily Working Life*, deals with the state of such problems and places an even stronger focus on the inside perspective of work in welfare state settings.

On the individual articles

Six articles are collected in the first part, *Accountability and Control*: in his essay entitled *Managerial Control of IT Professionals via IT Systems*, Clive Trusson addresses the implementation of information technology for controlling purposes in British public sector administrative establishments according to a professional-commercial model. He primarily pays attention to the reduction of opportunities for gaining autonomy in operating and making decisions in daily working life in the public sector. The author connects the restriction of the space for autonomy first and foremost with rationalised operational processes.

In the second article, entitled *Performance Targets as Negotiation Devices – Accounting Management in French Job Centres*, following Max Weber (1978), Jean-Marie Pillon understands NPM as the result of sustained modernisation and rationalisation processes in bureaucratic operations. Using the example of the French public job centres, he shows effects of the organisational readjustment in terms of NPM on the division of labour in the administrative organisation (here, between career advice, job placement and controlling), and discusses attempts by the operative staff to elude complete external control in order to maintain autonomous room for manoeuvre.

The article *Labour Market Experts and their Professional Practices: Technologies of Self-Control of Job Placement Professionals* by Frank Sowa and Ronald Staples takes a look at the transformation of German employment agencies, which were traditionally bureaucratic in nature, into service-orientated institutions aimed at increasing efficiency and effectiveness. The authors explain the measures for restructuring the organisational structures and administrative processes connected to this process (including introduction of controlling, management by objectives, computer-supported placement activities, service orientation, customer segmentation, action programmes) and then present essential consequences for the activities and daily working life in the German employment agencies.

With Helena Serras' chapter, the view shifts to a very precarious part of modern welfare states, the Health Care system. Serra focusses on: *Managerial Doctors: Professionalism, Managerialism and Health Reforms in Portugal*. The impact of neo-liberal and NPM health reforms on medical profession has also undergone comprehensive changes. The relationship between professionalism and managerialism indicates new emergent configurations of hybrid professionals and mixed forms of governance in health care. Although the underlying reasons are similar across western countries, concerning the Portuguese case the outcomes diverge, particularly due the influence of the medical profession on shaping professional practices and regulatory mechanisms. In Portugal, doctors' influence on state regulation seems to counter the dynamics that have been described in sociology of professions and organisations, which point out the increasing criticism of medical autonomy, the growing managerial control over medical authority and the state regulation of medical procedures. Doctors have succeeded in developing strategies to protect their professional position in the workplace, by reconfiguring their jurisdictions and influencing organisational structures and decision-making processes. The control of technologies along with the control of management instruments is an example of the intersection between state and medical regulation. The domination of a technology is important insofar as it boosts the self-regulation mechanisms of the profession whilst also allowing the organisation to attract investment that brings greater financial sustainability. From the notion of 'medical technocracies' and by following the Portuguese case, this chapter aims to analyse the way medical profession interpret and responds to the external pressures and managerial values imposed by state policies. The purpose is to provide a comprehensive explanation of how NPM health reforms impact on micro-level relationships on health organisations, namely the interplaying of doctors with other health professions, managers and patients.

Social work professionals have also been subject to NPM-driven reforms of the organization and regulation of their work, and this is the topic Jorunn Theresia Jessen's paper *Accountability requirements for social work professionals* is concerned with. Working in the frontline of public welfare services, social workers are entitled to make independent and discretionary decisions when determining eligibility claims, assessing needs and work abilities. In their role as institutional agents, the welfare professionals have to define, interpret and fulfil the ambitions of government policies and welfare reforms (Scott, 2008). However, the extent to which technical subordination has occurred in social work practice is much debated in terms of whether discretion still is part of the everyday decision-making (Harris & White, 2009). This chapter investigates how social work professionals experience and adapt to the new managerial regimes and accountability requirements in the Norwegian social services. A main issue is to assess the impact of external and internal mechanisms of accountability, imposed to regulate discretionary practice.

The contribution of Whyeda Gill-McLure concludes the first part. She sheds a light on a systematically overseen part of public services: *Key Challenges in the Complex Setting of Public Services: A case study of performance management in Local Museums*. Usually, museums do not get attention for the way they are managing their personnel. However, in the context of change of public services, museums are also affected by it. Although museums may not be typical welfare state organizations, they are conforming to the institutional function of public service. In this case the service is a cultural one. Performance management has long been a key challenge in public services with public servants traditionally keen to influence debate in terms of professional accountability and public service values. Public service reform and austerity have put performance management centre-stage with governments steering policy in terms of managerial values demanding more for less. Negative staff and service impacts have been highly publicised. This paper examines this complex and contested terrain, identifying critical dimensions of clumsy versus effective interpretations of performance management in the UK and Europe. It presents case study evidence that demonstrates the negative staff impacts of performance management on museum professionals.

The second part of this edited volume – *Acting and Coping Strategies* – starts with *Doing Meaning in Bureaucratic Organisations? Findings from the Public Service Sector* by Mascha Will-Zocholl and Friedericke Hardering. The authors deal with experiences of working in the continuum of sensemaking and alienation in the public sector against the background of changing organisational contexts. Their empirical material refers to employment relationships in German university clinics on the one hand, and different areas of application pertaining to social work on the other. Their focus lies on the influence of new developments in modern bureaucratic organisations, such as informatisation, commercialisation and the predominant implementation of project-related work.

In her paper entitled *From Client to Transaction Object. The Modernisation of Disability Insurance Administration and the Marketisation of the Personnel-Client Relation*, Eva Nadai outlines the effects of NPM on the interactive relationship between placement staff and clients. In the Swiss employment agency for people with disabilities, for example, NPM becomes concretised in the form of an increased customer and service orientation, the use of private sector marketing techniques, the introduction of fast-track decision processes and new teams for maintaining contacts with potential employers.

In the article, *Collective mobilization among welfare professionals in Sweden – the politicisation of caring*, Anna Ryan Bengtsson writes about collective mobilisation of voice in Sweden. Independently of the union to which they belong, different occupational groups protest in open letters or social media contributions against the deteriorating working conditions and the accompanying restriction of working in a professional manner. Departing from a feminist theoretical lens she draws attention to the historically gendered relations of power involved with care work and how these take new forms in the NPM work organisation. She suggests that this mobilisation needs to be understood as a politicisation of care. In this sense, to mobilise a collective voice serves to challenge NPM effects on professional groups, involving both work intensification and processes of deprofessionalisation. Furthermore, that this also needs to be understood as a way to collectively negotiate or safeguard a professional knowledge base that involves empathy and a caring commitment for patients or clients.

The third and final part of this volume, *Organisational Culture and Daily Routine*, compiles five more articles from Italy, Ireland, France and Sweden. The contributions show how important the relationship between organisational culture and everyday work is, if one wants to analyse organisational dynamics. In their paper entitled *Street-Level Bureaucracy under Pressure: Job Insecurity, Business Logic and Challenging Users*, Micol Bronzini and Diego Coletto deal with the change in the quality of the relationship between clients and Italian administrative staff that was affected by the introduction of NPM. They also elaborate on the changed self-image of the clients approaching the public institutions. Here, they use research material from different institutions in different scopes of duties and fields of activity of the public authorities (social work, health care, education, public security, housing and employment centres).

In their chapter *New Managerialism as the Organisational Form of Neoliberalism*, Kathleen Lynch and Bernie Grummel concern themselves with the influence of neo-liberal economic and welfare policy on the Irish education system. New Managerialism spans the account of a strategic change, the restructuring of public organisations with regard to establishing new values and practices and to introducing control mechanisms based on measurement and calculation. Consequent effects regarding gender inequalities are also considered in this context.

The central theme of the article *Framing Injury in a Changing Welfare State – Blaming and Naming* by Antoinette Hetzler is how NPM strategies change work of primary school teachers in Sweden. She accesses this highly contested field by analysing illness accounts. Changes at the Macro level, how compulsory education shall be organised following NPM principles, effects the professional identity of concrete teachers. With this original approach, Antoinette shows how professional identity, health and organisational restructuring are linked together. Her analysis culminates in the conclusion that these accounts tell a story of 'strategic violence' as an unintended effect of the changed management of Swedish school system.

Finally, the article *Comply or defy? Managing the inclusion of disabled people in the Netherlands* by Lieske van der Torre and Menno Fenger deals with the labour market activation of the disabled. The change in socio-political orientation within the EU has huge consequences for sheltered work companies – their management and their strategies – as these are now measured by the success with which disabled people are integrated. The paper offer insights into how work with and for disabled people is framed by the modern welfare state and what kind of effects the different welfare state traditions show dealing with these clients.

According to the empirical findings depicted and discussed in this volume, the assumption imposes on the observer that the NPM regime had a very strong impact on the form of welfare state organisations. It is widely accepted as state of the art management technique, but its success may also be an effect of normative isomorphism as Meyer and Rowan called it in their seminal paper on institutional isomorphisms (Meyer & Rowan, 1977). Undisputedly, the management of welfare state organisations and their clients has changed massively since the first occurrence of NPM techniques (Aucoin, 1990). However, and this may be the original contribution of this volume to the discourse on the change of the welfare state and its organisations, it is not worn out with it. Bureaucratic public services and the practices within and in contact with their clients is much richer than the tight corset of NPM would suppose. The key to further research on the change of public service organisations seems to lie in reframing the relations between organisational framework and the practices of their members as dynamic.

Notes

1 The idea of editing a book on transforming welfare state organizations arose during the 12th Annual Conference ESPAnet in 2014 in Oslo (Norway) and the Third ISA Forum of Sociology in 2016 in Vienna (Austria). The editors hosted two sessions dealing with the differences and similarities of changes in welfare state organisations. We agreed that an empirical approach to this phenomenon would have the potential to make a fruitful contribution rather than a theoretical one. The reader, working her way through the different studies assembled here, will, hopefully, recognise not only how tightly organisational structures, welfare state regimes and practices are knit together, but at the same time also how these kinds of social pattern enable specific degrees of freedom. Finally, the book is a compelling compilation of how members and clients of welfare state organisations are dealing with the varying demands of welfare regimes in modern Europe.
2 Full employment does not assume the absence of unemployment. Thus, phases in which it is unavoidable for unemployed persons not to pursue an occupation although they are available to the labour market in principle (for instance, during the transition from the education and training system into an occupation, or for brief periods when changing jobs) are treated as natural, or frictional unemployment, which is not evaluated to the detriment of the target of full employment. Here, there is room for interpretation. Not least depending on the economic situation as a whole, the definition of which unemployment rate still corresponds to full employment is variable.

References

Aucoin, P. (1990): Administrative Reform in Public Management: Paradigms, Principles, Paradoxes and Pendulums, *Governance* 3: 115–137.

Bäcker, G., Naegele, G., Bispinck, R., Hofemann, K., Neubauer, J. (2010): *Sozialpolitik und soziale Lage in Deutschland. Band 1: Grundlagen, Arbeit*, Einkommen und Finanzierung, Wiesbaden: VS-Verlag.

Boltanski, L., Ciapello, È. (2005): *The New Spirit of Capitalism*, London and New York: Verso.

Butterwegge, C. (1999): Neoliberalismus, Globalisierung und Sozialpolitik: Wohlfahrtsstaat im Standortwettbewerb? in: Butterwegge, C., Kutscha, M., Berghahn, S. (eds.): *Herrschaft des Marktes – Abschied vom Staat? Folgen neoliberaler Modernisierung für Gesellschaft, Recht und Politik*, 26–44, Baden-Baden: Nomos.

Castel, R. (2011): *Die Krise der Arbeit. Neue Unsicherheiten und die Zukunft des Individuums*, Hamburg: HIS.

Crouch, C. (2004): *Post-Democracy*, Cambridge: Polity Press.

Crouch, C. (2011): *The Strange Non-Death of Neoliberalism*, Cambridge: Polity Press.

Esping-Andersen, G. (1990): *The Three Worlds of Welfare Capitalism*, Princeton: Princeton University Press.

Foucault, M. (2008): *The Birth of Biopolitics: Lectures at the Collège de France, 1978–1979 (Lectures at the College de France)*, New York: Palgrave Macmillan.

Gilbert, N. (2005): The "Enabeling State?" From Public to Private Responsibility for Social Protection: Pathways and Pitfalls. OECD Social, Employment and Migration Working Papers 26.

Goffman, E. (1961): *Asylums: Essays on the Social Situation of Mental Patients and Other Inmates*, New York: Anchor and Doubleday.

Greve, C., Hodge, G. (2010): Public-Private Partnerships and Public Governance Challenges, in: Osborne, S.P. (ed.): *The New Public Governance? Emerging Perspectives on the Theory and Practice of Public Governance*, 149–162, Abingdon: Routledge.

Harris, J., White, V. (2009): *Modernising Social Work: Critical Considerations*, Bristol: The Policy Press.

Hood, C. (2005). The Idea of Joined-Up Government: A Historical Perspective, in: Bogdanor, V. (ed.): *Joined-Up Government*, 19–42, Oxford: Oxford University Press for the British Academy.

Jessop, B. (1992): Thatcherismus und die Neustrukturierung der Sozialpolitik – Neoliberalis-mus und die Zukunft des Wohlfahrtsstaates, in: *Zeitschrift für Sozialreform* 38: 709–734.

Jessop, B. (2002): *The Future of the Capitalist State*, Cambridge: Polity Press.

Kocyba, H. (2004): Aktivierung, in: Böckling, U., Krasmann, S., Lemke, T. (eds.): *Glossar der Gegenwart*, 17–22, Frankfurt a. M.: Suhrkampg.

Lessenich, S. (2012): *Theorien des Sozialstaats zur Einführung*, Hamburg: Junius.

Lessenich, S. (2013): *Die Neuerfindung des Sozialen. Der Sozialstaat im flexiblen Kapitalismus*, Bielefeld: transcript.

Meyer, J.W., Rowan, B. (1977): Institutionalized Organizations: Formal Structure as Myth and Ceremony, in: *American Journal of Sociology* 83: 340–363.

Mohr, K. (2008): Creeping Convergence – Wandel der Arbeitsmarktpolitik in Großbritannien und Deutschland, in: *Zeitschrift für Sozialreform* 54: 187–207.

Nassehi, A. (2014): Ökonomisierung? Politisierung? Differenzierung? Über das schwierige Verhältnis von Wirtschaft und Politik nebst einer Klärung der Frage, wer die Guten und wer die Bösen sind, in: Horster, D., Martinsen, F. (eds.): *Verbotene Liebe? Zum Verhältnis von Wirtschaft und Politik*, 36–52, Weilerswist: Velbrück Wissenschaft.

Newman, J., Clarke, J. (2009): *Publics, Politics and Power. Remaking the Public in Public Services*, Los Angeles: Sage Publications.

Offe, C. (2008): Some Contradictions of the Modern Welfare State, in: Pierson, C., Castles, F.G. (eds.): *The Welfare State Reader*, 66–75, Cambridge: Polity Press.

Olk, T. (2000): Weder Rund-um-Versorgung noch „pure" Eigenverantwortung. Aktivierende Strategien in der Politik für Familien, alte Menschen, Frauen, Kinder und Jugendliche, in: Mezger, E., West, K.-N. (eds.): *Aktivierender Sozialstaat und politisches Handeln*, 105–124, Marburg: Schüren.

Opielka, M. (2008): *Sozialpolitik. Grundlagen und vergleichende Perspektiven*, Reinbek bei Hamburg: Rowohlt.

Osborne, S.P. (2010): The (New) Public Governance: A Suitable Case of Treatment? in: Osborne, S.P. (ed.): *The New Public Governance? Emerging Perspectives on the Theory and Practice of Public Governance*, 1–16, Abingdon: Routledge.

Osborne; S.P., McLaughlin, K., Chew, C. (2010): Relationship Marketing, Relational Capital and the Governance of Public Services Delivery, in: Osborne, S.P. (ed.): *The New Public Governance? Emerging Perspectives on the Theory and Practice of Public Governance*, 185–199, Abingdon: Routledge.

Reichard, C., Röber, M. (2001): Konzept und Kritik des New Public Management, in: Schröter, E. (ed.): *Empirische Policy- und Verwaltungsforschung. Lokale, nationale und internationale Perspektiven*, 371–392, Opladen: Leske + Budrich.

Rose, N. (1996): *Inventing Our Selves: Psychology, Power, and Personhood*, Cambridge: Cambridge University Press.

Ruiner, C., Wilkesmann, M. (2016): *Arbeits- und Industriesoziologie*. Paderborn: Wilhelm Fink.

Sahlin-Andersson, K. (2001): National, International and Transnational Constructions of New Public Management, in: Christensen, T., Lægreid, P. (eds.): *New Public Management – The Transformation of Ideas and Practice*, 43–72, Aldershot: Ashgate.

Scott, W.R. (2008): Lords of the Dance: Professionals as Institutional Agents, *Organisational Studies* 39: 219–238.

Sowa, F., Reims, N., Theuer, S. (2015): Employer Orientation in the German Public Employment Service, in: *Critical Social Policy* 35: 492–511.

Sowa, F., Staples, R. (2016): Public Administration in the Era of Late Neo-Liberalism: Placement Professionals and the NPM Regime, in: Ferreira, A., Azevedo, G., Oliveira, J., Marques, R. (eds.): *Global Perspectives on Risk Management and Accounting in the Public Sector*, 25–48, Hershey: IGI Global.

Sowa, F., Zapfel, S. (2015): New Public Management und Aktivierung als globale Modelle der Weltpolitik? Zum Wandel der Arbeitsmarktpolitik in europäischen Wohlfahrtsstaaten, in: *Sozialer Fortschritt* 64: 47–54.

Urban, H.-J. (1995): Deregulierter Standort-Kapitalismus? Krise und Erneuerung des Sozial-staates, in: Schmitthenner, H. (ed.): *Der ‚schlanke' Staat. Zukunft des Sozialstaates – Sozialstaat der Zukunft*, 9–38, Hamburg: VSA-Verlag.

Voswinkel, S. (2011): Zum konzeptionellen Verhältnis von "Anerkennung" und "Interesse", in: *Arbeits- und Industriesoziologische Studien* 4: 45–58.

Weber, M. (1978): *Economy and Society*, Berkeley and Los Angeles: University of California Press.

Weick, K. E., Sutcliffe, K.M., Obstfeld, D. (2005): Organizing and the Process of Sensemaking, *Organization Science* 16: 409–421.

Weishaupt, J. T., Lack, K. (2011): The European Employment Strategy: Assessing the Status Quo, in: *German Policy Studies* 7: 9–44.

Wren, A. (2001): The Challenge of De-industrialisation. Divergent Ideological Responses to Welfare State Reform, in: Ebbinghaus, B., Manow, P. (eds.): *Comparing Welfare Capitalism. Social Policy and Political Economy in Europe, Japan and the USA*, 239–269, London and New York: Routledge.

Chapter 1

Managerial control of public sector IT professionals via IT systems

Clive Trusson

Introduction

This chapter explores the role played by IT systems comprising multiple information and communication technologies (ICTs) in placing public sector IT professionals under increasing pressures from managerialism (Fournier, 2000). It does this by reference to a case study of a group of public sector IT workers who might expect to have discretionary control over their work: a hallmark of professions. Specifically, it discusses how IT systems play a central role in managerial processes of rationalisation and control over the work of IT professionals.

In 1988, Shoshana Zuboff (1988, p. 388) wrote: "Technology makes the world a new place". As we now survey the 'world' of public sector work some three decades later, we can reflect upon how ICTs have slowly but surely made that 'world' a new place. Having first introduced ICTs in order to achieve efficiency benefits, the managements of local and national government bodies have become increasingly dependent upon ICTs for ensuring that public services are provided in the most cost-effective manner. This imposition of ICTs upon the public sector workforce has inevitably impacted upon how these workers, including professionals, perform their duties. Of specific interest is how forms of managerialism associated with the logic of the market have apparently been inscribed within these new ICT-enabled ways of working (e.g. Carvalho, 2014).

The profession that has been at the forefront of making this 'world' a new place are highly skilled IT technicians, now employed in large numbers by public sector organisations to oversee the IT systems that enable public services to be provided. It is these public sector professionals who are the subjects of this study. As reported on in this chapter, they have not been immune from the ICT-enabled managerialist agenda that aggrandizes a commercial-professional standpoint. The case study serves to illustrate how the technical-professional concerns (Spence & Carter, 2014) that have traditionally accorded status to these managed professionals are susceptible to being undermined by the ICTs imposed by managers. An argument is presented, supported by an inductively developed model, that a range of different ICTs are imposed upon IT professionals that in combination serve to undermine their professional status by operating as mechanisms that serve the managerial purposes of managers seeking to rationalise and control the practices of professionals.

The chapter straddles different streams of academic literature. First, in line with this volume, it relates to the literature on the transformation of public sector work through the diffusion of managerial ideas and practices of marketised service provision, commonly referred to as 'New Public Management'. Second, it relates to the literature that is interested in the relationship between managers and professionals (e.g. Abbott, 1988; Spence & Carter, 2014; Hodgson et al., 2015). Third, it relates to the literature concerning the impact of ICTs on professional work (e.g. Ford, 2015; Susskind & Susskind, 2015; Russell et al., 2015). At the interchange of these discussions are the issues of autonomy over decision-making being wrested from public sector employees with special knowledge and skills (Derber et al., 1990) and the managerial desire for the technological capture and control of such know-how (Reich, 2000; Ford, 2015).

In this chapter, these streams of enquiry are engaged in through a study of organisationally situated IT professionals as exemplars of 'managed professionals' (e.g. Noordegraaf, 2015; Russell et al., 2015) working in the public sector who to a great extent have their labour process imposed upon them. ICTs, typically selected by management, are an integral part of these predefined processes, both enabling them and structuring them with a managerial objective of optimising efficiency, productivity, control and consistency. Through analysis of qualitative data consideration is given to how ICTs used by these workers in their everyday work of investigating and resolving IT service incidents (also) serve a managerialist agenda that upholds a commercial/market logic (e.g. Carvalho, 2014), such that this logic impacts upon the concept of 'professional' work as primarily having an agenda with a contrasting technical, service quality logic.

As a theoretical development, consideration is given to how management-imposed ICTs used by public sector IT professionals might be alternatively associated with either the rationalisation of the professional experience or the rationalisation of their professional expertise. This theoretical contribution is supported by an inductively developed model that illustrates how management-imposed ICTs diminish the extent to which public sector IT professionals enjoy autonomy in their work. With reference to studies of other professionals working in the public sector it is further theorised how this model might be adapted to illustrate how ICTs operate as control mechanisms serving managerial purposes.

Before reporting the study, a brief commentary is presented to contextualize it. First, this serves as a reminder that ICTs have been central to the managerialist agenda of new public management initiatives; and second, it informs that those ICTs have typically been implemented across the public sector as an element of widely diffused service-oriented 'best practices'.

This is followed by an outlining of the methodology for the study. The findings of the study are then reported on and discussed, giving particular consideration to the implications for understanding the changing nature (or transformation) of managed professional work in public sector organizations. Specifically, this discussion reflects upon how ICT-enabled managerial controls imposed upon this group of professional workers impact upon core defining traits of professional work, specifically autonomy, authority and the acquisition and use of expertise. As a theoretical contribution an illustrative model is presented to show how a collection of different ICTs (i.e. rather than ICT as a singular entity) combine to assert the authority of management, operating from a commercial-professional logic, over the work of professionals, trained to operate from a technical-professional logic (Spence & Carter, 2014).

Context of the case study: public sector service-oriented IT professional work

In contemporary society, IT is intrinsic to government-funded public service provision as well as wider business practices (Greenhill, 2011) and as such the use of ICTs – often complex technologies that require intensive training and skilful operation – is part-and-parcel of the everyday experience of many workers, including those who would claim to be working in specific professions. Given the ubiquity and socio-economic importance of IT (Carr, 2003; McAfee & Brynjolfsson, 2008), the IT profession can be said to have played a vital role in the success of the neoliberal political agenda associated with new public management (Harvey, 2007). As such, we might understand the professional domain of IT to be intrinsically symbiotic with the techniques of efficiency-focused managerialism (Derber et al., 1990).

Public sector IT professionals are a distinct body of workers who develop and support ICTs used by other public sector employees and the public, recast as customers or service users. It is their technological expertise (Larson, 1977) and ability to use professional inference in responding effectively to circumstances (Abbott, 1988; Broadbent et al., 1997) that affords them the authority to practice and the trust and obedience of service recipients (Weber, 1947; Johnson, 1972; Starr, 1982) such that they can lay claim to professional status. Accepting that defining features of professionalism are contested (Broadbent et al., 1997), the performance of work investigating, and resolving IT service incidents that occur across complex governmental IT infrastructures particularly resonates with the assertion that professions perform socially significant work (Brock et al., 2014).'

In this study, focus is applied to public sector IT service professionals in the UK who support operational IT systems and are managed in accordance with the 'best practice' managerialist guidelines for managing IT systems as customer-oriented services: ITIL (formerly – but no longer – an acronym for Information Technology Infrastructure Library). These ITIL guidelines that have been globally adopted through processes of diffusion and institutionalisation have their origins within the UK civil service during Margaret Thatcher's third term of government (Cartlidge et al., 2007). They can be identified as compatible with – or indeed exhibits of – the new public management discourse. Specifically, they explicitly commodify public sector workers as 'people assets', such that their 'productive capacity' might be measured 'in units of cost, time and effort' (Cannon, 2011, p. 382), and promote the use of ICTs, within defined processes, as mechanisms of innovation, productivity and efficiency (Dutta & Mia, 2011) that inevitably assert control over practice.

The case study: methodological approach

The study reported on here is of public sector IT professionals working across several teams that provided and supported IT services for a county council (i.e. a local government authority) in the Midlands of England employing 12,000 people. It is referred to in this case study as Midshire County Council (MCC). Significantly, the IT management at this authority had implemented ITIL 'best practice' for managing IT services (e.g. Cannon, 2011). In public sector contexts, such as MCC, ITIL endorses an internal market approach, casting the IT systems users (i.e. other MCC departments and individual employees, and local authority-controlled schools) in the role of internal customers who receive IT services according to service level agreements (SLAs). As such, the MCC management not only confidently espoused IT service management 'best practice' (i.e. ITIL) but had also sought to organise work accordingly, imposing various ICTs – as advocated by the 'best practice' – upon their IT professional workforce.

Data were collected across three IT service support teams at MCC, all of which had responsibilities for investigating, diagnosing and resolving IT service incidents across a wide range of IT systems that supported the services provided by MCC. Table 1.1 provides further information on the three different teams visited for the study and Table 1.2 details the number of IT professionals interviewed and observed investigating, diagnosing and resolving IT service incidents.

The interviews were conducted using a semi-structured approach to access workers' 'descriptions, rationalisations and reflections' on their everyday work experience (Bloor & Wood, 2006, p. 71). In analysis of the fully-transcribed interview data, specific interest was taken in those narrative thoughts that concerned their individual experiences of working with the management-imposed technologies and the labour processes that were enabled by those technologies. Observation data were collected by a single researcher sitting alongside the selected IT professionals and watching what was done in practice, all the while recording in a notebook the small actions taken. It should be noted that the researcher (and author of this chapter) had

Table 1.1 Descriptions of the three Midshire County Council teams visited

Corporate Systems IT Service Desk (CSITSD): MCC's Corporate Services IT Service Desk was situated in an office on the second-floor of a cuboid pre-fabricated block (built in 1962 as temporary office accommodation) annexed to the rear of the Council Headquarters. This IT Service Desk team was a single point of contact for support of IT systems used by all of the County's service divisions except Education Services (e.g. Social Care; Leisure Services; Environmental Services). When a 'customer' contacted the Service Desk they were placed in a queue until a worker became available. When an incident or service request could not be completed or escalated to a second line team (e.g. Desktop Services) within 20 minutes, it was passed to a second-tier worker within the team who could work on the matter without the pressure of dealing with in-coming calls to the 'single point of contact' phone-number. The team comprised of ten IT professionals who sat alongside other (specialist) IT professionals in the open plan office space. Most of the team comprised of young men who, despite being equipped with headsets, engaged in a high level of social and work-related conversation. The only female workers on the team, Kate and Judy, both older workers, had specific responsibilities for setting up and modifying user access rights to the organisation's systems, and sat apart from the other Service Desk workers.

Corporate Systems Desktop Services (CSDS): The Desktop Services team were situated on the ground floor to the rear of the main County Council office building, an architecturally impressive 1930s structure. The five workers in the team generally congregated within one room which served as office space, technical workshop where computer equipment could be maintained and hardware store for new computer equipment and spares. As you entered the room, the first thing you noticed was the high workbench with stools for the technicians to sit on. The workbench was littered with computer hardware that was undergoing repair, screwdrivers and other tools. Above the workbench were a collection of manuals and materials for maintaining the hardware. The team were friendly towards each other and, while they worked on incidents individually, supported each other with the technical aspects of the work. They appeared to be highly conscientious as a team and, while they did not face constant interrupting phone calls, they worked assiduously throughout the periods of observation.

Education Services IT Service Desk (ESITSD): The Education Services IT Service Desk was located on the top floor of a converted Art Deco industrial building (built in 1936) in the Northern suburbs of the county's major city. The team was dedicated to the support of the IT systems provided to support the council's education services and typically operated by administrators in schools and colleges. The team were self-contained within one room with its own adjoining kitchen area. The team was effectively split into three parts. Three workers took the calls that came into the 'single point of contact' phone number and email address and via the Internet. One worker would take the lead on the phones at any given point of the week for a morning or afternoon session. The others would pick up additional calls that came in whilst this worker was handling a call. Calls were directly answered, rather than via an automated call response system. Where incidents could not be resolved over the phone within approximately 20 minutes they would be passed to a specific second-tier worker depending on the particulars of the incident. If the matter related to the SIMS system, then the matter would be referred to one of four specialist workers.

Table 1.2 Data collected at the three Midshire County Council teams visited

Team	Number of IT professionals interviewed	Number of IT professionals observed	Number of IT incidents observed being processed
Corporate Systems IT Service Desk	3	1	11
Corporate Systems Desktop Services	4	4	9
Education Services IT Service Desk	3	4	19
Totals	10	9	39

a professional background working in similar environments and as such was able to interpret those small actions, record the data and later analyse the data from a 'shared lifeworld' perspective (Schutz, 1953). The benefits here are similar to those advanced for insider research (Brannick & Coghlan, 2007). While the researcher here was not an insider, nonetheless familiarity with similar settings enabled in-situ interpretation and post-collection analysis to be conducted through the lens of the researcher's personal historical experience: "because we are close to something or know it well... we can research it... [and provide] important knowledge about what organizations are really like" (Brannick & Coghlan, 2007, p. 60, 72).

Additionally, a research journal was used to record broader ethnographic data from observations in the workplace, e.g. notes from unplanned conversations with employees. These research journal notes were particularly drawn upon in the preparation of this chapter as they were a reliable record of the IT systems that were observed being used by the IT professionals.

The interview transcriptions and journal notes were manually analysed through an iterative process of reading, reflecting and modelling to identify common themes and patterns relating to the meanings that the participants attached to their everyday work experiences, and specifically how they used and related to ICTs in their practice. Recurring themes were manually identified from the interview transcriptions such that convincing typifications might be theorised reflecting experiences common among IT professionals.

Through analysis of the complete dataset a formative theoretical model was inductively arrived at that illustrates how ICTs are exploited in the pursuit of a managerialist agenda to assert control over the work of IT technical professionals. This theoretical model is presented later in the chapter, and then used to reflect upon how other ICTs imposed upon other managed professionals in the public sector have similar effects associated with managerial control.

The case study: findings

In keeping with the holistic approach taken and in order to present our argument concerning how ICTs are employed by managers to enable the assertion of control over public sector IT professionals, our findings are structured into two parts representing two aspects of the IT professional labour process: the practice as experienced by the worker, and the professional expertise that enabled that practice to be conducted capably. Thus, first, data are presented to illustrate how ICTs are used to rationalize the everyday experience of IT professionals. Second, data are presented to illustrate management attempts to implement ICTs to rationalize and control their authority-giving expertise. Together these findings illustrate how management-imposed ICTs assert a two-pronged attack on the IT professional by enabling the rationalisation of both their experience and expertise.

ICT-enabled rationalisation of experience

The observed IT service professionals worked within tightly-defined processes built around an integrated ICT tool designed to support an Incident Management process. This tool – 'HP Servicecenter' – comprised computer telephony integration (CTI) technology, databases, a workflow management system (WFMS), a system-generated work queue and statistical reporting technology. WFMSs provide a structural framework to ensure that tasks are performed efficiently, according to a set of inscribed procedural rules, by the right people in the right order (Bocij et al., 2008). As such they are tools that are designed to optimize efficiency by rationalising the labour process into distinct stages. In the design of this process, 'the incident' (i.e. the reported service issue) is reified as a computer record and positioned as the central entity within the process. Consequently, by IT systems design, the IT professional is objectified as a system resource 'that' (i.e. who) is subordinate to 'the incident' and 'that' (i.e. who) generates labour activity that is consumed in the processing of that incident to bring about its satisfactory resolution and closure.

When coupled with managerial assertions of protocol (i.e. that workers must utilise these technologies) the everyday experience of these professional workers becomes structured (i.e. is prescribed) according to the rational process designed alongside the technological solution to meet the business/system requirement. Observation data from the study reveal that the IT professionals' labour process was heavily structured around a 'best practice' incident management process that is enabled by the integrated ICT tool. A significant proportion of time was spent working with this tool to record details of incidents and categorise them to meet a managerial demand for metrics and to enable similar incidents in the future to be addressed by reference to completed incident records. As such, while spending significant amounts of time recording data using this tool, the IT professionals were not spending that time using their technical-professional skills to investigate and resolve incidents. For some of the IT professionals, this was clearly not an issue of concern: they understood this aspect of the work as being integral to it. However, their variable engagement with the tool, as observed and as illustrated in the words of Adam, point to different IT professionals making different choices concerning the extent to which they adhered to the implied management command to fulfil the administrative tasks of generating accurate statistics and providing useful information/knowledge on how the incident was resolved:

> Some people seem to be completely averse to completing a call properly or putting any information or useful information in.... you will get one team just putting a few notes on it and others putting huge resolution information.
> (Adam, IT Service Desk Assistant, ESITSD)

The time spent collecting data for managers is significant to this study as this is time not spent practicing skillfully as professionals and as such the central role that the ICT tool plays can be seen to have an impoverishing effect on the professional experience. First, it can be seen to restrict the time available to thoroughly investigate technical problems to gain a deeper understanding of the underlying technological issues of the reported incident. Rather, it encourages a quick fix approach to incident management in order to generate higher productivity figures, even though this approach is likely to result in more incidents further down the line because the underlying issues are not being resolved. Second, the IT professionals have less time to develop their IT expertise, and therefore their individual capabilities (and by extension organizational capabilities) to resolve incidents quickly using professional inference (Abbott, 1988). Stephen, who had worked in IT for 23 years, was one of several IT professionals who recognised how time pressures were impacting upon his capacity to express his technical-professional inclinations:

> Because of the timescales we work to, we don't really have the ability to really get our teeth into interesting problems. We have to get things fixed... But it's a business at the end of the day.
> (Stephen, Support and Installation Engineer, CSDS)

The incident-related data entered by the IT professionals as mandatory procedural tasks, along with automatically generated (by design) quantitative data, enabled management reports to be produced to inform management decision-making and/or facilitate discussions concerning SLAs with the internal 'customers' (Hunnebeck, 2011). Thus, the integrated ICT was employed not only to structure and facilitate the work of the IT professionals but also to provide managerial statistical reporting (or 'dataveillance' (Clarke, 1988)) functionality as a facet of managerial surveillance of work activity.

Reading across the range of interviews, as exemplified by the extracts below, it becomes apparent that the work queue, as a rationalising facet of the integrated ICT, implicitly exerts disciplinary agency (Winner, [1980] 1999) to intensify the professional experience (Baldry et al., 1998). Contrary to Brock's (2006) suggestion that ICTs applied to professional work might offer a reduction in labour intensity, the data here suggest a surreptitious intensification of the professional experience via the role played by the integrated ICT for incident management in facilitating the kind of self-managing teams often advocated within the managerialist literature (e.g. Katzenbach & Smith, 1994). At all three sites there was not only an awareness of supervisory monitoring of the system-generated work queues, but also behavioural self-regulating and intra-team disciplining (specifically compliance with the process and prioritization rules) on account of the 'panoptican' surveillance functionality of the system (Foucault, 1975).

> I think I would be brought up about it if I didn't actually do anything and left loads in my queue.
> (Gareth, Support and Installation Engineer, ESITSD)

> I think the emphasis is very much quite often placed on us as the team to monitor the performance of ourselves and of other members of the team rather than it being done by management... It often falls down to myself, or to Jane, to monitor the work that is in the queue. We are supposed to pick up the stuff according to priority and according to how old it is... Whilst we're also doing the work, we also monitor the work and sort of say "Why aren't you picking this up?" or "Is there a reason why this has been sitting in the queue for a week?" or that sort of thing which is, to my mind, more of a managerial role.
> (Roger, Support and Installation Engineer, CSITSD)

> As a team leader... I don't want to micromanage or whatever; I like to be able to trust them to look at the queue, to pick up faults and to be able to go out on their own bat and do what is there.
> (Tom, Team Leader/ Support and Installation Engineer, CSDS)

Another ICT type was identified as placing restrictions upon the capability of IT professionals to develop their technical skills through problem-solving. Role-based Access Control (RBAC) Systems (Ferraiolo et al., 2007) are routinely used in organisations to manage which IT users of the corporate systems have access to specific IT applications and data. Analysis of the observation and interview data indicated that these systems were being employed as control mechanisms denying certain IT professionals from performing certain technical work or developing their skills in a particular area of technical specialism. Thus, for example, Adam (IT Service Desk Assistant, ESITSD) reported that "there's some stuff that just needs to be handed over straight away because it's quite a specialist system... because it's been custom-built for schools". Similarly, Roger (Support and Installation Engineer, CSITSD) alluded to the RBAC system being employed to assert managerial control over bureaucratic demarcation of work: "Being a council organization there are quite strict hierarchies about this goes to this department and they fix it, and that goes over there". These controls were actually administered by two of the IT professionals who were interviewed and observed: Kate and Judy (Service Desk Assistants, CSITSD). Through that observation it emerged that independent controls were placed on them such that they did not have access to, nor could they give access to, certain politically-sensitive parts of the corporate IT system.

The IT professionals operating in the two Service Desk teams had their working experience further prescribed for them by two other technologies. Firstly, calls were answered on the service desks via computer telephony integration functionality, which ensured that when taking receipt of incidents from 'customers' the IT professionals were able to enter the software-mandated information onto the incident record as they listened to that information being supplied by the customer. The headsets worn by the IT professionals on the Corporate Systems IT Service Desk that were wired to the desktop computer had the additional effect of restricting these professionals' spatial autonomy (i.e. freedom to move around). Spatial autonomy was also restricted by the use of remote access software (RAS) that they were expected to use as and when appropriate in order to investigate, diagnose and resolve incidents. Rather than attend the 'customers' site, the protocol was to use RAS technology to take control of users' computers. The observation data revealed that the IT professionals in the Corporate Services Desktop Services team necessarily practiced with greater spatial autonomy on account of their remit to visit 'customers' in other departments to investigate, repair and replace computer hardware.

ICT-enabled rationalisation of expertise

The study also serves to highlight how ICT-enabled control mechanisms are employed within ITSM work settings to capture and codify the human expertise developed and used during the performance of IT professional work within a KMS. This study reveals limitations to the success of such attempts.

Organisation-based IT professionals typically practice their professional skills within highly contextualised, complex and dynamic technical infrastructures (Trusson & Woods, 2017). Such complex operational IT systems that IT professionals are tasked with supporting are prone to failure (i.e. such that a service incident would be reported) in multifarious ways. This study of IT professionals confirms that the individualised and contextualised experiential knowledge (Barley, 1996) that they have acquired over time through their practice is of crucial importance to enable the development and then deployment of professional inference that Abbott (1988, p. 48–49) defines as "the middle game [of professional thinking]... undertaken when the connection between diagnosis and treatment is obscure". The data suggest that it is this 'obscurity' rather than any worker resistance that defies the managerial will to rationalise expertise through codification (Orr, 1996). The interview data supported the observation that the work was typically highly contingent and often extemporaneous, with know-how being developed slowly over time through practice. For example:

> The thing is with this environment… because of the way that it's all been fragmented it's a difficult environment to get to grips with.
> (Harry, Support and Installation Engineer, CSDS).

> We've got a couple of guys who are experts in some things and couple of people who are experts in others.
> (Roger, Support and Installation Engineer, CSITSD)

> We're not that knowledgeable about the sort of questions the boys on the service desk get asked. We are knowledgeable about our side (systems access).… They haven't got the knowledge that we've got on the systems.
> (Judy, Service Desk Assistant, CSITSD)

The study illustrates how the professionalism of these IT professionals relates to the individualized 'know-how-in-action' (Swart, 2011) they bring to the job, i.e. the fine-grained and creative application of previously learned knowledge in technical decision-making and subsequent action based on the particular complex context facing them at each point in time, thus making the work in large part 'uncommodifiable' (Abbott, 1988, p. 324). The observation data revealed IT professionals being autonomously self-reliant when actively engaged in the core task of processing incidents (albeit confined within the process), drawing on personalised knowledge gained from their heavily-contextualised experiential learning (Trusson et al., 2014):

> To laymen [the work] would probably seem excruciatingly complex, like a lot of things to me seem complex because I'm not doing it day in day out. It's second nature to me. It all seems pretty straight forward.
> (Stephen, Support and Installation Engineer, CSDS)

Such self-reliance is at odds with the aforementioned ITSM concerns of rationalisation and control, as epitomised in the 'best practice' advice given to IT service managers that they should 'reward the contribution of valuable knowledge assets' captured in a KMS (Rance, 2011, p. 242). KMSs designed to enable managers to increase their power and control (Gray, 2001) had been implemented at all the organisations visited. Consistently, IT professionals were expected to codify to a sufficient level of detail the knowledge they had used in investigating, diagnosing and resolving incidents either on the 'incident record' or as a separate 'knowledge article' for storage in a semi-detached knowledge database. Roger (Support and Installation Engineer, CSITSD) referred to this database in interview:

> We've got a central knowledge base with all the documents we've written. There's a lot of training documents in there that I've written and that other people have written that we use for induction and that's available to everybody who works in IT.

What is telling from this, along with the absence of any reference to use of the knowledge database from the collected observation data, is that the KMS is not being used routinely but for the more limited purpose of helping new recruits to 'get up to speed' so that they can become self-reliant.

Typically, the observation data showed that IT professionals, working under time pressures, recorded (as an integral stage of the processing of incidents) how they resolved the incident within the incident record – usually fairly brief notes – but eschewed use of the knowledge database (either writing to it or retrieving from it). It was also noted that the integrated incident handling system incorporated functionality to mark particular incident records as 'known errors' (notionally stored in a Known Error Database) with 'workarounds' to be implemented upon recurrence (Steinberg, 2011). This could theoretically be used as a rationalising technology when the service had been restored to the 'customer' but the underlying cause of the incident had yet to be determined. However, the observation data indicated that this functionality was not in practice taken advantage of by IT professionals, who, by default, preferred to use their technical expertise to find their own solution rather than look on the incident record database to see if a similar incident had previously occurred. Further, as Stephen (Support and Installation Engineer, CSDS) intimated, database 'solutions' are problematic when it comes to reusing the 'knowledge': "it's only as good as what you put into it".

Ideally, from the managerial perspective of cost-minimization, 'customers' experiencing incidents would choose to investigate, diagnose and resolve them themselves. Such self-help systems, which typically operate via a web interface (Steinberg, 2011), rely upon the commodification of expert knowledge so that it might be diffused to customers. Such diffusion of knowledge from 'professionals' to 'customers' serves the managerial agenda by removing the professional (as a human resource expenditure item) from the technical support process (Kanter, 1990; Fournier, 2000). Although such self-help arrangements at MCC were limited, there was a rudimentary intranet facility for 'customers' to consult. The implicit managerial objective of providing this was to reduce reliance on the IT professionals by shifting responsibility for investigation, diagnosis and resolution to the customer. Making the knowledge database that was used for training purposes (see above) available to people who didn't work in IT was not considered appropriate (interview with Roger) on account of the technical nature of the documents.

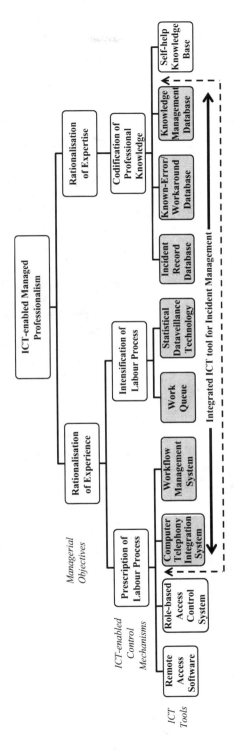

Figure 1.1 ICT-enabled 'Managed Professionalism' Model for Public Sector IT professionals.

Modelling ICT-enabled 'managed professionalism' of IT professionals

The technologies identified in this study are presented in model form at Figure 1.1, showing a division between ICTs for rationalising the individual professional experience by prescribing and intensifying the labour process in a way more typically associated with non-professional info-service work (e.g. Russell, 2009), and ICTs for rationalising (or attempting to) the individual's professional expertise via ICT-based knowledge management processes of codification and capture of 'knowledge' (as considered from an objectivist perspective (Hislop, 2013)).

Discussion of the case study

The case study illustrates how the professionalism of public sector IT professionals in the UK has been subjected to managerial discourses and ICT-enabled processes of rationalisation that are advocated by the leading professional bodies representing these IT professionals (i.e. BCS and ITSMF). We might then identify the professional discourse of these professional bodies and the related isomorphic implementation of 'best practices' by cadres of IT service managers (DiMaggio & Powell, 1983) as reflecting the 'organising professionalism' perspective recently theorised by Noordegraaf (2015, p. 200) in which "professional processes are privileged, in order to deal with multiple cases in demanding environments". The individual IT professional who processes those 'multiple cases' experiences this 'organising professionalism' as one of subjugation to the ICT-enabled processes as they negotiate between conflicting demands for ensuring reliability and quality (associated, according to Noordegraaf (2015) with a 'managed professionalism' perspective) and efficiency and meeting metrical targets (associated with a 'controlled professionalism' perspective). We might theorise here that an individual IT professional might respond to the imposition of ICTs in various ways. They might 'collaborate' by embracing the technology as the professionally-sanctioned (by their IT professional body), and therefore professional, response to the management will; or 'accommodate' by simply accepting and adopting the technology in accordance with their management's expectations of them; or 'resist' by attempting to circumvent the management will. The data point to flexibility in adopting these different approaches. The centrality of the integrated ICT tool to the incident management process effectively mandated an accommodating response although for some it was clear that this was tempered by a will to record only scant details on the incident record. In contrast, engagement with the semi-detached KMS that implicitly relied upon discretionary activity was more obviously resisted as part of the structured incident management labour process.

Through this study, management tactics involving the employment of IT systems for reducing the reliance upon human capabilities that are founded upon individually-held 'know-how-in-action' (Swart, 2011) have been highlighted. Specifically, the study illustrates how IT service managers operating from objectivist epistemological assumptions (Hislop, 2013) have attempted through the use of database technologies, to organize the codification and capture of the professional knowledge of IT professionals in order to place it under their control. The assumed prize for succeeding in this venture would be the promise of degrading the work so that it might be performed by lower cost 'people assets' utilising the 'knowledge' now theoretically under the control of management (Braverman, 1974; Taskin & Van Bunnen, 2015). The evidence from this study points to such an assumption being flawed on account of the embodied nature of the knowledge employed in practice (Collins, 1993).

The study points to the professional development interests of the IT professionals being undermined by the technology imposed upon them by their managers. Their autonomy is curtailed by the prescriptive demands of WFMSs and the spatial restrictions, synonymous with call centre work, imposed by CTI technology (Taylor, 2015). The dataveillance technology and ever-present work queues serve to intensify their work. And the labour-market value of their previously acquired professional knowledge is implicitly threatened by a managerial intent (albeit one based on a flawed objectivist epistemological assumption) to redistribute commodified 'professional' knowledge to other (potentially less expensive) employees or 'customers'/'-users' via self-help tools.

The managerialist influence upon professional projects, and thereby the very concept of professionalism, is then one that implicitly enlists ICTs in an imperative to reorient professional knowledge from the personal to the rationally bureaucratic, and with it, the trust of 'customers' from being personal (i.e. trust in the individual 'professional' [noun]) to impersonal (i.e. in the 'professional' [adjective] service being provided) (Russell et al., 2015). Drawing on Weber's ([1922] 1968) theory of bureaucracy and Mintzberg's (1983) division of the bureaucratic form into a process-oriented 'machine bureaucracy' and a skills-oriented 'professional bureaucracy', the effect of this imperative is thus one that both dehumanizes professionals and undermines their power base of expertise. Here this occurs through tightly defined, ICT-enabled labour processes that prioritise restoring the service to the customer to meet agreed service levels even where this entails the use of 'workarounds' that do not address the underlying technical problem. From this managerial perspective, giving an IT technician the time to fully understand and resolve the root cause of the reported incident jeopardizes meeting agreed service levels (Steinberg, 2011); the practice and development of their individual professional skills is of no concern. From the earliest conception of 'the professions', trust in the competence, reliability, dependability (McAllister, 1995; Zaheer et al., 1998) or 'gentlemanhood' (Haber, 1991) of 'the professional' has been an important principle. Here, though, the managerial objective is to establish a rationalised 'authority trust' in line with the defining words of Ward and

Smith (2003, p. 12): "only a completely consistent and reliable mode of service delivery can be trusted to give me what I need every time". Therefore, this imperative to rationalise 'trust' in competence (or professional authority (Weber, 1947)) via ICT-enabled 'best practices' that emphasise the corporate over the individual has implications for our understanding of professionalism from a sociological perspective. We might specifically consider the negative effect upon the status of the public sector IT professional. This status is likely to be diminished by the managerial insistence that an ICT-enabled process is adhered to that restricts their autonomy to the confines of that process, and that enlists the service recipients, 'transformed into empowered customers', as agents of control and discipline (Fournier, 2000, p. 67).

Analysis of the data collected for this study suggest that it is not that these empowered service recipients are apt to question the authority of IT 'professionals' [noun]. Rather, we might infer that the human professionals, and their mystery, are being removed from the picture and replaced by rationalised 'professional' [adjective] services provided by specialist functional units that, via diffusion and institutionalization of 'best practices' for managing IT services (DiMaggio & Powell, 1983), operate from corporate and managerial logics (e.g. Swart & Kinnie, 2010; Kipping & Kirkpatrick, 2013). Thus, we might observe how ICTs imposed upon managed professionals can play an important role in shifting the service recipient/consumer perception from one of trusting the authority of professionals to one of trusting the quality of 'professional' services within the remit and control of managers. From this changed perspective responsibility for measuring the quality of the work output shifts to the manager with the professional reduced to a commodity providing specialist 'intellectual capital' to the manager (Weber's ([1922] 1968); Stewart, 1998). Further research is needed to explore how IT professionals (and other 'managed professionals') are protecting (or might protect) themselves from the managerial assault on their professional status through such commoditization.

Further discussion: extending the model of ICT-enabled 'managed professionalism'

This article has illustrated how IT systems of multiple ICTs have become an integral part of a rhetorical managerialist discourse that situates IT professionalism firmly within a setting of assertive management. In an inductively built model, a theoretical contribution has been made that may assist in understanding how IT professional work performed in IT service support environments is typically controlled through the employment of a range of ICT tools. It is proposed that this model is adaptable to assist in understanding how management-selected and implemented ICTs support rationalised management of other public sector 'managed professionals'. To illustrate, consideration is given to how this model might be applied to recent studies of policing and nursing.

First, we might consider the study of Lindsay et al. (2014) that reports on how the issuing of mobile ICTs to police officers to use 'on the beat' re-prescribed the labour process such that officers had fewer opportunities to return to the police station and interact with colleagues. Figure 1.2 shows how these mobile technologies might be positioned within the framework of the hierarchical model previously presented at Figure 1.1.

Second, we might consider two studies of contemporary nursing. The first of these, Petrakaki and Kornelakis (2016), reports on the imposition of Care Record Service (CRS) systems in the UK National Health Service. Amongst the findings are observations that these systems prescribed standardised healthcare delivery and healthcare professional conduct and regularized interaction with patients. It also pointed to work intensification with increased workload resulting from unnecessary urgency of tasks being inscribed within the software, for example, requiring a time-consuming scanning task to be completed at a particular point in the sequence before being allowed to progress, whereas greater efficiency would have resulted had nurses been able to combine such scanning tasks into a single task. Another study of nursing (Russell, 2012) discusses the implementation of algorithmic clinical decision support software in the Australian health service as an enabler of a shift from face-to-face nursing to tele-nursing. Like the CRS systems, these systems that were provided to nurses working in these tele-nursing roles were built along the lines of a WFMS, prescribing a sequence to be followed in order to investigate and diagnose a medical complaint so that treatment might be prescribed. However, beyond the rationalisation of the professional experience induced by the WFMS functionality, the software also can be identified as having a rationalising effect upon professional expertise. Qualified nurses were required by the software to subordinate their agency to act using their personally acquired professional expertise and familiarity with the local health

Figure 1.2 Application of ICT-enabled 'Managed Professionalism' Model to study of mobile policing (Lindsay et al. (2014)).

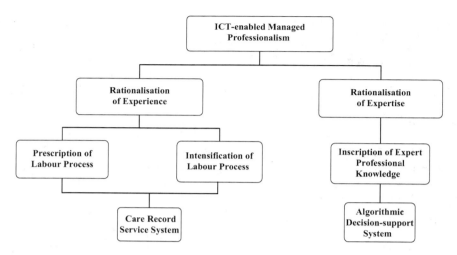

Figure 1.3 Application of ICT-enabled 'Managed Professionalism' Model to studies of nursing (Russell, 2012; Petrakaki & Kornelakis, 2016).

context. Instead they were expected to act according to the rationalised 'expert' knowledge that was inscribed within an algorithm that had been coded based on medical knowledge provided by medical informatics experts based in the United States. Figure 1.3 illustrates how the framework of the hierarchical model previously presented at Figure 1.1 might be employed to illustrate particular rationalising effects of these ICTs upon the nursing profession.

Concluding remark

These additional examples support the argument of this study that ICTs enable 'managed professionalism' in multifarious ways. Professional work has long been associated with the exercise of autonomous control over the work performed. As Freidson (1994, p. 63) wrote: 'management can control the resources connected with work, but cannot control most of what the workers do and how they do it'. This study illustrates that by asserting ICT-enabled routines that constrain work autonomy (Petrakaki & Kornelakis, 2016) managers are able to assert their authority over 'professional' work. Three decades ago, Abbott (1988, p. 325) suggested that, although professionalism had 'stayed ahead of commodification', control of work might over time be ceded by the professions to the organizations employing 'professionals'. This study, and the suggested expansion of the model induced from this study to other professional spheres practiced in the public sector, suggests that ICTs selected by managers and imposed upon professionals has altered professional practices such that they are increasingly inclined towards espousing the commercial/efficiency-focussed spirit of managerialism. For public sector organizations (or departments) that provide IT services (or other professional services), there is the promise of efficiency gains, but this comes at a cost to the 'managed IT professionals' as the protections, privileges and respect associated with their identity as professionals with considerable autonomy over their practice are eroded.

References

Abbott, A. (1988): *The System of Professions: An Essay on the Division of Expert Labour*, Chicago: University of Chicago Press.

Baldry, C., Bain, P., Taylor, P. (1998): 'Bright Satanic Offices': Intensification, Control and Team Taylorism', in: P. Thompson, C. Warhurst (eds.), *Workplaces of the Future*, 163–183, Basingstoke: MacMillan.

Barley, S. R. (1996): 'Technicians in the workplace: ethnographic evidence for bringing work into organization studies', *Administrative Science Quarterly*, 41: 404–441.

BCS [BCS, The Chartered Institute for IT] (2017): 'About Us' (online), available at: http://www.bcs.org/category/5651, accessed 19 May 2017.

Bloor, M., Wood, F. (2006): *Keywords in Qualitative Methods: A Vocabulary of Research Concepts*, London: Sage.

Bocij, P., Greasley, A., Hickie, S. (2008): *Business Information Systems: Technology, Development and Management*, 4th edn., Harlow: Pearson Education.

Brannick, T., Coghlan, D. (2007): 'In defense of being "Native": the case for insider academic research', *Organizational Research Methods*, 10(1): 59–74.

Braverman, H. (1974): *Labor and Monopoly Capital*, New York: Monthly Review Press.

Broadbent, J., Dietrich, M., Roberts, J. (1997): *The End of the Professions?: The Restructuring of Professional Work*, London: Routledge.

Brock, D. M. (2006): 'The changing professional organisation: a review of competing archetypes', *International Journal of Management Reviews*, 8(3): 157–174.

Brock, D. M., Leblebici, H., Muzio, D. (2014): 'Understanding professionals and their workplaces: the mission of the Journal of Professions and Organization', *Journal of Professions and Organization*, 1: 1–15.

Cannon, D. (2011): *ITIL: Service Strategy*, 2nd edn., Norwich: TSO.

Carr, N. C. (2003): 'IT doesn't matter', *Harvard Business Review*, 81: 41–49.

Cartlidge, A., Hanna, A., Rudd, C., Macfarlane, I., Windebank, J., Rance, S. (2007): *An Introductory Overview of ITIL V3: A High-level Overview of the IT Infrastructure Library*, Wokingham: The UK Chapter of the itSMF.

Carvalho, T. (2014): 'Changing connections between professionalism and managerialism: a case study of nursing in Portugal', *Journal of Professions and Organization*, 1: 176–190.

Clarke, R. (1988): 'Information technology and dataveillance', *Communications of the ACM*, 31: 498–512.

Collins, H. (1993): 'The structure of knowledge', *Social Research*, 60: 95–116.

Derber, C., Schwartz, W. A., Magrass, Y. (1990): *Power in the Highest Degree: Professionals and the Rise of a New Mandarin Order*, New York: Oxford University Press.

DiMaggio, P. J., Powell, W. W. (1983): 'The iron cage revisited: institutional isomorphism and collective rationality in organisational fields', *American Sociological Review*, 48(2): 147–160.
Dutta, S., Mia, I. (2011): *The Global Information Technology Report 2010–11: Transformations 2.0*, Geneva: The World Economic Forum/INSEAD.
Ferraiolo, D. F., Kuhn, D. R., Chandramouli, R. (2007): *Role-Based Access Control*, 2nd edn., Norwood, MA: Artech House.
Ford, M. (2015): *The Rise of the Robots: Technology and the Threat of Mass Unemployment*, London: Oneworld.
Foucault, M. (1975, reprinted 1977): *Discipline and Punish: The Birth of the Prison*, London: Allen Lane.
Fournier, V. (2000): 'Boundary Work and the (un)making of the Professions', in: N. Malin (ed.) *Professionalism, Boundaries and the Workplace*, 67–86, London: Routledge.
Freidson, E. (1994): *Professionalism Reborn: Theory, Prophecy and Policy*, Cambridge: Polity Press.
Gray, P. H. (2001): 'The impact of knowledge repositories on power and control in the workplace', *Information Technology and People*, 14: 368–384.
Greenhill, R. (2011): *Preface*, in: S. Dutta, I. Mia (eds.), *The Global Information Technology Report 2010–11: Transformations 2.0*, Geneva: The World Economic Forum/INSEAD.
Haber, S. (1991): *The Quest for Authority and Honor in the American Professions, 1750–1900*, Chicago: University of Chicago Press.
Harvey, D. (2007): *A Brief History of Neoliberalism*, Oxford: Oxford University Press.
Hislop, D. (2013): *Knowledge Management in Organizations: A Critical Introduction*, 3rd edn., Oxford: Oxford University Press.
Hodgson, D., Paton, S., Muzio, D. (2015): 'Something Old, Something New?. Competing Logics and the Hybrid Nature of New Corporate Professions', *British Journal of Management*, 26(4): 745–759.
Hunnebeck, L. (2011): *ITIL: Service Design*, 2nd edn., Norwich: TSO.
Johnson, T. (1972): *Professions and Power*, London: Macmillan.
Kanter, R. M. (1990): *When Giants Learn to Dance*, London: Unwyn Hyman.
Katzenbach, J. R., Smith, D. K. (1994): *The Wisdom of Teams: Creating the High-Performance Organization*, Boston: Harvard Business School Press.
Kipping, M., Kirkpatrick, I. (2013): 'Alternative pathways of change in professional services firms: the case of management consulting', *Journal of Management Studies*, 50: 777–807.
Larson, M. (1977): *The Rise of Professionalism: A Sociological Analysis*, Berkeley: University of California Press.
Lindsay, R., Jackson, T. W., Cooke, L. (2014): 'Empirical evaluation of a technology acceptance model for mobile policing', *Police Practice and Research: An International Journal*, 15(5): 419–436.
McAfee, A., Brynjolfsson, E. (2008): 'Investing in the IT that makes a competitive difference', *Harvard Business Review*, 86(7–8): 98–107.
McAllister, D. J. (1995): 'Affect- and cognition-based trust as foundations for interpersonal cooperation in organizations', *Academy of Management Journal*, 38: 24–59.
Mintzberg, H. (1983): *Structure in Fives: Designing Effective Organizations*, Englewood Cliffs: Prentice-Hall.

Noordegraaf, M. (2015): 'Hybrid professionalism and beyond: (New) Forms of public professionalism in changing organizational and societal contexts', *Journal of Professions and Organization*, 2(2): 187–206.

Orr, J. E. (1996): *Talking About Machines: An Ethnography of a Modern Job*, New York: ILR Press/Cornell University Press.

Petrakaki, D., Kornelakis, A. (2016): "We can only request what's in our protocol': technology and work autonomy in healthcare', *New Technology, Work and Employment*, 31(3): 223–237.

Rance, S. (2011): *ITIL: Service Transition*, 2nd edn., Norwich: TSO.

Reich, R. B. (2000): *The Future of Success: Working and Living in the New Economy*, New York: Vintage.

Russell, B. (2009): *Smiling Down the Line: Info-Service Work in the Global Economy*, Toronto: University of Toronto Press.

Russell, B. (2012): 'Professional call centres, professional workers and the paradox of the algorithm: the case of telenursing', *Work, Employment and Society*, 26: 195–210.

Russell, B., Trusson, C., De, S. (2015): 'The Ambiguities of 'Managed Professionalism': Working In and With IT', in: A. Wilkinson, D. Hislop, C. Coupland (eds.), *Perspectives on Contemporary Professional Work: Challenges and Experiences*, 165–186, Cheltenham: Edward Elgar.

Schutz, A. (1953): 'Common-sense and scientific interpretation of human action', *Philosophy and Phenomenological Research*, 14(1).

Spence, C., Carter, C. (2014): 'An exploration of the professional habitus in the Big 4 accounting firms', *Work, Employment and Society*, 28: 946–962.

Starr, P. (1982): *The Social Transformation of American Medicine*, New York: Basic Books.

Steinberg, R. (2011): *ITIL: Service Operation*, 2nd edn., Norwich: TSO.

Stewart, T. A. (1998): *Intellectual Capital: The New Wealth of Organizations*, London: Nicholas Brealey.

Susskind, R., Susskind, D. (2015): *The Future of the Professions: How Technology will Transform the Work of Human Experts*, Oxford: Oxford University Press.

Swart, J. (2011): 'That's why it matters: how knowing creates value', *Management Learning*, 42: 319–332.

Swart, J., Kinnie, N. (2010): 'Organisational learning, knowledge assets and HR practices in professional service firms', *Human Resource Management Journal*, 20: 64–79.

Taskin, L., Van Bunnen, G. (2015): 'Knowledge management through the development of knowledge repositories: towards work degradation', *New Technology, Work and Employment*, 30: 158–172.

Taylor, P. (2015): 'Labour and the Changing Landscape of the Call Centre', in: K. Newsome, P. Taylor, J. Bair, A. Rainnie (eds.), *Putting Labour in its Place: Labour Process Analysis and Global Value Chains*, 266–286, London: Palgrave.

Trusson, C. R., Doherty, N. F., Hislop, D. (2014): 'Knowledge sharing using IT service management tools: conflicting discourses and incompatible practices', *Information Systems Journal*, 24: 347–371.

Trusson, C., Woods, F. (2017): "An end to the job as we know it': how an IT professional has experienced the uncertainty of IT outsourcing', *Work, Employment and Society*, 31(3): 542–552.

Ward, A., Smith, J. (2003): *Trust and Mistrust: Radical Risk Strategies in Business Relationships*, Chichester: John Wiley and Sons.
Weber, M. ([1922] 1968): *Economy and Society*, New York: Bedminster Press.
Weber, M. (1947): *The Theory of Social and Economic Organization* (translated by A. M. Henderson and T. Parsons), New York: Free Press.
Winner, L. ([1980]1999): 'Do Artefacts have Politics?', in: D. McKenzie, J. Wajcman (eds.), *The Shaping of Technology*, 2nd edn., Buckingham: Open University Press.
Zaheer, A., McEvily, B., Perrone, V. (1998): 'Does trust matter? exploring the effects of interorganizational and interpersonal trust on performance', *Organization Science*, 9: 141–159.
Zuboff, S. (1988): *In the Age of the Smart Machine: The Future of Work and Power*, Oxford: Heinemann.

Chapter 2

Performance targets as negotiation devices – accounting management in French job centres

Jean-Marie Pillon

Introduction

This chapter sheds light on the relation between job counsellors, management accountants and managers at *Pôle Emploi* (the French job centre). Thereby, I would like to define the contemporary government of unemployment in France. The central question of this chapter is: how do management accountants rationalise and "frame" (Callon, 1998) counsellors' work to solve the so-called efficiency problem of the state in reducing mass unemployment?

Our research question derives from other field works addressing the contemporary transformations of the state. According to such literature, New Public Management actualises the long-lasting dynamics of rationalisation in public bureaucracies – revealed by M. Weber (Hood, 1995; Bezes & Musselin, 2015). Public organizations embraced an evidence-based steering and an objective measurement of their performance (Desrosières, 2003a). Accounting became more important than general interest to assess what a good work is. Means got subordinate to returns instead of needs. The concept of New Public Management often encompasses such transformations with a view to analyse the 1970s-born project of mimicking private corporations to rule the public sector (Bezes, 2009). "Institutional entrepreneurs" pointed out the autonomy and the immobility of public administrations, stressing the flexibility and the efficiency of private organisations (Kitchener, 2002). National-based studies about the implementation of the NPM show that this straightforward interpretation was an ex post recollection of events. There was no formal plan written from the beginning. Moreover, national importation processes varied widely depending on the importers' characteristics and the political configurations they had to deal with. In the French academic arena, for instance, the knowledge corpus coined as NPM aggregated step-by-step around heterogeneous pieces such as microeconomics (the public choice school, the transaction cost theory or the agency theory) or applied management (Bezes, 2005).

If too reified, a straightforward and mechanistic approach of the phenomenon risks putting aside the fact that administrations were already managed and performances measured before the 1970s (Maynard-Moody et al., 1986).

It risks emphasising a story in which optimisation procedures had suddenly overhauled "professional bureaucracies" (Mintzberg, 1980). The idea that New Public Management consists in a top-down imposition of new managerial tools downplays or avoids the political underpinning of management: when you try to optimise a *ratio*, you must state what you count as a benefit or as a cost (Vatin, 2011). Therefore, whether you study materials before or after the neoliberal turn, management tools are not "humanity-less machines". They are rather social procedures that real people elaborated. And the latter attempt to integrate what is worth – to them – into their tools. It's impossible to study such material such as returns, efficiency or productivity without mentioning that they proceed from disputed "conventions" cutting-out the world between what is worth and what is not (Desrosières, 2008). In that outlook, studying management accountants with a sociological imagination means unveiling the values and powerplays folded in the performance indicators.

At *Pôle Emploi*, management accountants produce and circulate scoreboards scoreboards among managers during the budget repartition process – the "performance dialog" – which lasts half a year from June to December. As in other fields, these drafts represent a scientific approach of management based on impartial data and figures (Miller & O'Leary, 1993). Management accountants see their mandate in a restrictive way, as if they only *"serve the organization by affecting the work of others [...] removed from the operating flow"* (Mintzberg, 1980). They claim for this position, aside from the decision process.[1] Nevertheless, measuring is an activity that is not only technical. It relies on a rhetorical process to enforce its legitimacy (Carruthers & Espeland, 1991; Hodgson, 2002).

There is an implicit postulate in management accounting: figures are "realistic". I define "realism" as the idea that statistics "measures objects and events whose status of reality is granted" (Desrosières, 2003b). Nevertheless, during our investigations, management accountants testified that they are not really sure of the matter they handle through scoreboards. They often suspect the data of being biased. Our point is not to study whether this statement is true or false but to understand – through a classic sociology of work (cf. Box 1) – how management accountants preserve themselves from this risk: steering using false data. To tackle this issue, I borrow to B. Latour the opposition between hot and cold science (Latour, 1993) to apply it to the bureaucracy (Weller, 2000). I consider as "cold bureaucracy" the outcome of public administration, the cold savour of a barely unquestionable enforced law. The "hot bureaucracy", on the contrary, refers to the endless negotiations, rearrangements and confrontations from which a decision derives. In other words, management accountants use informal manners to produce formal artefacts. This article thereby shows that, in the case of *Pôle Emploi*, the influence of management accounting on street level bureaucrats do not only derive from its efficiency – the objectivity and the materiality of the information system – but also from the way management accountants reheat the bureaucratic mechanisms to redefine other people's work. By "reheating", I intend to describe how management accountants interfere or keep their ears open, to collect qualitative information on what happens here and there. I suggest that those pieces of information frame their ability to translate numbers and charts in words and in organisational solutions they promote. Reheating enables them to understand the context into which data were recorded and interpreted. Thus, they comprehend the contingency from which measurements derive. They finally may then assume the bias or noise that scoreboards have recorded too. But this move toward knowledge is also a move toward power.

I first describe how management accountants collect qualitative information to do their official task: an objective analysis of figures and curves (I). I then point out to what extent management accounting is part of the decision-making process (II). I finally expose how job counsellors react to this frame in order to preserve their work from a complete external framing (III).

> **BOX 1 ADMINISTRATIVE STRUCTURE OF PÔLE EMPLOI**
>
> Pôle emploi is an administrative institution attached to the French Ministry of Labor. It negotiates its budget every year with the Ministry for the Budget. More than 50,000 employees work for Pôle Emploi, 1.9 times less than in Germany and 1.02 times less than in England, in proportion to the number of unemployed (Hespel et al., 2011). Unemployed are between 3 and 5 million in France, depending on the year and depending on the account conventions. Thirty-five thousand of Pôle emploi's employees work in local job centres, of which more than two-thirds are employment counsellors. Another third deals with unemployment benefits.
>
> Pôle emploi headquarters is based in Paris. The General Director is appointed by the President of the Republic. The General Directorate employs 1,000 people, and nearly one hundred of them are in charge of measuring the performance of the institution. Pôle emploi is then divided into 26 Regional Directorates. In terms of size, the regions are a French administrative level equivalent to the German Länder or the British Government Office Regions. There is an elected regional council, but these assemblies have very few responsibilities, as France is not a federation. In the case of Pôle emploi, the regional division is not even articulated with the political activity of the regional council. The Regional Directors are appointed by the General Director of Pôle emploi. Each Regional Directorate of Pôle emploi is divided into several departmental divisions – a tighter territorial division similar to a district. The Departmental Director is appointed by the Regional Director. Finally, each departmental directorate has several local job
>
> *(Continued)*

centre agencies that house between 25 and 90 employees. There are 912 local employment agencies in France. Pôle Emploi's managerial chain therefore has four levels: The General Director, the Regional Director, the Departmental Director and the Agency Director.

In France, scholars distinguish between "unemployed" – who are unemployed in the sense of the International Labor Organization – and the "jobseekers" – who are registered in the Pôle emploi registers. The two figures are positively correlated but the exact number can vary from one to two. Each employment advisor follows between 100 and 150 job seekers. According to a 2005 enforced law, each jobseeker should theoretically be received monthly by their counsellor. Due to a lack of time, it was decided in 2012 to introduce variable appointment schedules adapted to the employability of the people. Interviews with the unemployed generally take 30 minutes and relate to the jobseeker's job searches, vocational reorientation or vocational training opportunities.

This paper is based on qualitative materials. The analysis relies on a "conventionalist" theoretical framework that stresses the social construction of judgement and calculation devices. Consistently with Alain Desrosières' legacy and the galaxy he participated to bind (Thevenot or Boltanski in France, Bowker, Stars, Porter abroad and more generally all the participants to the "Bielefeld group"), our attention focused on measurement processes. I studied how performance indicators were designed, how they were enforced and how they were registered. Therefore, I interviewed managers to understand how strategies were elaborated. I interviewed management accountants to record their practices and way of thinking toward scoreboard interpretation. I did so with IT developers to understand how those two pressures (strategy and accountability) were incorporated into software. I finally observed daily work in local agencies to understand how figures were recorded in front of the unemployed. Management accountants' and managers' practices and way of thinking were collected through semi-structured interviews with upper, middle-ranking and local executives at Pôle Emploi ($n = 70$ from 2008 to 2015). Job counsellors' daily tasks and manners were collected through two two-month participant-observer periods in local job centres respectively in 2011 and 2012.

I. A sense of measurement: moving closer to get a better sight

In Pôle Emploi, management accountants shape figures to produce scoreboards. They then transmit notes to their manager so as to make those tables speak. As professional statisticians are eager to consult methodological appendices, management accountants appreciate knowing what was the context in which the figures they analyse were collected. Plus, their mandate of planning and forecasting assign a great value to qualitative and informal information: it could help in the analysis and prediction of tendencies. Management accountants therefore practice a delicate diplomacy so as to be aware of what really happens (I.1). This care strengthens a dilemma between collecting confidences from the subordinate managers they control and strongly prescribing them management reorganisations (I.2). I analyse this tension as rooted in an epistemological question about homogeneity and comparability.

I.1. Numbers and trust: analysing from confessions

In *Pôle Emploi*, management accountants alert their manager when econometric models point a delta between annual targets and forecasting based on actual results. They know well to what extent there is a difference between an event – e.g. an industry closure or a social movement in a local branch – and its consequences in the scoreboards. Management accountants I interviewed need subordinate managers to "confess" what really happens at the street level and at the district level for them to be able to produce more accurate forecasting and a better analysis of the figures. Management accountants would like to analyse before the trend reversal. For some of them, it is a necessary condition of a quantitative evaluation device. A former management accountant in a departmental directorate explains that he considers such a transparency as the condition for a rigorous monitoring of quantitative data:

> Management accountant at a district level (interviewed in 2011):
> "*It is the same things in every company. If we want to sincerely steer things at any level, we need confidence and maturity, between each corporate role. And management accounting has a major role to play in that process. Actually, we could embody* l'oeil de Moscou [Big brother] *but what is* l'oeil de Moscou [Big brother] *worth if disconnected from reality? He's going to steer illusions and you don't know what really happens on the ground. To know what happens on the ground you need to get confidence from lower managers. This confidence can arise if and only if lower managers are well advised to let management accounting develop.*"

To this management accountant, the normative aspect of quantitative evaluation may cause arguments and conflicts with lower managers (local managers in this case). But before and after the debate, information should be fully transparent, to certificate the figures analysis. In return, this management accountant makes a point of honour to elaborate specific tools that help local managers steer their own branch. What is at stake – in his mind – is the legitimacy of management accounting because the status of reality of figures cannot be granted. Without being as constructivist as the latter, every management accountant I interviewed should react when the curves collapse. In those cases, management accountants ask for more information and hold lower managers accountable. It's interesting to notice that when management accountants ask – firmly – for explanations, telling about a corrective action plan is a very effective "blame avoidance" (Hood, 2010) strategy. A Regional management accountant explains that, when he warns a Departmental manager of the disturbing evolution of an indicator, he waits in return to be warned of the actions planned to fix the figure:

> Regional management accountant (interviewed 2012):
> *"I think at some point we have to play our role of alert. We are alerting [upward] our Regional Manager to results that are not up to expectations. It is true that if we learn that [down there] there are plans of action that are being put in place, it softens the alert. We will plead: "There are things in the process of being put in place, it will be some time before it will bear fruit." softens the alert. We tell the upper boss that some things are about to settle and that within a week or a month it will pay off. Without explanations, we thump the table."*

The approach of this management accountant rests on different points that need to be distinguished. First, he asks for information to explain the fall of the indicator. Second, the deleteriousness character of this information is "mitigated" by the existence of operations set to correct the indicator. This last information preserves the departmental Director from the wrath of the Regional Director. This information makes it possible to relativise the sustainability of poor results. If the recovery operation works, the drop-out will no longer appear in the scoreboards at the end of the year. On the other hand, without reaction from the lower manager, the management accountant mobilises his own director, the Regional Director, against the Departmental Director. He uses the chain of command for information to be transmitted. Information about arising corrective action plans preserves the lower manager from the wrath of the regional manager. Bad results almost vanish. Without information, they use the chain of command to impose themselves but at the risk of embodying big brother and creating underground practices. Management accountants I investigated do not appreciate imposing blame and sanctions. They prefer "enrolment" (Callon, 1986) – i.e. a conviction that entails a conversion – because a bureaucrat who believes in your own cause is easier to control than a subordinate who just fears sanctions. From the local managers' point of view, it's anyway too risky to let the management accountant alone with bad results, because it is well known that the latter could use the chain of command to pass his alert. They therefore foresee bad news.

A former local director explains his relationship with the management accountant of the departmental directorate:

> Former local manager (interviewed in 2011):
> "*Yes, I was the one who was calling him* [the district management accountant]. *I used to tell him – "You know... We're completely screwing on this target" – I explained it to him because... It's like a banker. You shall better explain than letting him discover that you're overdraft*".

For this local manager, relaying the bad news to the upper management accountant does not change the fact that the targets won't be achieved. But foreseeing bad news gives the management accountant talking points to elaborate a buffer between the regional manager and the local one. This buffer is a rhetoric one, but it solidifies the analysis of the curves that climb the hierarchic ladder. A national management accountant explains the interest he finds in his visits in the Regional Directorates:

> A national management accountant (interviewed 2013):
> "*Last week a district manager told me – "At the second term that kind of things happened and we won't reach the target" – To me it's worth gold!*"

This management accountant finds it comforting to identify a mechanism explaining a score that falls. Naming issues fills management accountants' needs. They can suggest hypothesis to lower managers. They can explain a mechanism to upper managers. Those situations legitimate their monopoly upon information system. They thereby frame "bureaucratic problems" – in reference to the framing of "public problems" (Gusfield, 1984). They also use those situations – when a local manager experiences difficulty to reach his targets – to teach steering. First, they help them understand what could bias the figures. Then, they look for the most determinant variables. They do not elaborate plausible answers to those problems but are not very far from it.

1.2. Exploring or imposing? Tempted to decide

The tension between exploring and imposing becomes explicit when management accountants go downward to meet the managers they monitor. In such a layout, management accountants wonder if they should better impose an actual protocol – i.e. a normalisation of productive tasks designed to "logically adjust the means for the purposes" (Schön, 1991) – or carry out informal qualitative studies. When a management accountant wants to understand what really happens below, he somehow has to go through his computer screen to go beyond figures. Needless to say, within our panel, the favourite ways to look below vary depending on the person and his/her background. Nevertheless, each of them had a way to do so. They wanted to understand what professional tasks – the one carried out by job counsellors – were hidden behind the figures.

Some of the management accountants I interviewed climbed the hierarchic ladder to their actual position from the street level duties. They therefore gathered many contacts and a real network of workers, within *Pôle Emploi*, enabling them to understand how to read the figures. One of our interviewees uses the term "antennas" to name those relays. They enable him to collect specific examples, facts and practices:

> Management accountant at a district level (interviewed 2011):
> "I know all the productive processes, I'm at ease, I've got my network and it talks to me. I know how things happen. Those are my antennas."

In my interviewees' mind, qualitative inputs drawn from informal exchanges give more weight to the figures because such information make it possible to explain them. Some of the management accountants I interviewed even forced their co-workers – that had never been in a front office position – to make internships in local job centres in order to know what employment advising or placing means, why the phone rings, why some calls are made, what an unemployed looks like and what he is told. Informal investigations enable understanding: understanding as mastering the reality that meant to be behind the figures (the norm); understanding as mastering the process from which the figures actually come out (the practice).

> Regional management accountant (interviewed 2011):
> "There is a part of the production we do not master very well: Financial aids. We need to know. We need to see the work in local jobcentres and the organisation of the work. We need to build something to monitor those spendings".

This management accountant infers that different work organisation settings determine different results. Behind this questioning, "monitoring spending" means converging toward a common organisation. To him, it's difficult to forecast the aggregate evolution of the budget if there is too much variation in spending. But this remains a hypothesis. That is why he needs a qualitative investigation before modelling work and its evaluation. The final target is still enhancing the curves through an evolution of the organisation.

Through downward moves, management accountants thereby promote the "legitimacy" of the "statistic argument" (Desrosières, 2008) and defend the "auditability" (Power, 1996) of managers' decisions. They rhetorically promote counting, in a measured but decisive manner. This rhetorical activity functions on the following mechanisms: once they convince subordinate managers to think as optimizers, they are in a better position to persuade them to change the organisation of work toward a more effective one. In this process, the compliance between organisations and the information system is a necessary condition before counting. This process reminds us of the convergence between economy-rationalisation and economics-mathematisation in the 19th century:

> A. Cournot: *"Trade extension and business processes enhancement tend to bring the real state of things closer and closer to that particular order of abstract conceptions that allow theoretical reasoning."*
>
> (Cournot, 1980)

Rationalisation cannot operate *ex nihilo*. In Pôle Emploi, management accountants convey this process through a teaching of "conventions" (Desrosières, 1993). They do so without forgetting that there is always a *delta* between the reality and its representation in scoreboards. They do not take compliance for granted, they work for it.

Monitoring therefore represents a kind of protocol made to solidify and homogenise the data. For the management accountants I interviewed, interfering is worthy if and only if it participates in homogenising practices and thus, data. To analyse the figures, counted events must be equivalent. Equivalence and comparability take root in similar organisations. This is why they also tend to command, even when it is not a professional claim (Miller & O'Leary, 1993). They command, and frame the job counsellors' activity, in order to enhance their further objectivity. As E. D. Deming enhancement in error measurement forced the car industry to reengineer itself to comply with total quality management (Didier, 2000), our interviewees shape an organisation where it is possible to compare, to perform competitivity and to control the homogeneity of services. To put it another way, management accountants make benchmarking possible and relevant. I coin the interference of management accountants in the decision process as "protocol" as it enables measures and *ratio*. Through a homogenisation of conventions, management accountants turn the data collected in front of the unemployed into "boundary objects" – able to keep having sense on different stages (Bowker & Star, 1998).

II. For generous curves: accountants as organisers

Quantifying and analysing job counsellors' work lead management accountants to organise and decide. Through a comparison of how different organisations affect the figures, they try to elaborate work organisations that have the property – or the reputation – to improve the trend of curves. Nevertheless, they formally have no power to decide, due to the specific division of labour within *Pôle Emploi*. Imposing organisations is therefore based on conviction and valorisation: they make sure to frame their own manager's decision (II.1.); they find a way to congratulate the best pupils (II.2.).

II.I. Action plans: modifying work to get better results

Common *benchmarking* devices comprise action plans that formalise abstract strategies in practical applications. Most often, performance indicators monitor action plans to function as an evaluation of those general strategies. In *Pôle Emploi*, such mechanisms occur through the "performance dialog" – a budget repartition procedure that intertwines financial and physical indicators with a view to set next year's targets. A "performance contract", signed by an upper and a lower manager, e.g. a regional director and a departmental one or a departmental director and a job centre one, closes the negotiation. Within this process, notions such as "strategy" and "policy" refer to ideas that bind the diverse indicators consistently. When a manager proposes to his upper manager the action plans he intends to set up, he actually enters a more complex game than it seems. First, this game consists of proposing detailed actions that comply with the General director's strategy. Then, he must find proxies, i.e. indicators that sum the action plan up. Finally, he must predict the target his team is able to achieve. Each of those steps implies judgement and calculation operations, opening an opportunity for management accountants to impose their conception of the decision. A Regional management accountant explains how she interferes in this game:

> Regional management accountant (interviewed 2012):
> *"During the performance dialog we can tell the regional director: 'go on, put pressure on the departmental manager, his proposition is bullshit'. We give figures and analyses to both managers therefore if the lower manager is timorous we do not dread telling so. He has the capacity, he must propose a target adjusted to his potential."*

As this description of her work shows, even though they are not appointed to a decision-making position, management accountants are not reluctant to be authoritarian. As the future targets change, the actions elaborated to reach them also change. Work reorganisations gradually apply to new indicators or new targets. Even when the reorganisation only focuses on a specific part of the activity – such as vacancy prospecting or unemployed phoning – it affects the whole schedule. Indeed, job counsellors have to be more effective on the rest of their activities (Pillon & Quéré, 2014). As the human resources are stable, time repartition is a zero-sum game.

In *Pôle Emploi*, it remains important to distinguish two types of action plans: the annual action plans and the corrective action plans. Annual action plans derive from an iterative negotiation (6 months) and translate the General director's strategy or policy in various actions toward unemployed and recruiters. Conversely, corrective action plans occur between two rounds of negotiation, when scoreboards testify that the indicators of a division are crashing. Managers of this division are ordered to react by their upper manager. Depending on the level where the crash occurs — national, regional, departmental or local — corrective action plans skip the lower managers. Authoritarian reorganisations thus often bypass local managers since they are the last link in the chain of command. A local director describes how these operations weaken everyday work activity and daily work organization in his agency:

> Local manager (interviewed 2012):
> *"At the end of last year, when we had to adjust the schedule every day, it was pretty difficult to give sense to our action. They [upper managers] used to say: 'Put everybody on that target' but they only realized latter on that it could crash another indicator... and they therefore changed the action plan the next day. Me and my team we are not reluctants to break our backs on a brief period but if you do not settle the organisation this game won't last".*

Formerly powerless, management accountants sort the good and the bad action plans through a validation procedure within which they estimate the relevance of the reorganisation and its potential effects on the indicators. In their own language, they do not "play the tune". Implicitly, they mean that they composed the score.

Performance indicators frame the construction of bureaucratic problems: they are translated in a diagnosis of the situation. When the situation looks bad, they also shape the reaction to the problem, i.e. corrective action plans. Through such a process, management accountants interfere in the chain of command. The grammar of the scoreboards frames the decision process.

II.2. Steering changes: a power of translation

In *Pôle Emploi*, the General Director's strategy gives sense to the indicators and institutes a hierarchy between them. Thus, political bifurcations can change their signification. For instance, in 2011, two simultaneous events redistributed the values within scoreboards and the frame of the scoreboard itself. First, in November, the state enforced a new third year contract with *Pôle Emploi*. Then, in December, a new General director was appointed. He soon wrote a note called *Pôle Emploi 2015* corresponding to his own appropriation of the new contract. Management accountants reacted by delaying the performance dialog – waiting for the new strategy. They did not want to work for nothing and therefore paid attention to comply with the new strategy. The iconic decision integrated to the note *Pole Emploi 2015* was the end of the monthly supervision of the unemployed. Until then, unemployed people had to be seen every month by a personal counsellor. It was not possible anymore since the 2008 crisis, due to a lack of time. To maintain equity – and not equality – between unemployed the note put forward the following motto: "Do more for those who need more". Unemployed would be profiled and supervised depending on their employability. People with less difficulty would attend fewer appointments.

For the management accountants I interviewed, this step regarding supervision is risky for the matching mandate of *Pôle Emploi*. *Pôle Emploi* has to collect vacancies and place unemployed into it. Counsellors have time to do so and software to help them in that task: they can match the vacancy file with the unemployed file. Reducing the frequency of the appointment with the unemployed thus threatens the quality of the file matching. The information registered in each personal profile may be out of date and the matching – that entails a transmission of a letter to the unemployed telling him to apply – will be useless. People may have moved, found a job or entered a professional training institute, any event that could change the professional profile and the job search. Automatic matching may look like flailing at the air and management accountants are dreading a productivity decrease regarding the job placement indicators. To contend with this fear, they invited local managers to convoke most of the unemployed before the enforcement of the new strategy:

> Regional management accountant (interviewed 2012):
> *"We claim toward every local manager to keep on supervising appointment. We have to maintain a relation with the jobseekers before the new setup. It's important to maintain a certain monitoring with those we already received and it's important to meet the unemployed we have not seen for months. We have to clean the file to be the most effective we can in matching once the new strategy begins".*

The interference of management accountants in steering the changes goes further than this mere incitation. They also stand for a division of work between the counsellor in charge of the less unemployed and those assigned to the more autonomous. Local managers want to share the less unemployed between the counsellors. The reluctance of local directors to accept specialization is twofold. Frist, they risk losing the homogeneity of their "placing" workforce. As advisors become specialised, they may no longer be fully transferable between different workstations. Then, agency managers should manage the fact that part of their workforce would be emotionally affected by working only with the most "difficult" job-seekers, which can give way to a uselessness feeling. Against this mobilisation, management accountants achieve to impose a segmentation of counsellors. They actually point out that specialising on a specific task – e.g. supervising less employable unemployed – gives better yield.

> Regional management accountant (interviewed 2012):
> *"We did not want a job counsellor to have different kind of unemployed, that he could have convoke at different frequency. We wanted something we could steer through the schedule".*

Beyond the question of productivity, this citation also points out a power dimension in this decision: Schedules keep being a management tool, and a remote one furthermore. Work protocols are sometimes depicted like autonomous machines that have taken control over organisations (Bureau, 2011). But studying the norm incorporated into those devices and their appropriation process unveils social configurations within which people who have power seized the protocols, the tools and the technical instruments. In *Pôle Emploi*, at least, managers that believe in the power of quantification are more and more numerous and the last converted became the first supporters of quantification. If management accountants frame the daily work, it is just as much through their instruments as through their rhetoric interferences to comply the organisation of work with the measurement devices. They convince, they negotiate and they participate in the inner power struggle. They do not only calculate and quantify.

III. Make work pay: street level bureaucrats and the figures

Describing and analysing how management accountants work does not inform us on the way their interferences and interventions make their way to the job counsellors in local job centres. As local and middle-ranking managers claim to stand as buffers protecting their team, it is not sure that job counsellors are aware of the management accounting frame surrounding their work. Managers describe themselves as umbrellas, but do they achieve the protection the street level bureaucrats from scientific management? The answer is clearly negative. Coffee machine chats, cigarette breaks, informal discussions upon specific tasks, injunctive mails from the hierarchy or formal meetings in front of a "Power point", there are many places where discussions concern targets and performance indicators. Job counsellors know they are evaluated on a quantitative base. But how do they know so? The last part of this paper deals with specific agents who pass the grammar of the scoreboards in local agencies.

III.1. The importance of alley accountants

In *Pôle Emploi*, "Management accountant" is an occupation well delimited in the organisation chart. But workers move within the organisation in order to get a promotion or to live closer to their family. Consequently, some local managers or team leaders had position within management accounting department in district or regional directions. They then spread the management accounting culture in local agencies. They are not official accountants; I thus call them "alley accountants" – in reference to alley cats as opposed to domestic cats. What is at stake in their strategy is to make work pay – the job counsellors' work. Indeed, productivity does not only depend on the number of tasks performed but also on how tasks are recorded in software. Alley accountants commit to fit together, on the one hand, the "valorisation nomenclature" incorporated in the information system and, on the other hand, the professional conventions of job counsellors. The most important skill they try to teach is the ability to translate. Alley accountants do not try to erase the professional culture – based on social work tricks and consulting practices (Christensen et al., 2007) – they try to elaborate "coding conventions" between two grammars (Thévenot, 1983). This is the case of Christophe, whose reasoning is simple: since we, as counsellors, are evaluated by these devices, we must control how performance valuation works to defend us.

> Local agency team leader (interviewed 2011):
> *"According to the information system, only workshops and matching are meant to be efficient. If you give an address – and not a formal vacancy notification – to the unemployed, where he then finds a job, this is not efficient. If you rewrite his CV during an appointment – and not a collective workshop – this is not efficient... Unless you put wrong codes in the software, wrong codes that better describe what you did".*

Thus, from the point of view of Christophe, the methods of valuation mobilised by the counsellors are not the same as the evaluators' one. Counsellors do not do exactly what management expects of them. They act according to the way they see the information system. While the content of monthly appointments with the unemployed varies greatly depending on the specific characteristics of the unemployed and the labour market, the method of assessing the efficiency of counsellors' work is not very flexible. Labour market advice and guidance are not counted if they do not lead to a defined and identified service. Alley accountants such as Christophe stand for a recognition of counsellors' work and thus have an ambiguous effect on their subordinates' work. Through their mastery of the information system, they contribute to complying work with its representation into indicators and scoreboards. Contrarily, they also give weapons to their team mates – weapons to struggle against normalisation of tasks.

III.2. Clean scoreboards to pull the wool over managers' eyes – phony figures, true conventions

The investigations I conducted within the French employment system unveiled a triangle framework that binds together managers, management accountants and job counsellors, in which two sides are able to unite against the third. What is at stake is to organise work to comply with some specific targets such as performance targets, symbolic, or professional ones. This process occurs through a distribution of tasks in time – or schedules.

Management Accountants and Managers against Job Counsellors. This setup is the most common one. It occurs when action plans and corrective action plans reorganise the daily tasks without any debate or without taking the professional culture into account. In those cases, street level bureaucrats' submissiveness is taken for granted. But rebellions or at least resistance can also arise.

Job Counsellors and Managers against Management Accountants. Counsellors know part of the government science that monitors them. Above all, they know they take risks if figures are bad. Authoritarian corrective action plans could reorganise their work without any debate. To job counsellors, those reorganisations reduce the quality of their work both through work atmosphere and work results. Indeed, corrective action plans aim at formal targets, not real services. Corrective action plans skip professional conventions of what is fine-quality work. "I do not want to prostitute myself", once said a counsellor I was interviewing. In order to preserve their autonomy on their schedules, job counsellors therefore take control of the information system.

> Job counsellor (interviewed 2012):
> *"Figures are mandatory. Good figures mean more resources. If you want your agency to get more resources, you give your manager good results. It's a win-win agreement."*

This experienced counsellor is well aware of the budgetary dimension conveyed by the indicators. She engages in the diversion of the information system to offer her superiors a better bargaining power. But it is not a sacrifice. By playing this game, she tries to preserve her daily work from a loss of autonomy that could be more important. During the action plans, schedules are designed far from the local agencies. And such reorganisations reduce the ability of the most legitimate agents within the collective to negotiate their own schedules. Such an alliance, between counsellors and managers, allows counsellors to retain some of their own bargaining power. In that approach, performance indicators are not objective anymore and do not participate in describing what really happens on the ground. Figures turn into negotiation devices. Job counsellors code their tasks in the most efficient way to strengthen their position – so as to say their manager's position – in the *ratio* of power with the hierarchy. Job counsellors even elaborate "formal action plans" to disguise common daily work (such as big recruitment imposed by a recruiter) into aforethought aggressive strategies toward employers. That form of coding is called "regularisation" in the counsellors' *jargon*. A counsellor once said: "*Regularisation is tiresome but it is the best way to get recognition*". Some counsellors talk about "doping" to qualify such activities.

Those commitments to evaluation are rather problematic to management accountants. It reduces the quality of scoreboards and – thus – the quality of their analysis. "Regularisation" uncouples daily work and its representation in the information system, it threatens Management accountants' legitimacy.

Job Counsellors and Management Accountants against Managers. Job counsellors play with the science that monitors them. They use performance indicators as negotiation devices. They are then able to use the information system to frame bureaucratic problems. From 2008 to 2011, job counsellors in the biggest job centres – 90–120 counsellors – achieved a withdrawal of unemployed monthly supervision to make the managers aware of the gap between reality – economic crisis – and the targets – personal supervision of each jobseeker. Instead of doping, those specific counsellors decided to formally apply work procedure. The unemployed that could not be seen were not "regularised" and their register left blank. That kind of work-to-rule awoke management accountants' consciousness about the real aftermaths of economic crisis: too much jobseeker to supervise. Management accounting gradually convinced managers to abandon the performance indicators related to the proportion of jobseekers that were supervised. Strategic uses of counter-performance rest on an implicit union between job counsellors and management accountants against manager strategies to maximise results. What is at stake is to impose one specific interpretation of the curves: bad figures are due to a lack of resources, not a lack of organisation.

Conclusion

The situation described in this paper could let the reader think of a complete illusive configuration, an administration without steering or a fake employment policy. This interpretation may not lead to neglecting any sense of performance indicators. Those tools keep on being material measurement devices, strongly rooted in job counsellors' software. Arguing that those devices are "biased" by non-conform interventions could convey the idea that an objective and omniscient registration of real work is possible and desirable. Such an approach would resurrect a "realistic" – or positivist – vision of statistics (Desrosières, 2003b) that widely disappeared since the Second World War. I would like to suggest a more constructivist pattern. Management accountants tackle figures that circulate through multiple arenas of argumentation. In each arena, appropriation processes change the sense of the figures.

Among those processes, the most important one is the legitimisation one: every professional group (managers, job counsellors and even management accountants) use figures in a specific way to enhance its position. Measuring the work in an administration therefore opens onto an arena of controversies where what is at stake is what work is worth.

From this point of view, a study of management accounting in the French public employment service using the tools of the historical sociology of quantification largely fits to the results of neo-institutionalism. To explain the power of management by figures, "professional, cultural and political forces" (Shenhav, 1995, p. 557) appear at least as important as the technical dimensions of management tools (Meyer & Rowan, 1977). The study of the sets of actors within the organisations thus makes it possible to open the black box of institutional isomorphism (DiMaggio & Powell, 1983). This does not mean that technical devices do not contribute to these legitimisation process deployed by the measurement engineers. Nevertheless, it must be borne in mind that accounting systems develop jointly and mutually reinforce each other with rhetorical processes which are politically structured.Acknowledgements

The author would truly like to thank Mathilde Pillon for the translation of this text from French to English and Paul Lagneau-Ymonnet for his remarks and commentaries about the rationale.

Note

1 They even quote H. Mintzberg during interviews.

References

Bezes, P. (2009): *Réinventer l'État*, Paris: Presses Universitaires de France.
Bezes, P. (2005): 'L'État et les savoirs managériaux: Essor et développement de la gestion publique en France', in: Lacasse F. Verdier P.E. (Ed) *30 ans de réforme de l'État*, 9-40, Paris: Dunod.
Bezes, P, et Musselin C. (2015) : 'Le new public management', in: Boussaguet L., Jaquet S. Ravinet P. (Ed.), Une « French touch » dans l'analyse des politiques publiques, 125-152. Paris: Presses de Science po.
Bowker, G.C., Star, S.L. (1998): 'Building Information Infrastructures for Social Worlds – The Role of Classifications and Standards', in: Ishida T. *Community Computing and Support Systems, Social Interaction in Networked Communities*, 231–248, London: Springer Verlag.
Bureau, M.-C. (2011): 'Du travail à l'action publique : quand les dispositifs d'évaluation prennent le pouvoir', in: *Cahiers internationaux de sociologie*, 128–129(1): 161–175.
Callon, M. (1986): 'Éléments pour une sociologie de la traduction : la domestication des coquilles Saint-Jacques et des marins-pêcheurs dans la baie de Saint-Brieuc', in: *L'Année sociologique*, 36: 169–208.
Callon, M. (1998): 'An Essay On Framing and Overflowing: Economic Externalities Revisited by Sociology', in: Callon M. *The Laws of the Markets*, 244–269, Oxford: Blackwell.

Carruthers, B.G., Espeland, W.N. (1991): 'Accounting for Rationality: Double-Entry Bookkeeping and the Rhetoric of Economic Rationality', in: *American Journal of Sociology*, 97(1): 31–69.

Christensen, T., Fimreite, A.L., Lægreid, P. (2007): 'Reform of the Employment and Welfare Administrations – The Challenges of Co-ordinating Diverse Public Organizations', *International Review of Administrative Sciences*, 73(3): 389–408.

Cournot, A.-A. (1980): *Recherches sur les principes mathématiques de la théorie des richesses*, Paris: J. Vrin.

DiMaggio, P. J., Powell W. W. (1983): 'The iron cage revisited: Institutional isomorphism and collective rationality in organizational fields' in: American sociological review, 147–160.

Desrosières, A. (1993): *La politique des grands nombres : histoire de la raison statistique*, Paris: la Découverte.

Desrosières, A. (2003a): 'Historiciser l'action publique : l'État, le marché et les statistiques', in: Laborier P. and Trom D. (Ed.): *Historicités de l'action publique.* 207–221, Paris.

Desrosières, A. (2003b): 'Les qualités des quantités', in: *Courrier des statistiques*, 105(106): 51–63.

Desrosières, A. (2008): *L'argument statistique I Pour une sociologie historique de la quantification*, Paris: Mines ParisTech-les Presses.

Didier, E. (2000): *De l'échantillon à la population: sociologie de la généralisation par sondage aux États-Unis avant la Seconde Guerre mondiale*. Thèse de doctorat. École nationale supérieure des mines, Paris: France.

Gusfield, J.R. (1984): *The Culture of Public Problems: Drinking-Driving and the Symbolic Order*, Chicago: The University of Chicago Press.

Hespel, V., Lecerf P.-E., Monnet E, (2011): 'Etude comparative des effectifs des services publics de l'emploi en France, en Allemagne et au Royaume-Uni'. Inspection Générale des Finances.

Hodgson, D. (2002): 'Disciplining the Professional : The Case of Project Management', in: *Journal of Management Studies*, 39(6): 803–821.

Hood, C. (1995): 'The "New Public Management" in the 1980s: Variations on a Theme', in: *Accounting, Organizations and Society*, 20(2): 93–109.

Hood, C. (2010): The blame game: Spin, bureaucracy, and self-preservation in government. Princeton: Princeton University Press.

Kitchener, M. (2002): 'Mobilizing the Logic of Managerialism in Professional Fields: The Case of Academic Health Centre Mergers', in: *Organization Studies*, 23(3): 391–420.

Latour, B. (1993): *Petites leçons de sociologie des sciences*, Paris: La Découverte.

Maynard-Moody, S., Stull, D.D., Mitchell, J. (1986): 'Reorganization as Status Drama: Building, Maintaining, and Displacing Dominant Subcultures', in: *Public Administration Review*, 46(4): 301–310.

Meyer, J.W., Rowan, B. (1977): 'Institutionalized Organizations: Formal Structure as Myth and Ceremony', in: American Journal of Sociology 83(2): 340–363.

Miller, P., O'Leary, T. (1993): 'Accounting Expertise and the Politics of the Product: Economic Citizenship and Modes of Corporate Governance', in: *Accounting, Organizations and Society*, 18(2–3): 187–206.

Mintzberg, H. (1980): 'Structure in fives: A Synthesis of the Research on Organization Design', in: *Management Science*, 26(3): 322–341.

Pillon, J.-M., Quéré, O. (2014): 'La planification de l'action publique à l'échelle du planning', in: *Temporalités*, 19: 2–15.

Power, M. (1996): 'Making things auditable', in: *Accounting, Organizations and Society*, 21(2–3): 289–315.

Shenhav, Y. (1995): 'From chaos to systems: The engineering foundations of organization theory, 1879–1932', in: Administrative Science Quarterly, 557–585.

Schön, D.A. (1991): *The Reflective Practitioner: How Professionals Think in Action*, Aldershot: Arena.

Thévenot, L. (1983): 'L'économie du codage social', in: *Critiques de l'économie politique*, 23–24: 188–222.

Vatin, F. (2011): Évaluer et valoriser – Une sociologie économique de la mesure, Toulouse: Presses universitaires du Mirail.

Weller, J.-M. (2000): 'Une controverse au guichet: vers une magistrature sociale?' in: *Droit et Société*, 44(45): 91–109.

Chapter 3

Labour market experts and their professional practices technologies of self-control of job placement professionals

Frank Sowa and Ronald Staples

1 Introduction: organisations and 'rationalized institutional myths'

Organisations do not arise because they are functional to solve societal problems and therefore ensure society's survival, but organisations are the result of socially negotiated interpretations and classifications. Organisational action is therefore based on the idea circulating in society that actions of organisations are considered socially appropriate and rational. It is the result of social processes of negotiation and therefore changeable. Meyer and Rowan (1977) identify 'rationalized institutional myths' when they argue that organisations incorporate societally rationalised procedures to achieve legitimacy. These procedures are characterised on the basis that they contain largely unverifiable or taken for granted assumptions about rational organising, which are often unquestioningly accepted by the organisations. Organisations are then rational when they take on socio-cultural notions of rationality and visibly symbolise that they use the best means of achieving the purpose when processing a social concern, independently of the practices' actual efficacy: "Institutionalized products, services, techniques, policies, and programs function as powerful myths, and many organizations adopt them ceremonially" (Meyer & Rowan, 1977, p. 340).

In our case, from the early 1990s the public employment service (PES) in Germany was confronted with the threat of being broken up as unemployment levels increased significantly, with labour market policies and the national labour administration held responsible for those increases. The organisation of job placement and counselling was regarded as inefficient and ineffective. Consequently, a reorientation of labour market policies occurred, which considerably influenced the public institutions that process unemployment. The rational organisation of unemployment was influenced by environmental expectations that are, naturally, as a result of the different concepts of rationality in plural societies, conflicting and contradictory. These expectations contain ideas about the rational organisation and influence the organisational action. Organisations adapt to these rationalized institutional myths. Sahlin-Andersson (2001) spoke in terms of 'travelling ideas' (ideas, concepts and models) that are continually revised and changed by the organisations in an active process of translation. The survival of organisations will therefore be subject to obtaining societal legitimacy through the taking up of these myths.

Two of these myths or travelling ideas are 'new public management' (NPM) and the strategy of 'activation' that transformed the PES in the course of numerous reforms. NPM and administrative reforms (Hood, 1991, 1995; Sahlin-Andersson, 2001) have the common goal of introducing concepts, organisational structures and assessment criteria from the private into the public sector. Additionally, the PES has been affected by the introduction of economically driven control concepts, which resulted in increased managerialism and economic thinking within these services. These administrative reforms aimed to increase the efficiency and effectiveness of the PES (i.e. to improve the speed at which the unemployed entered employment and to reduce the number of individuals in receipt of unemployment benefits). However, at the same time, the PES reflected itself increasingly as service provider, as indicated by the use of the term 'customer' to address job seekers instead of 'client'. Addressing people who are seeking a new job and have to make use of their unemployment insurance benefits is changing the relationship between these two actors substantially. A 'contractual' relationship came into being between job seekers and the state (Sol & Westerveld, 2005), that confirms the 'welfare to workfare' strategy rooted in the British "new deal" of labour market policy (Walker & Wiseman, 2003). Integration contracts were created, which established rights and obligations on the part of individuals and the state (Born & Jensen, 2010; OECD, 2007; Tergeist & Grubb, 2006).

Research in PESs on the impact of these activation policies on job seekers has shown that it is difficult to provide services within a culture of legally prescribed compulsion. For example, Rosenthal and Peccei (2007) noted in their research on Jobcentre Plus in the UK that a highly mixed picture emerges after introducing customer language: the language of rights and choices is combined with the language of commitment, monitoring and control within the same documents. Therefore, the customer language in this organisation can be interpreted differently, depending on where the emphasis is put (Rosenthal & Peccei, 2007, p. 217). However, from the perspective of job seekers, activating labour market policies resulted in an individualisation of unemployment (Ludwig-Mayerhofer, 2010). In this context, activation is understood as a de-standardisation and individualisation of the duties and responsibilities of the job seeker. In place of involving them in the decision-making process of the PES, unemployed individuals are required – instead – to provide details of their availability for work, document their efforts to end their unemployment and demonstrate employability (Borghi & Berkel, 2007).

In order to secure the legitimacy needed to survive, the rationalised institutional myths of NPM and activation were taken up by the PES. Telling about what efforts one has made to end unemployment and to show employability by obeying the rules of this contractualised relationship can be analysed as subjectification (Foucault, 2009). On becoming a managerially driven labour administration, the formal structure changed. The organisation now encourages and – at the same time – makes demands on its 'customers' and deploys its financial resources more sparingly, having regard to cost-benefit considerations. The principle of activation together with the notion of mutual obligations is enforced through individual action plans (IAPs), set up during counselling interviews.

Previous studies on activation policies in a managerially driven PES avoided analysing the consequences of such policies for the actions of PES management and placement personnel. Focussing on the practices of the PES enables us to examine the new direction of labour market policy. Our case study of the German Federal Employment Agency (German acronym is BA), allows us to determine general trends resulting from activation, examining a 'special case of what is possible' (Bourdieu, 1998, p. 2). In our case study, the number of job placement officers at specific sites of BA was increased. Consequently, each placement officer worked with only 70 job seekers. As a result, each participating local office provided intensive support to every job seeker and, in one office, each placement officer was encouraged to identify a so called 'customer of the week' to whom particular support was provided. We examine the customer of the week exemplarily, assuming that herein the new quality of the relationship between job placement officers and their clients can be depicted properly. In our case study, we examine how PES management assesses an intensified relationship between job placement officers and the unemployed. How does the strategic improvement to the support ratio affect job placement practice? How are job seekers and placement professionals affected? As we show, the same organisational strategy is interpreted in different and, sometimes, contradictory ways by the individual actors and, if our assumption is correct, reflects an intensification of the subjectification as 'Unemployed' and as 'Job Placement Officer'. This contribution cautions against any simplistic mapping of specific actions to predetermined categories of labour market instruments. Namely, on the basis of the present empirical sample, we show that, within the framework of an organisation with the power to impose sanctions, rational action can produce particularly serious adverse consequences.

Before we discuss our case study empirically, we sketch out our theoretical framework by reflecting Michel Foucault's thoughts on the conditions of the disciplinary society and the concept of subjectification in Section 2 (Foucault, Martin, Gutman & Hutton, 1988). This framework enables an analysis of the data on intensive support to show a concretisation of societal disciplinary techniques. In Section 3, we present activating labour market policies and their implications for clients dealing with PES job placement personnel as the form of subjectification conceptualised before. These policies have been harnessed by many welfare states in central Europe, leading to reforms in their labour administration. We then describe our case, where we observed a project at PES that experimented with an increased support ratio in selected employment agencies (Section 4). This is followed by a discussion of the empirical analysis in relation to our theoretical framework (Section 5). Finally, we reflect our findings and problematise the issue of constant change in organisations of public welfare as an ambiguous governmental principle of organising (Section 6).

2 Disciplinary society and subjectification as analysis models for changes in 'organizing' job placement

Foucault's understanding of the development of disciplinary societies[1] and his reflections on subjectification as a twofold form of becoming a subject are the reference concepts that are used to analyse the specific activation variants and the resulting and observed practices. This combination of two main elements of Foucault's theory of power may shed a light on the complex interferences on a transsubjective (abstract) level of governmental power relations and concrete interactions. It seeks to explain how different and overlapping institutional structures can affect a rationally intended instrument of placement policy resulting in the (unintended) side effects observed in our empirical research and illustrate the productivity of modern power relations (Foucault, 1978).

The highly effective activation paradigm considered in this case study does not lead to action on the part of individual actors that is more reflective, i.e. more active. But it fosters a form of subjectification[2] that may be pointedly described, following Foucault (1995), as a radical form of individualisation and collectivisation at once (Rose, 1999), enacted during interactions of counselling interviews. In this paper, analysis of the disciplinary society occupies a key position, particularly because Foucault locates disciplinary techniques as developments of pastoral power (Foucault, 2009). Pastoral power is rooted in the early Christian ritual of confession, establishing and increasingly refining a highly specific power relationship in interactions. Foucault unveils in his analysis of confessional practices a strict system or economy that acts in an individualising way when actors subjectify themselves and obey (Foucault, 2009, p. 233). The relationship of dependency cannot be understood to descend from the pastor to a single member of the flock because the pastor is an inherent part of this differentiated reciprocal relation. Pastoral power and the anonymous discipline principles bridges Foucault in the concept of 'Governmentality'. It names the paradox of constructing a population and individualising at once (McKinlay, Carter & Pezet, 2012). How does this tight-knit order occur? To remain at the historical level, one is referred to the interaction between pastor and flock, and this ordering occurs in part linguistically. Therefore, the relationships outlined must occur or take effect through speech. As modern human sciences emerged in the late 18th century, the verbalisation became constitutive for forming a new self (Foucault et al., 1988). Moreover, the institutional surface of the pastoral power has changed a lot since the era of enlightenment and Foucault puts the state in the role of the pastor, where individualisation and governmental institutions knit a new form of pastoral power (Foucault et al., 1988, p. 380). But this pastoral dispositive does not perfect itself through a tightening of the controls on the unemployed (who are always suspected of idleness). Instead, it seems that in all societal conditions individual activity has become the central *normality*. Thus, from a genealogical perspective, the intensive support on *customers of the week* discussed here constitutes a preliminary culmination of pastoral power in which flock and sheep find themselves subjectified within the same *tactics* (Foucault, 1995) and become the object of a universal disciplining of individuals. Analysing this as part of a dispositive one can take into account that "the realized strategic pattern may not have been expressly intended by anyone, but comes into existence as the result of an ongoing interaction and stays subject to further modification" (Raffnsøe, Gudmand-Høyer & Thaning, 2014, p. 15). Time represents the central category of discipline. According to Foucault, the differentiation of time is the most productive means to implement the mechanics of disciplinary training.

In the intensive support examined in our case study, time differentiation appears to be a central dimension of the activating efforts. Foucault shows that the dissection of time (and thus its decreasing subjective availability) significantly intensifies the quality of disciplining techniques. The individual measures of external discipline, such as those concerning time allocation (requirements to attend meetings in person and telephone reporting), are successively internalised by individuals until the external, transformed to something internal, is externalised again (Deleuze, 1987). Foucault mentions that discipline produces a positive economy that relies on a principle assuming a theoretically endlessly increasing use of time (Foucault, 1995). In differentiating time as finely as possible, the most consistent and productive use of time is facilitated. For that reason, the necessary physical gestures of the activity are combined with the differentiation of time, with subject and object necessarily correlated as reciprocals.

Another question is whether, by means of the instrument of intensive support, the panoptical disciplinary society has not simply experienced an update of its own strategies, supplemented, however, by efficiency criteria conferring a new quality to the strategy of quantifiable time structures (Scheer, 1976). In fact, it seems that the justiciable disposability on individual time structure is the methodological key to achieving the obedience or manageability of not only the unemployed but also of society in general. In this special type of organisation, the BA as the subject of our case study, there are two other terms of importance for our analysis: the travelling ideas of IAPs and 'accounting' (Mäkitalo, 2003, 2006). These two phenomena, which are rooted in business administration, are representative for subjectification in labour, observed over many years in the social sciences. Above all, in industrial sociology and the sociology of work, a change in the construction of work subjects has been observed for some two decades or more. This change primarily concerns the phenomenon whereby increasingly more tasks, in the form of values or work ideals, are assigned to individual workers, who internalise these formerly external tasks or values and then externalise them again as a genuine component of a work subject. The most popular metaphors for this phenomenon are the 'labour entrepreneur' and 'the entrepreneurial self' (Bröckling, 2007; Pongratz & Voss, 2003).

Both the tactics of IAPs and accounting can be perceived as capillary techniques of modern pastoral power. The use of IAPs has become widespread as an instrument of the activating welfare state in Europe following the restructuring of many such regimes in particular with regard to placement of the unemployed (Rosenthal & Peccei, 2007). Recent studies note two effects. First, job seekers are constructed in dialogue as a specific form of subject,[3] who are subject to rules on activity and as experts reflect their own selves. The final contractual agreement then appears as a certificate of access to the labour market. The signature of the assistance-seeking subject under a contract-like agreement is constitutive of the unemployed person's role (Born & Jensen, 2010).

Second, this approach entails a contradiction for the welfare state bureaucracy. Verifiable and cost-effective administration and implementation of instruments contradicts a highly individualised consulting practice with very little potential for replication or generalisation of placement activities. The ambiguity of the notion of accountability is implicit in these two findings and clearly reflected in the empirical results of our research. In the context of managing the unemployed, 'to account for something' means that job seekers must subjectify themselves through the publication of their activities (in applying for jobs). At the same time, it provides placement officers, through additional human control of placement activities, with information on their performance in the form of standardized indicators (Lambert & Pezet, 2012; Mäkitalo, 2006).

In relation to the institutional system of the PES, we organise our analytical considerations in the following manner. Strategic actions of modern PES are subject to effects produced by other governmental relations, in particular, the Economy (the PES must act in a business-like manner) and Ideology (should the unemployed be *disciplined* or do they need to be *helped*). Finally, IAPs and accounting techniques designate a specific set of practices that subjectify individuals within this dispositive of 'Managerial Welfare'. But just to remember, these strategies, which look like well-coordinated actions, have not been determined by Governmentality Principles. Nevertheless, they demonstrate the productivity of pastoral power as our findings indicate (McKinlay et al., 2012).

3 The form of subjectification: activation in meetings with PES job placement professionals

The German PES has been under pressure to undergo reform since the 1990s. The loss of its monopoly on job placement and the introduction of private labour brokers in 1994 required a re-establishment of the legitimacy of a *public* service (Schmidtke-Glamann, 1995). The pressure for institutional reform increased and focused primarily on internal administrative restructuring, the computerisation of internal processes and services, the implementation of guidance and control systems, budgeting, the introduction of 'customer' and 'service' terminology and task specialisations. The internal administrative restructuring that began in 1994 resulted in the introduction of model PES offices, such as the testing of a new organisational idea, the 'Employment Office 2000', which was introduced nationwide in 2000. The objectives of these reform efforts were customer focus, efficiency and a focus on staff. Ultimately, therefore, they aimed to increase the efficiency and effectiveness of the PES in the shape of BA by introducing elements of NPM.

In a similar vein to Giddens' notion of "No rights without responsibilities" (Giddens, 1998, p. 66), the idea that the state should both encourage and make demands of individuals (in German, *Fördern und Fordern*) was established as a new principle in German labour market policy, now described as 'activating' and not 'active'. Activation, with its functional logics of self-control and social investment, unfolded in the German discourse (Lessenich, 2005) through the Blair-Schröder paper (Blair & Schröder, 1999) and *The Politics of the New Centre*, a book by the head of the Chancellery, Hombach (1998). The entry into force of new legislation (the Third Book of the Social Code, known as 'SGB III') in 1998 has been described in the literature as a major break in the continuity of German labour market policy, which assumed a new direction with the introduction of *activation*. Job seekers must now take responsibility themselves for their labour market situation and not simply rely on the placement efforts by the PES ('passive labour market availability'). Now, the focus was on an active search for employment, which had to be demonstrated to the PES (Schmuhl, 2003). As a core task of the German labour administration, PES activities were intensified by an increase in personnel and the adoption of a preventive orientation.

A scandal in 2002 concerning the rate of successful labour market integrations was the trigger for further reforms. The German PES, then renamed to BA, was expected to evolve from a public authority to a modern service provider on the labour market. This service provider is committed to a business logic that seeks primarily to increase the efficient and effective use of resources. To that end, a segmented job placement policy was introduced. That is, resources are allocated according to different action programmes that depend on the labour market chances of job seekers, now segmented into customer groups or profile layers (Kaltenborn, Knerr & Schiwarov, 2006).

In this reformed labour administration, counselling interviews with job seekers form the central task for employee-oriented placement professionals. These meetings take place in accordance within a legal framework setting out the relationship between the PES and job seekers. Internal requirements based on the business objectives of the Federal Employment Agency accompany this framework. At the level of placement officers these requirements crystallise as targets, process management and controlling and therefore affect interview practice. Thanks to the requirements of an activating welfare and labour market regime, counselling interviews take on a new quality. Because of increased staffing levels and the specialisation of placement officers, employee-oriented professionals are now responsible only for job seekers and, in addition, have considerably improved resources in terms of time. This improvement allowed meetings with job seekers to occur more frequently and to last longer. Now, during the first counselling interview, job placement specialists can determine the labour market fit of the job seeker using a software-based profiling tool. Usually they record specific knowledge and skills and search for appropriate vacancies. In this way, the 'travelling ideas' of activation and mutual obligations were implemented with the help of IAPs (Born & Jensen, 2010). Such obligations include, for example, attending counselling interviews, applying for jobs proposed by the placement officer, documenting efforts to find a new job, accepting a suitable job offer and participation in employment or training measures. The introduction of the IAP method places the counselling interview within a contractual framework.

4 The case study, data collection and methods used

Within the framework of the Federal Employment Agency's pilot project 'Increased intermediary capacity in selected types of region', from 2007 to 2010, the ratio of placement staff to clients was improved in 14 local offices of the PES. This pilot project constitutes our concrete case. During this period, one placement specialist supervised 70 unemployed individuals in receipt of Unemployment Benefit I (*Arbeitslosengeld I*). For offices taking part in the pilot project, this meant an increase of placement staff by 100% and in smaller agencies staff numbers quadrupled. The intention of the pilot project was that increased staffing alone would lead to better outcomes in terms of placing the unemployed. The pilot project aimed to verify how reasonable it is to expect that an increased contact density or intensity of counselling will significantly shorten the duration of unemployment, achieve additional labour market integration and increase correspondingly the number of vacancies successfully filled. The budget head for integration, in other words, for active labour market policy measures, was to remain unchanged.

The considerable decrease in the number of job seekers to support brought about significant change in the daily routine of placement officers. The relationship with customers was intensified, i.e. both the time spent counselling and contact frequency increased. In addition, most of the offices participating in the pilot launched their own efforts to harness these new resources productively.[4] For example, following the October 2007 staff increase, one local office experimented with particularly intensive support for unemployed individuals. Each employee-oriented placement officer was asked to identify from their pool of clients a 'customer of the week' (trans_04_10, paragraph 75) and to work with the selected customer more intensively than with other unemployed individuals to achieve a rapid integration into the labour market. This included the possibility to call the unemployed individual into the office every day for counselling interviews or to accompany the individual personally to job interviews with employers ('assisted placement'). Intensive support was provided for a period of 1 month.

The data used in this paper stems from a local office of the PES that was visited during the pilot period from September 2007 to November 2010. A total of 568 empirical ethnographic data were collected from regional agencies, regional directorates and the BA's headquarters: 254 interviews with job placement officers, 133 interviews with managerial personnel, 75 interviews with jobseekers and 12 interviews with staff councils. There are also 94 participatory observations of counselling interviews between placement professionals and jobseekers. The pilot project carried out by the PES took place in 14 local agencies spread over Germany. Our data originates mainly from one of these 14 regional agencies. In this regional agency, we conducted 10 qualitative interviews with placement professionals, eight with executive staff (including the chief executive of the branch, the departmental head and the team leader) and one with a member of the works council. The primary method of data collection chosen was a series of semi-structured interviews with experts (Brinkmann, Deeke & Völkel, 1995; Trinczek, 1995) with a view to examining both management and placement professionals at the level of action. In addition to gathering expert knowledge, the interviews sought to reveal knowledge of a subjective kind and patterns of interpretation and to reconstruct the collective discourse on the organizational changes resulting from the reforms. Nonetheless, in keeping with the notion of an 'understanding' interview, conversations were guided to focus on relevant stories raised by the interviewee. Therefore, the list of questions was used as 'flexible guidance' (Kaufmann, 1999). Additionally, to the interview data we present findings from participant observations of counselling interviews conducted in nine agencies that were part of the pilot project (36 observations in total). The observations focussed on the non-verbal corporal expressions during counselling interviews and asked if they do also shape the process of the IAP dialogue. For the purposes of the present article, all transcripts of the interviews and observations carried out with individuals working at the office experimenting with intensive support were thematically encoded and evaluated. Case reconstruction followed the utterances and interpretations expressed by management and placement staff involved in the intensive support experiment.

5 Loose ties between formal structure and actual activity: presentation of the case study and theoretical reflections

In the previous sections of this article, the motif of 'activation' was introduced as a strategy adopted by contemporary welfare state regimes and related to current academic discourse. Furthermore, as a theoretical framework for activation, we presented Foucault's idea of disciplinary techniques and subjectification, conceptualised as specific practices an individual is subject to in modern welfare to workfare systems (Borghi & Berkel, 2007). Following that, we set out the empirical basis for our research project and its embedding in the specific framework of the German welfare state bureaucracy. The current section reconstructs the present case study through selected statements of interviewees and examines those observations in the light of governmentality (Foucault, 2009). Fundamental to this reconstruction is the assumption that this special measure of 'intensive support' not only subjects job seekers to a significant discipline but that this discipline also affects the placement professionals themselves. The accounting practice[5] associated with intensive support has radically subjectified both groups of actors as our empirical findings show. Job seeker and placement officer subjectify themselves by playing the game within its frame of public welfare and bureaucratic artisanship, exerting pressure on both in the same way.

In the light of our empirical data, we show that organisational strategies used as a form of authority in implementing this strategy among the intensive support interaction networks of the organisation represents a complex mode of subjectification. The organisational instruction to pick a 'customer of the week' requires integrating this specific job seeker within a month and, if not, the job seeker will be deselected. We therefore believe that these guidelines increase the pressure not only on job seekers but also on placement professionals because the latter must choose week in, week out promising candidates and to justify why the integration deadline was not met. The gaps between the formal structure and actual activities are an example of complex organisational ties, resulting in unintended consequences for placement officers.

The specific experiences of placement professionals are contrasted pairwise in the following with the conceptual perspectives of executive staff, supplemented by relevant ethnographic data. The first set of material contrasts expectations surrounding the pilot project with narratives of staff experience. The placement specialists speaking here reflect on their experience, contrasting it with the organizational framework that usually governs placement practice. In the second part, supervisors provide an account of the development of the different variants of intensive support. The job placement specialist reflects on how the expectations of managers – as she sees them – have an impact on her working practices. From the first pair of quotations, we extrapolate how the practical entanglement of acute demands for business-like efficiency in welfare state bureaucratic action and the existing disciplinary techniques of activating labour market politics result, through changes to the use of the global resource[6] time, in the instrument of intensive support. The second pair of quotations shows the effects of intensive support on job seekers and placement professionals and reveals how this tactic constitutes an effective element of subjective governmentality.

5.1 Changes to the everyday routine of placement professionals as a result of the pilot project

The increased staffing resources within the pilot project made themselves felt through an ostensibly significant increase in the individual counselling time that could be provided to job seekers. Job placement professionals were able to schedule meetings with job seekers approximately every 2 weeks. Asked about the impact of staff increases on placement, a placement officer from the employee-oriented team gives the following response:

> Well, first of all, um, we have, we have much more time for client interviews. [...] There is definitely real trust now. That's because they have to come more frequently. I usually do every two weeks. [...] Um, you get to know each other much better. You really get to know their quirks; that's something you have to know. Um, customers' motivation, so that I know 'Okay, this one always misses appointments,' I don't need to send those to the top employers, because they would then probably be annoyed. These are things you get to find out. [...] Well, yes, advice, labour market instruments, such as training measures, trial positions, training. [...] That was done very superficially in the past. And now, [it is] so much more intense.
>
> (trans_04_03, paragraph 55)

It is noticeable that the placement officer speaks of a (newly acquired) trust, facilitated by the frequent personal contacts, while, at the same time, she refers to the unemployed in a strongly distanced and thus objectifying way, using either the generalised label 'customers' or simply the pronoun 'they'. However, this way of speaking unveils a specific practice of individualisation. In this practice, using those characteristics (or skills) deemed relevant by systemic requirements, the 'customer object' is individualised. The 'matching machine' reduces clients to their 'factor status as a worker' (Hielscher & Ochs, 2009), in which the subjective needs of individuals and their desires, motivations, interests and resources are relegated to the background. In addition, based on her comments, it appears reasonable to claim that the respondent used the word 'trust' to indicate that, as a result of the increased contact frequency and the attendant improvement in communication, she had acquired greater confidence in her placement strategy.

Almost as it appears in Foucault's analysis, the effect of (modern) power relations are observable in the process of intensive support, in which truths, the truths of the individual, are produced (Foucault, 2007). In other words, job seekers are subjected to a selective placement practice depending on their individual behaviour, as perceived by the placement officer (Born & Jensen, 2010; Mäkitalo, 2006). One of the managers interviewed states that the improved support ratio and the associated intensification of the support provided comes close to the ideal placement situation:

> <u>This</u> is how we always <u>really wanted</u> to work. And as a placement officer, quite honestly, I would only welcome this. <u>Intensive</u> support and really be able to take the <u>time</u> with customers. One and a half hours for the first meeting. That would have been a <u>dream</u> for me. Back in my day, I sometimes had ten-minute meetings.
> (trans_04_10, paragraph 89)

The executive associates the motif of 'taking the time' for individual job seekers with his seemingly positively connoted idea of intensive support. However, as he explains the benefits to the PES of this additional time, the pastoral-therapeutic theme of 'taking the time' is displaced in favour of a considerably more sophisticated gain of information. The individualisation of job seekers ('Where are the sticking points?') takes priority and in this regard follows the promise of the matching strategy, which suggests that for each individual job seeker there is a suitable job (and vice versa). If suitable jobs are lacking, obtaining more information about the abilities, skills, inclinations of the job seekers and the obstacles that they face may help to overcome this issue. The relationship between the placement officers and job seekers significantly intensified during the pilot project because meetings took place approximately every 2 weeks. As the observational sequence shows, the 'normal' ongoing relationship follows its own kind of conversational conventions (Goffman, 1982) and not only in this case the job seeker anticipates the meeting's routine. This may be not only an effect of routinisation, but also as disciplinary progress.

> Customer (C) 'So, next appointment in 14 days as it was this time or will it be a bit longer again?
> Placement officer (PO): Yes, I would say, let's see, under this set-up we can meet more often as, well, there are a few coming, uh, amongst the jobs coming in, there might be something there (C: Yes) so depending on that, if something really, if I see that there are more jobs available, then let's, well, then, as far as I'm concerned, we can increase the gap between meetings [...]
> PO: That's how we'll do it then. And as we had it before here's the target agreement for your records, yes, (C: Mm) it's the same as last time. And here we go, I need another signature again in that box. In fact, er, there's nothing really new, it's just the latest version. (C: Mm) Like last time.
> (trans_R_07_5_12_B; paragraphs 962–1046)

The job seeker's initial question is possibly uttered in the counterfactual hope that they will not have to come again in 14 days. However, the placement officer states unmistakably (without offending the job seeker directly) that this will be the mandatory routine until enough new vacancies arise.

In the following section, we analyse a selection of statements reflecting on 'intensive support' as a specific and existing practice within the scope of placement activities. Here again, both executives and managers of the organization and providers of intensive support were given the opportunity to speak.

5.2 Intensive support: the 'customer of the week'

As illustrated in the previous examples, the respondents had high expectations regarding the increased time available for each job seeker. In particular, the improvement or simply the establishment of trust was expected. In addition, the interviewees assumed that the improved relationship would lead to an increase in the detail and quality of the information and that the contexts and background of the job seekers could be explored and documented. Below, we discuss significant statements the practice of intensive support. *The following* sequence clarifies how a placement officer singles out a certain job seeker as 'customer of the week':

> Let me put it like this. Placement officers should choose someone every week, where they say [...], 'that's someone who's so motivated and committed and on the ball, we can get him placed very quickly. We are going to support him. We can do something here.'
>
> (trans_04_10, paragraph 75)

A feature worth noting in this sequence is the contingency that exists from the perspective of the organization. The placement professional can invite certain individuals to participate and exclude others. For the unemployed individual, intensive support does not constitute an 'opportunity' rather it is something that excludes opportunities (to do other things). In this connection, activity on the part of the job seeker is necessary to qualify for selection. According to this account, intensive support is something that has additional benefits for the unemployed person. It constitutes a reward for being active, which results in activity on the part of the organisation. For the management respondent, this strategy has a dual advantage. First, job seekers can be integrated more rapidly in the labour market and, second, this can be regarded as a placement success for the organization. Therefore, from the organisation's perspective, it is logical to select only job seekers already perceived as particularly active and to interpret this activity as a sign that such job seekers have both a greater interest and likelihood of achieving a rapid re-entry to the labour market. In practice, the executive continues, placement specialists have different interpretations for the use of intensive support.

> Intensive support, for sure! But sometimes you're understood slightly differently. That is, in a negative sense. They think 'someone wants to take advantage of me. Now we can take a good look at how motivated and

> committed he is.' That was not my approach. My approach would be more positive. I also think it makes more sense. Because, what's in it for me, if I suspend someone's benefits? Afterwards, he will still be with me and is still unemployed.
>
> (trans_04_10, paragraph 76)

In contrast to the previous statement, indicating that intensive support was a win-win strategy for all involved, this statement indicates that intensive support is also used in an opposite manner to exert control. Although management prides itself on its own intention to use intensive support positively, later in the interview, however, in discussing placement practices desired by the organisational hierarchy, the manager reveals how both placement officers and job seekers are bound within a control system.

> But <u>intensive support</u>, that's what's crucial. And, for example, amongst our placement officers, there are some that have an Excel spreadsheet, where they've listed all their clients. Containing everything they're doing with them. That's something that helps a lot. Right?
>
> (trans_04_10, paragraph 76)

The list mentioned in that passage does not indicate simply the measures benefiting a specific job seeker, but also the efforts of the placement professional. Consequently, intensive support appears to increase external and internal efficiency. Both job seekers and placement officers are disciplined. Contrary to management's description, the pool of candidates for 'customer of the week' appears extremely large. A placement officer described her criteria as follows:

> If in the conversation you notice that there is absolutely no motivation there, then that person is required to turn up every week, is presented with vacancies and has to detail their own efforts and this has legal consequences. And this builds up so much pressure, right, he then says, 'I'm fed up with this, I'll go and get a job.' Or in the case of other customers who really could be customers ready for the labour market given their qualifications but perhaps they have a short-term health problem or, I don't know, depression, a depressive phase, who perhaps in eight weeks only need one meeting because maybe they're going through a crisis, something like that, y'know those sorts of things. That [person] belongs in intensive support.
>
> (trans_04_08, paragraph 128)

The placement expert identifies both subjects who, from the organisation's perspective, show little cooperation and those who need psychological counselling as relevant. The ambivalence of this instrument is already clear. Likewise, we see the importance of a detailed (initial) conversation, in which job seekers bear witness in a ritualized form. The pastoral power and its confession instrument analysed by Foucault appear here in a modernised form.

There is a specific requirement for every placement team that between 10 and 12 customers must be in intensive support at any one time (trans_04_08, paragraph 132). This explicit requirement regarding the use of intensive support indicates the doubly disciplining character of the instrument and points to the performance evaluation of placement officer behaviour through a system of differentiated controlling. The role of 'accounting' now becomes explicit. Not only is the activity or inactivity of job seekers measured through specific 'accounting' practices, this also applies to those actors who perform such practices in relation to job seekers. The interaction between these two relationships of dependency would appear to be obvious. As its primary objective, intensive support seeks to achieve employability. Any job is better than no job. This claim is omnipresent in the counselling interviews observed.

> PO: I'll give you a bit of time and as long as I (C: Yes) can point you to something (C: Yes) that you're interested in and that I think might suit you, um, then we can let it go on like this, but as I say (C: Yes) after three months at the latest of course I'll be starting to get a bit impatient (C: Yes) Y'know.
>
> (trans_R_06_3_7)

In response to the question of whether intensive support resulted in a greater number of benefit claims being terminated, a placement officer answered:

> B: No, not in my opinion, no. ++ Not really. ++ The only thing we had, okay, what we had, if we really required them to come every week, those were the people who didn't show up for their appointment, and then after three weeks we could, y'know, terminate their claim because of their availability after the third appointment letter. Yes, that was the positive effect, and that's what they want here. But other than that, no..
>
> (trans_04_08, Abs. 133–142)

At first glance, this statement concerns an almost typical side effect. Terminations of claims do not occur because job seekers are annoyed by the increased frequency of personal meetings or because they can be placed more rapidly but because the formal obligation together with the power to impose penalties gives the organization a right to terminate claims. At the same time, this statement demonstrates that precisely by way of this practice the organisation will ultimately achieve a success, even if not intended. Namely, the organisational unit is also controlled by extensive 'accounting' practices and has to account to the parent organisation on the basis of their 'numbers' and must face consequences for ongoing 'below-target performance'. Another interviewee overgeneralises the intensive support but, at the same time, gives it legitimacy:

> Well you do select the people, either those who you get on with. Or those you find annoying. It's said that they now have to become a bit more active. I think that's something you do if time-wise there's a chance to do so.
>
> (trans_04_14, paragraph 72)

The additional time means that a more intensive form of support, involving both encouragement and making demands on individuals, can finally be put into effect. Although, in a quasi-normative sense, something is done that 'you' would do in any case, the interviewee excludes herself as an active participant. She does not state her opinion on the measure. Instead, she describes herself as a small cog turned by a larger wheel. Her only part as placement officer is the selection of the individuals.

In addition, from the counselling interviews observed, we note as a general finding that although placement officers have new possibilities to shape or individualise a specific interview, because of accounting requirements the framing of counselling interviews is far more structured than it used to be. This structure seems to produce more formal commitment to the active process of job seeking. The fact that time is disposable, which has to be filled with action by both participants, forces them to concentrate on small details of the job seeking process e.g. discussing extensively the details of job applications or filling out painstakingly sheets on professional skills. However, in none of the feedback interviews, carried out right after each observation, did a job seeker indicate that this use of time was helpful. It looks much more like a way of disciplining both job seekers and placement officers.

6 Conclusion: the dilemma of placement activity and time rationality

In this 'special case of what is possible' (Bourdieu) taken from current practice in German activating labour market policy, our analysis illustrates an exaggerated form of more generalised trends that have been associated in the critical labour market literature with the notion 'welfare to workfare' (Torfing, 1999). Tasks once seen as the responsibility of welfare states such as social stabilisation and labour market integration of the unemployed shift from the level of collective actors and turn into responsibilities of the individual. All social policy efforts focus on the empowerment of individual job seekers to restore their labour market suitability. The disciplinary consequences for job seekers are evident in the statements of the placement professionals and managers in our case study. The job seekers selected as 'customer of the week' must endure a rigidly repressive time management that substantially restricts an individual's agency with regard to their own 'working' time. However, the activation paradigm also affects the placement professionals: the activators are activated and henceforth subjectified.

In our case study, we note that the practice of choosing a 'customer of the week' involves a two-fold pressure of subjectification. Selected customers are forced to act according to the will of the activation agents, with an accompanying loss of individual agency. However, the individual placement staff subjectify themselves too due to the obligation to choose an individual customer. The disciplinary tactic implied by the 'customer of the week' scheme is that after 4 weeks of intensive support the client can be placed in the labour market or, in practice, is no longer a customer of the PES. Each placement specialist visualises in their selection of the appropriate customer, and the resulting failure or success of placement efforts, their own placement and counselling expertise. In the event of failure, the placement specialist regards herself exposed to greater pressure, because she has to justify the substantial expenditure of resources on a single individual. With this tactic, not only job seekers are forced into a specific form of subjectification, but also the relevant placement officers are permanently subjected to this form of individualization.

Finally, we would like to use this case study and our interpretations to show a connection between the level of situated action by individual job placement specialists and job seekers and the level of regulatory institutions. In relation to the case study set out above and its underlying data, we consider it reasonable to assume that in the light of an effective disciplinary apparatus and resulting technologies of the Self (Foucault et al., 1988) transversal power structures emerge, which – intended or not – contribute to intensified governing.

If one returns to the description of individualisation by time deprivation outlined above, it appears justified to conclude that the Foucauldian account concerning the (historical) formation of disciplinary society finds a contemporary equivalent in the labour market policy of activation and that 'intensive support' exemplifies a qualitatively new stage in the establishment of the disciplinary subject across different social spheres. The observed side effects of intensive support in terms of semantics, implementation strategies and action targets enable us to conclude that these unintended practices can affect the organization at the trans-individual level. Within the institution of the modern (Western) Welfare State, organisations operate across different institutions using proven organizational means to achieve their publicly legitimised objectives. The different practices of discipline spread across institutions; they are present in most. These practices are observable and refer to a specific new interstitial structure, which has begun to establish itself beyond the differentiation of traditional institutions.[7] To compare our particular findings with the results of other current studies seems necessary, to develop a comprehensive research design that considers the interstitial changes within (European) social administrations and asks which pivotal institutions or power networks are present in a post-disciplinary society.

Notes

1 For one of the first applications of Foucault's theory of power to the welfare state, see Hewitt (1983).
2 Foucault highlights the two-folded meaning of 'subject' several times in his work. A precise description can be found here:

> There are two meanings of the word subject: subject to someone else by control and dependence, and tied to his own identity by a conscience or self-knowledge. Both meanings suggest a form of power which subjugates and makes subject to.
>
> (Foucault, 1982, p. 212)

3 See also the German version of the conversation model contained in the '4-phase model' and the intensive individualisation of job seekers through questions regarding their professional achievements and personal characteristics. This approach establishes a binding structural framework in which placement professionals can manage cases fairly and individually.
4 The manner in which additional staff resources were used by local offices was largely left to their own discretion. In practice, three orientations were identified: a focus on job seekers, a focus on employers and the adaptation of internal processes.
5 We discuss the problem of accounting in Sowa and Staples (2014) and (2016).
6 In the PES, deploying more staff ultimately means that, as a result of redistribution, the individual placement professional has more time available for work tasks.
7 Coming from a different approach, Crouch (2004) has described the phenomenon of post-democracy, which – using our terminology – can also be described as an interstitial structure.

References

Blair, T., Schröder, G. (1999): *Europe: The Third Way/Die Neue Mitte, June 8, 1999*, London: The Labour Party.
Borghi, V., Berkel, R. van (2007): 'Individualised service provision in an era of activation and new governance', *International Journal of Sociology and Social Policy*, 27(9/10): 413–424.
Born, A.W., Jensen, P.H. (2010): 'Dialogued-based activation – a new "dispositif"?', *International Journal of Sociology and Social Policy*, 30(5): 326–336.
Bourdieu, P. (1998): *Practical Reason: On the Theory of Action*, Stanford: Stanford University Press.
Brinkmann, C., Deeke, A., Völkel, B. (1995): *Experteninterviews in der Arbeitsmarktforschung: Diskussionsbeiträge zu methodischen Fragen und praktischen Erfahrungen*, Nürnberg.
Bröckling, U. (2007): *Das unternehmerische Selbst*, Frankfurt am Main: Suhrkamp.
Crouch, C. (2004): *Post-Democracy*, Cambridge: Polity.
Deleuze, G. (1987): *Foucault*, Frankfurt am Main: Suhrkamp.
Foucault, M. (1978): *The History of Sexuality*, New York: Pantheon Books.
Foucault, M. (1982): 'The subject and power'. in: Dreyfus, H., Rabinow, P. (eds.), *Michel Foucault: Beyond Structuralism and Hermeneutics*, 208–226, Chicago: University of Chicago Press.

Foucault, M. (1995): *Discipline and Punish: The Birth of the Prison*, New York: Vintage Books.
Foucault, M. (2007): *Ästhetik der Existenz: Schriften zur Lebenskunst*, Frankfurt am Main: Suhrkamp.
Foucault, M. (2009): *Security, Territory, Population: Lectures at the Collège de France*, Basingstoke: Palgrave Macmillan.
Foucault, M., Martin, L.H., Gutman, H., Hutton, P.H. (1988): *Technologies of the Self: A Seminar with Michel Foucault*, Amherst: University of Massachusetts Press.
Giddens, A. (1998): *The Third Way: The Renewal of Social Democracy*, Cambridge: Polity Press.
Goffman, E. (1982): *Interaction Ritual: Essays on Face-to-Face Behavior*, New York: Pantheon Books.
Hewitt, M. (1983): 'Bio-politics and social policy: Foucault's account of welfare', *Theory, Culture & Society*, 2(1): 67–84. doi: 10.1177/0263276483002001007.
Hielscher, V., Ochs, P. (2009): *Arbeitslose als Kunden?* (Vol. Sonderband 32), Berlin: edition sigma.
Hombach, B. (1998): *Aufbruch*, 2nd ed., München: Econ.
Hood, C. (1991): 'A public management for all seasons?', *Public Administration*, 69(1): 3–19.
Hood, C. (1995): 'The "new public management" in the 1980s: variations on a theme', *Accounting, Organizations and Society*, 20(2–3): 93–109.
Kaltenborn, B., Knerr, P., Schiwarov, J. (2006): Agenturen für Arbeit: Systematisierung des Ressourceneinsatzes, *Blickpunkt Arbeit und Wirtschaft*, 2006(4), 1–6.
Kaufmann, J.-C. (1999): *Das verstehende Interview*, 2nd ed., Konstanz: Universitätsverlag.
Lambert, C., Pezet, E. (2012): 'Accounting and the making of Homo Liberalis', *Foucault Studies*, 67–81.
Lessenich, S. (2005): '"Activation without work". Das neue Dilemma des "konservativen" Wohlfahrtsstaats', in: Dahme, H.-J., Wohlfahrt, N. (eds.), *Aktivierende Soziale Arbeit. Theorie – Handlungsfelder – Praxis*, 21–29, Baltmannsweiler: Schneider Verlag Hohengehren.
Ludwig-Mayerhofer, W. (2010): '"Wenn sie nicht selber etwas wollen, dann passiert gar nichts". Aktivierende Arbeitsmarktpolitik und die Grenzen der 'Individualisierung' von Arbeitslosigkeit', *Zeitschrift für Rechtssoziologie*, 31(1): 21–38.
Mäkitalo, Å. (2003): 'Accounting practices as situated knowing: dilemmas and dynamics in institutional categorization', *Discourse Studies*, 5(4): 495–516.
Mäkitalo, Å. (2006): 'Effort on display: unemployment and the interactional management of moral accountability', *Symbolic Interaction*, 29(4): 531–555.
McKinlay, A., Carter, C., Pezet, E. (2012): 'Governmentality, power and organization', *Management & Organizational History*, 7(1): 3–15.
Meyer, J.W., Rowan, B. (1977): 'Institutionalized organizations: formal structure as myth and ceremony', *The American Journal of Sociology*, 83(2): 340–363.
OECD (2007): *OECD Employment Outlook*, pp. 281, Paris: OECD.
Pongratz, H.J., Voss, G.G. (2003): 'From employee to 'entreployee': towards a 'self-entrepreneurial' work force?', *Concepts and Transformation*, 8(3): 239–254.
Raffnsøe, S., Gudmand-Høyer, M., Thaning, M.S. (2014): 'Foucault's dispositive: the perspicacity of dispositive analytics in organizational research', *Organization*. doi: 10.1177/1350508414549885.
Rose, N. (1999): *Powers of Freedom: Reframing Political Thought*, Cambridge: Cambridge University Press.

Rosenthal, P., Peccei, R. (2007): "The work you want, the help you need': constructing the customer in Jobcentre Plus', *Organization*, 14(2): 201–223. doi: 10.1177/1350508407074224.

Sahlin-Andersson, K. (2001): National, international and transnational constructions of New Public Management, in: Christensen, T., Lægreid, P. (eds.), *New Public Management – The Transformation of Ideas and Practice*, 43–72, Aldershot: Ashgate.

Scheer, K.-D. (1976): *Zur Kritik der Rollentheorie. Versuch einer Rekonstruktion der Formbestimmtheit sozialer Interaktion*, Bremen, Univ., Diss., 1975.

Schmidtke-Glamann, W.-D. (1995): 'Die öffentliche Arbeitsvermittlung – Fremdkörper in einem "schlanken" Sozialstaat?: Versuch einer Standortbestimmung', *Arbeit und Beruf*, 46(12): 360–363.

Schmuhl, H.-W. (2003): *Arbeitsmarktpolitik und Arbeitsverwaltung in Deutschland 1871–2002. Zwischen Vorsorge, Hoheit und Markt* (Vol. BeitAB), Nürnberg: Bundesanstalt für Arbeit.

Sol, E., Westerveld, M. (2005): *Contractualism in Employment Services. A New Form of Welfare State Governance*, The Hague: Kluwer Law International.

Sowa, F., Staples, R. (2014): 'Accounting in der Arbeitsverwaltung: Vermittlungsfachkräfte zwischen Steuerungsimperativen und autonomem Vermittlungshandeln, *Zeitschrift für Sozialreform*, 60: 149–173.

Sowa, F., Staples, R. (2016): Public administration in the era of late neo-liberalism: placement professionals and the NPM regime, in: Ferreira, A., Azevedo, G., Oliveira, J., Marques, R. (eds.), *Global Perspectives on Risk Management and Accounting in the Public Sector*, 25–48, Hershey: IGI Global.

Tergeist, P., Grubb, D. (2006): *Activation Strategies and the Performance of Employment Services in Germany, the Netherlands and the United Kingdom*, Paris.

Torfing, J. (1999): Workfare with welfare: recent reforms of the Danish welfare state, *Journal of European Social Policy*, 9(1): 5–28.

Trinczek, R. (1995): 'Experteninterviews mit Managern: methodische und methodologische Hintergründe', in: Brinkmann, C., Deeke, A., Völkel, B. (eds.), *Experteninterviews in der Arbeitsmarktforschung: Diskussionsbeiträge zu methodischen Fragen und praktischen Erfahrungen* (Vol. 191), Nürnberg: Institut für Arbeitsmarkt- und Berufsforschung.

Walker, R., Wiseman, M. (2003): Making welfare work: UK activation policies under New Labour, *International Social Security Review*, 56: 3–29.

Chapter 4

Managerial doctors
Professionalism, managerialism and health reforms in Portugal

Helena Serra

This chapter aims to analyse the way the medical profession interprets and responds to the external pressures and managerial values imposed by state policies. The purpose is to provide a comprehensive explanation of how NPM health reforms impact on micro-level relationships on health organisations. The reflection on the interplaying of doctors with other health professions shows how the introduction of NPM reforms reinforces medical domination in the social division of work in healthcare and that multi-professional teams often fail to improve cooperation mechanisms between their members. These issues bring new challenges to professions theory and this chapter proposes to change the focus to the actor perspective in order to highlight and discuss individual engagement in organisations as an embedded process.

Introduction

Economic-driven policies are similarly shaping health reforms in Western countries. The impact of neoliberal and New Public Management (NPM) health reforms on the medical profession has also undergone comprehensive changes. The relationship between professionalism and managerialism indicates new emergent configurations of hybrid professionals and mixed forms of governance in healthcare. Although the underlying reasons are similar across western countries, concerning the Portuguese case the outcomes diverge, particularly due the influence of medical profession on shaping professional practices and regulatory mechanisms.

In Portugal, doctors' influence on state regulation seems to counter the dynamics that have been described in sociology of professions and organisations theory, which points out the growing managerial control over medical authority and the state regulation of medical procedures. Doctors have succeeded in developing strategies to protect their professional position in the workplace by reconfiguring their jurisdictions and influencing organisational structures and decision-making processes. The control of medical technologies along with the control of management instruments is an example of the intersection between state and medical regulation. Serra (2010) had already defined the notion of 'medical technocracies' to describe different systems of governance based on the physician's technical skills in a given medical area of expert knowledge. The control of a technology is important insofar as it boosts the self-regulation mechanisms of the profession whilst also allowing the organisation to attract investment that brings greater financial sustainability. From the notion of 'medical technocracies' and by following the Portuguese case, this chapter aims to analyse the way the medical profession interpret and responds to the external pressures and managerial values imposed by state policies. The purpose is to provide a comprehensive explanation of how NPM health reforms impact on micro-level relationships on health organisations, namely the interplaying of doctors with other health professions, managers and patients.

Bearing in mind this background, this chapter brings together conclusions of several researches in medical sociology in Portugal (Carapinheiro, 1993; Serra, 2008; Correia, 2012). These studies followed qualitative, in-depth methods on specific features of the medical profession that joined and reinterpreted here in the light of the following argument: the ability of doctors to influence the way health policies turn out in practice at the workplace level. Using data collected from physicians working in three different hospital settings in Lisbon (Portugal), continuous and extensive participant observation was therefore chosen as the central technique for data collection, whilst semi-structured in-depth interviews were used as a complementary technique, applied to the physicians, nurses and also hospital administrators represented in the field of observation.

The specific features of the medical profession on which this argument is drawn are: (1) the specificity of healthcare governance in Portugal and the medical colonisation of hospital management; (2) the interplaying of doctors with other health professions, and (3) the cooperation/tension mechanisms in multi-professional teams in healthcare.

The chapter is organised as follows: the next section gives a sociological perspective of the governance of healthcare in Portugal and its specificities. Section 2 discusses the interplaying of doctors with other health professions to show how the introduction of NPM reforms reinforces medical domination in the social division of healthcare work. Finally, by looking at multi-professional teams in healthcare, Section 3 discusses the cooperation/tension mechanisms associated with multi-professional teams, in contexts of NPM reforms, and the challenges these issues pose to both professions theory and organisation studies.

I The specificity of healthcare governance in Portugal: A sociological reading

Across European countries, the relation between professionalism and managerialism give place to new emergent configurations of hybrid professionals and mixed forms of governance in healthcare (Davies, 2004; Kuhlmann et al., 2011). NPM criteria reflect current public policies where states attempt to boost the bureaucratic-rationalistic control over public organisations and their workers. NPM criteria that emerged translated the deep-seated reconfigurations of the public sector in convergence with the private sector. The way in which the state has ensured policies implementation in healthcare providers takes well-known forms, such as cost containment, computerisation of information flows, and prospective models of professional and organisational performance. Principles of modern capitalist rationality, previously restricted to the private sector, are now extended to the functions of state provision and regulation (Santos, 1987; Ferlie et al., 1996), justifying the option for the objectivity and predictability of management as a way of controlling uncertainty and restoring the lack of transparency present in the discretionary knowledge (Slater, 2001; Gabe, 2004; Chamberlain, 2009). Thus, the current debate focuses on the consequences of these changes for medical autonomy and authority. Although several comparative studies have detected an increase in the strategies of state regulation of governance in health care (Burau & Vrangbæk, 2008; Kuhlmann et al., 2011), they find a set of effects in medical profession that vary between defending continued autonomy and greater professional accountability (Davies, 2004).

Studies concerning Portuguese case (Carapinheiro, 1993; Serra, 2008; Correia, 2012) show a specific situation not exclusive to Portugal; other countries have the same situation due to power of medical profession that still exerts over health regulation. Definitely, doctors' influence on state regulation seems to counter the dynamics that have been described in sociology of professions and sociology of organisations, which point out the increasing criticism to medical autonomy, the growing managerial control over medical autonomy, and the state regulation over medical procedures. Note that despite the attempts from the government and European health policies to force on this direction, we still do not have studies that can confirm these trends.

The control of technologies is an example of the intersection between state and medical regulation. Previous studies have already described different systems of governance based on physicians' technical skills in a given area of expert knowledge, designed as medical technocracies (Serra, 2010). Medical technocracies constitute systems in which medical experts are in control and where decision makers are selected for their skills and qualification. The need for public investment coexists with the relative inability to maintain state regulation over the effective control of medical technologies. The point is that for hospitals and medical specialities in particular, the domination of a technology is important insofar as it boosts the self-regulation mechanisms of professions, also allowing the organisation to attract investment that brings greater financial sustainability. So, one's proposal is to revisit the notion of 'medical technocracies' (Serra, 2010) to address the key question of technological dependence and control of management tools by medical profession which allows medical procedures to meet the demands of the three Es – economy, effectiveness and efficiency (Rhodes, 1994) – and simultaneously boosts the self-regulated professional power defined as technocracy. The argument is that to certain extent the increasing introduction of NPM criteria strengthens medical technocracies and reinforces medical domination.

Physicians' strategies boost authority, reputation, prestige and professional power, which results from state regulation, at least in part. And this could be seen not only in the hospital structure (in hospital-centric nature of healthcare system) where the medical profession continues to hold a strong structural position in terms of organisational division of work, but also in the colonisation of management instruments and the control of the state technological investments despite the increasing managerialism. It seems that the medical profession has taken advantage of the State regulation mechanisms by incorporating them into their own mechanisms, as internal regulation mechanisms. This means that the medical profession still defines professional jurisdiction in health: doctors influence the organisational model in the provision of healthcare services; they define how healthcare is provided and evaluated; they influence educational policies in medical training. Therefore, Portuguese case is quite specific due to the power that medical profession continues to have over regulation in health, by influencing State regulation, other health professions and public opinion (Correia, Carapinheiro & Serra, 2015). This is a paradox when compared with the dynamics that have been described in the sociology of professions, sociology of organisations and health policy studies, that point out the growing managerial control over medical authority.

Medical technocracies is one of the examples of the intersection between State regulation and medical regulation. In Portugal, the definition of medical quality involves a paradox. The need for public investment coexists with an inability to maintain state regulation over the effective control of these technologies. The access to technologies gives rise to different kinds of competition, between hospitals, medical specialities, hospital departments and patients. The domination of a technology is particularly important to hospital and medical specialities as it boosts the self-regulation mechanisms of medical profession and, at the same time, allows hospital organisation to attract investment and ensure financial sustainability. Therefore, the prestige of innovative hospital services is defined according to technological expertise as well as the nature of the health care produced.

Serra (2008; 2010) study on medical technocracies shows that these services bring new dynamics to the hospital where they operate. The nature of these services involves all other areas of the hospital acting as a motive or stimulus for the creation and development of new hospital services. On the other hand, this technical rationale reveals interdependence and shows what this entails: the position of innovative services in relation to a specific hierarchy of values makes them the driving force of the hospital. These medical elites, focused on the innovative medicine, hold a dominant position within the hospital. Depending on the scarcity of the special services and the level of technology, these centres have the economic and strategic advantage over other services in the health sector. They are rare services, *la crème de la crème*, that attract a significant slice of the health budget and have a different mission to that of other services insofar as they offer a national coverage. Serra (2008) also note that these services stand out because of their high level of technical differentiation in a very sophisticate area of medicine. That makes them immune to any unfavourable attitude or hostility from the Board of hospital directors. According to Serra (2008; 2010), these kinds of services are seen as exotic, elitist or exceptional, bringing prestige to the hospital and so they favoured with good working conditions and a very stimulating work environment. These services have priority over all other services; everything is made available to their professionals to do their work, confirming the dominance of these innovative services over the remained hospital services.

The discourse expressing scientific and technological level and development of hospital medicine remains the same as decades ago, as a Carapinheiro (1993) study showed about the Portuguese situation. However, now there are new principles articulated with effectiveness and efficiency. Medical autonomy and authority in terms of specialisation and patient selection remain unchanged and are the keys to determine the value of medical specialities. Like twenty years ago, doctors are still concerned about the profitability and productivity of medical activities, particularly those linked to strategies to make services specialised or hyper-specialised, in order to comply with the technical model of medical practice.

Therefore, the key question of technological dependence is that it allows medical procedures to meet the demands of three Es: Economy, Effectiveness and Efficiency, and then, at the same time, boost the self-regulated professional power of those in control, defined as technocracy (Serra, 2010). To a certain extent, it is the increasing introduction of NPM criteria that strengthens medical technocracy. Medical procedure that uses technologies transports us to a 'more scientific' side of medical knowledge, where notions of order and certainty prevail over chaos and where technology legitimises safe neutral and objective knowledge. Scientific knowledge is used by doctors as a resource to mobilise public opinion and the State, because it is the only profession capable of operating it with discretion.

2 The interplaying of doctors with other health professions

Not even the emergence of new professional areas of knowledge in Portugal, involving health technologies, threatens the medical control of technologies. In fact, professionalisation strategies based on legal and formal recognition through academic training have not changed the medical domination in the social division of work in healthcare. Professional autonomy of these different kinds of expertise is far from being achieved in other health professions, as is the case of health technology professions.[1] Despite the legal framework of health technology professions, the formal recognition and the high education training, these factors have not been sufficient to make this expertise a strategic resource to build professional autonomy.

Autonomy is a key element in understanding the processes of professionalisation of non-medical professional groups and in particular of the health technology professions. In general terms, it is assumed that all professional groups have autonomy, e.g. all actors belonging to socio-professional group have certain margins of autonomy (even if they are minimal) within their work contexts. This greater or lesser autonomy is visible in their professional practices. The different degrees of autonomy of the various professional groups are directly related to their status and the position they occupy in the organisation and division of work, which in turn is related to power. In this regard, it is important to underline that power issues assume a relational character; power is not in itself an attribute, but rather implies a relation (the power exercised over others). In this sense, all forms of autonomy are relative, and there are no absolute and non-relational forms of autonomy, the latter depending on external factors and not only internal to professional groups.

However, this aspect does not necessarily imply that autonomy is determined by the contexts in which it is exercised, insofar as it is not independent of the practices and strategies of the actors in the contexts. Actors' concrete actions imply various forms of interaction and highlight the inevitability of multiple expressions of inter-professional dependencies. Thus, the various autonomies are also elastic because there is no fixed domain of autonomy. In this way, Bucher and Stelling (1969) suggest the concepts of elastic autonomy, responsibility and monitoring in order to guarantee the interpretation and analysis of the diverse arrangements between autonomy, responsibility and professional regulation in the organisation of medical work.

It is important to reflect on what supports the autonomy of different professions. Several studies on medical profession (Freidson, 1986; Carapinheiro, 1993; Serra, 2008; 2010) have shown that doctors' autonomy is ensured by the domination of their knowledge and technical competence in the organisation of the division of work. The medical profession directs and evaluates the work of all other professional groups that are functionally articulated to physicians. However, in contrast, the medical profession is not subject to control and evaluation by any professional group; it is therefore, as already mentioned, the dominant profession in the structure of health care (Freidson, 1986).

Knowledge is assumed as the main resource of professional power. However, the space occupied by the different professional groups in the model of division of work is not limited to specific knowledge; it also implies the conquest of exclusive territories of autonomy, i.e. the monopoly over a certain field of activity. However, these factors inevitably refer to the issue of power relations where knowledge and power arise closely related in the sociological analysis of professions and of the healthcare professions in particular.

From the analysis of the nature of the specific knowledge of these new emerging professions, one can stand the distinction between indeterminate and technical knowledge. The former arises associated with a theoretical-scientific frame that contains a strong component of interpretation in the articulation between abstract and concrete. It is a non-routine or standardised knowledge whose resources are not capable of strict and unique codification. In this way, indeterminate knowledge ensures a barrier to any interference outside the profession that dominates them. On the other hand, technical knowledge, although also using theoretical and scientific knowledge, allows standardising its operationalisation in terms of concrete work situations. This is precisely the case of the transferable forms of knowledge that allow procedures to be standardised (Serra, 2011).

In previous studies, stressing the strategic importance of knowledge as a resource of power, Serra (2008) pointed out that the lower the weight of indeterminate knowledge is, the more vulnerable a profession is, with respect to external control and regulation. Consequently, the social visibility of a profession is lower. In the case of health technologies professions, as the specialisation and formalisation of knowledge has increased, the technical component has also been accentuated, which weakens the social visibility of the indeterminate knowledge.

In this sense, it is important to reflect on a potential opportunity that, in the context of day-to-day practices, can emerge in order to promote the translation of this indeterminate knowledge into strategic resources. This question links to Crozier and Friedberg's (1977) work, which put the uncertainty as a fundamental strategic resource. In a situation of uncertainty, the actors are able to control its use as a fundamental resource in their daily activities, as a strategic resource. Thus, what is uncertainty from the point of view of the constraints is power from the point of view of the actors. The relations between individual or collective actors and the issues that concern them are part of an unequal field, structured by relations of power and dependence. The actors are unequal in the face of the uncertainties, as each one, by their situation, resources and skills, controls the situation differently and uses his own power to impose themselves before the others. The actors who dominate will be those who are able to affirm and impose their mastery of the most crucial uncertainties (Serra, 2008; 2010). In this way, the zones of uncertainty (Crozier & Friedberg, 1977) constitute excellent opportunities for the construction of strategies by the actors. The greater the space available for indeterminate knowledge is, the more these zones of uncertainty are reduced, as well as the possibility for actors to transform this uncertainty into strategic resources. Therefore, power results from contingent factors and from the mobilisation of the sources of uncertainty that actors control in their relations with other professional groups in the context of their professional practices. In this sense, any structure reproduces power, that is, inequalities, dependency relations and mechanisms of social control (Serra, 2008). Since specialisation based on technical know-how is what persists in these emerging health professions, and it is associated with zones of uncertainty that can be standardised (where standardisation is almost non-existent), knowledge is not used as a strategic resource to reinforce and consolidate professional autonomy (Serra, 2011).

Another relevant issue pointed by Serra (2011) is the internal and external nature of professional knowledge: endogenous knowledge and delegated knowledge, respectively. The former is built within the profession itself; the second is produced by other professions and controlled by the profession. The autonomy of professions is precisely based on their ability to produce their own knowledge and to negotiate its exclusivity. Nevertheless, it is also the capacity to reconstruct the external knowledge of other professions in order to transform it into endogenous knowledge. That is the case of the medical profession when one looks at doctors' influence on State regulation. In the Portuguese context, what studies show is that the increasing introduction of NPM criteria strengthens medical autonomy and reinforces medical domination. Medical strategies boost doctors' authority, reputation and status, very well described in the so-called image of *Managerial Doctors*, which results from State regulation, at least in part. It seems that the medical profession has taken advantage of the NPM mechanisms by incorporating them into their own mechanisms, as internal regulation mechanisms, or endogenous knowledge.

3 Multi-professional teamwork in healthcare, in context of NPM reforms: challenges to professions theory

As stands above, strategies concerning autonomy will seek to reconvert delegated knowledge into endogenous knowledge. The technical complexity of professional work in healthcare and the expertise it requires involve levels of indeterminacy, i.e. necessarily include a control that involves triggering operational knowledge and practical skills exclusive of health professions. Along with professional intervention subordinated to the medical profession, emerges the construction of other spaces that constitute exclusive territories of social closure around technology and technical operations. It is a question of technical autonomy, although this primacy of technical competence, in the case of health professions, is contextually bounded, because they belong to a specific field (health technology) which is organised around medical profession. However, as seen in Serra (2011), this factor does not fail to introduce several discontinuities into the formal model of dependence on medical authority, since it emerges because particular conditions are created in order to trigger strategies to reconvert knowledge. These strategies also seem to work when the medical profession takes advantage of the NPM mechanisms by incorporating them into their own mechanisms, as internal regulation mechanisms, allowing the transition from the category of NPM criteria delegated, to that of medical work.

There are several examples of multi-professional teams in healthcare. According to Pietroni (1994), the notion of multi-professional teamwork between medical practitioners began with the growth of hospitals in the nineteenth century. Multi-professional teams in healthcare is established in hospital settings with its strong, hierarchical organisation where the medical profession is at the highest level, supported by the nurses, the nursing assistants and the social workers. Nowadays, multi-professional cooperation in healthcare implies a commitment between an old governing model, professional control, and NPM, a new model. NPM is then regarded as the context for the professionals' actions (Liff, 2011). In the same line, Hood (1991; 1995) stands that this new context reflects an ideological shift on how the public sector should be governed and controlled. Multi-professional teamwork in healthcare in the context of NPM reforms reflects the idea that teams consist of several professions within a common team where the care is customised. Multi-professional teams should be able to respond to patients just as businesses respond to customers in a way that meets the administrative demands originating in the NPM reforms (Liff, 2011). By fulfilling these demands, multi-professional teams are pointed out as an example of the NPM reforms in healthcare that require customised patient care provided in a resource-effective way. In this context, *managerial doctors* emerge as leaders of the team, applying management by objective principles to economic and performance matters, successfully combining their professional roles with their administrative roles.

Looking closely at multi-professional teamwork in healthcare, in contexts of strong economic and efficiency control resulting from NPM reforms, it is possible to understand what promotes and what stops or hinders cooperation between their members (Liff, 2011). Teamwork can be seen as a network of semi-dependent professionals who tend to represent their professional organisations and groups, despite sharing a mutual interest in their patients. According to Liff (2011), cooperation between different health professionals and workgroups often results in conflict and tension. Many of these problems are assumed as associated with, but not only with, differences between the several professional's self-governance mechanisms involved in the multi-professional teams. Most of these conflicts are built from the drawing of boundaries between healthcare groups and, when talking about medical work teams, between medical specialities.

Organisation of healthcare according to teamwork logic's focus on collaboration has struggled with difficulty practices dominated by independent and autonomous professionals (Scott et al., 2000; Reay & Hinings, 2009; Gadolin & Wikström, 2016). The normative sight of teamwork is rarely seen in practice in healthcare organisations (Payne, 2000; Larkin & Callaghan, 2005; Oborn & Dawson, 2010; Mitchell et al., 2011; Muzio, Brock & Suddaby, 2013). According to Gadolin and Wikström (2016), healthcare professionals follow specific institutional logics as they belong to separate professions (Scott, 2008) and interpret these logics in practice (McPherson & Sauder, 2013; Lindberg, 2014), which leads to distinct roles (Currie et al., 2015) and therefore different and diverse perceptions of what can be considered as high quality healthcare. This way, multi-professional teams often fail to improve cooperation mechanisms between their members. Difficulties associated with multi-professional teams in healthcare organisations have been identified along the literature. In their study, Gadolin and Wikström (2016) stand that the dominance of physicians governs interaction in the team, impeding the voices of representatives of other professional categories. As a result, other professions tend to perceive the notion of teamwork as a myth (Meyer & Rowan, 1977), confirming that a group of people does not automatically constitute teamwork.

Serra (2008; 2010; 2011; 2013) have shown that frontiers between different professional groups act, in one hand, as articulating mechanisms to be found in the division of health work and as barriers to the interaction of the various skills. The argument is that NPM reforms in healthcare may not have improved the situation. Given these conditions, there is a good reason to explore how cooperation between different health professions (including hospital managers) is constructed as they work together in the best interest of patients. However, it is also possible that the continued influence of professional self-governance and the increase of management mechanisms will resulting in new arrangements in terms of professionalism. Once more the idea that NPM reforms is regarded as destructive or harmless to professional autonomy. However, previous studies (Correia, Carapinheiro & Serra, 2015) showed that this is scarcely a realistic description of professionals' long-term behaviour. Portuguese case shows a specific situation where medical autonomy still exerts power over health regulation. Doctors' influence on state regulation seems to counter the dynamics that have been described in sociology of professions. What this study shows, in the Portuguese context, is that the increasing introduction of NPM criteria strengthens medical autonomy, reinforces medical domination; medical strategies boost authority, reputation, prestige, professional power which results, in part, from state regulation.

This brings new challenges to professions theory. Research on professions and professional groups seems not to deal with the fact that multi-professional cooperation is the same character as mono-professional cooperation to preserve collegiality through co-existence (Liff, 2011). Such professionals do not wish to challenge others approaches and practices, nor do they wish to learn from them. Looking at this issue from this angle seems that we are challenging professions theory, more exactly, the general idea of professional dominance. If we change the focus to the actor perspective, to look at these cooperation issues, what can happen? What is new when introducing a different perspective? The actor perspective or agent perspective from a neo-institutionalism approach offers a useful interpretation in understanding how agents (actors, individuals) built cooperation. Concepts as 'agency' enable to highlight and discuss individual engagement in organisations as an embedded process that links past, present and future (Emirbayer & Mische, 1998). It is to move to individual basis to understand cooperation issues and professions rather than professional basis.

From the reading of Crozier and Friedberg's (1977) approach, centred on the individual level, the 'actor' is conceptualised as an agent. This means that the performance of social roles in a given context is understood as a synthesis consisting of rules associated with the performance of these roles, personal interests, past influences and perceptions that agents hold about themselves and other agents with whom they relate to. Concerning professional groups, Scott (2008) refers that professions have assumed leading roles in the creation of institutions, acting as preeminent institutional agents. According to Muzio, Brock & Suddaby (2013) Scott brings the agency of professions to the theoretical debate, against the dominant tendency to put these discussion on the context of broader processes of exogenous change.

Also Benamouzig and Pierru (2011) refer that sociology of professions approach takes into account changes in professional work that are both endogenous and exogenous, especially institutional changes, in which the professions are now engaged. The authors propose to look the broader position that professions occupy in institutional contexts, including state and market, and not specifically professional sets. This contrasts with the idea of fragmentation or pluralisation suggested by professions theory, when having in mind professional reinforcement strategies. It means that the erosion of professional autonomy is less like a simple professional integration and more a reinforcement of their institutional integration (Benamouzig & Pierru, 2011).

In what ways do professionals reconcile different institutional influences with embedded individual preferences? Very often, it is assumed that new challenges to organisations, like NPM reforms, for instance, are transposed or translated into the mind of professionals. There is nothing wrong with this assumption. Although, we also need to look at individual professionals before assuming how they make sense and cope with external influences in their daily life in organisational settings. This is because we must see professions as one of the key elements of social differentiation, financially, symbolically and morally, since their existence is as institutional as individually experienced.

However, professions theory has usually focused on structural dimensions, knowledge or interplay among players (users, State, market and different professions) and less on professionals as individuals with mental processes when performing their duties. This is particularly evident and visible in the theorisation of certain key concepts as 'professionalism', which is built on normative value systems of professionalism in the workplace (Evetts, 2003; 2009), as automatisms over individual preferences. Therefore, it is not easy to balance the different social influences, present in the mind of professionals, and the aims that individuals have in mind while performing their roles, even when framed by similar training or similar work conditions.

Some neo-institutionalist theorists as Meyer and Rowan (1977) and DiMaggio and Powell (1983; 1991) have a long time since looked to such automatisms, standing the need to considerer institutional patterns as simultaneously external (institutionalised) and internal (present in individuals' minds). The proposal is to analyse actor's engagement with social structures, according to individuals' own interests and projects and with their own reflexive decisions. How do individuals internalise their surrounding context that can enable or constrain their individual action? Better to look with detail on the drivers of agent/individual action towards organisational functioning, exploring the role of structure features in how professionals relate to and make use of the contexts. How do actors create endogenous institutions, i.e. how professionals act under the influence of NPM reforms by incorporating these exogenous rules (NPM criteria) as strategic resources to boost professional power? How do professionals transform exogenous institutions in inside institutions, the so-called endogenous institutions?

At a micro-level, according to Muzio, Brock and Suddaby (2013), interaction between institutional work and identity work (Powell & Colyvas, 2008) constitutes an important direction for further research. Many questions remain unanswered and core issues remain unresolved in professions theory and in organisational studies. How do organisations seek to institutionalise professional roles and identities? What is the role of agency used by actors on the processes of institutional creation, preservation and change? How do actors use reflexivity when dealing with institutional pressure? Muzio, Brock and Suddaby (2013) also refer to the institutional role that includes, but is not limited to, strategies to control a particular professional jurisdiction, as implicated by the notion of professional project (Suddaby & Viale, 2011). Scott (2008) also points out the bases of institutionalism framework to identify how institutional role is exercised. Professions act as cultural-cognitive agents providing the mechanisms, principles, and conceptual instruments to define and frame issues. As normative agents, professionals provide the norms, standards and rules to guide individuals' actions. Although, professions are key actors in the implementation and interpretation of legal aspects and regulation through which external and coercive power is exercised. Therefore, professions act as regulative agents (Muzio, Brock & Suddaby, 2013).

Is it possible that cooperation problems, in highly controlled exogenous institutions, are caused by individuals who have not chosen to play 'by the rules' and, therefore, have not built endogenous institutions. This argument challenges three stands on professions theory (Liff, 2011): (1) the general idea of service ideal; (2) discretionary power, and; (3) professional dominance. Although all these three stands support the existence of professional autonomy, they allow us to explain only part of the tension/cooperation problems in multi-professional teams in healthcare. Professionals are strongly influenced but not determinate by professional logics.

According to professions theory, a main problem with multi-professional cooperation may be that professions seek professional dominance (Abbott, 1988; Freidson, 1984; 1986). Professional dominance results from the belief that professions alone know what is better for their clients who are shared with other professions. The feature that distinguishes professions from other occupations is their degree of self-control or self-governance. However, professions are also associated with the service ideal (Wilensky, 1964), the commitment to the best interest of their clients. Saying this, one needs to understand the effects of these three stands — service ideal, discretionary power and professional dominance — to explain the tension/cooperation issues among health professions and between them and administrative management. Therefore, whether cooperation prevails or fails in a given situation depends on the balance of these three stands. At least, professions theory allows us to believe that professions can cooperate in providing customised care, which is a primary goal of NPM reforms. Nevertheless, all these three stands support the existence of one profession's autonomy that may cause cooperation problems.

Professions' persistence on determining their own ways of working is expected to create control issues, from the viewpoint of democratic governance and of resource use (Ferlie et al., 1996; Freidson, 2001). Since the declared goal of NPM reforms is to make the public sector more effective, accountable and customer-oriented, such principles impose limits to professions' self-regulation. For instance, several authors (Tsoukas, 1997; Strathern, 2000; Levay & Waks, 2007) stand that, in healthcare, an increased concern for patient safety has resulted in demands for more transparency from professionals as well as additional and strict clinical guidelines and evidence-based healthcare (Power, 1997; Timmermans, 2008).

But as seen from the discussion above, unexpected effects appear once NPM criteria are introduced in professions (Freidson, 2001; Timmermans, 2008). Several explanations can be listed from organisational theory. Scott (2003) suggests there is a decoupling between the NPM criteria/reforms and the individuals' action, due to formal structures decoupled from core activities (loosely decoupled systems). In the same line, Orton and Weick (1990) contrast decoupling and ritualistic adherence to change, as a ceremony effect (Meyer & Rowan, 1977) or organisational hypocrisy (Brunsson, 1989). Other studies stress the necessity to protect core activities from external turbulence (Meyer & Rowan, 1977; DiMaggio & Powell, 1991). Therefore, organisational theory assumes one of two contrasting positions on discussing how professionals view the results of the introduction of NPM reforms on their professional autonomy: either professionals consider NPM reforms a threat to their autonomy or they see them to have little impact on their professional autonomy. Although, little focus has been put on actor-oriented explanations.

Concluding remarks

Several authors refer to NPM as an umbrella name for organisational reform methods, strongly determinated by solutions derived from the private business sector built on trust in managers and markets rather than in professions (Clarke & Newman, 1997; Barzelay, 2001; Almqvist, 2004). The argument put forward by the NPM is that the variation in medical practices is responsible for cost escalation and increased spending in the healthcare sector, and it is therefore important to establish principles based on pre-established quantifiable objectives that lead to standardisation of medical practices. Therefore, it is crucial to understand healthcare regulation and its implications in the dynamics of professionalisation of the health professions and, in particular, in the medical authority.

It is not new that the relation between professionalism and managerialism has been given place to emergent configurations of hybrid professionals and mixed forms of governance in healthcare, across Western countries. Although, a comprehensive explanation of how NPM health reforms impact on micro-level relationships on health organisations is needed. The specificity of the Portuguese case shows that medical profession still exerts over health regulation. Unquestionably, doctors' influence on State regulation seems to counter the dynamics that have been described in sociology of professions and sociology of organisations, which stand the increasing criticism to medical autonomy, the growing managerial control over medical autonomy and the State regulation over medical procedures. Despite the attempts from the government and European health policies to force on NPM reforms, medical professions seem to reinforce their authority and domination.

The reflection on the interplaying of doctors with other health professions shows how the introduction of NPM reforms reinforces medical domination in the social division of work in healthcare. Not even the emergence of new professional areas, involving health technologies, seems to threaten physicians' control of technologies. This means that the legal framework of health technology professions, the formal recognition and the high education training, along with professionalisation strategies, are not sufficient to change medical domination in the social division of work in healthcare. Professional autonomy in other health professions than doctors is far from being achieved. In the context of NPM reforms, the medical profession still directs and evaluates the work of all other professional groups that are functionally articulated to physicians. However, doctors are not subject to control and evaluation by any professional group, not even healthcare managers.

When looking at multi-professional teamwork in healthcare, in contexts of NPM reforms, again appears the same strategies, where doctors take advantage of NPM reforms. These strategies allow the transition from the category of NPM criteria delegated from State, to that of medical work. So, physicians still command as leaders of multi-professional teams, controlling NPM mechanisms.

Multi-professional cooperation in healthcare implies a commitment between an old model of governance, professional control and NPM tools. Managerial doctors comply with the new model from the control of NPM mechanisms, by incorporating them as internal to medical profession regulation mechanisms.

Yet, multi-professional teams often fail to improve cooperation mechanisms between their members. Difficulties associated with multi-professional teams in healthcare organisations have been identified. This way, other health professionals tend to see teamwork as a myth, as the dominance of medical profession governs the relationships in the team, hindering voices of other professional categories. These issues bring new challenges to professions theory. Research on professions and professional groups seems not to pay attention to the fact that multi-professional cooperation as the same nature as mono-professional cooperation: to preserve collegiality through co-existence. This perspective on professions theory has been challenged, or more exactly the general notion of professional dominance. The proposal is to change the focus to the actor perspective, to look to this cooperation issues. By introducing a different perspective, it enables to deepen our knowledge about doctor's influence in health policies, and about how it is transformed in practice at the workplace level. The actor perspective or agent perspective from neo-institutionalism approach offers a useful interpretation in understanding how agents, as individual actors, built cooperation.

Concepts as 'agency' enable one to highlight and discuss individual engagement in organisations as an embedded process. This approach can be very useful to clarify the interaction between professionalism and managerialism and the diversity of the emergent configurations of hybrid professionals and mixed forms of governance in healthcare. It is to bring a comprehensive explanation of how NPM health reforms impact on micro-level relationships on health organisations, moving to individual basis to understand cooperation issues and professions rather than professional basis.

Note

1 Health technologies professional groups are recognised by law since 1999 and consists of eighteen professional groups (not physicians) linked to several health areas, with intervention in diagnosis and therapeutics. They are called technicians (audiometrists, cardiopneumologists, dietitians, physiotherapists, etc.).

References

Abbott, A. (1988): *The System of Professions*, Chicago: University of Chicago Press.
Almqvist, R. (2004): *Icons of New Public Management. Four Studies on Competition, Contracts and Control*, Stockholm: Stockholm University, School of Business.
Barzelay, M. (2001): *The New Public Management: Improving Research and Policy Dialogue*, Berkeley: University of California Press.
Benamouzig, D., Pierru, F. (2011): 'Le professionnel et le "système": l'intégration institutionnelle du monde medical', *Sociologie du Travail*, 53(3): 293–348.

Brunsson, N. (1989): *The Organization of Hypocrisy: Talk, Decisions and Actions in Organizations*, Chichester: Wiley.
Bucher, R., Stelling, J. (1969): 'Characteristics of professional organizations', *Journal of Health and Social Behaviour*, 10.
Burau, V., Vrangbæk, K. (2008): 'Global Markets and National Pathways of Medical Re-Regulation', in: Kuhlmann, E., Saks, M. (eds.), *Rethinking Professional Governance*, 29–44, Bristol: The Policy Press.
Carapinheiro, G. (1993): *Saberes e Poderes no Hospital: uma Sociologia dos Serviços Hospitalares*, Porto: Afrontamento.
Chamberlain, J. (2009): 'The changing medical regulatory context: Focusing on doctor's educational practices', *Medical Sociology Online*, 4(2): 26–34.
Clarke, J., Newman, J. (1997): *The Managerial State*, London: Sage.
Correia, T. (2012): *Medicina: o agir numa saúde em mudança*, Lisboa: Mundos Sociais.
Correia, T., Carapinheiro, G., Serra, H. (2015): 'The State and Medicine in the Governance of Health Care in Portugal', in: Carvalho, T., Santiago, R. (eds.), *Professionalism, Managerialism and Reform in Higher Education and the Health Services: The European Welfare State and Rise of the Knowledge Society*, 151–171, Europe, USA: Palgrave Macmillan.
Crozier, M., Friedberg, E. (1977) : *L'Acteur et le Système: Les Contraintes de l'Action Collective*, Paris: Éditions du Seuil.
Currie, G., Burgess, N., Hayton, J. C. (2015): 'HR practices and knowledge brokering by hybrid middle managers in hospital settings: The influence of professional hierarchy', *Human Resource Management*, 54(5): 793–812.
Davies, C. (2004): 'Regulating the health care workforce: Next steps for research', *Journal of Health Services Research and Policy*, 9: 55–61.
DiMaggio, P. J., Powell, W. (1983): 'The iron cage revisited: Institutional isomorphism and collective rationality in organizational fields', *American Sociological Review*, 48: 147–60.
DiMaggio, P. J., Powell, W. (1991): Introduction, in: Powell, W., DiMaggio, P. J. (eds.), *The New Institutionalism in Organizational Analysis*, 3–41, Chicago: The University Press.
Emirbayer, M., Mische, A. (1998): 'What is agency?', *American Journal of Sociology*, 103(4): 962–1023.
Evetts, J. (2003): 'The sociological analysis of professionalism: Occupational change in the modern world', *International Sociology*, 18(2): 395–415.
Evetts, J. (2009): 'New professionalism and new public management: Changes, continuities and consequences', *Comparative Sociology*, 8: 247–266.
Ferlie, E., Ashburner, L., Fitzgerald, L., Pettigrew, A. (1996): *The New Public Management in Action*, Oxford: Oxford University Press.
Freidson, E. (1984): *La Profession Médicale*, Paris: Payot.
Freidson, E. (1986): *Professional Powers*, Chicago: The University of Chicago Press.
Freidson, E. (2001): *Professionalism – The Third Logic*, Cambridge: Polity Press Ltd.
Gabe, J. (2004): 'Risk', in: Gabe, J., Bury, M., Elston, M. A. (eds.), *Key Concepts in Medical Sociology*, 87–91, London: Sage.
Gadolin, C., Wikström, E. (2016): 'Organising healthcare with multi-professionalteams: Activity coordination as a logistical flow', *Scandinavian Journal of Public Administration*, 20(4): 53–72.
Hood, C. (1991): 'A public management for all seasons?', *Public Administration*, 69(1): 3–19.

Hood, C. (1995): 'The 'New Public Management' in the 1980s: Variations on a theme', *Accounting Organisations and Society*, 20(3): 93–109.
Kuhlmann, E., Burau, V., Larsen, C., Lewndowski, R., Lionis, C., Repullo, J. (2011): 'Medicine and management in European healthcare systems: how do they matter in the control of clinical practice?', *The International Journal of Clinical Practice*, 65(7): 222–224.
Larkin, C., Callaghan, P. (2005): 'Professionals' perceptions of interprofessionals working in community mental health teams', *Journal of Interprofessional Care*, 19(4): 338–346.
Levay, C., Waks, C. (2007): 'Professions and the pursuit of transparency in healthcare: Two cases of soft autonomy', *Organization Studies*, 30(5): 509–527.
Liff, R. (2011): *Professionals and the New Public Management. Multi-Professional Teamwork in Psychiatric Care*, Göteborg: Bokförlaget BAS.
Lindberg, K. (2014): 'Performing multiple logics in practice', *Scandinavian Journal of Management*, 30(4): 485–497.
McPherson, C., Sauder, M. (2013): 'Logics in action: Managing institutional complexity in a drug court', *Administrative Science Quarterly*, 58(2): 165–196.
Meyer, J. W., Rowan, B. (1977): 'Institutionalised organizations: Formal structure as myth and ceremony', *American Journal of Sociology*, 83: 340–363.
Mitchell, R. J., Parker, V., Giles, M. (2011): 'When do interprofessional teams succeed? Investigating the moderating roles of team and professional identity in interprofessional effectiveness', *Human Relations*, 64(10): 1321–1343.
Muzio, D., Brock, D. M., Suddaby, R. (2013): 'Professions and institutional change: Towards an institutionalist sociology of the professions', *Journal of Management Studies*, 50(5): 699–721.
Oborn, E., Dawson, S. (2010): 'Knowledge and practice in multidisciplinary teams: Struggle, accommodation and privilege', *Human Relations*, 63(12): 1835–1857.
Orton, D., Weick, K. (1990): 'Loosely coupled systems: A reconceptualization', *Academy of Management Review*, 15(2): 203–223.
Payne, M. (2000): *Teamwork in Multi-Professional Care*, London: Routledge.
Pietroni, P. C. (1994): 'Interprofessional Teamwork: Its History and Development in Hospitals, General Practice and Community Care (UK)', in: Leathard, A. (ed.), *Going Interprofessional: Working Together for Health and Welfare*, London: Routledge.
Power, M. (1997): *The Audit Society: Rituals of Verification*, Oxford: Oxford University Press.
Powell, W. W., Colyvas, J. (2008): 'Microfoundations of Institutional Theory', in: Greenwood, R., Oliver, C., Sahlin, K., Suddaby, R. (eds.): *The Sage Handbook of Organizational Institutionalism*, 276–298, London: Sage.
Reay, T., Hinings, C. R. (2009): 'Managing the rivalry of competing institutional logics', *Organization Studies*, 30(6): 629–652.
Rhodes, R. (1994): 'The hollowing out of the state: The changing nature of public services in Britain', *Political Quarterly*, 65: 138–151.
Santos, B. S. (1987): 'O Estado a sociedade e as políticas sociais: o caso das políticas de saúde', *Revista Crítica de Ciências Sociais*, 23: 13–74.
Scott, R. (2008): 'Lords of the dance: Professionals as institutional agents', *Organization Studies*, 29(2): 219–238.
Scott, W. R. (2003): *Organizations, Rational, Natural and Open Systems*, Upper Saddle River, NJ: Prentice Hall.

Scott, R., Ruef, M., Mendel, P., Caronna, C. (2000): *Institutional Change and Health Care Organizations: From Professional Dominance to Managed Care*, Chicago: University of Chicago Press.
Serra, H. (2008): *Médicos e Poder: Transplantação Hepática e Tecnocracias*, Lisboa: Fundação Económicas, Almedina.
Serra, H. (2010): 'Medical Technocracies in Liver Transplantation: Drawing boundaries in medical practices', *Health*, 14(2): 162–177.
Serra, H. (2011): 'Das tecnologias às tecnocracias: Novos protagonismos emergentes em saúde', in: Barbosa, A. C., Silva, J. R. (eds.), *Economia, Gestão e Saúde: As relações luso-brasileiras em perspectiva*, 187–202, Lisboa: Edições Colibri.
Serra, H. (2013): 'Learning from surgery: How medical knowledge is constructed', *Professions & Professionalism*, 3(1): 1–18.
Slater, B. (2001): 'Who rules? The new politics of medical regulation', *Social Science and Medicine*, 52(3): 871–883.
Strathern, M. (2000): 'The tyranny of transparency', *British Educational Research Journal*, 26(3): 309–21.
Suddaby, R., Viale, T. (2011): 'Professionals and field-level change: Institutional work and the professional project', *Current Sociology*, 59: 423–441.
Timmermans, S. (2008): 'Professions and their work. Do market shelters protect professional interests?', *Work and Occupations*, 35(2): 164–188.
Tsoukas, H. (1997): 'The tyranny of light. The temptations and the paradoxes of the information society', *Futures*, 29(9): 827–843.
Wilensky, H. (1964): 'The professionalization of everyone', *American Journal of Sociology*, 70: 137–159.

Chapter 5

Accountability requirements for social work professionals
Ensuring the quality of discretionary practice

Jorunn Theresia Jessen

Introduction

The work environment of welfare services is changing, resulting in more prescriptive policies, increased management of goals and methods and more control of procedures, outputs and costs (Healy & Meagher, 2004; Clark, 2005; White, 2009). Budgetary control, standard procedures and performance measures are being imposed, both to gain control over service production and to push implementation practices towards the desired policy aims. The trend is towards increasing standardisation in terms of internal manuals and guidelines to simplify work procedures and incentives to regulate practice. These changes address a shift towards new forms of control mechanisms and organisational regulations in most Western countries, and are associated with the new public management (Pollitt & Bouckaert, 2004; Hood, 1991).

In public welfare services, organisational control often appears in the form of codified bureaucratic rules and descriptions, as well as inbuilt technical systems to standardise the work process. The intention is to regulate practice to secure decisions that are correct and fair, and to shape actual decision-making in congruence with official policy (Hupe & Hill, 2007). The question is whether this trend towards increasing standardisation and externally defined targets and measurable outputs also represents a shift in management and organisation of social work practice (Harris & White, 2009; Banks, 2013).

New public management strategies have become increasingly popular methods of indirect control, favouring performance-based incentives over rules and regulations, in order to promote accountability in street level organisations (Brodkin, 2008). According to literature (Bovens, 2007; Christensen & Lægreid, 2017), one may distinguish between different kinds of accountability relationships to which that the caseworkers are accountable: first, the administrative or managerial accountability relationships between superior and subordinate levels and units, related to agencies or departments; next, professional accountability, related to peer relationships and professional competence or associations. Some of the core questions raised have been to whom, for what and how the leaders and front-line workers in various welfare services are held accountable.

This chapter investigates how social work professionals are held accountable in the Norwegian social services, by studying how they perceive the impact of management techniques and accountability requirements on discretionary practice. The primary focus is to assess the impact of both vertical managerial accountability and horizontal professional accountability mechanisms, and to address some potential consequences for social work practice.

The scope for autonomy and discretion in social services

Social work professionals are often characterised as street level bureaucrats, working in the front-line of public welfare. They provide public services, legitimise political decisions and new policies and buffer social conflicts. As street level professionals, they act as mediators between the state and its citizens, playing a key role in the translation and interpretation of social policy objectives into service deliveries (Hill & Hupe, 2008). Social work professionals have to interact with and make decisions about their clients, determine eligibility claims, consider options and decide the course of action. They are characterised as *agents of welfare* (Jewell, 2007). In their role as institutional agents, professionals have to define, interpret and fulfil the ambitions of government policies and welfare reforms (Scott, 2008). Working in the front-line of public services, they make decisions regarding what services to provide and how to respond to the issues that arise (Hjörne et al., 2010). In public services, they are entitled to make independent and discretionary decisions when determining eligibility claims, assessing needs and work abilities. However, the extent to which technical subordination occurs in social work practice is much debated in terms of whether discretion is still part of everyday decision-making (Harris & White, 2009).

According to Freidson (2001), professional employees possess technical autonomy or the right to use discretion and judgement in the performance of their work within certain limits set by management level resource allocation decisions. Professional autonomy[1] refers to the freedom of the professional practitioner to make choices and decisions about how to act (Banks, 2004). Discretion occurs whenever 'the effective limits on his [the public official's] power leave him free to make a choice among possible courses of action or inaction' (Davis, 1969, p. 4). In the public welfare services, professionals are formally allocated the freedom to make independent decisions by the authorities, having the official approval to decide a social right or entitlement (Evans, 2010). As social work professionals, the practitioners traditionally possess autonomy in their performance of work, having the authority to make independent decisions on certain technical issues such as what tasks to perform, how to carry them out and what the aim of the work should be. Thus, deliberate choices regarding policy and governance influence social work practice (Hupe & Hill, 2007). Professional *judgement* involves the capacity to balance a number of aspects and conditions when making decisions and prescribing adequate actions to be taken (Styhre, 2013). Professional decision-making and discretionary judgements thus depend on both the capacity to cognitively process existing information while simultaneously drawing on past experiences.

The delegation of discretionary autonomy is based on an assumption that the trustee is capable of passing judgment and making reasonable decisions (Molander & Grimen, 2010). In welfare services, the use of discretion intends to ensure proper treatment of individual cases, allowing professionals to consider what is particular and unique. Nevertheless, discretionary power can also be exercised in a negative way, serving as an entry point for unjust and unequal treatment.

A vast body of literature has shown that discretion plays a key role in the translation and interpretation of social policy objectives into service deliveries (Hupe & Hill, 2007). Lipsky (1980; 1991) argues that street-level bureaucrats exercise considerable discretion in determining the claims, means and sanctions requested. Discretionary decision-making occurs not only because technical limitations are in place to monitor street-level performance, but also because professionals are required to develop a workable policy in practice (Evans, 2011). Discretion is intentionally granted to ensure that assistance and means are responsive to individual needs, and to decide upon the methods of intervention. Hence, the work-related focus requires close and binding follow-up in a contractual manner that involves discretionary decisions. According to research (Jessen & Tufte, 2014), the perceived scope for discretion in the Norwegian welfare services has extended due to the activation policies and measures embedded in the Norwegian labour and welfare reform. Concurrently, the discretionary power of trained social workers is decreasing and challenged by the push for uniform practices and a managerially regulated role.

The mechanisms of accountability

Accountability is a complex and multifaceted term. One meaning of accountability is associated with the process of being 'called to account' to some authority for one's actions (Jones, 1992, p. 73). *To be accountable* means that people, if called upon, are obligated to give an account of their actions (Banks, 2013). In this sense, accountability may be understood as a specific social relationship: "between the actor and a forum in which the actor has an obligation to explain and justify his or her conduct, the forum can pose questions and pass judgement, and the actor may face consequences" (Bovens, 2007, p. 450). Such accountability has a number of features: it is *external,* in that the account is given to some other person or body outside the person or body being held accountable. It involves *social interaction* and exchange between the superior authority calling for the account and the persons held accountable. It also implies *rights of authority*, in that those calling for an account are asserting rights of superior authority over those who are accountable, including the rights to demand answers and impose sanctions (Mulgan, 2000).

Moreover, 'accountability' commonly refers to an *internal* feeling of individual responsibility and concern for the public interest expected from public servants, often referred to as 'personal' and 'professional'. Professional accountability is also an essential feature of social work. Professionals take on jobs with specific responsibilities and have a duty to account for what they do: to describe, justify and explain their actions in terms of publically agreed standards and values, often defined by the state in relation to the profession's public mandate (Banks, 2013). In addition to professional accountability to service users, the practitioners are accountable to the public for the effectiveness of the services they deliver.

However, the increasing tendency to regulate and control the working practice of social professionals by mechanisms imposed by employers and government refers to an external and new kind of accountability. According to Banks (2013), this 'new' accountability entails work that can be justified in terms of recognised standards of practice and in terms of its benefits and outcomes.

Dimensions and directions

Mulgan (2003) distinguishes between four main dimensions of accountability: the 'accounters' (individuals or organisations) who are held responsible for their actions and decisions, the account-holders to whom accountability is owed, the obligations and responsibilities of the agents and the external and internal mechanisms (processes and procedures) available to ensure accountability. The model (Table 5.1) provides a flexible framework of analysis in order to describe the relations between the accounters and the account-holders that involve complementary rights in several directions. The service providers or public officers are both accounters and account-holders, both accountable to an authority and/or superior with clear and comprehensive powers of command as well as to service users.

The accountability relationships and directions include vertical and horizontal, external (outwards) and internal (inwards) in order to identify the mechanisms involved to hold front-line workers legally answerable within the organisation. The *vertical* direction implies accountability both upwards to managers and central government, and downwards to citizens and the service users. The *horizontal* direction implies accountability to partners or an authority or organisations of a similar status. In line with this theoretical approach, Christensen and Lægreid (2017) distinguish between the two main directions in which accountability works: vertical (political, administrative, managerial, legal), and horizontal (social, professional) forms of accountability based again on the content of the obligation and the nature of the forum. While vertical accountability relationships tend to be mandatory and formal,

Table 5.1 Directions and mechanisms of accountability

	Vertical direction	Horizontal direction
External mechanisms	Formal rules, pre-defined targets, standard procedures, Performance measurement. External control and juridical review of administrative and discretionary decisions.	Improvement of knowledge and arrangements to ensure vocational training. Inter-agency cooperation between different kinds of services.
Internal mechanisms	Information and communication procedures (ICT). Guidelines and case-management procedures.	Professional guidance by colleagues and fellow workers. Agency routines and standards to ensure uniform practice.

and can result in sanctions, horizontal accountability relations are more voluntary, informal and indirect, and the consequences can be softer. However, the individual practitioner will always have to respond to external demands and expectations from politicians, managers, and the public.

The external and vertical dimension (often referred to as *managerial* or *administrative*), focuses on accountability to superiors and managers in the welfare bureaucracy. Vertical mechanisms often include formal rules, pre-defined targets, standard procedures[2] and performance measurements imposed to ensure measurable and beneficial outputs and outcomes. The administrative form of accountability is often oriented towards processes or procedures, while the managerial form is more focused on the monitoring of outputs and results based on agreed performance criteria.

Internal mechanisms of accountability may be exercised through collective or individual supervision and collaboration between colleagues and peers in order to improve knowledge and the discretionary decisions. In addition, inter-agency cooperation may take place between different kinds of welfare services and institutions. The internal mechanisms are variously described as personal and *professional* accountability, and they are evident in systems of professional peer review where the practitioners are accountable to professional bodies and professional associations of workers and their actions (Mulgan, 2003). Different professions are constrained by professional codes of conduct and scrutinized by professional organizations or disciplinary bodies. It is a system defined by trust in expertise, meaning the technical knowledge of experts. These are also essential features of social work professionals. The workers take on jobs with specific responsibilities and have a duty to account for what they do: to describe, justify and explain their actions in terms of publically agreed standards and values, often defined by the state, in relation to the profession's public mandate (Banks, 2013). In addition to professional accountability to service users, practitioners are also accountable to the general public for the effectiveness of the services they deliver.

The Norwegian welfare reform and social services

As in several other countries, the pressure to increase the capacity and efficiency of public administration and governance has led to organisational public reforms. In 2006, this pressure led to the 'Norwegian national labour and welfare reform'. The reform implies a change towards a 'whole-of-government' approach that has taken place in several countries as a means to achieve shared goals and performance regulation and bring about increased quality of service (Christensen & Lægreid, 2011). One main intention was to establish comprehensive, integrated and seamless services based on the collaboration between governmental employment, insurance services, and social assistance services, as well as the implementation of a 'one-door' policy through coordination of the former administrations (NOU, 2004, p. 13). This partnership model aimed to combine the principles of local self-government and the ministerial responsibility in order to improve cooperation and coordination between services (Askim et al., 2010)[3]. The main goals were to get clients off welfare benefits and into work, to create a more efficient administrative apparatus and to make the administration more service oriented (Royal Propositions No. 46, 2004–2005).

Over and above these changes, the transformation of integrated services into the new joint administration called for managerial interventions, whereby local managers were granted an important role in implementing the reform, responsible for budgetary control, coordination of services and the promotion of the changes required. Administrative leaders and bureaucrats thus became managers who were held accountable for their performance on given objectives. During the reform, managers became responsible for the coordination of services, for achieving results and promoting the developmental changes required (Askim et al., 2010). Also, they were both accountable to the main efficiency targets and responsible for the quality of services provided by the modern welfare administration (Harris & White, 2009). The role of local managers as key agents has been strongly emphasised in recent years. Audits and inspections, as well as efficiency indicators, aim to ensure that political and organisational goals are fulfilled, making welfare services more efficient and responsive to the demands and preferences of consumers.

Following the Norwegian labour and welfare reform, there has been a shift in the steering focus from overall goals to details of control and increased bureaucracy (Byrkjeflot et al., 2011). Requirements are set for more efficiency and outputs defined in measurable and quantifiable performance indicators. Since the reform, performance management has become the dominant principle for steering and control (ibid.). The instruments for this purpose are achievement targets and performance indicators: aspects that promote organisational and managerial objectives. In order to achieve concrete production targets, performance measurement tools have been introduced to monitor the processing time and to increase efforts to activate the recipients of social assistance.

In line with the main objectives of the reform, the use of activation measures has increased in all parts of the Norwegian welfare administration, as a result of more locally organised and tailored programs. At the front-line, the welfare workers are expected to translate activation policy into daily practice by implementing governmental strategies, emphasising the responsibilities and obligations of every recipient (Johanssen & Hvinden, 2007). Some of the requirements for receiving social assistance during unemployment involve meeting the terms and conditions set by the local administration. Social assistance recipients are enabled through instruments for testing work capacity and readiness through stricter follow-up and individual plans. Social service workers are increasingly required to enforce activation policies and to take measures towards clients, assessing and determining activation measures and sanctions as well as eligibility claims. In addition, the activation measures are targeted at more groups than before, including long-term recipients of social assistance with substantially reduced work and earning capacity.

The Norwegian Social Services are mainly discretionary based, and the administration of social assistance is largely means-tested. Unlike many other countries, the functions of cash allocation and social work are not separate. The trained core of social workers who administer the Norwegian Social Services are responsible for both financial assistance and assistance in kind[4]. While the educational level and background of caseworkers handling the social insurance and unemployment benefits varies, Norwegian social service workers are mainly educated as trained social workers. According to the enactment of the Social Services Act in 1991, their purpose is to promote financial and social security, to improve the living conditions of disadvantaged persons and to prevent social problems. Social assistance services provide a safety net for individuals in need by ensuring adequate resources and helping clients to become self-supporting. Financial assistance is means-tested and only granted when clients have exhausted their possibilities to obtain income from work or other social insurance benefits.

Data and methods

The empirical data used in this chapter come from a survey conducted in 2011 among different groups of front-line workers employed in the Norwegian Labour and Welfare Administration (NAV), counting both practitioners and local managers of the different services involved. The research was conducted during spring 2011 through a random sample comprising 25 per cent of all the municipalities in Norway. The respondents were front-line workers selected from local NAV offices situated in randomly selected municipalities. A 25 per cent sample of municipalities with a population below 100,000 people was randomly selected, as well as a 40 per cent sample of the local district administrations in each of the five large municipalities counting a population above 100,000 people.

The research was based on an online questionnaire financed by the Norwegian Research Counsel. The questionnaire included 20 research context questions, including work place and administrative positions, educational background, work tasks and conditions of work, autonomy and decision-making, managerial and administrative control, experiences related to activation requirements and the quality of work.

From a total sample of 2960 front-line workers, we received answers from 1758 respondents (59.4 per cent), of which 15 per cent were local managers and 85 were practitioners. The gender distribution shows a predominance of female workers with 79 per cent. The mean age of respondents were 46 years. About 64 per cent ($n = 1131$) were caseworkers working mainly within the social insurance and employment services, and 36 per cent ($n = 627$) were social service workers employed in the local authority administration of NAV. The new Auditor General's offices, established as a central part of the organisational reform in 2006, are not represented in this study.

The data are based on an online survey of several questions concerning different issues, such as autonomy and discretion, organisational and individual resources, professionalism and knowledge, management and accountability mechanisms, targeted at the front-line services in NAV. The subgroup selected for this analysis are 627 trained social workers, employed in the social services and responsible for handling cases and applications for social benefits, guidance and follow-up on recipients with special needs.

The following five questions and statements concerning the political, managerial and occupational control (Table 5.2) were analysed to examine the impact of various external and internal control mechanisms:

- *To what extent do rules and directives govern you?*
- *To what extent do politically defined targets govern you?*
- *The choices and judgments that I make are influenced by work procedures and agency routines.*
- *The choices and judgments that I make are influenced by my colleagues*
- *I am instructed to achieve results and production targets.*

The first, second and third question/statement was based on a 5-point scale ranging from 1 ('not at all') to 5 ('a very high degree'). The next statement concerning work procedures was based on a five-point scale ranging from 1 ('not at all') to 5 ('always'), while the two last statements concerning occupational control in terms of peer influence (colleagues) and management in terms of results and production targets were based on a 4-point-scale ranging from 1 ('disagree completely') to 4 ('agree completely'). In the survey, the respondents were asked to indicate the extent to which they agreed with each statement.

The next *seven* statements/prompts (Figure 5.1) concerning the mechanisms of accountability were analysed to examine how social work professionals perceive different strategies to improve and regulate the discretionary decisions and practice of work:

- *What are the best mechanisms to improve the quality of discretionary practice and decision-making in the front-line services?*

All of the *seven* prompts put forward in the survey were based on a on a five-point scale ranging from 1–5 (1 = 'not at all', 2 = 'small degree', 3 = 'to some degree', 4 = 'high degree', 5 = 'very high degree'). The statements presented in Figure 5.1 are an attempt to capture some of the accountability mechanisms and various directions presented in Table 5.1.

Experiences of managerial and occupational control – some empirical results

The questions and statements presented in the following Table 5.2 show the perceived degree of managerial and occupational control of social workers. Here, the impacts of accountability mechanisms are examined in the context of the Norwegian social welfare services.

As shown in Table 5.1, most practitioners in the social services completely agree (91 per cent) in being 'instructed to achieve results and production targets' (i.e. performance measurements), as put forward by the central welfare administration. Moreover, social workers are to a high degree subject to political defined goals (77 per cent). On the other hand, social workers report a higher level of administrative control by rules and directives (82 per cent) than by work procedures and agency routines (53 per cent).

The findings confirm the demands for efficiency and management in service delivery, both in terms of performance measurements and administrative procedures. Although management by objectives and results (MBOR) is the most widely used public management style in Norway, as in several countries (Lægreid et al., 2006), the Norwegian management model is characterised as a *hybrid* of traditional rule-oriented administration and new public management strategies and tools, elevated to principles for steering street-level practice (Christensen & Lægreid, 2011). The MBOR has only *supplemented* the traditional rule-based mode of governance and created an

Table 5.2 The experiences of managerial and occupational control (N = 620–626). Per cent

Managerial and occupational control	Low degree/ Seldom/Disagree	Some degree/ Sometimes	High degree/ Always/Agree
Governed by rules and directives (1–5)	1	16	82
Governed by political defined goals (1–5)	4	19	77
Influenced by administrative work procedures and agency routines (1–5)	11	36	53
Influenced by colleagues and professional standards (1–5)	13	60	27
Instructed to achieve results and production targets (1–4)	9	—	91

Note
Originally, the responses varied on different scales from 1 to 5, and from 1 to 4. In the presented table, the response categories are re-coded: 'High degree' and 'Often' combine the response categories 4 and 5 and 'Low degree" and "Seldom" combine the categories 1 and 2 on the five point scales. 'Agree' combine the categories 3 and 4 and 'Disagree' combine the categories 1 and 2 on the four point scales.

integrated model entailing bureaucratic procedures and performance management techniques.

In spite of the bureaucratic rules and managerial control, the new management regime still allows professional discretion and some autonomy in choosing means and measures. These kinds of decisions are often influenced by internal practices and advice given by colleagues and peers. According to the findings in Table 5.1, 60 per cent of front-line workers are influenced by fellow workers 'to a certain degree', while 27 per cent report to be 'always' influenced by fellow colleagues. The high degree of influence reported indicates that collegial support plays a significant role in providing professional standards for decision-making. In the Norwegian welfare administration, social workers are included in a range of professional relationships with fellow workers in other parts of the administration. Working in the same collegial structure and settings, social service workers will most likely be responsive to internal practice and professional advice when consulting their colleagues about decisions in complex cases, regarding social assistance services and interactions with clients.

Mechanisms to regulate discretionary practice

Figure 5.1 shows the social workers' perceptions of how to improve the quality of discretionary practice and decision-making in front-line services. The answers indicate that social workers in general prefer the horizontal mechanisms (described by the fifth and six and seven issues shown in Figure 5.1). First, the social service workers prefer professional guidance and advice by colleagues (mean 3.8), among other mechanisms, to improve and strengthen the decision-making process. Also, the need for more qualifications and knowledge in field of law and rules is strongly emphasised (mean 3.5). Social workers also believe that inter-agency cooperation is a good mechanism (mean 3, 6).

Since the work tasks of social services are often complex, practitioners need to discuss their cases with colleagues and other experts representing other fields of social security, health and care to ensure that the decision-making process is thorough and fair. Thus, they are depending on inter-agency cooperation as an important mechanism to improve the quality of decisions made in the more compounded cases.

The last two mechanisms of 'increased control and juridical review of decisions' and 'standard procedures to assess needs' were given the lowest mean scores of 2.7 and 2.8 respectively, while administrative rules including procedures, guidelines and formal instructions was given the mean score 3.2. According to our sample of respondents, these mechanisms strengthen the quality of decisions to a lower degree. On the whole, respondents prefer horizontal mechanisms of professionalism and cooperation rather than the vertical mechanisms of managerial accountability.

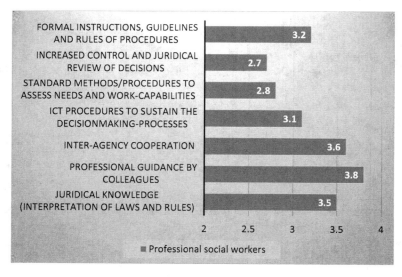

Figure 5.1 Mechanisms to improve the discretionary decision-making of social work professionals. (*N* = 626.) Mean

Discussion and final comments

The findings indicate that professional fellowship and collegial authority play a significant role in guiding and regulating social work practice, as the preferred mechanisms. The collective knowledge and shared beliefs of colleagues working within the social services provide the framework and support for interpreting individual cases and events. This in turn may justify decisions and increase the consistency of discretionary judgement across workers. Professional standards provide the basis for understanding and defining the appropriateness of action or the justification for inaction (Sandfort, 2000). Unlike new public management based on rational-legal and hierarchical authority, this collegial authority is based on professional knowledge and ethics and exercised by practitioners (Svensson, 2010). Social service workers develop shared norms and collective understandings from daily experiences. These norms and understandings, together with professional knowledge, then shape their interpretations and provide a common standard for rational action. Within the Norwegian welfare administration, social service workers are involved in a range of professional relationships with colleagues and co-workers in other parts of the administration. Working inside the same structural settings and services, social workers are responsive to professional norms and standards when consulting their colleges about decisions in complex cases regarding social assistance services and interactions with clients. The best way to ensure accountability and improve the quality of decisions is for them to follow the professional norms and standards of colleagues.

Cultural standards in terms of norms, professional standards and collective understandings in general affect social work practice. Professional expertise is applied to individual cases based on a comprehensive approach, using analytical tools that provide guides for different types of interventions and provisions (Johnson & Yanca, 2001). Collegial advice and professional standards therefore affect social work practice by regulating the decisions made by practitioners in an enabling way. These kinds of processes have structural implications for how the practitioners carry out their tasks. Professional norms and ethical codes that influence and guide the practitioners' discretionary judgements may therefore be more conducive to social work practice than management measures and standard procedures.

The demands to act in accordance with protocols and standard procedures, work manuals and guidelines may have both practical and ethical implications. In a *positive* direction, standard procedures may be necessary to push implementation practices towards the desired policy aims, provide more clarity and focus and enable front-line workers to be more inclusive in the way they use and share information (Banks, 2004). In addition, the standards and procedures to regulate case management may help ensure fair decisions and good practice to achieve equity for service users and protection for recipients against arbitrary decisions and misjudgement. In a negative direction, formal regulation, standardisation and the monitoring of outputs gives professionals fewer opportunities for exercising discretion and choose broad objectives. Within the Norwegian welfare and social services, social work professionals play a significant role in the way activation measures are applied. A primary strategy prescribed by the central government is to provide more closely tailored programs and promote the flexible use of activation services to improve employability. At the same time, social workers are accountable for reaching the policy objectives that were adopted in accordance with the main reform targets. Subjected to performance targets, the practitioners' focus may shift in order to fulfil the quotas numbers, pushing clients into activation programmes and arrangements. Consequently, the conflicting demands challenge the ability and opportunity for the individual practitioners to exercise discretion according to the ethical and technical standards of social work.

Standard procedures and instrumental approaches may decrease flexibility and reduce the complexity of social problems. Too many procedures and emphasis on predefined targets may transform the welfare services into a field of more regulatory practices. The expanding use of predefined targets, quality standard procedures, standardised assessment forms, plans and contracts introduced in welfare services, all challenge the ability and opportunity for the individual practitioners to reflect on the ethics of individual choices and decisions.

Notes

1. The term 'professional autonomy' is related to an individual practitioner's freedom to act according to the professionally defined norms and standards of social work, different from the freedom to act in accordance with their own personal moral values and judgments about particular situations.
2. Standards are criteria for judging how well something fits with the accepted norm, set by the central government, local authority or other agencies. Procedures describe how to do a set of tasks or outline the steps to be undertaken, in order to manage a situation. Standard procedures are often implemented to control and review administrative and discretionary decisions.
3. The Norwegian Parliament passed the NAV reform in 2005 (White Paper No. 9). In the following period from 2006 to the end of 2010 when the process was completed, a joint front-line service was established in all municipalities. Over all 457 local offices (one-stop-shops) were established in each municipality (430 in total). At the regional level, both administrative units and back-office units with special competencies was established, handling services defined as individual rights, primary concerning pensions.
4. Caseworkers employed in the social insurance and employment services are responsible for various benefits and supplements related to sickness and childbirth, unemployment, rehabilitation and disability, single parenthood, family and pension services, etc.

References

Askim, J., Christensen, T., Fimreite, A. L., Lægreid, P. (2010): 'How to assess administrative reform? Investigating the adoption and preliminary impacts of the Norwegian welfare administration reform', *Public Administration*, 88(1): 232–246.

Banks, S. (2004): *Ethics, Accountability and the Social Professions*, New York: Palgrave Macmillan.

Banks, S. (2013): 'Negotiating personal engagement and professional accountability: Professional wisdom and ethics work', *European Journal of Social Work*, 16(5): 587–604.

Bovens, M. (2007): 'Analysing and assessing accountability: A conceptual framework', *European Law Journal*, 13(4): 447–468.

Brodkin, E. Z. (2008): 'Accountability in street-level organisations', *International Journal of Public Administration*, 31(3): 317–336.

Byrkjeflot, H., Lægreid, P., Christensen, T. (2011): *Changing Accountability Relations in a Welfare State–An Assessment Based on a Study of Welfare Reforms*, Bergen: Uni Rokkan Centre.

Christensen, T., Lægreid, P. (2011): 'Democracy and administrative policy: Contrasting elements of New Public Management (NPM) and post-NPM', *European Political Science Review*, 3(1): 125–146.

Christensen, T., Lægreid, P. (eds.) (2017): *The Routledge Handbook to Accountability and Welfare State reforms in Europe* (Part II), London: Routledge.

Clark, C. (2005): 'The deprofessionalisation thesis, accountability and professional character', *Social Work & Society*, 3(2): 182–190.

Davis, K. C. (1969). *Discretionary Justice: A Preliminary Inquiry*. Baton Rouge, LA: Louisiana State University Press.

Evans, T. (2010): *Professional Discretion in Welfare Services: Beyond Street-level Bureaucracy*, Aldershot: Ashgate.

Evans, T. (2011): 'Professionals, managers and discretion: Critiquing street-level bureaucracy', *British Journal of Social Work*, 41(2): 368–386.

Freidson, E. (2001): *Professionalism: The Third Logic*. Cambridge: Polity press.

Harris, J., White, V. (2009): *Modernising Social Work: Critical Considerations*, Bristol: The Policy Press.

Healy, K., Meagher, G. (2004): 'The reprofessionalization of social work: Collaborative approaches for achieving professional recognition', *British Journal of Social Work*, 34: 243–260.

Hill, M., Hupe, P. (2008): *Implementing Public Policy: An Introduction to the Study of Operational Governance*, 2nd ed., London: Sage.

Hjörne, E., Juhila, K., van Nijnatten, C. (2010): 'Negotiating dilemmas in the practices of street-level welfare work', *International Journal of Social Welfare*, 19(3): 303–309.

Hood, C. C. (1991): 'A public management for all seasons?' *Public Administration*, 69(1): 3–19.

Hupe, P., Hill, M. (2007): 'Street-level bureaucracy and public accountability', *Public Administration*, 85(2): 279–299.

Jessen, J. T., Tufte, P. A. (2014): 'Discretionary decision-making in a changing context of activation policies and welfare reforms', *Journal of Social Policy*, 43(2): 269–288.

Jewell, C. J. (2007): *Agents of the Welfare State: How Caseworkers Respond to Need in the United States, Germany, and Sweden*, New York: Palgrave Macmillan.

Johansson, H., Hvinden, B. (eds.) (2007): *Citizenship in Nordic Welfare States: Dynamics of Choice, Duties and Participation in a Changing Europe*, London: Routledge.

Johnson, L., Yanca, S. (2001): *Social Work Practice: A Generalist Approach*, 7th ed., Boston: Allyn and Bacon.

Jones, G. W. (1992): 'The search for local accountability', in: Leach, S. (ed.), *Strengthening Local Government in the 1990s*, 49–78, London: Longman.

Lipsky, M. (1980): *Street-Level Bureaucracy: Dilemmas of the Individual in Public Services*, New York: Russell Sage Foundation.

Lipsky, M. (1991): 'The paradox of managing discretionary workers in social welfare policy', in: Adler, M., Bell, C., Clasen, J., Sinfield, A. (eds.), *The Sociology of Social Security*, 212–228, Edinburgh: Edinburgh University Press.

Lægreid, P., Roness, P. G., Rubecksen, K. (2006). Performance Management in Practice: The Norwegian Way. *Financial Accountability and Management*, 22(3), 251–269.

Molander, A., Grimen, H. (2010): 'Understanding professional discretion', in: Svensson, L. G., Evetts, J. (eds.), *Sociology of Professions. Continental and Anglo-Saxon Traditions*, 167–187, Gothenburg: Daidalos.

Mulgan, R. (2000): 'Accountability: An ever-expanding concept', *Public Administration*, 78(3): 555–573.

Mulgan, R. (2003): *Holding Power to Account: Accountability in Modern Democracies*, Basingstoke: Palgrave Macmillan.

NOU no. 13. (2004): En ny arbeids- og velferdsforvaltning (A New Employment and Welfare Administration).

Pollitt, C., Bouckaert, G. (2004): *Public Management Reforms. A Comparative Analysis*, 2nd ed., Oxford: Oxford University Press.

Royal Proposition No. 46. (2004–2005): Ny arbeids og velferdsforvaltning (The New Employment and Welfare Administration).

Sandfort, J. R. (2000): 'Moving beyond discretion and outcomes: Examining public management from the front lines of the welfare system', *Journal of Public Administration Research and Theory*, 10(4): 729–756.

Scott, W. R. (2008): 'Lords of the dance: Professionals as institutional Agents', *Organisational Studies*, 39(2): 219–238.

Social Services Act 2007. 1991–12–13, no. 81.

Styhre, A. (2013): *Professionals Making Judgments: The Professional Skill of Valuing and Assessing*, Basingstoke: Palgrave Macmillan.

Svensson, L. G. (2010): 'Professions, organizations, collegiality and accountability', in: Evetts, J., Svensson, L. G. (eds.), *Sociology of Professions*, 123–145, Gøteborg: Daidalos.

White Paper No. 9. (2006–2007): *Arbeid, Velferd og Inkludering (Work, Welfare and Inclusion)*, Oslo: Ministry of Labour and Social Affairs.

White, V. (2009): 'Quiet challenges? Professional practice in modernised social work', in: Harris, J., White, V. (eds.), *Modernising Social Work: Critical Considerations*, 129–144, Bristol: Policy Press.

Chapter 6

Critical perspectives on accounting, audit and accountability in public services

A study of performance management in UK local museums

Whyeda Gill-McLure

Introduction

For over three decades, public services across Europe and the US have undergone major reforms including privatisation, marketisation and managerialism. These trends have intensified since the international economic crisis of 2007–2008 with austerity imposing intolerable strains on public services and public employment (Labour Research 2010). These multiple pressures – from reform and cutbacks – mean that public servants must provide 'more for less' in an increasingly unstable political and economic environment (Arnaboldi et al., 2015).

A key element in public service reform is the New Public Management (NPM). NPM aims to make the public sector behave more like the private sector, and a key tool for achieving this is performance management (Heinrich, 2014, p. 32). However, measuring performance presents fundamental challenges in the public sector (Frey et al., 2013). Public services across Europe and internationally are the historical outcome of complex cultural influences, distinctive political formations and economic philosophies (Gill-McLure, 2013; Peters & Pierre, 2014; Rouban, 2014). This complexity is sometimes insufficiently acknowledged in the burgeoning literature on performance measurement. Critical and nuanced accounts of NPM are available (Pollitt, 1993; Arnaboldi et al., 2015), but the 'science' of performance management is full of typologies and 'what-to-do' lists (Hood, 1998, p. 12). Neglect of this complexity in public service performance management leads to negative impacts on public servants; addressing this complexity poses a major challenge to researchers, public service managers and policy makers.

This chapter contributes to the debate on performance management by offering a critical examination of some key features of this activity in public services. First, it discusses some critical perspectives on performance management in public services. The section argues that the attempt to managerialise public service professionals through performance management systems and tools that replace specialist professional skills with generic management skills are highly problematic in the complex and political setting of public services. It then critically evaluates the impact and processes of performance management in public services across three key dimensions: (1) The labour problem – staff morale (2) Critical perspectives on accounting and audit in public services (3) Performance management in the complex setting of museums – a case study. The concluding section summarises the main challenges facing performance management in the UK. It recommends a need for theoretical and empirical research to determine best practice in refining performance management practice to reduce the negative impacts on staff morale.

Critical perspectives on performance management in public services

Arnaboldi et al. (2015, p. 5) argue that complexity theory provides useful insights for addressing the challenges of performance management in the complex setting of public sector organisations. In particular, they see the latter as 'complex adaptive systems' and while there is an urgent need for effective performance management in public services, a major challenge to its success has been the neglect of complexity. Performance management is also silent on what management in public services means (Arnaboldi et al., 2015, p. 18) – a silence that needs to be addressed urgently if the nature of the 'effective public manager' is to be understood (ibid.).

Other commentators echo these concerns, arguing for the urgent need for a broad and articulated framework to shed light on the 'Whole' of public sector management reform: on the relationship between reform policy and its implementation both within government and between the various levels of government (Toonen, 2014, p. 496). Bejerot and Hasselbladh (2013) sketch out a 'holistic' framework to identify and articulate a 'cluster of interventions': political, regulatory, evaluative, managerial and professional. This *holistic* approach permits one to see that public management, and its reform, is infused with politics as the regulation, budgeting and content of public services is determined by political decisions (Bejerot & Hasselblad, 2013).

Another critical perspective on public management comes from the *politics of bureaucracy* school of thinking (Peters & Pierre, 2014; t'Hart & Wille, 2014). This approach also sees public management as distinctive due to its political dimension whereby public services are paid for out of taxation that must be justified to the electorate. Indeed, not only is 'public administration, in a broad sense, a political institution' but the politicisation of the French civil service has been debated for over two centuries (Rouban, 2014, p. 341). Yet, understanding of public management 'remains at the exploratory stage at the dawn of the twenty-first century' (ibid.).

The politicisation of public servants may be traced to three main sources: their participation in political decision making, political control over recruitment and political involvement (Rouban, 2014; Peters & Pierre, 2014). These considerations apply to professional and manual public servants working at the national or local level such as dustmen, park keepers, social workers, teachers and museum curators. Indeed, public servants form the crucial nexus between state and society with two important consequences for government (Peters & Pierre, 2014, p. 2). First,, daily implementation of policy by these workers 'defines what the laws actually mean for citizens' and second, the 'substantial discretion' these workers have affects 'who actually gets what from government' (ibid.). This view is also echoed by the street-level bureaucracy approach (Lipsey, 1980). The resulting contested and political nature of the terrain (Rouban, 1998) differentiates public employment from private sector employment. Frey et al. (2013, p. 952) detail three other such differences: the existence of 'pro-social' motivation, ambiguity over who has overall responsibility for staff performance and lack of market price and competition for services. These insights point to the distinctiveness and complexity of public management, and the potential for problems when performance management policy and practice fails to take these into account.

These considerations have been the subject of debate since the nineteenth century when, although a managerial model was mooted, the preferred model for dealing with the political complexities of public service, by government and civil servants, was the professional bureaucratic model (Mill, 1867; Tawney, 1921; Weber, 1947). This model suited the progressive approach to public administration during a period when state intervention to create and sustain a public sector was considered necessary to the successful functioning of a liberal political economy (Mill, 1867; Keynes, 1973). Historically, the professional model, characterised by autonomy, specialism and standardised careers, produced a cadre of local and central government professionals with expertise in specialisms such as town planning, finance, accounting and administrative law. In addition to expertise, a professional bureaucracy 'makes policy through the exercise of discretion' that 'gives the administration a political quality' (t'Hart & Wille, 2014, p. 330).

The assumptions of the performance management systems underlying New Public Management (NPM) thinking contrast starkly with those of the professional model. Crucially, NPM reverses the progressive approach to public services: it prefers a results-driven public sector modelled on private sector lines. The rationale behind this shift is that bureaucracies are inefficient in allocating resources, generic management skills are to be preferred to specialist professional skills and market mechanisms lower costs and explicate performance standards. Private sector-type performance management, it is claimed, on the other hand, in tandem with the production of league tables or other indicators of success, allows parents and citizens a more informed basis for choice.

NPM thus attempts to simplify public service accounting by replacing political and professional accountability with 'managerial accountability' (Stoker, 1996, p. 19; Lewis & Neiman, 2009). Critics, however, argue that NPM, with its preference for private solutions to welfare issues, writes out complexity replacing it with the kind of *instrumental rationality* in which political questions of priorities are transposed into apparently scientific or technical issues' of measurable and quantifiable results (Gruening, 2001, p. 19; Mattei, 2007, p. 614).

The perspectives on performance management in public services, sketched above, are all critical of its over-simplistic use and assumptions in a complex and political setting. This is an important and emerging area of research employed here to examine the challenges facing performance management in a complex public sector setting that we reflect on in the conclusion. The next section shows that results-based, private-sector type reforms, in the context of budget cuts and austerity, have resulted in serious negative impacts on staff: job loss, work intensification, low staff morale and resentment.

The labour problem – pay, performance and staff morale

Government attempts to control pay and performance have a long history in UK public services. This is because public sector pay and performance are deeply political issues for a number of reasons: public services are labour intensive with labour costs amounting to 60–70% of overall costs, the pay bill is paid for out of public expenditure which must be justified to the electorate and the government as paymaster can interfere in national pay determination. Total local government employment in England and Wales stood at 2.68 m in 2012 or one-eighth of overall employment. This large workforce is costly. Indeed, public services across Europe and the US are quantitatively significant in the overall economy and labour intensive according to a recent study (Gill-McLure & Thörnqvist, 2018). In addition, the professional bureaucratic model enshrined in the Whitley arrangements for pay bargaining since 1947 embodied a compromise involving lower pay than the private sector but better conditions of employment. According to a retired researcher for the Local Government Employers' Organisation,

> The good employer concept was integral to the bi-partisan, pluralist notion whereby employees were valued.
> (interview by author, September 2015)

This 'good employer' formula was under pressure from the 1970s as central government linked pay to performance through productivity bargaining to meet its incomes policy guidelines. However, it came under more sustained pressure from the neoliberal turn to NPM post-1979 ushered in by the Conservative government of Thatcher in the UK.

In local government, marketszation took the form of compulsory competitive tendering (CCT) from 1988. CCT took the sector back to the late nineteenth century by ending the 'good employer' assumption that all manual services (for example, refuse collection, parks and recreation, street cleaning) would be delivered using public staff directly employed by the council.

Instead, councils had to compete with the private sector. CCT was accompanied by a radical organisational restructuring: departmental structures were replaced by a dual structure of cost-centres and clients/contractors. A major aim was to reduce politicisation of decisions around service levels and needs through bypassing traditional departmental structures involving elected members, professional and unions (Audit Commission, 1989).

CCT was also aimed at reducing labour costs, which it succeeded in doing through job losses and outsourcing. Between 1988 (when CCT was introduced) and the mid-1990s, 300,000 manual jobs were lost. Union and employer figures show a reduction in total local government employment from 3 m to 2.7 m between 1979 and 1993 (UNISON, 1994). The Labour government of 1997 replaced CCT with the Best Value regime which imposed a general duty on authorities to 'secure continuous improvement'. An authority's performance was measured using 'performance indicators' and 'performance standards'. Authorities undertook reviews of functions and produced performance plans each financial year. New Labour, reinforced and recalibrated performance tools as part of its centrally imposed system of targets and performance indicators to be regularly audited by the Audit Commission (Gill-McLure, 2014).

The CCT and Best Value reforms resulted in job losses and transformed the sector by introducing NPM principles aimed at reducing local government autonomy to make local decisions through professional and political decisions about levels of service and labour management. The two initiatives were followed by austerity policies post-2008, which led to further job losses with more than 700,000 jobs lost in local government alone to date. The basic pay bill for England and Wales (excluding teachers and chief officers) fell by around 9% in real terms between 2010/11 and 2012 to £25.1b and continued to fall with the coalition government's policy of freezing pay in the sector.

The overall impact of job loss, frozen or deteriorating pay levels and doing more for less caused much anger amongst staff that erupted in industrial conflict and a rise in sickness absence. It also had negative impacts on staff morale, as under NPM, the function of the public organisation (school, council, university) is transformed (Ball, 2008, p. 52). It moves from being a multi-layered complex of conflicting political positions, rooted in distinct professional interests and expertise, to one that is there primarily to implement centrally imposed targets. The 'logic' and the real-life effects of this transformation become apparent from a *holistic* perspective, that is, one that examines the relationship between central reform policy and local implementation (Kirkpatrick et al., 2005; Gill-McLure, 2007, 2014; Bejerot & Hasselbladh, 2013; Rouban, 2013).

According to a major local government inquiry, determining citizen needs is an inherently political process (Widdicombe, 1986). Performance management, however, attempts to transmute this inherent complexity into a quasi-scientific activity through quantitative metrics and measurable performance indicators. Bevan and Hood (2006) have dubbed the Best Value regime one of 'targets and terror', and Bach and Kessler note the 'unintended consequences' of performance management on the workforce: it was unpopular in schools where it created recruitment and retention problems and fear of dismissal (2012, p. 50). Staff felt uninvolved in establishing targets that were seen as unrelated to local realities (Bach, 2004). Against this, one study asserted that Best Value in Scotland was more responsive to local priorities, but this study was based on interviews with council leaders, heads of policy and service heads rather than staff (Downe et al., 2008). In contrast, a comparative study of performance auditing in the UK and Australia was more sceptical about the concept and practice of BV (Barrett, 2010).

As noted above, managing pay and performance in public services is a deeply political issue. This makes pay determination complex (Priestley, 1955). NPM attempts to erase or conceal this political dimension by making the public sector behave more like the private. This move has negative impacts on staff morale as organisations and governments attempt to write out the complexity and political dimension involved in public service delivery and when they fail to consult with staff. The next section presents some critical observations on a number of key performance tools in public services, with particular reference to the public museums arena.

Critical perspectives on accounting and audit performance tools

Performance management is made up of a number of metrics and tools rooted in the assumptions underlying the NPM model's critique of the professional bureaucratic model. Arnaboldi et al. point out the difficulties for public service managers in selecting and mobilising performance management tools (2015, p. 7). Out of the five commonly used tools identified, the present study focuses on budgetary control, KPIs (key performance indicators) and lean management. It adds two more tools used in museum management and other public services – cost-benefit analysis and generic management (See Table 6.1, adapted from Arnaboldi et al., 2015). Examples below from English authority museums date from the period when Best Value was implemented and its effects started to be documented, that is, from about 2000.

Performance management has dramatically altered the context of public museum management with a 'shift towards income generation, customer orientation and increased efficiency' (Jackson, 1991, p. 41; Lawley, 2003, p. 75). The introduction of spending limits (capping) to local authorities has impacted negatively on museum finances as museum services are discretionary, under sections 12 and 14 of the Public Libraries and Museums Act 1964 (Museums and Galleries Commission, 1991). With 'standstill' budgets, restructuring and, more recently, austerity cuts and reduced staffing, public museums are under immense pressure regarding their long-term survival. Analogous trends are reported across Europe and internationally (Lindqvist, 2012; Lusiani & Zan, 2010; Zorloni, 2010; BBC, 2010, 2011).

Table 6.1 Performance management technologies

Technology	Key attributes	Comment
1 Budgetary control	Traditional accounting	Crude; Limited; open to manipulation
2 KPIs & benchmarking	Partial performance indicators in comparable settings	What gets measured gets included; centrally imposed; flawed comparisons
3 Lean management	Toyota production model; Continuous improvement	Negative side effects; Short-termism; Staff resentment
4 Cost-benefit analysis	Evaluates market price for cost and benefits of public service	Neglects political and long-term dimension of public service
5 Generic management	NPM-inspired attempt to merge professional activities	Neglects professional ethos/identity; Staff resentment

There are over 2,500 museums in the UK with large museums like Glasgow, Aberdeen, Dundee and Edinburgh accounting for 75% of total local authority museum expenditure in Scotland (Museums and Galleries Commission, 1991, para 3.1). Yet, 40% of registered museums are operated by councils (Lawley, 2003, p. 76) with funding thinly spread across around hundreds of very diverse organisations. This variety means that performance management tools need to be finely tuned if they are to meet these diverse needs.

However, *Budgetary control*, as Arnaboldi et al. (2015) point out, is a crude accounting tool for a number of reasons. First, it is difficult to accurately estimate museum expenditure partly because of accounting inconsistencies and partly due to disaggregating museum costs from the larger units they sit in. Public service budgets are increasingly operationally devolved to local cost-centres – university departments, council departments, museums – but strategically controlled by the centre. In local government, devolved budgets are particularly open to manipulation as elected members need to justify spending to constituents at election time and to central government in order not to be penalised for overspend. They can too easily fail to capture, like other NPM performance tools, the variety of service-user and staff requirements which are subject to political and professional judgements. For example, there are significant variations in expenditure per inhabitant across museums. This variety is partly due to the variation in size and function of local museums and the communities they serve and to the political nature of local authority provision and management.

Cost-benefit analysis similarly neglects the political dimensions of conservation decisions as it focuses on *allocative* and not *distributive* aspects of conservation policy (Frey & Obelhozer-Gee, 1998, p. 44). They also found that while the costs of inputs like building prices can be traded in competitive markets, the benefits of conservation are far more difficult to measure under conventional economic analysis. This is partly because this type of analysis is apolitical (ibid.) and does not factor in the long-term benefits to future generations of public service benefits (ibid.)

Key performance indicators (KPIs) were intrinsic to the Best Value regime of New Labour for local government. These plus targets and league tables were introduced to improve performance in schools, ambulance response times and waiting times for receiving treatment in a hospital accident and emergency facility. Centrally imposed KPIs were intended to increase effectiveness through proxy market measures. However, commentators note the unintended consequences and flaws of these ranging from gaming (manipulating targets) and synechdoche (taking the part to represent the whole) to distortion (altering behaviour to meet targets) (Bevan & Hood, 2006). Examples of these types of indicator abound and include increases in exclusions of children from school to make the school more competitive vis-à-vis other schools in league tables for pupil performance and manipulation of hospital waiting lists.

Benchmarking and the service reviews conducted under Best Value (BV) have caused some museums to reconsider their expenditure through comparisons with other authorities. However, identifying appropriate comparators is problematic as public organisations will vary in size and political context. For example, Ipswich, a small authority, had its museum budget of £1 m cut with a move to de-accessioning of collections (considered too expensive) and fewer exhibitions, but an increase in customer facilities like coffee shops (Lawley, 2003, p. 79). Staff felt the exercise had been used as a cost-cutting one rather than a serious review of the service (ibid.). One manager contacted by the Group for Museum Directors in October 2000 felt that:

> Best Value is fundamentally flawed, with an assumption of year on year "efficiency savings", meaningless performance indicators, and inconsistency in data capture. Discretionary services will be worst hit. There's also a lack of "joined-up thinking". Social inclusion work is labour intensive, with very little obvious immediate return.
>
> (Lawley, 2003)

This observation echoes the critical perspectives outlined above. For example, the reference to 'year on year efficiency savings' can be linked to the requirement of continuous improvement under *Lean Management*. In the context of centrally funded and politically determined public services, this is a flawed and unachievable assumption, as the respondent notes.

Finally, *generic management* denotes a rejection of the specialist expertise decried by NPM as part of the silo mentality underlying the bureau-professional state. This tool is now widespread in public services: in the NHS, with the rise of clinical managers; in universities and local government, with the emergence of merged departments. This move creates tensions by pitting clinical/professional expertise/opinion v. managerial decisions, and increasing workloads and professional stress and resentment.

The case study presented below shows how these performance management tools impacted negatively on museum professionals. The findings show an urgent need for staff consultation and social dialogue to minimise such negative effects. This is discussed in the concluding remarks.

Performance management in the complex setting of museums: Scotcity museums 2010–2013

Fieldwork for the case study involved over 35 semi-structured interviews with three curators, a senior personnel manager and a UNISON branch official over three years. Council documents were examined as well as authority and national policy documents and reports into museums.

Scotcity Council covers a geographical area of 140 square miles with a population of 150,000 and employs 8,500 staff. This large geographical area has a significant impact on the workload and responsibilities of museum curators. The museum service was traditionally located in four areas spread across the county, each with a museum and curator(s) (Table 6.2).

With CCT, manual services were removed from a departmental structure and reorganised on the client-contractor model. Outsourcing was witnessed across Scotland and driven by budget cuts:

> I hate to say there were financial advantages to a local authority doing things in this way, to balance the books for example, but like other authorities we put these services out. So, driven by budgetary constraints.
>
> (Senior Personnel Officer)

As with the rest of Scotland, the authority had a two-tier structure (introduced after the reorganisation of local government in Scotland (1975) and the rest of the UK (1974)) made up of regional and districts councils until the mid-1990s when a unitary structure was introduced. Figure 6.1 shows that the two-tier structure meant services, including museums, were managed across the two tiers with a strategic presence at Directorate level and an operational presence at Area/District level. This structure permitted museums to have central support in terms of a strategic officer with responsibility for commissioning manual support services post-CCT, amongst other duties. This officer provided support for example with building maintenance and cleaning services for museums. He was also responsible for external arts-funding applications.

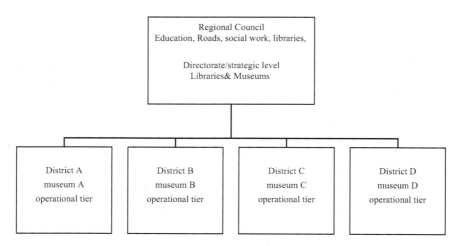

Figure 6.1 Scotcity, two tier structure 1975–1996.

He saw the core of his strategic role as one of 'acting as a buffer between the centre and local museums'. There were two levels of budgets:

> The four areas had four separate museums budgets and one central strategic budget. The local budget covered Collections management, staff, property management and exhibitions. The central budget was for single acquisitions. Local museums would put in bids to the centre for acquisitions.
> (Strategic museums officer)

The two-tier system allowed the money to be spread and targeted across the council's museums and art galleries; it also gave overworked curators some administrative support. But this arrangement broke down due to budget cuts that hit the council around 2009–10. The cuts, in tandem with a poor Best Value report from the Scottish Audit Commission in 2009, were major drivers for a council restructuring. Another driver included pressure for 'efficiency gains' under the Gershon Report, transposed to Scotland under the Labour-led Scottish executive (Gershon, 2004; Midwinter, 2010, p. 213). The curators felt that until 2008/9, although workloads were high and core tasks difficult to achieve due to lack of staff, they were left alone to manage their museums. This kind of relative autonomy was interpreted by the Audit Commission Report as a lack of hands-on centralised performance management, which it urged the authority to improve:

> Performance management is poor. There is little political or senior management leadership on performance management and there is no corporate culture of continuous improvement. Performance reporting is also weak.
> (Audit Commission Scotland, 2009, Part 2, p. 23)

The negative impact of performance management: work intensification, service deterioration, low staff morale

The recently appointed Scotcity Chief Executive introduced a programme of radical restructuring. A Performance and Development Review pack was produced consisting of a set of prescriptions including 360-degree appraisals, 'performance wheels' and 'core competencies' with over 60 elements in them. The curators felt much of this bore little resemblance to how they perceived their core tasks and were anxious and cynical over the lack of consultation over the exercise:

> Consultation now means we [sic.the management] are doing something and we are telling you we are doing it.
> (Strategic officer)

A lack of consultation over implementing cuts and restructuring was found across UK museums:

> The consultation period was a farce; our union agreed it was bordering on illegal.
> (Assistant curator – a local authority museum in the South West, Newman & Tourle, 2011)

At Scotcity, the restructure involved the delayering of management as well as a move to generic management. Performance indicators were introduced some years earlier at Scotcity. However, the Audit Commission found them inadequate and ineffective (Audit Commission Scotland, 2009, Part 2, p. 80). For Museum Services (as for other services such as Libraries and 'Sports and Leisure (SL)', the most common performance indicator used is 'Number of visits to/usages of council-funded or part-funded museums'. The curators found this to be a very crude measurement for capturing the variety of ways in which the public uses the museum service:

> In museums, what doesn't come out in the performance indicator of 'number of visits' is: …emails from America or Canada or New Zealand; or the BBC ring you for a picture of such and such for a programme… and the value that that has potentially in highlighting the region. … I mean how do you measure civic pride, sense of place, cultural facilities, it's like trying to apply production methods… it's like saying how many cars have you made…
> (Curator X)

There was concern that the social/educational value of public service delivery and its benefits are difficult to measure/evaluate quantitatively:

> The other parameter is how much does the visit cost… you've got 100 visitors let's say and it costs you £1,000 for staff, heating and lighting, so it costs £10 per visit. Is it a good thing or not? This has

happened recently with the budget reviews and the need for savings. If you go to outdoor activities – you've got 30 kids with one officer, one session a week. The subsidised cost is 50p per kid. He might get 150 kids a week if he's lucky and overall pools are dealing with 5,000 a week... But how do you assess the added value to kids of orienteering or swimming?

(Curator X)

The curators' views demonstrate that performance management cannot be un-problematically transported into the public sector where there is no straight link between consumers and least-cost performance. This creates problems for public services as it 'washes out the diversity of preferences and the conflicts of democracy' (Jackson, 1991). Performance measurement does not factor in 'value to society/community', nor does it reflect the need for long-term evaluation when it comes to public service. The value and effectiveness of cultural and education services can only be assessed as children grow into adults and then it cannot be divorced from other factors such as political, economic and industrial policies of the governments of the day.

The curators also had little confidence in generic management: they saw it as a flawed concept and as an attempt to compensate for the loss of managers through delayering. Staff resented the lack of consultation and felt that the performance management tools were inappropriate and over-simplistic.

Generic management involved the merger of SL with Museums. All curators and SL managers were to apply for new posts combining museum and SL duties. There was much stress amongst all affected staff. All felt the move was unworkable and damaging to museums and SL as they did not have the time or skills to run two disparate services. Curator X already ran a number of museums and art galleries. He was the only qualified curator in his division, and administrative support had been withdrawn due to cuts. He spent 41% of his time on 'core duties' (collections, information and exhibitions); 26% on 'non-core' duties (for example, special exhibitions, one of which brought in over 20,000 visitors over the summer months); and 30% of his time on managerial tasks (administration, organising and managing staff and volunteers, corporate meetings). Work intensification is widespread in the museum sector:

New funding priorities are fundamentally changing our working practices, with less of what the public expect us to do, e.g. enquiries, talks, research.... Fundamental work such as collections care and documentation is under threat.

(Assistant curator, local authority museum, South. – Evans, 2011, p. 13)

Despite working Saturdays, Curator X struggled to clear the backlog of work on cataloguing the collections. He was anxious as to how he could find more time to do the extra work involved in running two services:

> ...it's literally spreading us more thinly. Underlying this is the principle that it if you're a manager you can do anything, that management is about managing people and resources to deliver a service and if you're a generic manager (whatever that may be!), the implication is that you don't need to be a specialist, which is a problem for us in that we are [specialists]....
> (Curator X)

Thus, it can be seen that performance management and generic management are related strands of NPM with shared and inter-related aims: getting more for less; the dilution and undermining of specialist knowledge and professional autonomy through generic management and centrally imposed performance management tools. The case study shows how these aims were played out locally: pressure to get more for less was intensified under austerity; pressure from the Audit Commission meant the imposition and clumsy interpretation of performance tools. Under these circumstances, there was no evidence of any attempt to fine-tune these tools to meet staff concerns and service needs.

This lack of consultation caused staff anxiety, stress and resentment over what they perceived as the council's disregard for the realities of the museum service:

> Council policies done without regard for service realities. So our work is done in spite of the council, not because of the council... Problems with defining generic management...These problems not thought out by senior management, so everybody is being pushed beyond their knowledge base...that's got to be a worry... The whole move to generic management is driven by budget cuts and poor audit report.
> (Strategic museums officer)

Budget-driven, centrally imposed performance management has negative impacts on staff morale across the museum service:

> Morale [is] very low due to announcement of 25% staff cuts plus slashed running budgets and blocks on programmes planned for 2012/13.
> (Education manager, national museum, North – Evans, 2011, p. 13)

The strategic museums officer applied for a generic position as his post was being deleted. This caused him much stress and resentment as the specialist knowledge he had spent years building up would no longer be required. The deletion of his post also meant the disappearance of an essential support for local museums.

Museum staff met with senior managers to express their concerns with little effect. All affected staff from SL and museums re-applied for new generic posts. The four area museums and SL departments were merged into two divisions – West and East – spreading fewer staff more thinly across the county (Figure 6.2). Curators W and X (with no knowledge of SL) became generic managers for SL and museums in West division. An arts manager V and a Sports Manager Y (both without museums knowledge) became generic managers for museums and SL in East division.

Curator W struggled in his new generic post. Having 'always enjoyed going to work', he was stressed as he was totally untrained for the SL duties which involved large amounts of administration and the 'nitty-gritty of performance measures and figures' for both museums and sports and leisure:

> When you are managing sports and leisure, you don't [sic.as a curator] know what you are doing. And, I can't see any advantage in that. You expect [that] if people create a job, they know what they are doing but nobody knows what they are doing…it is all bafflement and bewilderment…all post ad hoc. That's where it's gone wrong… They are making cuts but calling it generic management.
>
> (Curator W)

Generic management creates increased workloads and stress across the museum service:

> Paid staff now work well beyond their job descriptions and contracted hours just to keep things going.
> (Director, independent museum, Wales – Evans, 2011, p. 13)

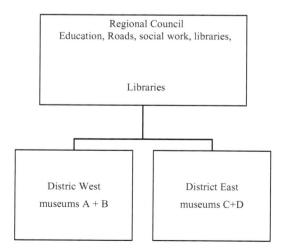

Figure 6.2 Scotcity East and West museum districts 2010–present.

Curator W's stress levels were so high that, despite loving his job, he took early retirement. But, he was deeply concerned about the future of the service:

> Part of me feels bad because I am creating an imbalance in the structure and they will have to devolve my responsibilities to people below me.
> (Curator W)

Curator X also struggled. His new post required that he cease or reduce time spent on curatorial duties but as sole curator, this was not possible. Curator Z (from Museum C, East Division) was thus tasked to him out at museum B, and when Curator W retired, she took over his duties at museum A.

This tortuous approach to museum management under austerity and NPM created immense upheaval and extra work for all concerned as all curators ended up driving around the county in all directions to do other people's jobs. Curator Z was forced to relocate to reduce the daily three-to-four-hour drive involved in her new duties. Curators X and W had to train Curator Z to take over their duties; Curator Z had to train Manager V to take over her duties. Another restructure took place in 2012 when Curator X retired despite loving his curator's job.

Table 6.2 Museum staffing pre and post restructure 1996–2014

	Museum A	Museum B	Museum C	Museum D
1996–2010	1 Curator (W) Exhibitions officer Education officer Admin officer (Shared with sports and leisure)	1 Curator (X) 1 clerical officer + volunteers	1 curator (Z)	Exhibitions officer; 2 curators; Education officer Admin officer Documentation officer
2011 Merger	District West (museums A+B)		District East (museums C+D)	
2011–2012	Curator W retires. Curator Z runs Museum A and Museum C	Curator X runs Museum B + Sports and Leisure dept. Curator Z helps out	1 Generic arts manager (V) with no museum training	Exhibitions officer + 1 Generic arts manager (V) with no museum training
2012–present	Curator X retires 2013. Curator Z runs A and B		1 Generic arts manager (V) with no museum training runs museums C+D	

Table 6.2 shows the reductions in museum staff from a very few people to even less. Indeed, after the latest restructure, there are 1.5 qualified curators to cover this large county as opposed to 3.5 pre-merger. This has meant increased workloads and an inability to get the job done:

> Not only is my job going but the posts of the 'doers', the curators are going...There has been an assumption made at the top that the service has a critical mass and that the manager of that location will be able to devote time to doing many other tasks but the reality for museums [Table 4: museums B and C] is that there is only one person anyway.
>
> (Strategic officer for museums)

The above findings demonstrate the negative impacts on staff of budget-driven, centrally imposed performance management systems in the public sector. They highlight an important fact: that lack of local consultation is a major source of low staff morale, resentment and stress.

Concluding discussion

Austerity across Europe has increased pressure on public services to maintain service levels and quality whilst cutting back on staff and public spending. Inspired by NPM, performance management has been a key tool for meeting such challenges. However, case study evidence at Scotcity shows the significant negative impacts on staff morale when performance management is driven by centrally imposed performance targets under diminishing budgets.

At a theoretical level, the paper has outlined a number of critical perspectives to argue that serious failings of performance management occur due to its neglect of the distinctive nature and complexity of public service organisations. This neglect creates immense pressure on public servants as the discretion and autonomy they require to meet politically determined user needs is seriously undermined/under-valued.

At an empirical level, the case study of Scotcity museums provides a 'closely grained' and 'holistic evaluation' (Arnaboldi et al., 2015, p. 18) of the local implementation and impacts of performance management on museum professionals. It shows how performance management was introduced as a knee-jerk reaction by local management to a poor Best Value report by the Scottish Audit Commission. There was a complete lack of consultation centrally (between the Audit Comission and the authority) as well as locally (between management and staff or their union). The performance management tools introduced were taken from a generic tool kit and the whole exercise was a box-ticking exercise.

Staff were stressed and over-worked but their chief resentment was at the lack of consultation and neglect of the complex, distinctive needs of public service professionals (Orr & Vince, 2009). Staff felt that the educational, long-term economic, cultural value and specialist nature of museum work and outputs cannot be captured by KPIs or generic management, which are more suited to unskilled assembly-line production work. These significant findings need to be deepened by further theoretical and empirical research to understand how the competing values of efficiency and social responsibility can be managed in practice by public service professionals under performance management. There is an urgent need, that is, for a more holistic understanding of the complexity involved in a key sector like local government that does not just deliver key infrastructural public services but is the locus of local politics and local democracy (Leach et al., 1995, p. 4–6).

Finally, there is an urgent need to look at whether a more sophisticated approach to public service performance management can be or has been deployed or developed. What would be the essential ingredients of such 'best practice'? Some examples can be found in Northern Europe where management have used consultation and social dialogue with staff and unions. Discussion with key stakeholders would enable the refinement and development of performance management tools. This would permit staff to both 'own' and influence the tools in ways which improved 'real' performance rather than some centrally-imposed notion of improved performance. Used in this way, performance indicators could potentially,

> …be a useful source of management (and union) information. For example, to set a target for the proportion of women in senior roles. But they can often be too coarse.
> (retired LGEO officer, Sep. 2015)

Local consultation and design would offset the two major problems with performance indicators under Best Value, viz. that

> they were centrally imposed and used in conjunction with targets. They don't have to be used in tandem with targets or be imposed centrally. A target-based regime shows a lack of trust in local management
> (retired LGEO officer, Sep. 2015)

Performance management thus need not inherently have negative impacts on staff and services. A new research agenda is urgently required if the ongoing negative impacts on staff are to be redressed. At a theoretical level, this agenda would need to highlight the ideological assumptions underlying NPM-style performance management that hinges on privatisation and marketisation as well as rebalancing the employment relationship towards employer/state interests. In addition, this agenda employs accounting and audit tools anchored in neo-classical economic orthodoxies which fail to reflect the complexity of public services. It is this that ultimately drives low-cost, labour-intensifying, skill-depleting approaches to performance management aimed at wresting professional control and political discretion from public servants.

Exposing these neoliberal ideological assumptions is a *sine qua non* for a scientific and nuanced evaluation of what is wrong with the current performance agenda. This is also essential to building alternatives based on a political understanding of the crucial role of professional autonomy, specialism and discretion to meeting citizen and social needs. A close empirical study of the latter 'in practice' through detailed case study and survey work would then show the kind of financial and organisational supports the state and public managers must foster in order to underpin truly efficient public services delivered by the 'real experts'. In sum, we need to redefine the current neoliberal agenda through theoretically-informed empirical research.

References

Arnaboldi, M., Lapsley, I., Steccolini, I. (2015): Performance management in the public sector: the ultimate challenge, *Financial Accountability & Management*, 31: 1–22. doi:10.1111/faam.12049

Audit Commission (1989): *Preparing for Compulsory Competitive Competition*, London: HMSO.

Audit Commission (1991): *The Road to Wigan Pier? Managing Local Authority Museums and Art Galleries*, London: HMSO.

Audit Scotland (2009): *The Audit of Best Value and community Planning*, Edinburgh: Scotcity Council, March.

Bach, S. (2004): 'Employee participation and union voice in the National Health Service', *Human Resource Management Journal*, 14(2): 3–19.

Bach, S., Kessler, I. (2012): *The Modernisation of Public Services and Employee Relations*, Basingstoke: Palgrave Macmillan.

Bain, M.A. (1972): *The New Local Authorities: Management and Structure*, London: HMSO.

Ball, S.J. (2008): 'Performativity, privatisation, professionals and the state', in: Cunningham, B. (ed.), *Exploring Professionalism*, London: Institute of Education, University of London.

BBC (2010): 'Italian cultural attractions go on strike over cuts'. www.bbc.co.uk/news/world-europe-11741506.

BBC (2011): 'Fifth of museums hit by 25% funding cuts, finds survey'. www.bbc.co.uk/news/entertainment-arts-14189864.

Barrett, P. (2010): 'Performance auditing – what value?', *Public Money & Management*, 30(5): 271–278.

Bejerot, E., Hasselbladh, H. (2013): 'Forms of intervention in public sector organizations: generic traits in public sector reforms', *Organization Studies*, 34: 1357–1380.

Bevan, G., Hood, C. (2006): 'What's measured is what matters: targets and gaming in the English public healthcare system', *Public Administration*, 84(3): 517–538.

Cochrane, A. (1986): 'Local employment initiatives: towards a new municipal socialism?', in: Lawless, P., Raban, C. (eds.), *The Contemporary British City*, London: Harper & Row.

Clarke, J., Gerwitz, S., Laughlin, E. (2000): 'Reinventing the welfare state', in: Clarke, J., Gerwitz, S., Laughlin, E. (eds.): *New Managerialism, New Welfare?*, London: Sage.

Downe, J., Grace, C., Martin, S., Nutley, S. (2008): 'Best value audits in Scotland: winning without scoring', *Public Money & Management*, 28(2): 77–83.

Du Gay, P. (2008): 'Without affection or enthusiasm: problems of involvement and attachment in responsive public management', *Organization*, 15(3): 335–353.
Evans, G. (2011): *The Impact of Cuts on UK Museums*, London: Museums Association.
Frey, B.S., Homberg, F., Osterloh, M. (2013): 'Organizational control systems and pay-for-performance in the public service', *Organization Studies*, 34: 949–972.
Frey, B.S., Obelhozer-Gee, F. (1998): 'Public choice, cost-benefit analysis and the evaluation of cultural heritage', in: Peacock, A. (ed.): *Does the Past have a Future? The Political Cconomy of Heritage*, London: The Institute of Economic Affairs.
Gershon Report (2004): *Releasing Resources to the Front Line: Independent Review of Public Sector Efficiency*, London: HMSO.
Gill, W. (1994): 'Decentralisation and devolution in local government: pressures and obstacles', *Industrial Relations Journal*, 25(3): 210–221.
Gill-McLure, W. (2002): 'Towards a political economy of local government industrial eelations: a study of union and management resistance to compulsory competitive tendering 1979–2000', Ph.D. thesis, Keele: Keele University.
Gill-McLure, W. (2007): 'Fighting marketization: an analysis of manual municipal labor in the UK and the US', *Labor Studies Journal*, Spring issue, 41–59.
Gill-McLure, W. (2013): 'The political economy of public sector trade union militancy under Keynesianism: the case of local government', *Capital & Class*, 37(3): 417–436.
Gill-McLure (2014): 'The politics of managerial reform in UK local government: a study of control, conflict and resistance 1880s to present', *Labor History*, 55(3): 365–388.
Gill-McLure, W., Thörnqvist, C. (2018): 'Reconstructing resistance and renewal in public service unionism in the twenty-first century: lessons from a century of war and peace', *Labor History*, 59(1): 3–14.
Gruening, G. (2001): 'Origin and theoretical basis of New Public Management', *International Public Management Journal*, 4: 1–25.
Heinrich, C.J. (2014): 'Measuring public sector performance and effectiveness', in: Peters, B., Pierre, J. (eds.): *The Sage Handbook of Public Administration*, London: Sage.
Hood, C. (1998): *State of the Art: Culture, Rhetoric and Public Management*, Oxford: Oxford University Press.
Ingraham, P.W. (2007): 'Striving for balance: reforms in human resource management', in: Ferlie, E., Lynn, L.E., Pollitt, C. (eds.), *The Oxford Handbook of Public Management*, Oxford: Oxford University Press.
Jackson, P.M. (1991): 'Performance indicators: promises and pitfalls', in: Pearce, S. (ed.): *Museum Economics and the Community*, London: Athlone Press.
Jackson, P.M. (2001): 'Public sector added value: can bureaucracy deliver?', *Public Administration*, 79(1): 5–28.
Kawashima, N. (1997): Museum Management in a Time of Change: impacts of cultural policy on museums in Britain 1979–1997, Centre for Cultural Policy Studies, Research Papers, No.3, Warwick: University of Warwick.
Kelly, J. (2009): 'Book Review' of Chisholm, M. and Leach, S. (2008) 'Botched business: the damaging process of local government reorganisation 2006–2008', *Public Administration*, 87(3): 707–709.
Keynes, J.M. (1973): *The General Theory of Employment, Interest and Money*, London: Macmillan.
Kirkpatrick, I., Ackroyd, S., Walker, R.M. (2005): *The New Managerialism and Public Service Professionals: Change in Health, Social Services and Housing*, London: Palgrave Macmillan.

Labour Research (2010): *'Coalition slash and burn begins'*, December, p. 12.
Lawley, I. (2003): 'Local authority museums and the modernizing government agenda in England', *Museum and Society*, 1(2): 275–286.
Leach, S., Stewart, J., Walsh, K. (1995): *The Changing Organisation and Management of Local Government*, London: Macmillan.
Leach, S. (forthcoming 2015): 'The relationship between central and local government', in: Leach, S., Robert, M., Copus, C. (eds.), *The Marginalisation of English Local Government*, London: Palgrave Macmillan.
Lewis, P.G., Neiman, M. (2009): *Custodians of Place: Governing the Growth and Development of Cities*, Washington, DC: Georgetown University Press.
Lindqvist, K. (2012): 'Museum finances: challenges beyond economic crises', *Museum Management and Curatorship*, 27(1): 1–15.
Lipsey, M. (1980): *Street-Level Bureaucracy Dilemmas of the Individual in Public Services*, New York: Russel Sage Foundation.
Local Government Management Board (1997): *Pay in Local Government*, London: LGMB.
Lusiani, M., Zan, L. (2010): 'Institutional transformation and managerialism in cultural heritage: Heritage Malta', *Museum Management and Curatorship*, 25(2): 147–165.
Marx, K. (1967 [1867]): *Capital*, Vol. 1, London: Dent.
Mattei, P. (2007): 'From politics to good management? Transforming the local welfare state in Italy', *West European Politics*, 30(3): 595–620.
Meier, S., Frey, B.S. (2003): 'Private faces in public places: the case of a private art museum in Europe', *Cultural Economics*, 3(3): 1–16.
Midwinter, A. (2010): 'New development: Efficiency savings in the Scottish budget – problems of accounting practice', *Public Money & Management*, 30(5): 313–317.
Mill, J.S. (1867 edn.): *Principles of Political Economy*, London: Longmans, Green, Reader and Dyer.
Moynihan, D.P. (2014): 'Identifying the antecedents to government performance: implications for human resource management', in: Peters, B., Pierre, J (eds.), *The Sage Handbook of Public Administration*, London: Sage.
Museums and Galleries Commission (1991) *Local Authorities and Museums: Report by Working Party 1991*, London: HMSO.
Museums Galleries Scotland (2011): *National Strategy Consultation: Working towards a National Strategy for Scotland's Museums and Galleries: Your chance to shape your future*, 16th September.
Newman, K., Tourle, P. (2011): *The Impact of Cuts on UK Museums*, London: Museums Association.
Niskanen, W.A. (1971): *Bureaucracy and Representative Government*, New York: Aldine-Atherton.
Orr, K. Vince, R. (2009): 'Traditions of Local Government', *Public Administration*, 87(3): 655–677.
Peters, B., Pierre, J. (2014): 'The role of public administration in governing', in: Peters, B., Pierre, J. (eds.), *The Sage Handbook of Public Administration*, London: Sage.
Pollitt, C. (1993): *Managerialism and the Public Services: Cuts or Cultural Change in the 1990s?*, Oxford: Blackwell.
Public Services Privatisation Research Unit (PSPRU) (1992): *Privatisation – Disaster for Quality*, London: PSPRU.

Rentschler, R., Shilbury, D. (2008): 'Academic assessment of arts management journals: a multidimensional rating survey', *International Journal of Arts Management*, 10(3): 60–71.
Resource (2001): *Renaissance in the Regions: A New Vision for England's Museums*, London: The Council for Museums, Archives and Libraries.
Roth, M. (2012): 'Keynote Speech', *Museums Association Conference*, Edinburgh.
Rouban, L. (1998): *The French Civil Service*, Paris: La documentation Francaise.
Rouban, L. (2013): 'Back to the nineteenth century: the managerial reform of the French civil service', *Labor History*, 54(2): 161–175.
Rouban, L (2014): 'Politicization of the civil service', in: Peters, B., Pierre, J. (eds.), *The Sage Handbook of Public Administration*, London: Sage.
Scotcity (2011): *Performance and Development Reviews: Guidance Note for Managers*, Scotcity Council.
Seifert, R., Gill-McLure, W., Gale, J., Mathers, K. (forthcoming 2015): *Resisting Reform: Public Sector Workers against the State*, Policy Press: Bristol.
Seifert, R., Ironside, M. (2013): *An Alternative Vision for the Cultural Sector*, London: PCS.
Smith, A. (2012): 'Local funding for arts to be cut by 90% by 2020', *The Stage News*, Thursday, July 19.
Stoker, G. (1996): 'The struggle to reform local government 1975–1995', *Public Money and Management*, 16(1): 17–22.
Talbot, C. (2007): 'Performance management', in: Ferlie, E., Lynn, L.E., Pollitt, C. (eds.), *The Oxford Handbook of Public Management*, Oxford: Oxford University. Press.
Tawney, R.H. (1921): *The Acquisitive Society*, London: Bibliobazaar.
t'Hart, P., Wille, A. (2014): 'Bureaucratic Politics: Opening the Black Box of Executive Government', in: Peters, B., Pierre, J. (eds.), *The Sage Handbook of Public Administration*, London: Sage.
Thomson, A.W.J. (1983): 'The contexts of management behaviour in industrial relations in the public and private sectors', in: Thurley, K., Wood, S. (eds.), *Industrial Relations and Management Strategy*, London: Cambridge University Press.
Thornqvist, C. (2007): 'Changing industrial relations in the Swedish public sector: new tensions within the old framework of corporatism', *International Journal of Public Sector Management*, 20(1): 16–33.
Toonen, T.A. (2014): 'Administrative reform: analytics', in: Peters, B., Pierre, J. (eds.), *The Sage Handbook of Public Administration*, London: Sage.
Traxler, F., Blaschke, S., Kittel, B. (2001): *National Labour Relations in Internationalized Markets: A Comparative Study of Institutions, Change, and Performance*, Oxford: Oxford University Press.
UNISON (1994): *Budget Briefing*, London: UNISON.
Weber, M. (1947): *The Theory of Social and Economic Organization*, Trans. Henderson, A.M., Parsons, T., New York: The Free Press.
Widdicombe Report (1986): *The Conduct of Local Authority Business*, Cmnd. 9797, London: HMSO.
Zorloni, A. (2010): 'Managing performance indicators in visual arts museums', *Museum Management and Curatorship*, 25(2): 167–180.

Chapter 7

Doing meaning in work under conditions of new public management? Findings from the medical care sector and social work

Mascha Will-Zocholl and Friedericke Hardering

Introduction

During the last decades, processes of marketisation or economisation mark a central aspect of societal changes (Pelizzari, 2001; Boltanski & Chiapello, 2007; Çalışkan & Callon, 2009).[1] Marketisation and economisation both refer to an expansion of market logics into non-market domains. Nearly every sphere of everyday life is affected. Marketisation is accompanied by processes such as informatisation,[2] efficiency orientation, assessing and standardisation (Moldaschl & Sauer, 2002; Çalışkan & Callon, 2010). All together, these processes are fostering reorganisation processes, which have consequences especially to the public sphere and its specific logic. The marketisation of public goods is framed by neoliberal modernisation efforts of the political agenda to reduce the influence of the state and to subjugate the public sector to economic principles.[3] The invention of 'New Public Management' (NPM) stands for this sustainable transformation in the course of marketisation that changed the logic of how public service has been understood so far (Christensen & Lægreid, 2002). Before, former forms of bureaucracy have been criticised for being inflexible, retrograde and ineffective. Now, under the umbrella term of NPM, bureaucratic principles should be replaced by commercial ones, including a stronger market and competitive orientation, an outcome and output oriented control, decentralised organisation and a change from internal orientation of public service to customers and citizens (fundamentally: Mintzberg, 1996; Evans & Rauch, 1999; critically: Pelizzari, 2001; Czerwick, 2007). A 'market-centred mode of control' (Marrs, 2008) is the outcome, even in public service.

Those changes have an impact on work and working conditions for employees especially in the public sector (Flecker et al., 2014). Economisation or marketisation are introduced as a threat for preservation-worthy ingredients of work, industrial relations and employment. Mostly, the negative consequences are discussed. This is especially discussed in the context of public goods like health and social care. A crucial transformation takes place there, for example the turning away from a patient-centric medicine or from a helping orientation in social work (Borgetto, 2006; Schultheis et al., 2010). The conditions of employment changed as well, towards an increasing insecurity among employees in public service sectors caused by an expansion of fixed-term contracts and negative wage developments, with increasing precarity as an outcome (Marrs 2008; Hermann & Flecker 2012; Schultheis et al., 2014; Gottschall et al., 2015). Further, self-optimisation and subjectification of work, as already mentioned in the introduction of the book, are leading to an increasing pressure on employees in the public sector. Nowadays they have to deal with similar ambiguities as in the economic sector. A recent analysis of the German Trade Union Confederation (DGB) found out that employees are affected by the decreasing job security, less attractive wages and worsening job conditions. One crucial aspect is that employees feel more rushed in their work caused by a work intensification and rising demands in work. This is the more true, the better the employees are qualified. In addition the results show that civil servants (75%) are more affected than employees (63%; DGB, 2017, p. 14). One consequence is that half of the employees feel 'very often' or 'often' physically and mentally exhausted (DGB, 2017, p. 30). In particular, the mental changes and ethical issues that bring about a change in work are particularly challenging (Schultheis et al., 2010). Increasing shares of mental illnesses and work-related stress are discussed as consequences of the changing working conditions (Angerer et al., 2008; Seithe, 2012; Maio, 2014; Vogd, 2014). The appropriation to one's work is questioned and the danger of alienation from work seems to be coming up (Rosa, 2013; Voß & Handrich, 2013; Kämpf, 2015). These studies show that the criticism of poor working conditions and the threat to the quality of work present a predominantly negative reading of changes in the context of marketisation. In this normative perspective, it remains unclear how employees interpret the changes indicated by marketisation and how they attach new meanings to these processes.

In this paper, we address the question of perception, embedding and evaluation of marketisation processes by high-skilled employees in the public sector.[4] The attachment of meaning to macro-processes such as marketisation also has implications for meanings individuals attach to work for one's own experience of meaningfulness at work. We will therefore refer to the process of attaching new meanings to structural changes at work and its effects on the experience of meaningfulness. These questions are part of a research project[5] that is embedded in research on 'meaning of work' and 'meaningful work' (Rosso et al., 2010; Budd, 2011; Hardering, 2015). During the last decades, research on both 'meaning of work' and 'meaningful work' has received attraction in different disciplines like psychology, organisation studies and business ethics. Many authors have highlighted the distinction between the 'meaning of work' or 'meaning' and 'meaningful work' (Rosso et al., 2010; Bailey et al., 2017). Building on Rosso et al. (2010), we define meaning as 'the output of having made sense of something' (p. 94). Work can have different meanings for individuals; it can be seen as a most important life domain or it can be seen as necessary evil (Budd, 2011). Thereby, attaching new meanings to work can be seen as a process of sense-making (Pratt & Ashforth, 2003). The terms 'meaningful work' or 'meaningfulness' refer to a positive construct, defining ones' work as meaningful in a way 'that the work and/or its context are perceived by its practitioners to be, at minimum, purposeful and significant (Pratt & Ashforth, 2003, p. 311). By this, meaningfulness is mostly understood as an outcome of the interplay between individual work values and the work environment (Lips-Wiersma et al., 2016). Both concepts, meaning and meaningfulness are connected: By changing meanings of certain aspects of work, the experience of meaningfulness can be influenced.

In this article, we show how different meanings are attributed to the concept of marketisation by high-skilled employees in the public sector. Our aim is to get a deeper understanding of the 'inside views'. In order to understand different meanings attached to marketisation processes by the interviewees, we use the methodological concept of 'orientation frames' (Nohl, 2010) to identify different views on marketisation. The evaluation of marketisation by the interviewees is much more heterogeneous than is reflected in the previous discourse on marketisation. Further, we will present the results of experiences of meaningfulness at work and show that employees often succeed in experiencing their work as meaningful despite many difficulties and barriers.[6] In a first step, relevant aspects of the German health and social care system are presented. In a second step, the methodological approach and the interviews sample is described, before the findings are introduced.

Economisation of public goods: impact on health and social care system

In Germany, as one of the classic welfare states in Europe, the state plays a major role in the organisation of health care and welfare, as is the case in other countries, such as the Nordic States, the United Kingdom and France. Health care insurance is obligatory for the vast majority of the German inhabitants and most of the social care services are free of charge. Neoliberal tendencies and structural challenges have led to a transformation in welfare policies throughout the welfare states: the marketisation of public goods (Rothgang et al., 2010a; Flecker et al., 2014). The main maxim of this reorientation, the reduction of costs in the public sector, affects all possible areas of the public service, public administration, education and especially various fields of care: children, elderly, health and social. During the last two decades, the health system and the system of social care (especially social security) have been in the center of reforms. Responsibility was transferred to the citizens and subjects reorganised under criteria of efficiency. The following section provides a brief overview of the developments in the two fields of analysis: healthcare in public hospitals and social work in public and social service.

The German healthcare system[7]

The process of marketisation of hospitals services in Germany goes hand in hand with the outcomes of the health care system reform of 2003[8]: Diagnosed Related Groups (DRG) were invented to price the services offered in the health care systems (hospitals and medical practitioners). The reimbursement of performance with fixed lump sums replaces a reimbursement system that takes the patient's real lying times into account. The diagnosis defines which amount of money the health insurance company has to pay. The invention the DRG system is discussed as a turning away from understanding health as a common good. It is seen as part of a major development in which the health care system is subjected to market-based principles (Kälble, 2005; Manzei et al., 2014; Schultheis & Gemperle, 2014).[9]

Another indicator of a further marketisation and privatisation of the health sector is the shifting ownership of hospitals in Germany. Three types of organisations can be found: public corporation, third sector organisations like churches or public welfare organisations and private investors. The share of privately owned hospitals has risen continuously during the last decades from 14.8% in 1991 up to 35.8% in 2015. During the same time, the share of public hospitals decreased from 46% to 29.5%, still offering the highest amount of beds (Statistisches Bundesamt, 2015). The legal forms of public hospitals also changed during this time. They are increasingly organised in limited liability companies (GmbHs), a further sign of the increasing economisation.

The structural changes in medical care are also reflected in the number of employees. 1.2 million employees are working in hospitals in 2015; about 190,000 of them are physicians with increasing tendencies.[10] A further look at the 2015 figures shows an increase in temporary employment up to 22,700 full-time-equivalents including 3,000 physicians (Bundesärztekammer, 2015; Statistisches Bundesamt, 2015).

Social Work in Germany[11]

Healthcare reforms have a similar impact for hospitals and doctors' work as social policy reforms under Agenda 2010 in the field of social work. The paradigm shift of social policy and further principles of NPM changed the logic of social and public service. Processes of marketisation led to more competition, short-term financing prospects and an increasing projectification of social work. In sum: an increasingly insecure organisation of permanent duties. This outcome means a reversion of social work logics. The privatisation of supplies and services, the introduction of quasi-economic principles in the course of new financing models form the basis for the emergence of a 'social service production' (Galuske & Thole, 2006, p. 12).

The number of people working in the field of social work is not that easy to determine. In 2014, about 286,000 academics were employed in social work.[12]

Regarding the profile of job requirements in social work, it even shows up that around 343,000 employees take on highly qualified tasks, including management functions. This means that nearly one fifth is working in higher positions without an academic degree. Every second job is part-time and about 50% of the advertised new positions are fixed-term contracts (Bundesagentur für Arbeit, 2016). The share of part-time work has risen during the last decade. This is a serious problem in social work, because the wages are low,[13] compared to other fields of work. Those circumstances lead to a debate about a precarisation of work in social work (Stolz-Willig & Christoforidis, 2011).

A comparison of the two fields of investigation reveals that marketisation is a major driver for changing working conditions. The changes in health care reform and the introduction of the DRG system are similar to the reform of social legislation within the Agenda 2010 for Social Work. In addition, both fields are subject to consolidation efforts of public budgets. Under given conditions, it is a challenge to ensure the possible treatment and recovery for the patients and clients – – in healthcare and social work. High individual efforts are necessary to deal with these challenges. As a consequence, both groups of professionals are located in a specific melange between high workloads, burden and burnout risks and a high amount of resources (autonomy, sovereignty and professional background) (Angerer et al., 2008; Badura et al., 2011; Seithe, 2012; Burisch, 2014; Maio, 2014; Vogd, 2014).

One important difference in both fields of research is the recognition of work: Social workers face low monetary recognition and social recognition for emotionally strenuous and responsible work. Nevertheless, employees in the field of social services estimate their workplace more positively than the average of all employees in Germany. The importance of the social contribution of their work, the pride in their work and the identification with their work is emphasized in a recent WZB-Study (Schmeißer, 2013). Physicians are still highly socially recognized. They are no longer the 'gods in white', but still highly recognized, as the annual occupational prestige scale implies (Allensbacher, 2017). Salaries are still higher than in comparable professional fields of health care or psychologists. In sum, the causes of new stressors and identity conflicts are discussed as closely connected with the challenges invented by the marketisation of the working spheres.

Methodological Approach and Interview Sample

This contribution is based on data that was collected in a research project on meaningful work. In this project, we aimed at understanding meaning-making processes of high-qualified professionals. A qualitative approach was chosen in order to reconstruct the subjective views of work, work experiences and on economisation processes. We conducted 40 interviews (24 women and 16 men) with physicians and social workers in leading positions in Germany between 2014 and 2015. The age of physicians we interviewed ranged from 33 to 63 years (50 on average). We included physicians with different specialities like gynaecology, neurology, neurosurgery, palliative medicine and cardiovascular surgery and different workloads. The age of the social workers ranged from 35 to 63 (53 on average). The social workers work in different sectors like social service, youth welfare, family counselling, addiction care or probationary services.

We conducted semi-structured biographic-narrative interviews that are based on the semi-structured, problem-centred interview (Witzel & Reiter, 2012) and on the narrative interview (Schuetze, 1983). The interviewees were asked to speak about their recent working experience, and then to tell their professional biographies. We also asked for their work experience in general, their expectations towards work and their resources and strains. We also included questions directly related to the changes in work organisation and on economisation processes at work. The interviews lasted 60 minutes on average and were conducted at the workspaces of employees. All interviews were fully recorded, transcribed verbatim and coded with MAXQDA. In our analysis, we combined the grounded theory approach[14] (Glaser & Strauss, 1967) with theory-driven analysis. In a first step, we identified codes in an open coding process. In a second step, we used the created categories and – in addition to categories that derived from existing results and theories corresponding with the topics of the interview guide. Based on those categories we were able to compare similar themes and identify patterns and similarities between cases. To identify perspectives on economisation, we analysed all passages that were related to economisation processes and identified distinct orientation frameworks. Orientation frameworks can be understood as different perspectives on a certain topic. The term is used in Documentary Method (Bohnsack, 1989; Nohl, 2010) to describe the idea that every topic within an utterance in an interview is framed by a socio-cultural framework, a so-called orientation framework. To identify orientation frameworks, one has to compare different thematisations on a specific topic within different interviews (Nohl, 2010). One can understand them as a kind of lens that economisation processes are viewed trough. To analyse experiences on meaningfulness, we identified all narrative passages referring to meaningfulness at work and looked for similar patterns. On this basis, we could identify three major complexes of meaningfulness at work.[15]

Findings: New meanings of marketisation and meaningfulness at work

In this section, we first take a closer look on physicians and social workers understandings of marketisation processes. The interviews show that the term 'marketisation' is associated with heterogeneous phenomena. Three frames of interpretation can be distinguished: work, functionality and care. Some interviewees interpret marketisation as a process that changes their working situation: work is accelerated and intensified, or the content of the work is changing. Others focus on outcomes of efficiency and organisational restructuring. Again, other interviewees reflect on the situation of the patients or clients when thinking about economisation. Their focus is to highlight the problems or benefits for the aid recipients. Overall, the interview partners not only have one perspective, but their view is also influenced by the context in which marketisation is discussed. In the interviews we can observe how they attach new meanings to marketisation processes. The understanding of marketisation is just one element of the perception of the work, which influences the experience of meaningfulness at work. Based on our material, we assume that the perception of marketisation plays an important role in the evaluation of work. Nonetheless, it is only one aspect of the work that is considered in the general work evaluations.

Attaching new meanings to marketisation

Based on the interviews, we identified three interpretative frameworks that are mostly used when the interviewees reflected on the economisation process. In the following, we describe these three interpretation frameworks and evaluations.

Work: worsening of working conditions

The orientation framework 'work' conceptualises marketisation processes primarily as a change of employment conditions, work organisation, workload, tasks and work content. The physicians and social workers reflect about their position as employees and especially about the financial situation of their organisation and beyond. This includes thinking about consequences for themselves and others. Economisation is viewed as a temporal process of change that leads to a worsening of working conditions. The increasing pressure at work plays a particularly important role in this context and is seen as the most crucial challenge for the younger and future generation, as the quote of a social worker describes:

> Financial resources are becoming narrower. [...] Demands have also risen and this has an impact on the work content. We work differently than ten years ago, twenty years ago. At that time, when I started, I had older colleagues who had been working there twenty years ago, and who told me about the working conditions and it seemed to me like other worlds. And when I say how we have been working twenty years ago compared to today. It is also another world to those who work now, the young colleagues who have now begun last year, who are already arriving at quite a different level. Twenty years ago, this was not foreseeable, no.
>
> (IM34)

The changes of the past 20 years are characterised as unpredictable and also very fundamental. The interviewee does not even reflect on a specific aspect of change, because it seems that the whole transformation is experienced as worsening. In a very similar way, some physicians report about conversations with elder colleagues, who told them that in the past, although the work was hard, they had a kind of golden times: They had enough time for patient care as well as time for conversation with colleagues and a joint lunch. Financial aspects did not dominate their work. Social workers are especially hit by these developments as they experience a projectification of their work, which is accompanied by a constantly uncertain financing of positions and services provided. This fosters precarious working constellations like fix-term contracts and forced reductions of working hours, with consequences for the employees and their clients:

> I think we're a pretty good team here. Although we don't have many times that overlap, because we all work part-time here. More or less voluntarily. The money has just been cut, so I say more or less voluntarily.
> (IM39)

This is a specialty in social work. Among the majority of the physicians the problem is the other way around. They complain about long working hours and less options to work within working hours. In both cases, a high workload can be a consequence. In hospitals, high workloads arise because doctors have to compensate for the lack of nursing staff and take on additional tasks. The physicians have to prioritise the different tasks they are working on. Permanently they have to make decisions about what is currently important and what tasks can be done at the end. In social work, because there is more work for existing jobs than can be done within the framework of employment, the latter aspect is being compensated by a high level of commitment in the acquisition of funds to protect workplaces. This leads to another aspect of the work orientation framework: New tasks in acquiring financial resources and new forms of documentation tasks lead to a higher degree of administrative tasks – – and marketing and publicity tasks. One female social worker reports about these new tasks:

> You have to see, nowadays you always have projects, and a project has a beginning and an end. And we have to work on that, that there is a continuity, you know. We have to look for financing, find sponsors. [...] And they want to know exactly, which kind of services we provided. And we have to document this, we have to document all the services and show them to the sponsors.
> (IM21)

The development of brands and the promotion of special skills is also commonplace in hospitals in order to get attention in lucrative fields of activity.

In both fields, the interviewees describe a change in the composition of tasks that they associate — despite their leadership responsibilities — with processes of economisation: increasing managerial, documentation and calculating tasks.

From the perspective of the overwhelming number of interview partners, the economisation leads to a worsening of the quality of work. Within the orientation framework 'work', the evaluation of marketisation tendencies is predominantly negative.

Functionality: increasing process orientation

In the light of the orientation framework 'functionality', marketisation means an increasing importance of processes which have an impact on the entire organisation. Their aim is efficiency and effectiveness improvements, measuring how far the organisational objectives are achieved successfully within the organisation. In this way, functionality is directly linked to the motifs of the rolling out of NPM values, with the introduction of efficiency criteria, business ratios, target agreements and the implementation of controlling. Further standards of processes and procedures as well as for documentation are initiated.

The development inside the orientation framework 'functionality' is assessed very ambiguously and cannot be defined uniformly. In the field of social work, the interviewees emphasise that process orientation was carried out simultaneously with a professionalisation of social work. Work processes are now clearer and more structured. Some social workers report, in the past there was a lack of organisational and operational structures to make sure that aid arrives. Today, the documentation of consultation success, frequencies of use or the identification of needs help to adapt structures in an efficient manner. If the requirements are exaggerated, this advantage is reversed, as the example of a social worker in the field of addiction consulting illustrates:

> A lot of things have changed. At the moment, we are in a certification delusion [...] All processes that take place must be documented, all procedures must be structured. [...] All procedures must be checked and so on. That is difficult. A paradigm shift has taken place. Everybody must look: ' What has happened? What did I do? Is that, what I'm doing still up-to-date? Has the aid reached people?' All these things happened during the last years, yes, case management. And those case control things.
> (IM21)

The quote shows the dilemma: the problem is not so much the process orientation itself, but rather excessive control and exuberant quality management systems. In medicine, the increase in functionality is positively assessed, too, when new processes and control mechanisms are used to contain the possibilities of misconduct — but only in this context. This is shown by the example of a neurosurgeon:

> I see this (the introduction of the DRG system) not necessarily negative, because in the past it was like this, and I have experienced it as assistant physician, that a medical director did absolutely not deal with the economic aspects of the clinic. He had a budget, he managed the household somehow, they spent the money somehow, in the end of the year they were in deficit and then the clinic administration has cursed and simply balanced the deficit and then he started again at zero.
> (IW08)

While from the physicians' point of view, missing control mechanisms have led to the neglect of economic aspects of the treatment, it can be an advantage of the DRG system that the management of the departments have to take care of the hospital budgets. Contrary to this point of view, however, it is often emphasised in the interviews that the marketisation does not lead to the functional gains that are actually associated with. Criticised above all is the short-term nature of the control mechanisms introduced and that those new criteria may lead to false needs. One social worker points it like this:

> I criticise when so-called social corporations arise when any new requirements are interpreted somewhere. That is — So also in our ranks, there is a lot of crap, you have to say for the sake of fairness, right. So the worst is when social facilities, so to speak, take over models from the business and then lose sight of the essentials.
> (IM21)

He points out to the fact that the establishment of key figures means that the utility of the institution is only measured along these factors. The real needs of the aid recipients are therefore put into the background. Although the system reacts functionally on process levels, it is not able to respond to the actual requirements. Further, the financing of permanent needs with temporary resources is a negative aspect that has been highlighted several times. On the whole, the economisation within the interpretative framework "functionality" is evaluated extremely ambivalently.

Care: aid delivery at risk

The orientation framework 'care' considers marketisation the light of its consequences for the aid recipients, focussing on the care of the needy and the maintenance of health and quality of life. From the point of view of the overwhelming number of interview partners, the provision of care services has deteriorated as a result of economisation. The restricted or rare financial resources are in the centre of this orientation framework, additionally strengthened by a difficult personnel situation. Together, they lead to extraordinary challenges in order to ensure the quality of care. A physician summarises this as follows:

> In the meantime, we treat patients badly, superficially and not adequately. We are at the limit. We also have hardly any staff yet.
>
> (IM04)

This quote also demonstrates the connection of the 'work' and the 'care' framework: the quality of care is in danger because of bad working conditions in the hospital. However, this view is not the only one; rather, some interviewees see quite a profit for the care situation. In the hospitals, the reduction of lying times is mainly mentioned here. Some interviewees highlight that the old system has provided incentives to keep patients longer in the hospital than medically induced and because of these incentives, patients were sent into rehab or home later. Due to such misguided controls, many interview partners see an ethical problem in marketisation processes. From their point of view, good care and economic success are not compatible. One female social worker puts it this way:

> Um, and that (economisation processes) makes me worried, yes, I think so uhm. Just where people are represented who cannot defend themselves. So that is not so extreme in the self help, but in dementia or where people need care, I find it very bad.
>
> (IW40)

The statement indicates that maybe there is not enough help for those in need, especially for those where the 'success' of consulting, a treatment or therapy cannot be determined. The danger of leaving people alone is always virulent. That is also true for patients in hospital who have to leave the hospital due to DRGs although they don't feel prepared or don't get enough help at home. In the area of social work, the critical view of the care situation prevails. Here, the interviewees have to look on the situation of their staff first and in a next step on the care situation of the clients. Therefore, they have to deal with the finance management. A social worker summarises this as follows:

> I have an attitude, the attitude means, I am there for the (people) with whom I work. And so I can do the work with the people, I must necessarily have to cope with the financing problem and have to try to get as much financial resources as it can.
>
> (IM26)

This quote illustrates that the professional understanding to care for clients and people to work with can put a bite on those who are at the same time responsible for colleagues and the ethical dimension of work. The time spent to get the financial means to keep the employees employed and professionally important projects running leads to a lack of time to look after the clients. To deal with new forms of financing will be the means to ensure an optimal client care. In the field of social work, interviewees further mentioned the shortcoming of offering help due to financial restrictions. This can mean that assistances are cut to a minimum, the quality of help is reduced (coaching instead of therapy) or specific offers are discontinued. In both groups, interviewees mentioned that they try to compensate for reductions or restrictions according to their ethical and moral perceptions and their professional self-identity. This means, employees use their private resources to cope with these conditions in an acceptable way, for example, by paying for things they consider absolutely necessary out of their own pockets or by working longer hours without being paid.. The latter leads to the sequences executed in the first orientation framework 'work'. Somehow, the implications of economisation are being adopted to the professional self. Overall, viewed through the lens of 'care', economisation processes are evaluated mostly critical.

Experiences of meaningfulness at work and meaning-making

In our study, the interviewees not only report about new demands at work, an increase of negative working experiences and further experiences of meaninglessness resulting from the changes of work organisation, but they also report about experiences of meaningfulness at work. The vast majority of the interviewees state that they define their work as personally meaningful. Some also state that they have experiences of meaningfulness on a daily basis. To understand the experiences of meaningfulness, we asked the interviewees about specific moments at which they felt their work was meaningful (Hardering, 2017a). As a result, three different sources of meaningfulness show up. The first source, 'being good and effective in one's work', means that work is experienced as meaningful when one can see one's own productivity and talents in one's work results. In the second source, 'produce visible results with a greater good', work is seen meaningful when one can see a contribution to socially shared values (like health or quality of life). The last source, 'recognition', means that the interviewees experience meaningfulness when colleagues, clients or patients appreciate one's work.

Additionally, we found that the experience of meaningfulness is interlinked with different ways of meaning-making. In our sample, we identified different forms of meaning-making: While some interviewees tried to change their work in order to create a better person-job fit, other interviewees did not want to change their work that much. Some interpreted the changes of the system and also economisation processes more than an unchangeable fact, while others identified potentials to work against new instructions (Hardering & Will-Zocholl, under review; Hardering, 2017b).

Our findings according meaning-making are supported by other research on meaningful work. Different studies provide evidence that people are able to experience work as meaningful, despite difficult working conditions (Senghaas-Knobloch et al., 1997; Ashforth & Kreiner, 1999; Isaksen, 2000). Research using the concept of job crafting emphasises that employees are willing to use potentials to design their work in a way that enables an experience of meaningfulness on a subjective level (Wrzesniewski & Dutton, 2001; Berg et al., 2013). In this debate, it is also argued that employees wish to find a positive relationship between their identity and work (Dutton et al., 2010). In order to remain able to act, employees must seek positive relationships between their work and their identity. Therefore, the meanings of work-related phenomena are renegotiated repeatedly. The experience of meaningfulness can therefore always be interpreted in relation to the use of personal resources and individual coping processes.

Conclusion

The aim of this article was twofold: First, by analysing the new meanings the professionals attach to marketisation processes, we could give insights to the inner views of the high-skilled workers on NPM processes. Second, we demonstrated that although there are many barriers of meaningfulness, both groups still define many aspects and moments of their work as meaningful. Based on the three interpretative frameworks, it becomes clear that the interviewees look very differentiated on marketisation. In addition to the literature, in which economisation processes are often criticised in a generalising way, it shows up that a shortening of the discussion to the negative consequences fails. The findings illustrate how the physicians and social workers differentiate between several aspects. Work, functionality and care stand for three different view axes, each with own interpretations.

In the framework of 'work', the focus is on the comparison with better times in the past. The introduction of business ratios creates new incentives that are partly directed against the medical or social worker ethos. This creates both temporal and emotional stress. The exception here is the passages dealing with the professionalisation of social work. While the doctors have always known themselves as a profession, this is a long-discussed but still new and controversial aspect in social work. Some aspects of marketisation on work foster the professionalisation of social work. Other outcomes like the interpretation of a long-lasting process of worsening conditions in the course of marketisation refers to the results already mentioned in this paper: increasing pressure in work (Schultheis et al., 2010; Flecker et al., 2014) and psychological distress (Angerer et al., 2008; Badura et al., 2011; Seithe, 2012; Burisch, 2014; Maio, 2014; Vogd, 2014).

In the orientation framework 'functionality', marketisation is seen more ambivalent. While some of the interviewees make an argument for advantages through new management structures and clearer action instructions. Others argue that functionality leads to higher workloads and does not provide any real help to help recipients. The danger of an over-bureaucratisation is permanently given by excessive documentation duties. This has to do with limited time due to limited personnel and/or restricted paid working hours. Further, the standardisation of processes may not reflect the individuals needs and procedures. This development is breaking down into a new division of labour between social workers and financial managers or doctors and coding staff, for example, as is mentioned in other work (Pfeuffer & Gemperle 2014). If business ratios get more important than helping people, this is leading to problems targeting everybody not only the employees working in these fields.

The question of 'care', the third orientation framework, seems to be under conditions of marketisation the most crucial issue in this context. Ethical and professional standards as well as humanity in general are strongly affected by these developments and illustrates the dilemma of an ongoing marketisation of public goods. Similar, results have been found in Schultheis et al. (2010) for employees in public administration or social workers. The same is true for nurses in Marrs (2008) study and for physicians (Flecker et al., 2014). In this orientation frame, a coping with outcomes of marketisation would mean to throw one's ethical guidelines and moral ideas overboard or the limited possibilities have to be compensated by an employee's own resources. In his expertise, Struijs (2007) described the ethical dimension as a major issue in healthcare under conditions of economisation. So, the assumption is plausible that it depends on how demanding these challenges are if employees manage to deal with them or lose track of their work (and health).

However, the findings regarding the orientation frames work and functionality show that the outcomes of marketisation processes cannot be judged in a general manner. A subjective perspective offers new insights on how differentiated people reflect on their work and evaluate the consequences. Those perspectives have an impact on the experience of meaningfulness. Looking at this experience, we were able to show that despite difficult working conditions the high-skilled professionals are able to experience work as meaningful. They redefine meanings of different work-related aspects and try to create connection between their selves and their work. Even against resistance, they try to gain positive experiences in their work in order to protect their feeling of meaningfulness. As we have also shown, the described processes are reinterpretations that are always accompanied by the investment of subjective resources. They are individually exhausting, and whether they are sustainable in the long term cannot be said in advance. Thus, the inner working life of the high-skilled employees remains highly fragile.

Notes

1. We use the terms economisation and marketisation interchangeably.
2. Informatisation understood as a socio-historical process of systematic handling of information leading to the establishment of an information layer in organisations, nowadays is represented by the use of IT-systems (Schmiede, 2006).
3. Examples of these efforts are the health or social security reforms (2000–2010) in Germany.
4. In this study, we are focusing on two groups, leading physicians and social workers with management responsibility.
5. The research project "Societal conceptions about what makes work meaningful and individual's experiences of meaningfulness at work" is funded by the German Research Foundation, DFG, and the first part ran from 04/2014 and 04/2016. We analysed perceptions on meaningful work and strategies of meaning-making in the fields of medical care and social work. We focused on high-skilled actors, physicians and social workers with management responsibility and a high level of autonomy at work.
6. The remarks in this text on meaningfulness at work and practices of meaning-making are based on Hardering (2017a) and (2017b).
7. For a detailed overview, see Rothgang et al. (2010b).
8. The law was passed in 2000, it took another three years to invent DRGs.
9. The consequences cannot be assessed uniformly, they belong to the perspective of the observer and the context of the specific scientific debate (s. contributions in Manzei et al., 2014).
10. For the ninth year in a row, the German physician statistics showed this development (Bundesärztekammer, 2015).
11. For a detailed overview, see Henriksen et al. (2012).
12. The public statistics count some occupations together in one category who do not all belong to the core of social work (for example special education).
13. The exception are the employees who are assigned to the public service.
14. Grounded theory is a qualitative approach to develop new theories based on empirical evidence. Practices of coding, categorisation and comparison are central in their concept as well as the principle of openness to new aspects in a research field.
15. For analysis of meaningfulness at work, see Hardering (2017a).

References

Allensbacher (2017): *Institut für Demoskopie Allensbacher (IfD Allensbach). Berufsprestigeskala.* Allensbach.

Angerer, P., Petru, R., Nowak, D., Weigl, M. (2008): Arbeitsbedingungen und Depression bei Ärzten, *Deutsche medizinische Wochenschrift*, 133(1/2): 26–29.

Ashforth, B.E., Kreiner, G.E. (1999): 'How can you do it? Dirty work and the challenge of constructing a positive identity', *Academy of Management Review*, 24: 413–434.

Bailey, C., Madden, A., Alfes, K., Shantz, A., Soane, E. (2017): The mismanaged soul: Existential labor and the erosion of meaningful work. *Human Resource Management Review*, 27(3): 416–430. doi:10.1016/j.hrmr.2016.11.001

Badura, B., Ducki, A., Schröder, H., Klose, J., Macco, K. (2011): *Fehlzeiten-Report 2011. Führung und Gesundheit*, Wiesbaden: Springer.

Berg, J.M., Dutton, J.E., Wrzesniewski, A. (2013): 'Job crafting and meaningful work', in: Dik, B.J., Byrne, Z.S., Steger, M.F. (eds.), *Purpose and Meaning in the Workplace*, 81–104, Washington, DC: American Psychological Association.
Bohnsack, R. (1989): *Generation, Milieu und Geschlecht. Ergebnisse aus Gruppendiskussionen*, Opladen: Leske and Budrich.
Boltanski, L., Chiapello, E. (2007): *The New Spirit of Capitalism*. New York/London: Verso.
Borgetto, B. (2006): 'Ökonomisierung, Verwissenschaftlichung und Emanzipation. Die Reformen im deutschen Gesundheitswesen und das Rollengefüge von Arzt und Patient', *Sozialer Sinn*, 7(2): 231–250.
Budd, J. W. (2011): *The Thought of Work*. Ithaca, NY: Cornell University Press.
Bundesagentur für Arbeit. (2016): Gute Bildung – gute Chancen. Der Arbeitsmarkt für Akademikerinnen und Akademiker. Nürnberg.
Bundesärztekammer (2015): Ärztestatistik 2015, www.bundesaerztekammer.de/ueber-uns/aerztestatistik/aerztestatistik-2015/im-krankenhaus-taetige-aerzte/ [Accessed 30 November 2017].
Burisch, M. (2014): *Das Burnout-Syndrom*, Wiesbaden/Heidelberg: Springer.
Çalışkan, K., Callon, M. (2009): 'Economisation, part 1: Shifting attention from the economy towards processes of economisation', *Economy and Society*, 38(3): 369–398.
Çalışkan, K., Callon, M. (2010): 'Economisation, part 2: A research program for the study of markets', *Economy and Society*, 39(1): 1–32.
Christensen, T., Lægreid, P. (2002): 'New public management: Puzzles of democracy and the influence of citizens', *The Journal of Political Philosophy*, 10(2): 267–295.
Czerwick, E. (2007): *Die Ökonomisierung des öffentlichen Dienstes. Dienstrechtsreformen und Beschäftigungsstrukturen seit 1991*, Wiesbaden: Springer VS.
Deutscher Gewerkschaftsbund (DGB) (2017): *DGB-Index Gute Arbeit. Sonderauswertung Beschäftigte im Angestellten- oder Beamtenverhältnis im öffentlichen Dienst*, Berlin. http://index-gute-arbeit.dgb.de/++co++4e445a72-4c48-11e7-8958-525400e5a74a [Accessed 1 July 2017].
Dutton, J.E., Roberts, L.M., Bednar, J. (2010): 'Pathways for positive identity construction at work: Four types of positive identity and the building of social resources', *Academy of Management Review*, 35: 265–293.
Evans, P., Rauch, J.E. (1999): 'Bureaucracy and growth: A cross-national analysis of the effectiveness of 'Weberian' state structures on economic growth', *American Sociological Review*, 64: 748–765.
Flecker, J., Schultheis, F., Vogel, B. (2014): *Im Dienste öffentlicher Güter. Metamorphosen der Arbeit aus Sicht der Beschäftigten*, Berlin: edition sigma.
Galuske, M., Thole, W. (ed.) (2006): *Vom Fall zum Management. Neue Methoden in der Sozialen Arbeit*. Wiesbaden: Springer VS, 9–14.
Glaser, B. G., Strauss, A.L. (1967): *The Discovery of Grounded Theory*. Chicago, IL: Strategies for Qualitative Research Aldine.
Gottschall, K., Hils, S., Kittel, B., Streb, S., Tepe, M., Briken, K. (2015): *Public Sector Employment Regimes: Transformation of the State as an Employer*, London: Sage.
Hardering, F. (2015): 'Meaningful work: Sinnvolle Arbeit zwischen Subjektivität, Arbeitsgestaltung und gesellschaftlichem Nutzen', *Österreichische Zeitschrift für Soziologie*, 40(4): 391–410.

Hardering, F. (2017a): 'Wann erleben Beschäftigte ihre Arbeit als sinnvoll? Befunde aus einer Untersuchung über professionelle Dienstleistungsarbeit', *Zeitschrift für Soziologie*, 46(1): 39–54.

Hardering, F. (2017b): 'Sinnvolle Arbeit unter Druck? Markterfordernisse, Organisationslogiken und die Verteidigung professioneller Handlungsautonomie', in: Börner, S., Bohmann, U. (eds.), *Praktiken der Selbstbestimmung. Zwischen subjektivem Anspruch und institutionellem Funktionserfordernis*, 3–24, Berlin: Springer.

Henriksen, L.S., Smith, S.R., Zimmer, A. (2012): 'At the eve of convergence? Transformations of social service provision in Denmark, Germany, and the United States', *VOLUNTAS: International Journal of Voluntary and Nonprofit Organizations*, 23(2): 458–501.

Hermann, C., Flecker, J. (eds.) (2012): *Privatization of Public Services. Impacts for Employment, Working Conditions and Service Quality in Europe*, New York: Routledge.

Isaksen, J. (2000): 'Constructing meaning despite the drudgery of repetitive work', *Journal of Humanistic Psychology*, 40(3): 84–107.

Kälble, K. (2005): 'Between professional autonomy and economic orientation – The medical profession in a changing health care system', *GMS Posychosocial Medicine*, 2: 1–13.

Kämpf, T. (2015): '"Ausgebrannte Arbeitswelt" – Wie erleben Beschäftigte neue Formen von Belastung in modernen Feldern der Wissensarbeit?', *Berliner Journal für Soziologie*, 25(1–2): 133–159.

Lips-Wiersma, M., Wright, S., & Dik, B. (2016): Meaningful work: Differences among blue-, pink-, and white-collar occupations, *Career Development International*, 21(5): 534–551. doi:10.1108/CDI-04-2016-0052

Maio, G. (2014): *Geschäftsmodell Gesundheit wie der Markt die Heilkunst abschafft*, Berlin: Suhrkamp.

Manzei, A., Schnabel, M., Schmiede, R. (2014): 'Embedded competition – Oder wie kann man die Auswirkungen wettbewerblicher Regulierung im Gesundheitswesen messen? Eine methodologische Perspektive', in: Manzei, A., Schmiede, R. (eds.), *20 Jahre Wettbewerb im Gesundheitswesen. Theoretische und empirische Analysen zur Ökonomisierung von Medizin und Pflege*, 11–33, Berlin: Springer VS.

Marrs, K. (2008): *Arbeit unter Marktdruck – Die Logik der ökonomischen Steuerung in der Dienstleistungsarbeit*, Berlin: edition sigma.

Mintzberg, H. (1996): 'Managing government – Governing management', *Harvard Business Review*, May–June, 75–83.

Moldaschl, M., Sauer, D. (2002): 'Internalisierung des Marktes – Zur neuen Dialektik von Kooperation und Herrschaft', in: Minssen, H. (ed.), *Begrenzte Entgrenzungen: Wandlungen von Organisation und Arbeit*, 205–224, Berlin: edition sigma.

Nohl, A.-M. (2010): 'Narrative interview and documentary interpretation', in: Bohnsack, R., Pfaff, N., Weller, W. (eds.), *Qualitative Analysis and Documentary Method in International Educational Research*, 195–217, Opladen: Budrich.

Pelizzari, A. (2001): *Die Ökonomisierung des Politischen. New Public Management und der neoliberale Angriff auf die öffentlichen Dienste*, Konstanz: UVK.

Pfeuffer, A., Gemperle, M. (2014): 'Die Kodierfachkräfte: Eine Beschäftigtengruppe des Krankenhauses im Spannungsfeld zwischen medizinisch-pflegerischen und betriebswirtschaftlichen Ansprüchen', in: Flecker, F., Schultheis, F., Vogel, B. (eds.), *Im Dienste öffentlicher Güter. Metamorphosen der Arbeit aus Sicht der Beschäftigten*, 89–106, Berlin: edition sigma.

Pratt, M. G., Ashforth, B. E. (2003): 'Fostering meaningfulness in working and in work,' in: Cameron, K.S., Dutton, J.E., Quinn, R.E. (eds.), *Positive organizational scholarship: Foundations of a new discipline*, 309–327, San Francisco, CA: Barrett-Koehler.

Rosa, H. (2013): *Beschleunigung und Entfremdung. Auf dem Weg zu einer kritischen Theorie spätmoderner Zeitlichkeit*. Berlin: Suhrkamp.

Rosso, B. D., Dekas, K. H., Wrzesniewski, A. (2010): On the meaning of work: A theoretical integration and review, *Research in Organizational Behavior*, 30: 91–127.

Rothgang, H., Cacace, M., Frisina, L., Grimmeisen, S., Schmid, A., Wendt, C. (2010a): *The State and Healthcare. Comparing OECD Countries*, London: Palgrave Macmillan.

Rothgang, H., Schmid, A., Wendt, C. (2010b): 'The self-regulatory german healthcare system between growing competition and state hierarchy', in: Rothgang, H., Cacace, M., Frisina, L., Grimmeisen, S., Schmid, A., Wendt, C. (eds.), *The State and Healthcare. Comparing OECD Countries*, 119–179, London: Palgrave Macmillan.

Schmeißer, C. (2013): Die Arbeitswelt des Dritten Sektors. Atypische Beschäftigung und Arbeitsbedingungen in gemeinnützigen Organisationen, WZB Discussion Paper, SPV 2013–302, Berlin: WZB.

Schmiede, R. (2006): 'Knowledge, work and subject in informational capitalism', in: Berleur, J., Nurminen, M.I., Impagliazzo, J. (eds.), *Social Informatics – An Information Society for All? In remembrance of Rob Kling. Proceedings of the 7th International Conference "Human Choice and Computers"*, IFIP-TC9 "Relationship between Computers and Society", 333–335, Heidelberg: Springer Science and Business Media.

Schuetze, F. (1983): Biographieforschung und narratives Interview, *Neue Praxis*, 13(3): 283–293. http:// nbn-resolving.de/urn:nbn:de:0168-ssoar-53147

Schultheis, F., Gemperle, M. (2014): 'Das Gesundheitswesen im Spannungsfeld von Gemeinwohlorientierung und betriebswirtschaftlichen Imperativen', in: Flecker, J., Schultheis, F., Vogel, B. (eds.), *Im Dienste öffentlicher Güter. Metamorphosen der Arbeit aus Sicht der Beschäftigte*, 23–33, Berlin: edition sigma.

Schultheis, F., Vogel, B., Gemperle, M. (eds.) (2010): *Ein halbes Leben. Biografische Zeugnisse aus einer Arbeitswelt im Umbruch*, Konstanz: UVK.

Schultheis, F., Vogel, B., Mau, K. (eds.) (2014): *Im öffentlichen Dienst. Kontrastive Stimmen aus einer Arbeitswelt im Wandel*, Bielefeld: transcript.

Seithe, M. (2012): *Schwarzbuch Soziale Arbeit*, Wiesbaden: VS Verlag für Sozialwissenschaften.

Senghaas-Knobloch, E., Nagler, B., Dohms, A. (1997): *Zukunft der industriellen Arbeitskultur. Persönliche Sinnansprüche und Gruppenarbeit*, 2nd ed., Münster: LIT.

Statistisches Bundesamt (2016): *Gesundheit. Grunddaten der Krankenhäuser 2015*. Wiesbaden.

Stolz-Willig, B., Christoforidis, J. (eds.) (2011): *Hauptsache billig? Prekarisierung der Arbeit in den sozialen Berufen*, Münster: Verlag Westfälisches Dampfboot.

Struijs, A.J. (2007): *Economisation of Healthcare and Professional Ethics*. Research Report of the CEG, The Hague.

Vogd, W. (2014): 'Stress im System. Oder wie verändern sich die Handlungsorientierungen von Krankenhausärzten unter den neuen organisatorischen und ökonomischen Rahmenbedingungen', in: Manzei, A., Schmiede, R. (eds.), *Gesundheit und Gesellschaft. 20 Jahre Wettbewerb im Gesundheitswesen. Theoretische und empirische Analysen zur Ökonomisierung von Medizin und Pflege*, 241–262, Wiesbaden: Springer Fachmedien.

Voß, G. G., Handrich, C. (2013): 'Ende oder Neuformierung qualitätsvoller und professioneller Arbeit?', in: Haubl, R., Hausinger, B., Voß, G.G. (eds.), *Riskante Arbeitswelten: Zu den Auswirkungen moderner Beschäftigungsverhältnisse auf die psychische Gesundheit und die Arbeitsqualität*, 107–139, Frankfurt am Main: Campus.

Witzel, A., Reiter, H. (2012): *The Problem-Centred Interview.* Sage: London/Thousand Oaks, CA/New Delhi/Singapore.

Wrzesniewski, A., Dutton, J.E. (2001): Crafting a job: Revisioning employees as active crafters of their work, *Academy of Management Review*, 26(2): 179–201. doi:10.1007/s10551-013-1894-9.

Chapter 8

Marketing without moralising

Service orientation and employer relations in the Swiss disability insurance

Eva Nadai

Robert Castel's observation that, historically, physical impotence, incurable diseases and visibly insufferable ailments have always been the best passes for welfare benefits (Castel, 2000, p. 45) has become obsolete. Castel included these marks of disabilities in what he termed "handicapologie" (ibid., p. 27), i.e. the catalogue of legitimate reasons for being exempt from the social obligation of work. He also noted, however, that the boundary between ability and inability to work is always contested. With the activating turn of social policy in the 1990s, disabilities lost the status of an unquestionable legitimation for welfare. More precisely: disabilities no longer conferred entitlements to so-called "passive" benefits – rather, in the context of productivist labour market and social policy people with disabilities were now also seen as human capital potential and prospective workers to be steered towards the labour market by means of "active" measures. With a series of internationally comparative reports, the OECD was a driving force of the reorientation of disability policy (e.g. OECD, 1992, 2006, 2010). In these reports, the focus was on correcting disincentives and establishing active support systems to promote the labour market inclusion of the individuals concerned, but at the same time, the lack of coordination, efficiency and effectiveness of the respective public administration and service providers was also deplored. As remedies of these problems New Public Management strategies were recommended such as quasi-competition by benchmarking, monitoring by performance evaluations of outputs and outcomes, outcome-based funding of service providers, profiling customer-clients, customer orientation and the like (Clarke, Gewirtz & McLaughlin, 2000; Newman & Clarke, 2009; OECD, 2010, p. 145ff.).

In Switzerland, the primacy of occupational integration over pensions has been a guiding principle of disability insurance since its inception in 1960 (Canonica, 2017; Germann, 2008). In fact, the very concept of disability is defined with respect to a person's work capacity or, more precisely, to his or her earning capacity: in the context of the insurance, disability is constituted by diminished earning capacity of a specified degree due to medically confirmed lasting health impairments (Nadai, Canonica & Koch, 2015, p. 34ff.;

Tabin, Piecek-Riondel & Perrin et al., 2016). Nevertheless, in the wake of the welfare state crisis discourses in the late 20th century, disability insurance, too, became the target of alarmist debates focussed on rising costs for pensions and the fact that pensions were most often one-way streets without return into the labour market (Lengwiler, 2007; OECD, 2006). Since 2004 there have been three major reforms of the Disability Insurance Act with the aim of cost reductions by curbing the number of pensions. The main focus of these reforms was on activating clients by restricting access to pensions and by enforcing participation in rehabilitation measures (Nadai et al., 2015; Probst, Tabin & Courvoisier, 2015), yet at the same time the administrative apparatus of the insurance itself was put under scrutiny. In the political debate, disability insurance was criticised for being inflexible, too slow and bureaucratic in processing applications for pensions and integration measures. Thus, it was argued that disability insurance ought to be transformed from "pension insurance with insurance mentality to integration insurance with a *service culture*" (Guggisberg, Egger & Künzi, 2008, V, italics added).

While service orientation pertains to all 'customer' groups (clients, doctors, private insurers, employers), the service rhetoric is most prominent with regard to employers. Although activation strategies target first and foremost insurance clients, their success is actually just as much, if not more, dependent on employers as gate-keepers to the labour market. Consequently, in disability policy reports and research, *employers* are identified as *key actors* (Marin, Prinz & Queisser, 2004; OECD, 2010). Since there are no legal obligations such as employment quota or rehabilitation duties in Switzerland, disability insurance must work with persuasion to win employers for the goal of occupational integration. In this context, *modernising the bureaucratic organisation* is seen as essential: in order to cooperate with business actors on an equal footing the welfare state administration has to become more business-like itself. Yet, prior to delivering its services disability insurance is faced with the issue of *creating a demand* for them at all. For employers, disability insurance clients and people with health impairments in general range far down the labour queue. Many employers rather avoid hiring or retaining them and simply have no experience in handling the problem (Baumgartner, Greiwe & Schwarb, 2004; Domzal, Houtenville & Shartma, 2008; Heymann, Stein & Moreno, 2014; Shaw, Daraz & Bezzina et al., 2014). Therefore, the first challenge is to establish the labour market inclusion of people with disabilities as a pressing concern for employers – only then will they become the customers the service-oriented insurance might actually serve.

Based on empirical data from ethnographic research this chapter analyses the structural and cultural remodelling of disability insurance and its implication for the work of disability insurance staff on the ground.[1] In particular, the focus is on the "market imagery" (Newman & Clarke, 2009, p. 79) and the "win-win"-rhetoric used in addressing employers both on the level of marketing the insurance as such and on the case-related level of 'selling' particular clients to particular employers. As I will show, in the context of the currently pervasive conflation of market and society (Crouch, 2011; Shamir, 2008), disability insurance *repackages a normative issue in market terms*. Below this surface of market imagery, I contend, however, that disability insurance must make use of less obviously economic rationales and strategies, because market logic alone is inadequate to mobilise employers. These seemingly 'non-economic' justifications can best be understood within the theoretical framework of the Economics of Conventions (EC).

The interdisciplinary, pragmatist approach of EC is focused on the problem of coordinating action in situations of uncertainty. Social situations are seen as characterised by "cognitive indeterminacy" (Eymard-Duvernay, 2002, p. 62), because in most situations there is a plurality of rationales available to interpret and justify actions. Therefore, actors need to assess which rationales provide an appropriate frame for action under particular circumstances. These rationales ("conventions") are anchored in overarching societal "orders of worth", which each centre on a specific notion of the common good and provide principles of equivalence to judge and rank the value of social objects (Boltanski & Thévenot, 2006; Eymard-Duvernay, Favereau & Orléans et al., 2005; for an overview of conventions, see Diaz-Bone, 2015, pp. 139–153). In the economic sphere, conventions refer to the construction and assessment of the quality of goods, services and labour. Quality conventions rest on an infrastructure of socio-cognitive and material forms such as classifications, technologies, norms, standardisations and the like (Thévenot, 1984). The premise of the co-presence of a plurality of rationales in social situations implies that economic organisations represent compromises between different conventions – generally, at least between the market and the industrial convention (Boltanski & Thévenot, 2006). In the market convention, the value of economic objects is determined by supply and demand, and cost-benefit-calculations, whereas the industrial convention values expertise, efficiency, planning and standardisation. Disabled workers, for example, may appear unprofitable in market terms inasmuch they may be less productive as non-disabled workers. Assessed according to the industrial convention they may be rated as less valuable because they may not fit neatly into the given coordination of work, so that adjustments of the material infrastructure or of work routines may be needed. As I will show, the employment of disabled people is also justified with respect to the domestic and the civic convention. In the domestic convention, the worth of a person is determined by his or her position in networks of interdependencies, loyalties and trust (Thévenot, 2001), while the civic convention ranks actors according to their engagement for the common good as opposed to pursuing self-interest only. In the economic sphere, this valuation frame is manifest in calls for equality and non-discrimination (Diaz-Bone, 2015, p. 147). Thus, to engage employers, disability insurance must deploy these conventions in situationally appropriate ways, both in public campaigns and in case-related interactions.

The activating turn and the reorganisation of disability insurance

In Switzerland, disability insurance is regulated by a federal law while the administration of the insurance is managed by 26 cantonal disability insurance offices. The transformation from welfare bureaucracy managing pensions to service provider evolved with three major reforms of the Disability Insurance Act between 2004 and 2012. These reforms were twofold: on the one hand, they pertained to the regulation and handling of entitlements, on the other hand, to the governance of disability insurance. With respect to governance, disability insurance and its cantonal offices were gradually reorganised by borrowing New Public Management ideas. Among other amendments, the reforms strengthened the job placement services, which had existed before but were now redefined as an "entitlement". Active job placement includes initiating contacts to employers or negotiating the terms of employment on behalf of clients. Thus, employer relations necessarily come to the forefront, and counselling and information of employers regarding integration and social insurance questions were added as new tasks of disability insurance. Employer networks and respective databases were created, and many cantonal offices designated specialised staff to handle these networks (Geisen, Baumgartner & Ochsenbein et al., 2016, p. 104).

The new tasks ensuing from the three *activating reforms required additional staff* and moreover *changed the nature of work* in the disability insurance offices. With each reform the offices were accorded more personnel for occupational integration and job placement. The new integration jobs go hand in hand with new *job profiles*. Following the activating reforms the basically administrative task of handling claims for pensions and medical or technical aids had to be complemented by interactive work in relations with clients and employers. On the one hand, activation involves people-changing work (Hasenfeld, 2010, p. 21), which is akin to professional social work and necessitates an orientation to the needs of clients (van Berkel & van der Aa, 2012; Marston, Larsen & McDonald, 2005; Nadai & Canonica, 2012). On the other hand, handling employer relations also requires interactive skills albeit not quite the same ones. Above all, in dealing with employers, staff need a "salesman's mentality" and a "realistic" attitude to the possibilities and limits of occupational integration (Nadai, 2017, p. 117f., see also Guggisberg et al., 2008, p. 39ff.; Geisen et al., 2016, p. 101). In one of the disability insurance offices of our study, for example, integration specialists are often university graduates with a degree in psychology or other social sciences (e.g. social work), while job placement specialists are expected to be solid "practitioners" with professional experience in various industries and good contacts to private businesses. Whereas the profile of the former is oriented to understanding the needs of clients and support them in the often-difficult return to work, the skills of the latter are geared to negotiating with employers. The interviewed disability insurance managers and staff all agree that dealing with employers requires a distinct blend of qualities and knowledge, namely "economic understanding" and "a feel" for employers: "You need to know how to speak their language and to understand the problems of those businesses". Understanding businesses includes an unsentimental assessment of how the clients' limited work capacities might or might not match employers' demands. Furthermore, keen perception of a situation and swift decision-making are considered crucial to countervail the bureaucracy-stereotype. Knowing the appropriate business language and economic thinking as well as acting efficiently is believed to be indispensable in order to be taken seriously in the business world and to win employers' trust, which again is seen as the decisive factor for mobilising employers. So, merging the necessary employer orientation and client orientation instead of assigning them to separate functions like, for instance, in German public employment services (Sowa, Reims & Theuer, 2015, p. 8) results in "a very complex job profile that no one can really fit" as the head of an integration department said. Whereas in relations to clients disability insurance staff acts in the *role of social worker and counsellor*, vis-à-vis employers they find themselves in the *roles of advertisers of disability insurance services and sellers of labour*. Although client-oriented social skills are acknowledged as important, the interviewed managers and staff emphasise above all the qualities and knowledge needed to cooperate with employers, because "employers are our main focus".

From bureaucracy to service provider: cultural modernisation

"When I started here", the communication manager of a disability insurance office recalls, "employees told me they never mention in public that they work for disability insurance". Staff did not want to talk about their job because they were afraid of having to defend themselves against the widespread criticism of disability insurance. The notoriously *negative image* of the insurance not only troubled frontline workers but was also identified as a *major obstacle to reforms* by management and by the Federal Social Insurance Office. The following diagnosis in the communication concept drafted by the communication manager cited above is quite typical:

> The brand IV has a negative connotation.[2] There are prejudices (bureaucratic, complicated, slow, inefficient, inflexible, too harsh, too lenient, not transparent). The tasks of IV are not sufficiently known (legal mandate, integration measures, role of medical services). Representation in the media is mostly negative, presentation of individual cases provoke negative emotions.

The negative image was believed to be pervasive in public, but most detrimental to the cooperation with employers. As a communication concept of the national Conference of Disability Insurance Offices summarises, employers associate "work incapacity, problems, billions of deficit and red tape" with the insurance. The paper concludes that disability insurance has to create a new "corporate brand". To this end, a national *employer campaign* was launched in 2009 to communicate the 5th reform of the Disability Insurance Act, which had introduced new financial incentives and support for employers. The campaign, designed by a commercial marketing agency at costs of several million Swiss francs, was soon deemed ineffective by the federal authorities, however, and replaced by activities initiated by cantonal offices with federal funds. Instead of communicating some rather general slogans to an undefined mass audience by means of posters and media advertisements these activities should target employers on a local level and in more specific ways. The cantonal offices of our in-depth case studies, for example, organise networking events and seminars for employers, participate at regional trade fairs, publish electronic newsletters and information brochures, present good practice-examples on their websites, thank cooperative employers with small "give-aways" and the like (see also Geisen et al., 2016, p. 19). Again, professional marketing agencies and techniques are involved, developed by in-house communication departments or by commercial agencies commissioned for specific marketing activities.

The core messages of these marketing activities are, first, to establish disability insurance offices as "professionals for job retention and reintegration", who fully "meet the demands of a modern service enterprise" (communication concept, cantonal office). Second, occupational integration is presented as a "win-win"-affair. Yet, the idea that employers should consider buying or retaining a 'flawed commodity', i.e. the labour of workers with limited work capacity, is not an inherently economic view, but a normative societal goal.[3] The topic of disabled people's access to the labour market has been successfully put on the political agenda by the disability rights movement as a matter of justice, citizenship and social inclusion (Heymann et al., 2014; Maschke, 2004; Wansing, 2005). When disability insurance publicly promotes occupational integration, it somewhat reluctantly joins these "moral entrepreneurs" (Gusfield, 1996) to *advocate the common good*. Yet, against the backdrop of the economisation of political discourse and public administration, it must not too obviously appear as moral agent (Nadai & Canonica, 2016). Disability insurance offices try to avoid appearing obtrusive or idealistic, as the director of a cantonal office declared: "We don't evangelise or moralise". Rather, with the omnipresent catchphrase of integration as a win-win-affair the essentially normative issue of the labour market inclusion of marginalised people is repackaged in the economic language that is supposedly more appealing to actors of the economic world.

Presenting occupational integration as unequivocal success is the core message of national and cantonal public relations activities. Indeed, "success stories" with testimonials of clients and employers appear as a distinct communicative genre on websites, in glossy brochures and in short videos available on the websites of the cantonal offices and of the Conference of Disability Insurance Offices. Success stories and other elements of the campaign in general promise the *reconciliation of economic and social benefits*. In concrete instances, however, the latent message is ambivalent. This is apparent in the main video of the current employer campaign (entitled "success stories"), in which four employers talk about their experiences with disabled workers and, to a lesser extent, with the services of disability insurance.[4] In fact, only in the last 10 seconds of the three-minute video are the services of disability insurance explicitly mentioned. Moreover, disability insurance remains an abstract and mute entity, i.e. we do not see or hear any job placement or integration staff. Rather, it is exemplary employers, who address an audience of other employers thereby realising the idea, that disability insurance needs to speak the language of employers to win them over. The focus of the video is on employers' reflections about the rewards of "giving these people a chance". Disabled workers are described as "top workers", whom the employer would not want to "give away". But they are also "different" from other staff, because they show "ups and downs", they "can't always deliver 100%", they need more supervision than other workers and sickness absences occur at unpredictable intervals. Therefore, employing people with health impairments is also "a bit of an adventure" that, nevertheless, "pays off" because – out of gratitude for having a job at all – disabled workers are highly motivated and loyal employees. On the manifest level, the video posits an unequivocal profit for employers. Latently, however, considerable risks are also apparent, namely inconsistent performance levels including unpredictable absences as well as the extra effort for close supervision. From an economic point of view, these risks translate into financial costs and losses: loss of productivity, costs for maintaining production despite absences and performance fluctuations, and supervision costs.

The real pay-off, the video suggests, is to be found elsewhere, namely on the level of *social relations* within the company and between the company and society. The socially minded employer who gives disabled people a chance acts as the patriarch assuming responsibility for the 'company family' and is rewarded by the loyalty and hard work not only of the disabled workers but of all of his staff.[5] In this way, employing disabled people is legitimised with respect to the hierarchic interdependencies of the *domestic convention*. Moreover, the paternalist employer gains public reputation for showing solidarity and assuming social responsibility, i.e. the *civic convention* is also brought into play. Tapping into the civic convention, over the last 10 years at least a dozen awards for 'integration-friendly' businesses has been created in Switzerland, more than half of them with the participation of cantonal disability offices. Awards generate honour for the recipient as well as for the donor and at the same time they create the diffuse mutual indebtedness inherent in social exchange (Vogt, 1997, p. 238). The award enhances the symbolic capital of the honoured companies but also commits them to exemplary behaviour towards people with health impairments in the future.[6]

By explicitly inviting the businesses to use the award as a marketing tool, the institutions awarding the prizes actively construct the link of social and economic gains implied in the win-win argument, which is a mainstay of the popular corporate social responsibility discourse (Brejning, 2012; Crouch, 2011; Shamir, 2008). In this way, disability insurance avoids inappropriate "evangelising and moralising" on behalf of the disabled, while still launching moral appeals albeit in the modernised form of "market-embedded morality" (Shamir, 2008). As Shamir argues, the more the distinction between society and the market is dissolved in neoliberal thought, the more socio-moral issues "become 'the business of market actors'" (ibid., p. 3). But in contrast to legal obligations, market-embedded morality is based on self-regulation: businesses freely choose to assume social responsibility and by doing so they simultaneously further their own interests. Instead of moralising disability, insurance thus 'argues the business case' to induce employers to take normative societal considerations into account (Nadai & Canonica, 2016).

Employer relations on the ground: market deals and networking

The public campaign uses employers to market the normative goal of disabled people's labour market inclusion as well as the disability insurance services to other employers. On the case-level disability insurance staff cannot stay discretely in the background and when it comes to finding employment for specific clients the 'sales pitch' must be more specific than the rather general arguments used in public campaigns. Especially the job placement process is actually described as a sales act or "human trafficking", as one job placement specialist called his task, adding apologetically: "We deal in people. Human trafficking may sound brutal, but these people need a job after all". Dealing in people may start with sending anonymised client profiles to businesses and inquiring for possible job openings. But most often it happens in direct interaction with employers. In these personal encounters, job placement staff basically argue along the same lines as the media campaign. In particular, they also stress *economic advantages*, which are spelled out in more detail and tailored to the case at hand. For example, they promise to "find the needle in the haystack", i.e. to propose job candidates with the perfect profile for a given job thus helping to save search costs and risks and enabling smooth operations. By emphasising how the fit between worker and job enables the efficient coordination of work, the matching argument draws on the *industrial convention*. The screening function of disability insurance's job placement service is furthered by offering different types of work trials provided by the Disability Insurance Act. Work trials are used to test the work capacity of clients in the realistic setting of a normal job as opposed to sheltered employment. For businesses they constitute *free labour*, because clients receive disability insurance benefits (daily allowances) instead of a salary paid by the employer.[7] Since employers are not obliged to offer the client a regular job afterwards, the trials also constitute a kind of 'product warranty' – in case of insufficient performance the 'defective' labour can be returned (Nadai, 2017). Temporary wage subsidies during the adjustment period of newly hired insurance clients are another financial incentive, which job placement staff use as extra "candy", when an employer seriously considers offering a regular job to an insurance client but is still somewhat hesitant (Gonon & Rotzetter, 2017). Work trials and wage subsidies use the market mechanism of price-cuts to stimulate demand for a 'non-competitive commodity' i.e. the labour of disabled people.

Although the law and the respective ordinances define entitlements to work trials and subsidies in some detail, job placement staff believe that it is crucial to decide fast and to be flexible and generous instead of being "a stickler for the letter of the law". Being generous and using these incentives "creatively" means granting or prolonging work trials even if either the client or the employer does not meet all the conditions. Likewise, in the case of temporary wage subsidies for newly hired employees in regular jobs – meant as compensation for lower productivity during the adjustment period – we observed that insurance staff was ready to offer or prolong them in cases where they were not convinced that the particular client actually needed extra adjustment time (for an example, see Gonon & Rotzetter, 2017). Yet, because "regular employment is worth its weight in gold for these people", generosity is seen as a successful integration strategy:

> I try to empathise with the employer and to feel what might be appropriate. (...) I'm generous with daily allowances. I don't haggle, I think, hey, you have to support an employer who has the stamina and understanding [for a long rehabilitation process].
>
> (integration specialist)

Although the law specifies the terms of daily allowances (conditions, duration, amount), the integration specialist here uses the term "haggling" to describe how she decides about granting allowances. She thereby frames the negotiations with employers as a *market deal* – moreover, a deal to support the employer not the client.[8] In the eyes of the integration specialist cited here, the negotiation is not an instance of haggling, presumably because she is generous and is not openly trying to get a better deal for disability insurance or her client. As sociological observers, however, we might come to the conclusion that haggling is not needed because the employers' wishes are anticipated and factored into the deal without the employer actually having to quote a price. In our study, we only observed one interaction between disability insurance staff and employer, in which a job placement specialist bargained in favour of the client (in this instance for a higher wage). Usually, however, either the explicit demands of employers were accepted or – like in the quotation – disability insurance staff proposed terms that they felt were "realistic" and acceptable to employers in the first place. To remain with the market metaphors, disability insurance staff is well aware that employers dispose of a rare good, namely jobs for people with limited work capacity. Moreover, insofar as occupational integration has become the overriding concern and the most important benchmark for disability insurance there is no way around the cooperation with employers, so these can dictate the price.

Even though case-level cooperation with employers is predominantly framed as market transactions, disability insurance staff believes that ultimately employers' willingness to hire or retain disabled workers is not motivated by economic calculation but by a *moral sense of social responsibility* (Nadai, Gonon & Rotzetter, in press). Moreover, they are convinced that this moral motivation is intrinsic and cannot be generated by extrinsic incentives or persuasion.[9] Rather, they see social responsibility as rooted in corporate culture and tradition, in paternalist conceptions of the employer's duty of care, in personal experiences with disabled people and the like, i.e. in factors outside the control of disability insurance. In other words, despite the market imagery used to describe negotiations with employers the readiness to even consider dealing with disability insurance is attributed to non-market determinants, namely to employers' social bonds within the 'company family' and with society. On the one hand, the social ties of the enterprise as a hierarchically structured community create reciprocal obligations between employers and employees.[10] Inasmuch a company is seen as part of a wider (local or national) community, on the other hand, obligations extend to that community, e.g. by "giving a chance" to a disabled job applicant or provide temporary workplaces for a work trials in order to "contribute to society".

Consequently, the main strategy of disability insurance staff is *to build long-term personal relations with particular employers* in order to generate the diffuse reciprocal obligations inherent in social relations. Successful cases of job retention support or job placement are deemed the most effective means to secure long-term loyalties – the satisfied customer will come back and do business again. Therefore, interactions with employers are constantly assessed with respect to maintaining the relation. If, for example, the job placement specialist realises that a particular case will not result in successful integration he or she redirects the focus of the interaction to keeping up the relation to the employer in view of a potential cooperation in the future. "Building trust" is seen as essential for maintaining relations. This involves being a reliable partner, relieving employers of "paperwork", listening and being sympathetic to their concerns, being honest (i.e. not foisting unsuitable clients on them) and accommodating employers' demands: "We accept the terms of the employer, because this is the free labour market."

Even though disability insurance would like to see itself as professional "partner" on a par with employers there is a fundamental asymmetry in the relationship. In general, employers dictate the terms and disability staff accepts them or even anticipates them. There are, however, *differences according to company size*. All disability insurance offices in our sample agree that gaining access to SMEs is easier than cooperating with big companies. Big companies usually have health management systems and in-house social services with expertise in handling the problem of workers with health impairments. They see disability insurance only as a last resort for employees, when in-house rehabilitation attempts have failed and they expect disability insurance to then accept this outcome and grant a pension.

> I simply expect a smooth service. I told the director of the disability office, look, if I want something of you, you can be sure that I really need it. We save you so much work, you don't have much to do with us, so if I need your help, you can be sure that we have tried everything and I want your staff to know that and to toe the line!
> (Head of in-house social services, multinational company)

Even if disability insurance does not always "toe the line", it finds itself in a structurally weak position, because big companies do not need support for dealing with their own employees while almost never accepting insurance clients as job applicants. Neither do financial incentives carry much weight: the big companies "pick them up" whenever they are entitled to them, but these incentives are not a decisive factor. The relations with SMEs are more symmetrical. On the one hand, disability insurance is just as dependent on their willingness to accept disabled workers as it is on big companies. On the other hand, especially small businesses do not have the expertise or the resources to manage long-term sickness absences or workplace adjustments. Disability insurance here serves as a kind of substitute health management. Insurance staff sometimes describes the relations with these small businesses in almost therapeutic terms with the employer appearing more like a client than like a customer. It is important to "listen to" employers, to have "sympathy" for their concerns and to be there for them, so "the employer feels I have a backing, they don't shunt it off to me, but IV is still there for me". In the context of counselling insecure employers, the aforementioned work trials also function as a lever for disability insurance to influence the terms of a possible employment, e.g. by suggesting workplace adjustments and negotiate expected performance level and pay. During and after the trial period there are evaluation meetings between disability insurance and employers; the trial thereby provides a reason to keep in touch with businesses and to strengthen long-term social ties.

When disability insurance sees employers as the focus of its new service culture and conceptualises the task of occupational integration as "human trafficking" the clients seem to disappear from the picture. They seem to be mere *transaction objects* within a sales act on the one hand and within the social relations disability insurance wants to establish with businesses on the other hand. Indeed, the strategy of building long-term social ties with particular employers gives them structural precedence over clients, since clients change faster than businesses – clients' entitlements to job placement services for example normally do not exceed six months. Moreover, long-term relations with clients are undesirable because this would be an indicator of failed occupational integration. Furthermore, clients are in a weaker position since they are legally obliged to participate in any occupational rehabilitation measures, while employers are not: businesses cannot be sanctioned for not cooperating with disability insurance. Nevertheless, clients cannot be reduced to passive objects of negotiations between employers and disability insurance. Just like any worker, they are an "abstract unity of labour power substitutable by other such units", in other words, a commodity, but at the same time workers are also "concrete individual[s] with specific skills, knowledge, and creativity" (Jessop, 2017, p. 4). While being dependent on selling their labour power – a necessity, which has been reinforced by activation policies (Gilbert, 2002; Lessenich, 2013; Tabin, Probst & Waardenburg et al., 2013) – clients still have *agency* with respect to how they 'market' themselves. Disability insurance staff regards the motivation and self-presentation of clients as decisive factors for successful integration. Thus, the self-will of clients has to be taken into account. If the clients are not able or not willing to project confidence in their own work capacity job placement staff cannot persuade employers to purchase their labour power. Moreover, their own standing as competent service providers is jeopardised, because their judgment of the client's employability proves inaccurate. Therefore, prior to putting clients on the market, i.e. to contacting an employer on their behalf, insurance staff needs to assess not only their work capacity but also their attitude. Are they motivated and do they have a "realistic" understanding of their options and their value in the labour market – if not, can their attitude be influenced? Therefore, *employer orientation and client orientation cannot be separated* completely. Even though employers are the more powerful customer group, clients have at least the negative power to obstruct the deal – albeit by putting their own labour market access at risk.

Conclusions

In Switzerland, disability insurance was affected rather late by the transformations observed throughout Western welfare states since the late 20th century, both with respect to the redirection of policy goals and to the redesign of public services. Profound changes were not initiated until the first decade of the 21st century, when the primacy of labour market inclusion over pensions was reinforced by a series of reforms aiming at the activation of clients. Likewise, New Public Management as the neoliberal strategy to infuse public administration with market principles reached disability insurance cantonal offices long past its heyday and in diluted forms. The main elements of NPM such as the marketisation of public services or installing "quasi-consumer choice mechanisms" to stimulate competition (Newman & Clarke, 2009, p. 79) are notably absent. None of the customers (clients, employers, doctors) can choose his or her preferred social insurance office – allocation is simply given by residence – neither has the core function of disability insurance (the management of pensions) been handed over to private providers.[11] Furthermore, controlling cantonal offices by benchmarking seems to be largely without consequences. The target agreements between the Federal Social Insurance Office as supervising body and the cantonal offices may have "strengthened competition between cantons" (OECD, 2010, p. 151), but in the absence of sanctions (e.g. cuts in funding) the competition amounts to "naming and shaming" only (ibid., p. 150). Instead, change happened primarily on the level of *discursive modernisation*, whereby the use of market imagery marks the transition from inefficient and legalistic bureaucracy to modern service provider with customer focus. Employers as gatekeepers to the labour market became the most important customer group, even more so because they also represent the business world from which the public administration is supposed to learn to become an efficient service provider.

Yet, before professionally serving employers, disability insurance first has to create the demand for its services and the 'commodity' it deals in, namely the labour of people with health impairments. In pure market logic, it is unreasonable to hire or retain workers with permanently limited work capacity, but in the face of the cultural predominance of market imagery it seems just as unreasonable to appeal to economic actors with non-economic arguments. Therefore, disability insurance makes use of the *win-win rhetoric* to anchor a normative societal issue – the social inclusion of disabled people – in "market-based morality" (Shamir, 2008). This discursive strategy simultaneously reaffirms the "infusion of the capitalist ethos in the realm of social protection" (Gilbert, 2002, p. 42) and the concept of "voluntariness" of Swiss disability policy, i.e. the idea that the employment of disabled people ought to be a self-chosen social responsibility for employers, not a legal obligation (Canonica, 2017).

However, market rhetoric and market mechanisms alone are not sufficient to stimulate the respective demand. In cost-benefit terms, it may pay to retain sick employees to save costs for personnel turnover and to preserve human capital. But when it comes to hiring, the calculating employer may come to the conclusion that in terms of supply and demand of labour "no one really waits for [disabled] people, because I can get 10 other people who bring me 100% [performance]", as an interviewed supermarket manager said. Therefore, disability insurance is more successful regarding job retention than in helping jobless clients to get hired (Bolliger, Fritschi & Salzgeber et al., 2012; Guggisberg, Bischof & Jäggi et al., 2015). Insurance staff on the ground, while fully accepting the necessity of acting as a business-like service provider, do not believe that employers act primarily on market rationales. They attribute employers' openness to disabled workers to *moral values and social ties*.

In interactions with employers, they situationally switch between the market, domestic and civic conventions in their arguments, thus acknowledging that market logic is not the only framework for economic action. Likewise, their dealings with employers are not modelled on the fleeting contacts between anonymous buyers and sellers in the market place. Instead, they follow the template of long-term social relations entailing reciprocity by building personal relations with particular employers who – in the case of SMEs – may even be seen as clients in need of support rather than customers. So, both disability insurance as an institution and its frontline workers engage in market imagery while implicitly or explicitly relying on non-market forces. Still, market discourse has an effect: it puts employers in the position of customers exerting the consumer choice of buying or discarding the labour of disabled people. Welfare state support thus marks disabled workers as residual labour that the customer-employer will only buy at a state-sponsored discount, if at all.

Notes

1 The research under direction of the author was funded by the Swiss National Science Foundation (grant 153638); Anna Gonon and Fabienne Rotzetter collaborated as research assistants. The study analysed employers' rationales with respect to the hiring and retention of disabled workers and the persuasion strategies of disability insurance. We conducted in-depth case studies in two disability insurance offices and two business companies, which were complemented by data from additional disability insurance offices and businesses. Overall, the database comprises observational fieldnotes, 19 interviews from 7 different disability insurance offices, 32 interviews from 15 companies and various textual and visual documents.
2 IV is the commonly used acronym for the official term "Invalidenversicherung" (invalidity insurance).
3 Of course, not every disability affects work capacity in significant ways: depending on the job and the kind of disability an impaired worker may be as productive as any non-disabled person. But the work capacity of clients of disability insurance's integration or job placement services must by definition be reduced, otherwise they would not be entitled to these services.
4 The video is available on different websites https://youtube.com/watch?feature=player_embedded&v=gCba4zxQPhw. Employer quotes are from the video; the disabled employees are shown in the video but they do not speak for themselves.
5 In our study respondents from the economic field often described their companies as a "family" and this occurred not just in small family businesses but also in big (multinational) companies.
6 One company of our sample experienced the downside of honour when it was attacked as "hypocritical" for dismissing a sick employee exactly with reference to the social award obtained a few years before the incident.
7 The law specifies different forms of trials depending on the phase within the rehabilitation process and on the purpose of the trial. For one type of trial employers even get a financial compensation on top of the free labour, which is meant as compensation for the extra-time and effort needed to instruct and supervise insurance clients.

8   Daily allowances are financial entitlements for clients, so it is even more striking that the integration specialist stresses the support for the employer.
9   The employers in our sample share this belief and explain their engagement with a moral commitment to social responsibility. Yet, both sides also point to the limits of social responsibility set by "economic reality".
10 Our data show that these informal social obligations go beyond the statutory periods of protection against dismissal during sickness leave – the companies of our sample tend to retain sick employees longer than they must according to the law (Nadai/Gonon/Rotzetter, in press).
11 Job placement and coaching are to some degree outsourced to private agencies.

References

Baumgartner, E., Greiwe, S., Schwarb, T. (2004): *Die berufliche Integration von behinderten Personen in der Schweiz. Studie zur Beschäftigungssituation und zu Eingliederungsbemühungen*, Bern: Bundesamt für Sozialversicherungen.

Bolliger, C., Fritschi, T., Salzgeber, R. et al. (2012): *Eingliederung vor Rente. Evaluation der Früherfassung, der Frühintervention und der Integrationsmassnahmen der Invalidenversicherung*, Bern: Bundesamt für Sozialversicherungen.

Boltanski, L., Thévenot, L. (2006): *On Justification: Ecnomies of Worth*, Princeton: Princeton University Press.

Brejning, J. (2012): *Corporate Social Responsibility and the Welfare State*, Farnham/ Burlington: Ashgate.

Canonica, A. (2017): 'Konventionen der Arbeitsintegration. Die Beschäftigung von Behinderten in Schweizer Unternehmen (1950–1980)', *Zeitschrift für Unternehmensgeschichte*, 62: 233–255.

Castel, R. (2000 [1995]): *Die Metamorphosen der sozialen Frage. Eine Chronik der Lohnarbeit*, Konstanz: UVK.

Clarke, J., Gewirtz, S., McLaughlin, E. (2000): *New Managerialism, New Welfare?* London: Open University.

Crouch, C. (2011): *The Strange Non-Death of Neoliberalism*, Cambridge: Polity Press.

Diaz-Bone, R. (2015): *Die "Economie des conventions". Grundlagen und Entwicklungen der neuen französischen Wirtschaftssoziologie*, Wiesbaden: Springer VS.

Domzal, C., Houtenville, A., Shartma, R. (2008): *Survey of Employer Perspectives on the Employment of People with Disabilities: Technical Report*, McLean, VA: CESSI.

Eymard-Duvernay, F. (2002): 'Conventionalist Approaches to Enterprise', in: Lazega, E., Favereau, O. (eds.), *Conventions and Structures in Economic Organization*, 60–78, Cheltenham: Edward Elgar.

Eymard-Duvernay, F., Favereau, O., Orléans, A. et al. (2005): 'Pluralist Integration in the Economic and Social Sciences: The Economy of Conventions', *Post-Autistic Economics Review* [online] 34: article 2. www.paecon.net/PAEReview/issue34/Thevenot34.htm.

Geisen, T., Baumgartner, E., Ochsenbein, G. et al. (2016): *Zusammenarbeit der IV-Stellen mit den Arbeitgebenden*, Bern: BSV Bundesamt für Sozialversicherungen.

Germann, U. (2008): '"Eingliederung vor Rente". Behindertenpolitische Weichenstellungen und die Einführung der schweizerischen Invalidenversicherung', *Schweizerische Zeitschrift für Geschichte*, 58: 178–197.

Gonon, A., Rotzetter, F. (2017): '"Zückerchen für Arbeitgeber". Sozialstaatliche Anreize zur beruflichen Eingliederung von Menschen mit gesundheitlichen Einschränkungen in der Schweiz', *Soziale Passagen*, 8: 153–168.
Gilbert, N. (2002): *Transformation of the Welfare State. The Silent Surrender of Public Responsibility*, Oxford: Oxford University Press.
Guggisberg, J., Bischof, S., Jäggi, J. et al. (2015): *Evaluation der Eingliederung und der eingliederungsorientierten Rentenrevision der Invalidenversicherung*, Forschungsbericht 18/15, Bern: Bundesamt für Sozialversicherungen.
Guggisberg, J., Egger, T., Künzi, K. (2008): *Evaluation der Arbeitsvermittlung in der Invalidenversicherung*, Bern: Bundesamt für Sozialversicherungen.
Gusfield, J.R. (1996): *Contested Meanings. The Construction of Alcohol Problems*, Wisconsin: Wiconsin University Press.
Hasenfeld, Y. (2010): 'The Attributes of Human Service Organizations', in: Hasenfeld, Y. (ed.), *Human Services as Complex Organizations*. 2nd Edition, 9–32, London: Sage.
Heymann, J., Stein, M.A., Moreno, G. (2014): *Disability and Equity at Work*, Oxford: Oxford University Press.
Jessop, B. (2017): Revisiting Offe's Paradox in the Light of Neoliberalism: Ricardian and Schumpeterian Workfare Regimes. Paper presented at the Conference "Economies of Welfare", 26–27.1, University of Basel.
Lengwiler, M. (2007): 'Im Schatten der Arbeitslosen- und Altersversicherung: Systeme der staatlichen Identitätsversicherung nach 1945 im europäischen Vergleich', *Archiv für Sozialgeschichte*, 47: 325–348.
Lessenich, S. (2013): *Die Neuerfindung des Sozialen: der Sozialstaat im flexiblen Kapitalismus*, 3rd edition, Bielefeld: transcript.
Marin, B., Prinz, C., Queisser, M. (2004): *Transforming Disability Welfare Policies: Towards Work and Equal Opportunities*, Aldershot: Ashgate.
Marston, G., Larsen, J., McDonald, C. (2005): 'The Active Subjects of Welfare Reform: a Street-Level Comparison of Employment Services in Australia and Denmark', *Social Work & Society*, 3: 141–158.
Maschke, M. (2004): 'Behinderung als Feld wohlfahrtsstaatlicher Politik eine Systematisierung der Behindertenpolitik', *Berliner Journal für Soziologie*, 14: 399–420.
Nadai, E. (2017): 'Asymmetrische Responsibilisierung oder wie man Arbeitgeber vom Wert von "Behinderten" überzeugt', in: Bilgi, O., Frühauf, M., Schulze, K. (eds.), *Widersprüche gesellschaftlicher Integration - Zur Transformation Sozialer Arbeit*, 111–128, Wiesbaden: Springer.
Nadai, E., Canonica, A. (2012): 'Arbeitsmarktintegration als neu entstehendes Berufsfeld: zur Formierung von professionellen Zuständigkeiten', *Schweizerische Zeitschrift für Soziologie*, 38: 23–37.
Nadai, E., Canonica, A. (2016): The Moralisation of Labour. Rationales for the Employment of People with Disabilities, Paper Presented at the Workshop "Moral Struggles in and around Markets", 11.-12.11, University of Neuchâtel.
Nadai, E., Canonica, A., Koch, M. (2015): *... und baute draus ein grosses Haus. Interinstitutionelle Zusammenarbeit (IIZ) zur Aktivierung von Erwerbslosen*, Konstanz: UVK.
Nadai, E., Gonon, A., Rotzetter, F. (in press): 'Costs, Risks and Responsibility. Negotiating the Value of Disabled Workers between Disability Insurance and Employers', *Swiss Journal of Sociology*, 44.
Newman, J., Clarke, J. (2009): *Publics, Politics and Power. Remaking the Public in Public Services*, London: Sage.

OECD (1992): *Employment Policies for People with Disabilities*. Labour Market and Social Policy Occasional Paper No. 8, Paris: OECD Publishing.

OECD (2006): *Sickness, Disability and Work: Breaking the Barriers*, Vol. 1, Norway, Poland and Switzerland, Paris: OECD Publishing.

OECD (2010): *Sickness, Disability and Work. Breaking the Barriers*, Paris: OECD Publishing.

Probst, I., Tabin, J.-P., Courvoisier, N. (2015): 'De la réparation à la réversibilité. Un nouveau paradigme dans l'assurance invalidité?' *Revue suisse de sociologie*, 41: 101–117.

Shamir, R. (2008): 'The Age of Responsibilization: on Market-Embedded Morality', *Economy & Society*, 37: 1–19.

Shaw, L., Daraz, L., Bezzina, M.B. et al. (2014): 'Examining Macro and Meso Level Barriers to Hiring Persons with Disabilities: A Scoping Review', in: Altman, B.M., Barnartt, S.N. (eds.), *Environmental Contexts and Disability*, 185–210, Bingley: Emerald.

Sowa, F., Reims, N., Theuer, S. (2015): 'Employer Orientation in the German Public Employment Service', *Critical Social Policy*, 35: 1–20.

Tabin, J.-P., Probst, I., Waardenburg, G. et al. (2013): 'Decommodification and Welfare State: The Case of Workplace Accident Victims', *Swiss Journal of Sociology*, 39: 129–146.

Tabin, J.-P., Piecek-Riondel, M., Perrin, C. et al. (2016): 'L'invalidité comme catégorie administrative', *Revue suisse de pédagogie spécialisée*, 13–19.

Thévenot, L. (1984): 'Rules and Implements: Investments in Form', *Social Science Information*, 23: 1–45.

Thévenot, L. (2001): 'Organized Complexity. Conventions of Coordination and the Composition of Economic Arrangements', *European Journal of Social Theory*, 4: 405–425.

van Berkel, R., van der Aa, P. (2012): 'Activation Work: Policy Programme Administration or Professional Service Provision?', *Journal of Social Policy*, 41: 493–510.

Vogt, L. (1997): *Zur Logik der Ehre in der Gegenwartsgesellschaft*, Frankfurt a.M.: Suhrkamp.

Wansing, G. (2005): *Teilhabe an der Gesellschaft. Menschen mit Behinderung zwischen Inklusion und Exklusion*, Wiesbaden: VS Verlag.

Chapter 9

Collective mobilization among welfare professionals in Sweden – the politicisation of caring

Anna Ryan Bengtsson

> We have had enough! The midwives of Stockholm have had enough! The midwives of Sweden have had enough! We demand the preconditions to be able to give a safe and secure care! We have gathered here today to clearly state that we are no longer accepting a situation where we have to perform care that is not secured. We are many. We are strong. We are loved and sometimes hated. Because we stir up emotions since we work with life itself. The human existence!
> (Speech held at demonstration 19th of March 2013, Midwives for a safe and secure delivery care)

This chapter addresses gendered labour struggles and collective action following neoliberal restructuring of human service organisations. In contemporary Sweden, contentious mobilisation is taking place among different occupational groups working within welfare services and in the health care sector. Contention is a broad term to capture processes where claims are raised that interfere with someone else's interest, ranging from small matters happening in your everyday life to big events (Tilly and Tarrow, 2007). Personnel, acting both inside and outside the workers' unions are trying to draw attention to changed conditions for their work and difficulties to guarantee the safety of patients and/or clients. Open letters are being published, demonstrations and manifestations held and contentious groups have mobilised taking advantage of both offline and online forms of organising.

Linda Briskin (2011, 2012, 2013, 2013) theorises women's labour militancy departing from a dialectic understanding of the relation between occupational gender segregation and gendered modes of labour struggle. Through empirical studies of nurses' militancy in different countries, she shows how both traditional strikes as well as untraditional methods e.g. mass resignations and sick outs are common practices among nurses regardless of their geographical location. Briskin connects the unorthodox forms of militancy to processes of power involving *professionalism, gendered subordination* and a *proletarianisation* of work following neoliberal transformation of the health care sector. These processes of power, she argues, have had a significant impact on the nursing profession and shaped an occupation-specific form of resistance, and a militant discourse regarding the *public interest* that she names as *a politicisation of caring*. The quotation above reflects the rhetoric used in the mobilisation taking place in Sweden and how the safety for patients is used to draw public attention to changed pre-conditions for work in the welfare sector.

The aim in this chapter is first of all to present an argument as to why the concept of a politicisation of caring is analytically useful in order for us to explore and understand the collective contentious mobilization that is taking place in Sweden. Allowing us to take an analytical entry point in untraditional forms of collective mobilisation as well as offering a theoretical lens to relate this mobilisation to the processes of power mentioned above. The politicisation of caring according to Briskin target three dimensions: the recognition and claim of a collective responsibility for caring in the society, the rejection of an essentialist notion of women as being responsible for care work by the virtue of being women and, interconnected to this, the demand that skills involved with care work needs to be both recognised and rewarded (Briskin, 2012). Based on data from two cases of contentious collective mobilisation initiated in Stockholm among social workers (active between 2011–2015) and midwives (2013–2014) I also show that the concept a politicisation of care can be developed by *adopting a broader empirical scope*. The mobilisation shortly described above does not only involve nurses, or personnel within the health care sector. Several occupational groups working in different human service organisations, such as social workers, home-care personnel, midwives and pre-school teachers are mobilising collectively in contemporary Sweden.[1] Taking the dialectic approach seriously and understanding occupational gender segregation as related to modes of labour militancy, this implies that other occupational groups in similarly gendered positions theoretically might also engage in mobilisation addressing similar issues and relations of power. Hence, adopting a broader empirical scope involves both *who* (subjects engaged), *how* (what practices that are used) and *why* (which issues that are addressed). By connecting theoretically with the previous literature on how the implementation of NPM affects human service organisations and welfare professional work (Astvik et al., 2014; Dellgran, 2015; Evetts, 2011; Lauri, 2016) the crucial role of knowledge is brought into the discussion on why a politicisation of care is undertaken by these occupational groups in contemporary Sweden. Before moving into the finer grains of the study at hand, there is a need to historically situate and contextualise these processes of power. This means addressing the historically *gendered* and intimate relationship between care work, welfare professional projects and the changes in the welfare state (Henriksson et al., 2006; Wrede et al., 2008).

Changing welfare states and the gendered paradox

The welfare state in Sweden is often referred to a Scandinavian or Nordic welfare regime, with political and economic welfare institutions highlighted in terms of equality and equity (Esping-Andersen 1999; Kuisma 2016). The expansion of the welfare sector, with its comprehensive tax-based welfare system and the central role of publically produced social services in the implementation of social rights, have, on the one hand, paved the way for women-dominated professional groups. By creating comprehensive opportunities for higher education and public-sector jobs as well as for work-related social rights, this has led to a process of professionalisation and formalising of social – and care work (Henriksson et al., 2006; Wrede et al., 2008). On the other hand, the same processes are shown to have withheld assumptions about women's responsibility for caring practices and its association to femininity have been used to devalue this kind of work (Waerness, 1984). Feminist scholars have brought attention to how gendered inequalities are institutionally produced and maintained and how processes of gendering shape hierarchies, jobs, organisational culture and relationships (Acker, 2006; Kanter, 1977). The embeddedness of welfare professional projects and women-dominated occupational groups in the realm of the welfare state hence calls for a multi-level understanding of the institutional matrix of welfare service work, including welfare policies, the industrial-relations as well as the state organisation (Henriksson et al., 2006).

Even if one should be careful with epochalism in welfare state research highlighted by e.g. (Kuisma, 2016) and (Wrede et al., 2008), the "golden age" of Nordic welfare state history ended in the beginning of the 1980s following ideological and political changes (Ferrera, 2008; Hemerijck, 2013). Sweden was heavily affected by the financial crisis in the beginning of the 1990s and this set off a series of neoliberal reforms. Political consensus was built around the need to reduce public deficits and to drop political goals of full employment, which were replaced with goals of low inflation.The social insurances were cut, and surplus-goals in the public sector implemented at the same time as a much of the responsibility for welfare services (and economic costs) were decentralised to the municipality level (Bergmark and Minas, 2007). Starting in the 1980s the public sector in Sweden also began a transformation in line with New Public Management (NPM) (Hall, 2012; Johansson et al., 2015). NPM is an umbrella term to describe how public institutions are (i) changed through the adoption of private sector business models and result-oriented management, and (ii) how welfare services are subjected to market competition by outsourcing and privatization (Hood, 1991; Johansson et al., 2015). There is a vast literature from different fields, geographical and institutional contexts describing and problematising NPM and managerialism, for example, how these changes have had a significant impact on both *work content* and *working conditions* for those working within these human service organisations, causing a situation of an intensified work pace as well as a sense of changed professional autonomy and loss of discretional power (Astvik and Melin, 2013; Dellgran, 2015; Evetts, 2011). It is crucial to any professional project to gain legitimacy, status and control over a certain knowledge base and the societies' mandate or jurisdiction over certain tasks or duties (Brante, 2014; Dellgran and Höjer, 2005). Discretion is an abstraction to capture how professional work is based on judgements and that professionals within certain areas are given the jurisdiction to make these judgements based on having special knowledge within a special field of expertise. Hence, the professional contract (jurisdiction) builds on the idea that professionals themselves (as a collective) define what constitutes good work (Ahlbäck Öberg et al., 2016; Hasselberg, 2012). Having the societal trust is therefore a prerequisite for such contracts and the professionals' ability to organize their own work are crucial to this informal contract (Ahlbäck Öberg et al., 2016; Brante, 2014). Professionalism is this way intimately connected to processes of knowledge, which are in turn also institutionally embedded in and shaped by the historic and social context. Placing analytical focus on the collective and individual strategies that occupational groups deploy in order to organise its relations with and boundaries to the state, other professions or occupations and the public (Freidson, 1994; Larson, 1977). With regards to gendered power relations, both the literature on and the historic processes of professionalisation are shown to be structured by masculininty and assumptions about rational, distant and objective knowledge, which have consequences for the perception of care work and welfare professional projects (Davies, 1996). Attention has been brought to the tendency to describe welfare professional projects as semi-professions, being defined by what they lack in terms of e.g. theoretical status rather than what they have (Dahle, 2012). Furthermore, in analyses of how care is framed in the context of the welfare state, the "irrational" and "dirty" aspects of care are often regarded as both non-professional and inferior work (Wrede et al., 2008).

These gendered relations of power involved with care work and welfare professional projects are shown to take on new shapes under the neoliberal regime (Lauri, 2016; Selberg, 2013). The turn towards managerial control has been analytically linked to masculinised archetypes of rationality, enhanced through specific ideas and norms of professionalism, evidence-based practice and a shift towards administrative capacity and documentation (Lauri, 2016). This draws attention to how organisational changes following the implementation of NPM are not only directed at the roles, duties and tasks of the professional but aim to reorient the professional identity in itself, into one that is much more managerial in nature (Thomas and Davies, 2005). This is often discussed in the terms of professional ethics and values based on an occupational professional identity that might stand in conflict with tasks that you are expected to pursue within work organisations subjected to managerialist ideas and practices (Dominelli, 1996; Evetts, 2011) within which attempts to safeguard professional status or utterances of empathy and/or a professional commitment to care for clients can be read as shivers of resistance by professionals on the street-level (Carey and Foster, 2011; Lauri, 2016). However, the effects and role of work intensification needs to be brought into the picture. One of the key assumptions in the neoliberal ideology is that better results can be achieved without additional resources and/or that equivalent outcomes reached despite measures of austerity (Hasselblad et al., 2008). Rebecca Selberg's (2013) ethnographic study of nurses in a Swedish hospital ward and Astvik et al. (2014) study of social workers in two Swedish municipalities draw attention to the un-paid and compensatory labour that is needed in order for this system to work. Departing from the Hirschman (1970) concepts of exit, voice and loyalty the social workers tend to stay loyal with the organisation by trying to balance the checks for lacking resources. At the same time, to save one's own health, compensatory strategies, such as lowering your professional ambitions, accepting less quality in your work and/or shying away from social relations in the work place, are used, strategies that in turn risk deprofessionalisation as well as moral stress, alienation and a sense of loss of meaning and are shown to, in the long run, also lead to exits either through sick-leave or staff turnover (Astvik et al., 2014). Similar compensation for lacking resources are shown in Selberg (2013) in order to maintain vocational or professional commitments in line with caring rationales (referring to Waerness). Taking her analytical entry point in the literature on the historic and gendered notion of nursing as a calling she argues that individual acts of resistance against the NPM logics of care, at the same time include covering for lacking resources in the organisation. This in turn risks reproducing the patriarchal notions of women's responsibility for caring in societies, and inherently the historic virtue script where care work is understood as a calling based on an essentialist understanding of gender and care (pp. 27–29). This draws attention to how the gendered paradox involved with care and caring is highly present in the contemporary human service work organisations, and how these relations of power are entangled and complex. Especially highlighting how they are hard to negotiate or resist individually, risking to either reproduce a historic virtue script or to slowly by slowly cause deprofessionalisation. This is also the reason to why I find the concept a politicisation of caring analytically useful, allowing us to both acknowledge and explore collective mobilisation that is taking place and to interrelate these with the deeply entangled the process of power involved with professionalism, proletarianisation and gendered subordination.

The politicisation of caring – towards a broader scope

This literature review serves as an argument to why the theory of the *politicisation of caring* is analytically useful in order for us to explore and understand the contentious mobilization that was shortly described in the introduction.

It also serves as a background to why a broader scope might deepen our theoretical understanding of these processes of power. Empirically, this has effects for both *how* (practices undertaken) and *who* (subjects) are involved in the mobilisation of a politicisation of caring. The analysis presented in this chapter builds on a qualitative case study of two cases of contentious collective mobilisation initiated in Stockholm among social workers (active between 2011–2015) and midwives (2013–2014). The cases were strategically chosen based on their relative similarities (Yin, 2014). Taking the dialectic approach seriously and understanding occupational gender segregation as related to the modes of labour militancy, other occupational groups in similarly gendered positions would in theory be relevant objects of study. Briskin (2011) also argues that the concept is relevant for the broader category of health care workers. Midwives and social workers are with regards to this understood as two cases of women-dominated welfare professional groups responsible for care work, and occupations intimately related to the expansion of the welfare state (Dellgran, 2015; Henriksson et al., 2006; Wrede et al., 2008). Having said this, there are differences that needs to be noted before we move on. The primary employer of social workers in Sweden is the municipality and the contentious mobilisation is in this case directed towards the city of Stockholm, whereas the health care is managed by the regional political level. Furthermore, the hospital organisations are also explicitly organised and steered through different professional groups where the medical doctors has the highest status. This is of course also a gendered story based on the understanding that such relations of power are institutionally produced and maintained through organizational hierarchies (Acker, 2006; Kanter, 1977). These differences are important to take into account and are open for further inquiry in the future.

With regards to the issue of *how*, the two cases for this study were chosen based on the fact that they have mobilised in a fairly similar manner: meaning collectively and over a certain period of time, addressing issues of changing working conditions and how this affects the quality of care and safety for patients or clients. The broadened scope in this sense refers to practices that are undertaken during contention and allows us to explore other ways to politicise caring aside from strikes or the militant practice of mass-resignations (Granberg, 2014; Granberg and Giritili Nygren, 2017; Henttonen et al., 2013). Furthermore, the gendered paradox involved with care work and welfare professional projects are shown to take on new shapes in neoliberal societies and does not only, or even necessarily, involve the issue of wages. By connecting with the literature on professionalism and NPM, the crucial role of *knowledge* inherent in these processes of power are addressed. Theoretically, this allows me to deepen our understanding of *why* the mobilization of a politicisation of caring is taking place. Inspiration is with regards to this taken in Paula Mulinari (2016) who frames the mobilization of protests among health care personnel in general standing up against racism in their work places, as a politicisation of caring. Showing how anti-discrimination laws, public statements and official rhetoric of organizations can be used to legitimise protests in the health care sector and collective mobilisation to safeguard a professional practice based on professional ethical values in an hostile environment. The analysis builds on a thematic content analysis of eleven semi-structured qualitative interviews with activists from the two networks, five social workers and six midwives, conducted within the time frame November 2015–June 2016. The names of the activists are fictious and the quotes are chosen to illustrate both the process of mobilisation as well as the key dimensions with regards to the issues of how and why the mobilisation has taken place.

Midwives for a safe and secure delivery care (MSDC)

The spark that set off the mobilisation of *"Midwives for a safe and secure delivery care"* (Barnmorskor för trygg och säker vård) was a formal complaint made to the work environment agency (Arbetsmiljöverket) regarding one of the obstetric clinics in Stockholm. The reason for the complaint was related to the conditions for work, and no longer being able to take breaks, and prior to the complaint the missed breaks were systematically documented. In connection with the complaint process, an open group was started on Facebook called *"It's enough"*. This group quickly became a forum for midwives all over the country, and included about 2000 members at the time. When the formal complaint wasn't met with any changes in the hospital this resulted in the mobilization of MSDC.

> It was the end of the year 2012/2013, and I contacted (…) she was one of the contact persons for the group started via the Health care union, with midwives from all the delivery clinics in the area and the goal or the theme was that it is enough – referring to the work environment and the patient security in the delivery wards. The high pressure, too much to do and the too few co-workers (…) Then I know that this came from the fact that they (…) in 2012 made one of those complaints to the work environment agency because of the situation but that nothing concrete came out in the employer's response to this complaint. So, they chose to move along this road and to try and meet across clinics and talk midwife to midwife – how is it at yours? And what can we do? What is our professional responsibility?
>
> (Eli, MSDC)

The union (Vårdförbundet) initiated the first meeting in response to the large activity online and midwives working in the delivery care in Stockholm were invited. In this initial meeting, the decision to act was taken: to act as midwives and to address their situation at work publicly. The local union (in Stockholm) offered organisational resources such as meeting facilities and access to competences, e.g. PR strategies and media-training. Since the initiative partly came from the union, the group also gained support from two officials in structuring the discussions and dileneating the aim with their mobilisation. The MSDC was at the same time free-standing from the union and the activists owned the issue themselves. The concept of *member-activism* was invented by Vårdförbundet (Health care union) as a way to host and support activities that doesn't follow the usual or traditional structures within the realm of the union. MSDC is one form of member-activism and the group was active between January 2013 and December 2014. One of the key strategies in their work was to create a collective platform for midwives over organisational boundaries in Stockholm. The internal organisation included appointing a "strategy group" where the goal was to have two representatives from each delivery clinic. The strategy group met at least twice a month for the whole period and consisted of between 10–15 persons. Social media (Twitter and Facebook) were used both for organisation of their work between meetings as well as an important communication channel towards the public. The Facebook-page "*Support the Midwife struggle*" was launched in connection to their first public appearance in the newspaper and these first steps into the public were strategically planned together with the officials and PR-department at the union. MSDC raised the following claims:

- To upheave the saving plans for the obstetric care immediately
- To have one midwife per one woman when in active delivery
- More midwives in the delivery care and on the deciding bodies of organs
- To raise the economic vouchers or price tags for deliveries, since these had been on the same level for many years
- More delivery rooms
- Take a long term economic responsibility in the planning of the delivery care

Breaking the silence among social workers (BSSW)

Another spark to mobilise was set in Stockholm among social workers, following an open meeting with the local politician responsible for the social services in the municipality, held in the beginning of 2011. The open meeting was jointly arranged by the unions for social workers, Vision and Akademikerförbundet SSR. When the politician was confronted with the social worker's experiences from their work places, such as effects of budget constraint or the inability to oversee work tasks, the response from the politician was that the social workers were very noble and decent, but that they needed to become more efficient in their work. Being met this way, three social workers initiated the mobilisation of the cross-union network called "*Breaking the silence among social workers*" (Nu bryter vi tystnaden bland socialarbetare) and their first meeting was held in on of the union premises in connection to the international day for social workers, on the 15th of March 2011.

> There were social workers from different parts of the city and everyone agreed on that the work load and the working conditions had been very tough for social workers for years. It has been a race to the bottom and become harder and harder and harder to work professionally. This has both to do with us being too few, and that we don't have the resources needed, not enough money for clients, too many errands and very ponderous administrative systems. We are not able to make it on time (...) And this was the case already back then and we tried to explain the situation (...) And then she says with a happy voice "you can always become more efficient" (...) And then we just, this is enough. It's enough now.
>
> (Chris, BSSW)

BSSW decided to be a cross-union network for social workers based in Stockholm, even if people working in the surrounding area also attended sometimes. The meetings in BSSW were open for members in either of the two unions and held once a month. BSSW wasn't a formal organisation with charters but you had to be a member in one of the unions in order to attend. Even if the unions were explicitly targeted in the BSSW critique, they were also a prerequisite for mobilisation, offering access to organisational resources such as printing, small financial support and a place to hold meetings as well as media training. In large, the network also decided upon their own issues and acted free-standing from the unions, but they also searched for both the two union's approval with regards to their official claims. BSSW met once a month, and these meetings were prepared by an appointed "steering group" that consisted of six persons. The steering group were also responsible for the external communication, where the use of social media was an important channel. Facebook, Twitter and a blog were used not only to break the silence and reach the public, but also as an arena for discussions with other professionals in the field, and for internal organization. BSSW wanted to bring political attention to how their work situation affects the clients and their rights. Their aim was both to reach the political level, but also to influence the work of the unions. The network raised thirteen claims directed towards both the work situation and the welfare system as a whole (here brought together in six clusters).

- Reasonable delegation and a formal ceiling for the amount of errands
- Introduction for new employees where they are given a lower stack of errands and a mentor who has time for this work
- To get rid of unnecessary administration and control systems that don't contribute to the social work and to rebuild a comprehensive approach
- That the amount of work is adapted to normal working hours, to have time to prepare and reflect and have access to skills development
- Administration staff and substitutes should be available and the budget should contain compensation for rising prices and salaries
- Make budget-periods longer than one year since social work is a long-term pursuit

Politicising caring through the mobilization of a collective voice

The concept of a politicisation of caring takes the gendered paradox of care work and welfare professional projects seriously. Drawing analytical attention to untraditional forms of collective action, unorthodox collective strategies that are used in order to negotiate the preconditions for professional work in the contemporary human service organisations in Sweden are in the following analysis explored further. The mobilisation of BSSW and MSDC started following specific events or a situation of trying to use the formal channels in order to raise concerns with regards to both working conditions and work content. However, when met with ignorance or a non-response from management or politicians, they did not remain loyal with their organisations and/or through compensatory strategies keep on balancing the checks (Astvik et al., 2014). Nor did they threaten with or pursue with mass-resignations (Granberg, 2014; Granberg and Giritili Nygren, 2017). Rather, these two cases of collective mobilisation present us with another strategy, namely, to mobilise collectively in order to raise a *collective voice* as professionals.

> What breaking the silence focused on, which the unions haven't done (…) is the welfare political issues and not only the working conditions for social workers but also the clients, yeah but why are the clients in this situation to begin with and how does this relate to our situation? That our situation is related to the clients, when the remunerations – the whole social policy or the social services has crashed due to a certain political agenda (…) Well, we made that connection much clearer and were in that sense more political, without taking a stance in every issue, we took a stance with regards to the welfare institutions. That they should function as good as possible and to be on the client's side in a sense.
>
> (Pim, BSSW)

> And we saw early on that this involves both dimensions both the health care and the work environment. And the Health care union, that is our union organisation but they also work with how the care is. Somewhere it was obvious to also include, what this means for the women. That's what we need address publicly because that is the severe with this and that's why we decided on this banner:" Midwives for a secure and safe care". That was the thing that we wanted to address.
>
> (Robin, MSDC)

In these excerpts, the strategic use of the *public interest,* in terms of the rights of clients and/or safety for patients is shown. The mutual interests between patients/clients and professionals are used rhetorically and stated as one of the primary reasons to why the mobilisation has taken place. Furthermore, taking an entry point in the recognition of and emphasis on a collective responsibility for caring in the society and that the collective mobilisation undertaken in these cases served as a means to draw public and political attention to how deteroriated working conditions in turn risks the safety and/or the rights of patients and clients. At the same time, the politicisation of caring, in these two cases, is aiming for the preconditions for work and other aspects than wages, addressing the need to have the preconditions for taking such collective responsibility in a qualitative way. This is also connected to the gendered paradox of welfare professional projects and how this take new shapes in contemporary human service organisations and how the processes of proletarianisation, professionalism and gendered subordination places the welfare professional in an intricate and complex nexus of powers.

The professional knowledge base at stake

Both in the claims raised in their mobilisation, as well as in the narratives of the activists, several dimensions regarding changed working conditions are brought up. These descriptions resemble the results shown in the previous literature on how NPM challenges the professional practices and power both individually and collectively.

> It was hopeless and it was, we only felt that we weren't doing the job that we could or wanted to. It was just a giant factory of women in labour, yeah, that were ready to be delivered, yeah (...) As a coordinator, there is no idea that you call another clinic because everyone is in the same situation. You try to juggle it, you know when you juggle and you feel like – okay I'll try another ball. That's how it is like all the time.
>
> (Alexis, MSDC)

> So, you see, the repression, the control – it's goes all the way down. The care administrator that has perhaps 150 errands and then John brakes his thigh and is in need of 15 minutes more every day – they have a budget. Then you have to pick 2 minutes from Jenny, five minutes from Amina, three minutes from Noor so that you get those fifteen minutes. It's so crazy. So, the need to restore the comprehensive approach in social work was a given….
>
> (Mio, BSSW)

The effects of budget-constraints are shown through these quotes and how both the social workers and the midwives are caught in the cross-fire between demands from patients and available resources within their work organisation (Astvik et al., 2014; Selberg, 2013). In the MSDC quote, the work place is referred to as a giant factory, within which the professional practice of midwives includes juggling women in labour both within and between clinics that are already filled to the breaching point, describing how their time is spent trying to keep patients away from the clinic as long as they can due to the lack of space and to handle three births simultaneously. Similar processes of being expected to re-arrange the client's needs based on the economic resources available in the organisation is shown in the social worker's account. Analytically this is an example of how the interrelated processes of power involved with proletarianisation and professionalism play out within these organisations. Showing how budget-constraints challenges the ability to control your work, both in terms of work intensification (the increased amount of errands or patients) as well as with regards to professional judgements, which are shown to be subordinated strict economic boundaries. To not be able to meet the needs of the clients or patients due to budget constraints seems to slowly challenge and change the discretionary powers held by these professions, highlighting the importance of having the preconditions to be able to make decisions based on a certain area of expertise (Ahlbäck Öberg et al., 2016; Hasselberg, 2012). The lack of space and personnel due to budget constraints changes the practices of midwives into something that stands in direct opposition with their professional training and research in the field. For instance, not being subjected to stress when in labour or the continuous presence of midwives are shown as highly important factors in the research on delivery care. Hence, the crucial issue of *knowledge* needs to be brought centre-stage in the analysis and how these contentious processes are intimately related to gaining legitimacy, status and control over a certain knowledge base and the societies' mandate or jurisdiction over certain tasks or duties (Brante, 2014; Dellgran and Höjer, 2005). In the claims that are raised and in the activist narratives, these processes of proletarianisation are also explicitly related to maintaining their professional jurisdiction and keeping control over their professional knowledge base.

> It's like they believe – well, we can develop certain methods, and it is like you take this little boy and you place him on an assembly line, because we are organised like Volvo or the Toyota-lines. No Friday cars here, no – everything is the same. So then you put one of these youngsters in basket A, who moves to station B where he gets to jump into another basket and over to conveyer C and then he comes out as a new human being, preferably within three months. This doesn't work, life doesn't work that way.
> (Mio, BSSW)

The obstetric clinics in Stockholm belong to the reproductive council, this deciding body functions as an advisory organ to the politicians and to the health care administration and that's when we understood that it wasn't strange at all that our truths and our needs and our ideas and our professional needs to develop the care didn't reach all the way up to those holding the money (...) So, the truth from the floor during summer becomes an evaluation in the county council in the autumn saying mm. "But it went alright after all", despite the fact that we might have died along the way. And when we got that, that's when we decided that we had to get through somehow.

(Juno, MSDC)

These descriptions echo results from literature on NPM in human service organisations and how the implementation of administrative documentation systems and standardised methods challenges professional power and practices (e.g. Dominelli, 1996; Evetts, 2011; Lauri, 2016). With regards to corporate models of management this is being explicitly targeted in the social workers description of LEAN-managament and how the rationality of these models are not taking into account how human beings or how social life works. The midwife, on the other hand, address the distance that is built into these organisations and how the knowledge or experiences from the floor rarely reaches the political level. Instead, they base their decisions on post-evaluations or data from administrative documentation, which doesn't necessarily or even closely correspond with the situation described by the social workers or midwives. The professional knowledge base is in this sense challenged both with regards to the discretionary room of manoeuvre following deteroriated working conditions, as well in terms of jurisdiction and the possibility to have collective control over their respective field of expertise (Ahlbäck Öberg et al., 2016; Hasselberg, 2012). It is also in this sense the mobilisation of a politicisation of caring needs to be understood as a collective strategy among occupational groups involved with care work, that serves to negotiate not only the working conditions but the professional jurisdiction and its boundaries to the state, other professions or occupations and the public in the contemporary society (Freidson, 1994; Larson, 1977).

> We needed to from the profession, say no and it's enough. This is not working anymore. And that it happened around this time was probably because it had gone so far that the social workers themselves had to say no, this is not working anymore (...) But you say that social workers are very loyal and that they don't give up with the first. That they sort of try to compensate for the system as a whole, struggle on and work more than you should. And it was from this that we came to some sort of tipping point where we felt that we didn't have the politicians with us on this at all. Then it was the time to put our foot down and say that this isn't working anymore.
>
> (Lex, BSSW)

That you have to say, if one should categorise it, and we do insist on the fact that this is a professional issue, in what ways do midviwes want to

work and ought to work in the delivery clinics and this is not really a local but a national issue and can be easily translated to a national level. Because it is the same everywhere, the only thing that differs are the number of women in delivery each year, and that the size of the clinics are different.
(Robin, MSDC)

With regards to the theory on a politicisation of caring, the strategy chosen in these cases is to mobilise a collective voice as professionals, outside or semi-connected to the unions and by taking advantage of new technology for both communication and internal organisation. The primary reason for mobilisation is not the gendered wage gap or to explicitly reject an essentialist notion that women by virtue are responsible for care in the society in the traditional sense (Granberg, 2014, 2016; Henttonen et al., 2013). It is rather related to how gendered relations of power permeate the contemporary human service organisation, undergoing transformations in line with neoliberalism, and the gendered paradox discussed above. One of the key points being that the politicisation of caring in these cases is mobilised in order to claim a collective responsibility for caring in the society as well as to collectively negotiate the professional jurisdiction and control over work. This in turn involves politicising how skills involved with caring work is recognized and rewarded (Briskin, 2012). In both cases, the activists refers to experiences of being patronised by politicians with regards to a historic virtue script, reproducing an essentialist view of care and gender. Being positioned as good and noble when addressing the conditions for work was in turn met with anger and urged the will to mobilise further. At the same time, the activists in MSDC or BSSW are not explicitly mobilising against the image of a historic virtue script (Granberg, 2014; Granberg and Giritili Nygren, 2017). As is described above, it was rather a reaction towards being *obedient* and to not on an individual basis keep compensating for a system with lacking resourcses. This also involved challenging the normative ideals of managerialism, where loyalty with the organisation is both proscribed and emphasised (Lauri, 2016). As well as to collectively resist the tendency to balance the checks for lacking resources, shown to risk both deprofessionalization or to reproduce the notion of care work as a calling (Astvik et al., 2014; Selberg, 2013). Based on his analysis of one contentious process involving mass-resignation, Granberg (2014) argues that the context of care might be expanded through a discourse of professionalism. Showing how nurses based on this notion were able to craft a subject position from which compliance could be criticized and protests framed as a form of caring of both oneself and the patients. Based on the analysis in this chapter one might just as well argue that the notion of *professionalism* might be expanded through a discourse of *caring*. Hence, the politicisation of caring undertaken by the social workers and midwives in this study can be seen as collective strategies used to negotiate a professional jurisdiction and professionalism that has room for empathy and a caring commitment for patients and clients (Dominelli, 1996; Lauri, 2016). This is also an argument that goes in line with Mulinari (2016) who frames protests among health care personnel standing up against racism, as a politicisation of care. Arguing that practices that serve to safeguard a professional practice based on ethical values can be seen as an attempt to maintain an occupational professionalism within an increasingly hostile and managerialist environment.

Conclusions

In this chapter, two cases of contentious collective mobilisation in the Swedish contemporary society are presented and analysed as a politicisation of caring. The theorisation involves taking the analytical entry in unorthodox methods and militancy outside of the formal structures. Based on a dialectic understanding, the theory on a politicisation of caring allows us to acknowledge and explore collective mobilisation and analytically relate this to relations of power involved with professionalism, proletarianisation and gender. As is shown and argued throughout this chapter the concept a politicisation of caring might also be developed further by adopting a broader empirical scope.

One of the arguments as to why a broadened empirical scope is undertaken in this study is based on the previous literature that problematise how gendered relations of power are intimately related to care work in societies. Historically this has been shown in how the welfare professional projects are defined by patriarchal power as well as how these relations of power take new shapes in the contemporary human service work organisation. This was captured through the concept "a gendered paradox" which throughout the chapter is shown to place the individual in a fairly complex position, due to processes of proletarianisation and work intensification, risking either deprofessionalization (Astvik et al., 2013) or to reproduce the gendered notions of care work as a calling (Selberg, 2013). Hence, to understand the contentious and collective mobilization as a politicisation of caring, this offers a theoretical entry point that allows us to both acknowledge and explore the collective mobilisation and relate these actions to the power relations that produces cross-fires and challenges the professional knowledge base. The form that is presented and explored here is the *collective voice* in order to politicise caring.

In these two cases, the reason to mobilise has been to draw public and political attention to *deteriorated working conditions* following neoliberal restructuration of work organisations. Based on the analysis another dimension can be added to why the politicisation of caring is undertaken, namely, to collectively mobilise and raise claims towards the preconditions provided to be able to take the collective responsibility for caring in the society. This dimension includes a broader notion of working conditions than the issue of wages, targeted in the previous literature on a politicisation of caring. Furthermore, by connecting theoretically with the sociology of professions the issue of knowledge and the challenged professional knowledge base is put centre-stage in the analysis at hand, showing how the professional jurisdiction is being circumscribed due to proletarianisation involved with work intensification and budget-constrains as well as through the turn towards managerialism and NPM. To add another dimension or reason to mobilise a politicisation of caring, this allows us to deepen our understanding of the interlinkage between processes of proletarianisation and professionalism in contemporary human service work organisations. Within which, the *politicisation of caring* undertaken in these two cases can be understood as a collective strategies aimed to safeguard a professional knowledge base and to negotiate a professional jurisdiction that involves empathy and a caring commitment for patients and clients in an increasingly hostile environment.

At the same time, this leaves us with several questions to be addressed in future research. In this chapter, one of the key issues in Briskin's theorisation is left out of the analysis, namely how a politicisation of care might offer new paths to union revitalization besides already identified entry points such as the vexed relationship between professionalism and union militancy and the masculinist assumptions embedded in the political culture of unionism (Briskin, 2011). Also the role of social media needs to be addressed, both its role in the mobilisation that is targeted in this chapter, but also how the hybrid organisational forms of online and offline mobilization might open up other paths to the politicisation of caring, forms that might also take other shapes than the mobilization of a collective voice. In the introduction, different contentious actions were described such as the writing of open letters, arranging demonstrations and manifestations. The argument presented in this chapter in this sense also opens for further analyses of these practices or forms to politicise caring in the future. Addressing issues of how these processes and practices might both challenge and revitalise established and institutionalised forms of political action in the contemporary society.

Note

1 These different forms of collective mobilisation are the focus of my PhD-thesis at the Department of Social Work, Gothenburg University (2014–2019). Based on mixed-methods, the data for the thesis include two qualitative case studies, netnographic data from observations online and an event catalogue constructed from social media communication.

References

Acker, J. (2006): 'Inequality Regimes: Gender, Class, and Race in Organizations', *Gender & Society*, 20(4): 441–464.

Ahlbäck Öberg, S., Bull, T., Hasselberg, Y., Stenlås, N. (2016): 'Professions Under Siege', *Statsvetenskaplig tidskrift*, 118(1): 93–126.

Astvik, W., Melin, M. (2013): 'Överlevnadsstrategier i socialt arbete: Hur påverkar copingstrategier kvalitet och hälsa?', *Arbetsmarknad & Arbetsliv*, 19(4): 61–73.

Astvik, W., Melin, M., Allvin, M. (2014): 'Survival Strategies in Social Work: A Study of How Coping Strategies Affect Service Quality, Professionalism and Employee Health', *Nordic Social Work Research*, 4(1): 52–66.

Bergmark, Å., Minas, R. (2007): 'Decentraliserad välfärd eller medborgerliga rättigheter? Om omfördelning av makt och ansvar mellan stat och kommun', *Socialvetenskaplig tidskrift*, 2–3, 220–241.

Brante, T. (2014): *Den professionella logiken: Hur vetenskap och praktik förenas i det moderna kunskapssamhället*, Stockholm: Liber.

Briskin, L. (2011): 'The Militancy of Nurses and Union Renewal', *Transfer*, 17(4): 485–499.

Briskin, L. (2012): 'Resistance, Mobilization and Militancy: Nurses on Strike', *Nursing Inquiry*, 19(4): 285–296.

Briskin, L. (2013): 'Nurse Militancy and Strike Action', *Workers of the World: International Journal of Strikes and Social Conflicts*, 1: 105–134.

Carey, M., Foster, V. (2011): 'Introducing 'Deviant' Social Work: Contextualising the Limits of Radical Social Work Whilst Understanding (Fragmented) Resistance within the Social Work Labour Process', *British Journal of Social Work*, 41(3): 576–593.

Dahle, R. 2012: 'Social Work – A History of Gender and Class in the Profession', *Ephemera – Theory and Politics in Organizations*, 12(3): 309–326.

Davies, C. (1996): 'The Sociology of Professions and the Professions of Gender', *Sociology*, 30(4): 661–78.

Dellgran, P. (2015): 'Människobehandlande professioner', in: Johansson, S., Dellgran, P., Höjer, S. (eds.), *Människobehandlande organisationer: villkor för ledning, styrning och professionellt välfärdsarbete*, Stockholm: Natur & Kultur.

Dellgran, P., Höjer, S. (2005): 'Rörelser i tiden. Professionalisering och privatisering i socialt arbete', *Socialvetenskaplig tidskrift*, 12(2–3): 246–267.

Dominelli, L. (1996): 'Deprofessionalizing Social Work: Anti-Oppressive Practice, Competencies and Postmodernism', *British Journal of Social Work*, 26(2): 153–175.

Esping-Andersen, G. (1999). *Social risks and welfare states. Social foundations of postindustrial economies.* Oxford: Oxford University Press.

Evetts, J. (2011): 'A New Professionalism? Challenges and Opportunities', *Current Sociology*, 59(4): 406–422.

Ferrera, M. (2008): 'The European Welfare State: Golden Achievements, Silver Prospects', *West European Politics*, 31(1–2): 82–107.

Freidson, E. (1994): *Professionalism Reborn*, Oxford: Blackwell Publishers.

Granberg, M. (2014): 'Manufacturing Dissent: Labor Conlict, Care Work, and the Politicization of Caring', *Nordic Journal of Working Life Studies*, 4(1): 139–152.

Granberg, M. (2016): Care in Revolt: Labor Conflict, *Gender, Neoliberalism*, Sundsvall: Mid Sweden University.

Granberg, M., Giritili Nygren, K. (2017): 'Paradoxes of Anti-austerity Protest: Matters of Neoliberalism, Gender, and Subjectivity in a Case of Collective Resignation', *Gender, Work and Organization*, 24(1): 56–68.

Hall, P. (2012): *Managementbyråkrati – Organisationspolitisk makt i svensk offentlig förvaltning*, Malmö: Liber.

Hasselberg, Y. (2012): *Vetenskap som arbete: normer och arbetsorganisation i den kommodifierade vetenskapen*, Möklinta: Gidlund.

Hasselblad, H., Bejerot, E., Gustafsson, R. Å. (2008): *Bortom new public management: institutionell transformation i svensk sjukvård [Beyond the new public management: institutional transformation in Swedish healthcare]*, Lund: Academia Adacta.

Hemerijck, A. (2013): *Changing welfare states*, Oxford: Oxford University Press.
Henriksson, L., Wrede, S., Burau, V. (2006): Understanding Professional Projects in Welfare Service Work: Revival of Old Professionalism?, *Gender, Work & Organization*, 13(2): 174–192.
Henttonen, E., Lapointe, K., Pesonen, S., Vanhala, S. (2013): 'A Stain on the White Uniform: The Discursive Construction of Nurses' Industrial Action in the Media', *Gender, Work and Organization*, 20(1): 56–70.
Hirschman, A. O. (1970): *Exit, voice, and loyalty: responses to decline in firms, organizations, and states*, Cambridge, MA: Harvard University Press.
Hood, C. (1991): 'A Public Management for All Seasons?', *Public Administration*, 69(1): 3–19.
Johansson, S., Dellgran, P., Höjer, S. (2015): *Människobehandlande organisationer: villkor för ledning, styrning och professionellt välfärdsarbete*, Stockholm: Natur & Kultur.
Kanter, R. M. (1977): *Men and women of the corporation*, New York: Basic Books.
Kuisma, M. (2016): 'Oscillating Meanings of the Nordic Model: Ideas and the Welfare State in Finland and Sweden', *Critical Policy Studies*, 11(4): 433–454.
Larson, M. S. (1977): *The rise of professionalism. A sociological analysis*, Berkeley: University of California Press.
Lauri, M. (2016): *Narratives of governing: rationalization, responsibility and resistance in social work*, Doctoral Dissertation, Umeå universitet.
Mulinari, P. (2016): 'När SD kom till arbetsplatsen – en professionalism som antirasism', in: Holmqvist, M. (ed.), *Makt och inflytande i arbetslivet*, Stockholm: Premiss förlag.
Selberg, R. (2013): 'Nursing in Times of Neoliberal Change: An Ethnographic Study of Nurses' Experiences of Work Intensification', *Nordic Journal of Working Life Studies*, 3(2): 9–35.
Thomas, R., Davies, A. (2005): 'What Have the Feminists Done for Us?', *Feminist Theory and Organizational Resistance Organization* 12(5): 711–740.
Tilly, C., Tarrow, S. (2007): *Contentious politics*, Boulder, CO: Paradigm Publishers.
Waerness, K. (1984): 'The Rationality of Caring', *Economic and Industrial Democracy*, 5(2): 185–211.
Wrede, S., Henriksson, L., Höst, H. (2008): *Care work in crisis: reclaiming the Nordic ethos of care*, Lund: Studentlitteratur AB.
Yin, R. K. (2014): *Case study research: design and methods*, London: Sage.

Chapter 10

Street level bureaucracy under pressure

Job insecurity, business logic and challenging users

Micol Bronzini and Diego Coletto[1]

Introduction

Since the introduction of New Public Management (NPM) in the public sector in the late Seventies and early Eighties the 'business-like' 'market-oriented' strategy, and its rhetoric, has long been discussed. It was supposed to streamline the delivery of public services, improving efficiency, effectiveness and responsiveness. The idea was that of transforming a "rigid, inward-looking, slow-moving bureaucratic hierarchy into a 'flat', responsive, multi-disciplinary agency" (Pollitt, 2000, p. 194). Workers, especially frontline ones, were expected to become empowered, flexible and proactive, instead of being rule-bound, and to care for customer service. Nevertheless, a mixed picture emerges from international researches underlying contradictory results and side effects such as work intensification and disheartenment of the workforce, or the dismantling of the 'traditional public service ethos' (Kirkpatrick, 1999; Haque, 1999; Jørgensen, 1999; Pollitt, 2000; Kirkpatrick et al., 2005; Diefenbach, 2009). Staff members have often suffered degenerating conditions with the risk of "a high output/low commitment public sector workforce" (Kirkpatrick et al., 2005, p. 5).

The possibility for street-level practitioners to exercise discretion under the top-down and bottom-up pressure for more accountability has also been questioned (Taylor & Kelly, 2006). The ensuing debate has focused on how the 'articulations' and hybridisation of bureaucratic, professional and managerial logics have been affecting discretion (Newman, 2005; Van Berkel & Van Der Aa, 2012). Discretionary practices may indeed be subject to much more intensive forms of control and standardisation through performance-based incentives (Fuertes & Lindsay, 2015; Bach & Bordogna, 2017). Nevertheless, many scholars (Taylor & Kelly, 2006; Brodkin, 2011; Durose, 2011) argue that street-level workers continue to act strategically, especially when they belong to professional groups (Evans, 2011), and that discretional practices remain an important aspect of policy implementation. Professional and occupational groups do not go through the aforementioned changes passively but do respond to the reforms and translate them in different ways, not always in accordance with policy makers' intentions. In particular, they devise informal practices to cope with both changing working conditions and diminishing resources, and users' demand, (re)interpreting higher level orders within organisational constraints.

Drawing on this background, we present two pieces of research on street level bureaucrats working in different organisational contexts in Italy with the purpose of understanding whether street-level bureaucrats adapt the implementation of NPM principles mediating top-down and bottom-up pressures. We employed a qualitative design, combining ethnographic observation of street-level workers-service users' interactions, by shadowing the former, semi-structured interviews and documentary analysis. Our study is based on *key* cases (Yin, 1994; Stake, 1995; Thomas, 2011), i.e. public employment offices (PEOs) and public housing managing bodies. The rationale for selecting these two sectors was that they have some similarities. First, they both address vulnerable segments of the population. Second, they have been traditionally more bureaucratic than other welfare areas, as a large portion of those employed do not claim fully fledged professional status. Third, both of them depend on the regional government and act on a provincial scale (which is a sub-regional unit including several municipalities). But they also differ in many respects. Specifically, as we will see in the next paragraph, while PEOs have been deeply affected by the new logic inspiring activation measures, this has not influenced the public housing sector. As a consequence, it is likely that public housing front-line workers still perform a mainly administrative role concerned with 'people processing' or bureaucratic technology (Hasenfeld, 1972). By contrast, the introduction of new welfare-to-work measures has changed (or should have changed) the nature of street-level practitioners of PEOs who have partially become 'caseworkers' dealing with 'people changing' (or professional) technologies.

The analytical framework: theorising the contradictory pressures on front-line officers

Since Michael Lipsky coined the expression 'street-level bureaucracy' around 35 years ago, a growing body of literature on bureaucratic discretion has been developed in different fields. Most of the studies have emphasised the importance of discretion in shaping how policies are delivered at the frontline. In this sense, the street-level bureaucrats not only act as intermediaries, implementing policies and bringing them directly to people, but also do policy work (Brodkin, 2011).

In recent years, the debate has more developed by considering the basis of discretion, how it is used, and its consequences. Discretion may concern the exercise of responsibility and judgment in decision making, which stems from the necessary adaptation of laws and regulations to individual cases. This kind of discretionary power especially involves professionals – teachers, healthcare workers, policeman, social workers, and the like – who deal with unexpected and complex situations on a daily basis (Taylor & Kelly, 2006). But discretion can also derive from the interpretation and the social construction of ambiguous or incomplete rules. Moreover, street-level workers can use their leeway of discretion to violate rules in order better to achieve policy goals or, on the contrary, to oppose them (Saruis, 2013). Gofen (2014) focused on the 'choice set' underpinning the exercise of discretion: rationality, i.e. the rational calculus of costs/rewards (Brodkin, 2011), ethics (Hutchinson, 1990; Evans & Harris, 2004; Loyens & Maesschalck, 2010; Evans, 2013), professionalism (Haynes & Licata, 1995) and workers' motivations (May & Winter, 2009).

Another much debated issue is the outcome of discretion (Hill & Hupe, 2009), which is neither good nor bad in itself (Evans, 2013). Some underline its positive effect in balancing the demands of communities with the formal stated policy (Lipsky, 1980; Maynard-Moody & Musheno, 2000; 2003). On the other hand, critics underscore the possible negative consequences of discretion, especially when it is used for self-serving motives (Evans, 2013) rather than to be responsive to user/client needs (Brodkin, 2011). According to these different views, the discretionary power of street-level workers is something to be enhanced through their empowerment or something to be controlled and reduced (Denhardt & Denhardt, 2000; Evans & Harris, 2004).

An increasing number of studies focussed the attention on the relationship between discretion at street-level and reform processes of public services basically based on NPM values. In this regard, Taylor and Kelly (2006) differentiate among three elements of discretion: rule-making discretion, value discretion and task discretion. According to the authors, rule discretion – which in Lipsky's view was at the core of policy making – has been eroded in recent years as a consequence of NPM techniques. However, task discretion persists and has also increased because street-level bureaucrats 'are required to consider the implications of their tasks for targets, managers and customers' (Taylor & Kelly, 2006, p. 640).

Furthermore, in many sectors of welfare, the everyday work of street-level bureaucrats now entails actively involving service users and engaging with the community (Durose, 2011). Lipsky's conception has been thus revisited, suggesting that the new ideal type of the 'civic entrepreneur' (ibid.) or 'citizen agent' (Maynard-Moody & Musheno, 2000) will replace the traditional 'street-level-bureaucrat' (Durose, 2011).

Much of the research has concentrated on the sectors of social work (Baldwin, 1998; Evans & Harris, 2004; Evans, 2011; 2013) and welfare-to-work (Wright, 2003; Brodkin, 2011; Fuertes & Lindsay, 2015).

In particular, there are various recent sociological studies that pointed out the tension between the personalisation and tailoring of employment services – which are among the key features of recent activation policies in many economically-advanced countries – and NPM pressure to hit targets and minimise costs through more standardised services (Rees et al., 2014; Fuertes & Lindsay, 2015).

Similar reform processes have recently affected various parts of the Italian welfare system (and specifically employment services), however, *street-level* studies have not been yet developed in Italy (with few exceptions, Ferrazza, 2008; 2010; Barberis, 2010; Saruis, 2013). Our study starts to fill this gap focussing the attention, as already said, on two specific sectors: public housing and public employment services. Social housing in Italy has to date been mainly provided by the public sector and, specifically, by local authorities and former Autonomous Institutes for Public Housing (IACPs). A wide reorganisation process occurred in 2001 with the reform of Title V of the Constitution, when housing competences were devolved from the central State to the Regions (decentralisation). Former IACPs thus assumed a variety of organisational structures and legal status in each Italian Region: some remained non-economic public authorities; others became public utilities or were privatised. This reorganisation occurred in the wake of a huge process of residualisation of the housing stock as a consequence of recurring 'right to buy' schemes for sitting tenants and the impoverishment of the remaining ones.

Also, the reforms of public employment services have been based on decentralisation of functions, which was combined by de-monopolisation of employment services and transformation of the public agencies delivering such services. The main purpose of these changes has been to transform job placement into a system with new active labour-market policy functions designed to meet the needs of various user categories. New public employment services have been created, operating through 'new' public employment offices established by the provincial administrations. The main aim of this reform has been to increase the degree of responsibility of those directly involved. Consequently, activation, individualisation and responsibility have become the core principles on which reform of the job placement system has been structured.

With these reforms, the Italian public employment offices (PEOs) have assumed an important role in managing services, but the increase of tasks has not been matched by an increase in public funds.[2] Moreover, during the recent economic crisis, the Italian PEOs have been faced with new challenges concerning management of some provisional anti-crisis measures that have combined, for the first time in Italy, passive labour market policies (economic benefits) with active policies (training schemes and various employment services). Specifically, we refer to the so-called 'exceptional' wages guarantee fund (*cassa integrazione guadagni in deroga*, CIGD): to qualify for the CIGD benefit, the worker must accept various sets of services divided among basic and administrative services (*servizi minimi*), employment services (including tutoring, counselling and coaching) and training services (Berton et al., 2009).[3] PEOs are thus public offices where the organisational structure has been recently put under pressure. This is true especially in Italy where the introduction of activation policies is an innovative aspect (Heidenreich & Aurich-Beerheide, 2014).

More in general, in both cases a huge effort for the absorption of institutional changes and for mediation between contrasting goals seems to emerge, and this will be the subject of next paragraphs.

Public housing organisations between residualisation and social concern

The research on public housing organisations was conducted in the Marche Region where former provincial IACPs have been unified (Regional Laws 36/2005 and 22/2006) into the 'Regional Body for Public Housing – Marche' (henceforth ERAP Marche). This is an instrumental body of the Regional government, tightly regulated by regional rules and laws, whose main task is to provide and manage the public housing stock. Within the reorganisation of ERAP Marche, managerial principles have been emphasised, at least formally, as demonstrated by the adoption of the first Performance Plan (2014–16) that focussed on strategy, planning and evaluation. This is in line with one of the NPM milestones: accountability for results. However, interviewees confirmed that performance measures were complied only ritualistically (Kirkpatrick et al., 2005). Customer-oriented practices, such as the service chart, customer satisfaction and certification of quality, had also been adopted. As regards the rationalisation of expenses, some activities, such as prompt repairs, IT services, the sending of forms for the payment of rents, had been contracted out.

Our analysis focussed on one territorial unit of ERAP Marche and, specifically, within it, on the so-called Users' Sector. This participates in the local committees for housing allocation, sets the rents and collects them on the basis of the regional legislation, and takes all decisions concerning the tenants. In order to improve the service, a 'Public Relations Office' (henceforth PRO) in charge of the front-line relationship with users was set up in 2007. In this context, we observed many informal practices intended to streamline the processes in line with NPM principles. The line manager explained:

> Some workers, in the past, thought that if they let people wait, this was a way for their work to be considered worthy. Initially, the idea was that the ERAP shouldn't answer immediately, but now that we have new personnel we can have different strategies.
>
> (Marco, Line manager)

On the other hand, however, old bureaucratic aspects still persist: users cannot submit the various requests online; nor have the dealings with different administrations been simplified. Moreover, the 'business-like' mentality seems to derive from the previous autonomy of IACPs more than being a consequence of a 'managerial turn'. A direct economic relationship has always regulated, in fact, the interactions between ERAP officers and users, as a formal owner-tenant contract defines the 'expected standards and behaviour'

(Kirkpatrick et al. 2005, p. 128). This can explain why in this sector the staff are 'more comfortable with the discourse of managerialism and consumerism' (ibid., p. 150) than in other areas of welfare. As explained:

> We have an 'education' that stems from when we were IACP, we were an autonomous Institution, and we had to think about management of the dwellings on the basis of the rents we collected; we had to repair the roofs with those rents... The concern about how the money could be better spent is something that we have in our DNA.
> (Franco, PRO)

However, as we shall see, staff loyalties, values and orientations were far from being closely aligned with business logic. In many circumstances, they showed partisanship on the part of tenants, legitimating their actions with affective, value-based claims (Newman, 2005):

> For me, doing my work means doing an activity that is useful for people and solving and satisfying their needs within the institutional constraints.
> (Sabrina, PRO)

These features make this sector an interesting case study for observing how NPM, on the one hand, and the challenges in the relationship with users, on the other hand, are reflected in everyday practices of front-line workers.

Working at the street-level: human touch and proactive behaviour

During the period of our research,[4] the Users' Sector consisted of nine employees overall, strongly affected by the following conditions envisaged by Lipsky (1980). First, the manpower/client ratio was very low, as the renters numbered more than 6,000 and in many situations officers found it difficult to collect relevant information in order to make informed decisions. Second, they sometimes worked under the threat of both physical and verbal abuse, especially when dealing with problematic users or trouble makers. Finally, role expectations were often ambiguous as public housing has been allocated to two jurisdictions: that of Local Authorities and that of ERAP. The latter should be in charge exclusively of managing the dwellings and of the relationships with tenants, while the Social Service, within each Local Authority, should attend to 'social issues'. However, the work of Users' Sector officers was often influenced by social concern for their tenants' situations. Moreover, they were increasingly experiencing the 'conflicting and ambiguous role expectations stemming from divided community sentiments' (Lipsky, 1980, p. 8), such as the trade-off between equity and reverse discrimination, or between impartiality and personalised, individualised consideration.

The tension between social concern and managerial issues has amplified in recent years. Increasing numbers of tenants in arrears, with insufficient rents collected to cover maintenance costs, generated problems of financial sustainability. This economic concern widely affected Users' Sector officers during our observation. They expressed a lingering worry, for example, about empty or under-utilised dwellings. Moreover, the trade-off between the institutional mission, i.e. housing the less well-off, and housing those who can afford the expenses has become more evident. In a respondent's view:

> it is morally disgusting, but we wouldn't survive without these tenants.
> (Marco, Line manager)

Given these surrounding conditions and contradictory imperatives, day-to-day practices are often at odds with formal role expectations. We will briefly mention the main ones, before dealing with the issue of discretionary power.

According to Kirkpatrick et al. (2005, p. 133) 'housing management is a techno-bureaucratic profession [...] the primary claim of expertise being the administrative skill or the ability to run things'. However, relational skills are becoming more and more necessary as many tenants do not raise only technical issues and are often 'welfare dependent'. For some of them, indeed, going to the PRO was a sort of weekly or monthly routine – so much so that they were dubbed 'habitués', 'regulars', 'most affectionate users' or even 'fans'. Officers encouraged a kind of personal relation and usually caught up with the habitués. However, even in the case of first-time users, the care for a personalised relationship could be noted also in small details. Furthermore, irony and quips were other frequent ingredients in the operator/user relationship. This 'human-touch' working style could respond to 'consumer orientation', in line with NPM; or, alternatively, it could be a compensatory strategy for helplessness and a way to experience a satisfactory relationship. Officers complained, indeed, that they were in an awkward position, caught between (more) demanding citizens and powerlessness. As an interviewee explained:

> My task is the first step of a procedure that, I know, will not necessarily lead to achievement of the goal. We mediate users' demands. It may be uncomfortable, but we understand both sides of the coin. We stand on both sides and sometime we compensate some shortcoming with words. It is almost a psychological work.
> (Sabrina, PRO officer)

This calls for more research on the pressures that the balancing of NPM and public service ethos puts on civil servants. Moreover, the fieldwork frequently highlighted a process of 'categorisation' of users and requests that meant distinguishing whether or not they deserved help. Deserving users were basically those who complied with the expected behaviour:

> When I see that they do their best then I also try to meet their needs. [...] We see if someone deserves help... This is also based on our experience. When a tenant creates difficulties these difficulties come back to us.
> (Franco, PRO officer)

This discourse was a way to rationalise problematic practices (Brodkin, 2012), perfectly in line with NPM logic. For instance, we followed a telephone call between an officer and a social worker: they were discussing the case of a tenant in arrears who did not provide the Equivalent Economic Situation Indicator (ISEE), and therefore had to pay a higher rent. In this case the officer, irritated, commented:

> If one wants to be considered worthy of help, he should deserve it.
> (Marco, Line manager)

On the other hand, officers showed responsiveness to deserving users' needs through 'proactive behaviour' beyond the sphere of competence and the 'silo mentality'. An example was provided by an officer working in close relation with Social Services to solve the situation of some tenants in arrears through work experience grants or applying for the national fund for involuntary arrears. Moreover, they often gave unrequested advice, such as suggesting to inquire about the deductions provided for tenants or the granting of a subsidy for certain refurbishment expenses. Again, according to interviewees, this proactive behaviour was not a positive effect of NPM but it stemmed, rather, from the history and the culture of this specific organisation. Moreover, giving advice sometimes turned into a paternalistic behaviour, when it was a means to encourage users' responsibilisation and compliance.

Shifting discretionary power

Both PRO officers and the other personnel of the Users' Sector defined their work as characterised by certain 'discretion'. Interpretative work was also considered inevitable, according to some statements that we heard many times during the fieldwork (for example, "the law is made by people who don't know how things work" and "laws shouldn't be written in a way that can be interpreted"). As regards allocation, each Local Authority issues its own rules for eligibility, in accordance with the regional law but with some leeway in the criteria. ERAP Users' Sector officers participated, together with Local Authorities' staff, in the local committees for housing allocation. These committees should merely have to verify the formal correctness of the applications, and to rank the applicants according to the rules. However, they admitted that there was room for some degree of discretion because:

> Half a point in the scoring may mean getting the house.
> (Marco, Line manager)

They also provided examples of how they built in restrictions on eligibility:

> There is a variety of possible behaviours, for example, before granting the score to those applicants who received the 'notice to quit' from a private owner. Similarly, some committees have decided that no-income applicants should prove they have received institutional subsidies, in order to obtain the maximum score, a measure intended to exclude those who live with the revenue from illegal activities.
> (Franco, PRO)

Whereas discretion in allocation was rather limited, ERAP officers had greater discretionary power when sitting tenants needed to move to another dwelling – because of new family members, bad quality of the dwelling, health needs, etc. They might help some applicants to 'climb' the special list for mobility drawn up on the basis of internally established criteria of priority (e.g. accrediting the score envisaged in the case of condominium contentiousness, regardless a formal charge). Sometimes officers helped users by rapidly skimming the list in order to show them a possible match with someone who wanted to swap, or facilitate it, mediating the relationship. In particular circumstances, *mobility ex officio* could also be disposed. This was intended to eliminate conditions of under-utilisation, for renovations, for sale to third parties or for other serious reasons. However, it was little used because it might mean disappointing those unwilling tenants who had been living in the dwelling for a long time. The line manager explicitly admitted that he preferred not to take on the responsibility of an unpopular, albeit fair measure. In so doing, he avoided exercising a broad area of discretionary power that would have solved many problems, as in the case of insolvent tenants under-occupying the dwelling.

However, officers appealed to it in particular circumstances as in the case of a young tenant with mental health problems who, after the death of his mother, continued living in their big house, having to pay high rents. The officer knew that there was a smaller empty dwelling in the same building that would have be suitable for him. However, with the 'standard procedure' of mobility, he could not ensure that the man would have remained in the same area. Moreover, the smaller dwelling had already gone through the maintenance that should not be provided for in the case of mobility. Nevertheless, he made an exception, suggesting to the psychiatric and social services that they should emphasise the need for an urgent change because of the man's emotional distress, specifying that it would have been better for him to remain in the neighbourhood he already knew. This story, like similar ones, was recounted as an example of a heroic effort 'to bend the rules in responding to the needs of selected individuals' (Brodkin, 2012, p. 4).

Another area of discretionary power that has been limited is that of tenancies. The Regional government defines the rules for setting rents. Users no longer present their documentation on income to ERAP. They have to go to the Centre for Fiscal Assistance (CAF), which calculates the ISEE and provides it to ERAP through data transmission. If the ISEE is not sent on time, tenants are automatically placed in a higher income bracket than the year before, having to pay higher rents. However, if they provide the ISEE to ERAP, though late, they can obtain the recalculation of rents. Here discretion continues to play a role. In fact, in these cases, the person in charge of rent setting immediately re-calculates the correct (and usually lower) rent and usually applies it to the current month (and sometimes even to previous ones), although, according to the rules, it should become effective from the following one.

Both self-serving and other-serving motivations contribute to this practice. On the one hand, the officer pointed out that recalculating the rents immediately was a 'time management strategy' (Brodkin, 2011) to speed up completion of paperwork. On the other hand, this was done in order to meet tenants' needs, regardless of the lower revenue for the organisation. This behaviour can be considered a form of resistance to a regulation that ascribes to tenants the responsibility to present their documentation on time, thus penalising 'those that are least well equipped to navigate the barriers of bureaucratic red tape and confusing or complex agency process' (Brodkin, 2012, p. 6). Given the increasing number of tenants in arrears, being rigid when it comes to applying the legislation regarding evictions is also becoming more and more difficult. We observed that the officers tended to give time to recover from economic hardship, accepting payments with very low instalments, and sometimes not intervening if tenants failed to pay one instalment. Again, this responds to both the interest of tenants and that of the organisation, for which it is better to recover immediately, even if gradually, part of the credit, than to start the long procedure for eviction.

Another area of discretional power concerned the requests for the enlargement of the household, which might be refused, among other reasons, in case of overcrowding. In these circumstances ERAP officers do the policy together with social workers of Local Authorities, echoing the notion of multi-layered discretion (Newman, 2005; Evans, 2011). We observed two opposite situations. In the first case, a social worker called asking the officer what was the size of the house required for a (foreign) family with 11 members. They discussed the regulation, and then ERAP officer asked: "What do you want us to do? I should bend the rules anyway because the size of the house is not sufficient. I'll follow your line". Then he wrote: "The Local Authority disagrees. Reject the request". In the other case, in order to please the social worker, the very same officer agreed for a new submission regardless having already denied the request. The day-to-day management of discretion entailed reflexivity on one's own work. During the shadowing the officers often asked "What could/should I do in such a case?" and all of them confessed that sometimes they were wondering if their actions were adequate or not. This is not exempt from psychological costs. During the 'backtalk', an officer complained about the difficulty of his job because of role conflicts deriving from discretion:

> I'm in a *limbo*, as I can and I can't decide, I can decide but I shouldn't. If I was the chief I could make some choices, taking the responsibility. But there is the top-down pressure; the higher levels want us to perform better some tasks, for example evictions. Our chief has been reprimanded for this issue. But I can't do it, I feel shattered. Even if you have 20,000 euros in arrears and you are a crook I can't do it light-heartedly, although I understand that we have to do something... I'm thinking to go to a psychologist for this dissatisfaction...We are caught in the middle.
> (Gianluca, Users' Sector Officer)

The previous excerpt shows the risk of a high-demand low-control situation that can lead to work strain. As argued by Lipsky (2010), in order to handle these overburdening situations, street-level practitioners elaborate coping strategies like routinising and standardising. This was evidenced when the very same person, while speaking with a depressed woman, who had just told him of her deceased husband and imprisoned son, interrupted her many times to answer the phone, never comforting her nor addressing a supportive gaze.

New principles of activation and old daily practices in the public employment offices

Lombardy is one of the regions that most rapidly implemented the reforms of the job placement system (Colombo, 2008). It is characterised by a system of employment services that combines public and private agencies, conforming to the principles of quasi-market and horizontal subsidiarity (Trivellato et al., 2015). The regional administration has established general rules, defined employment services and identified the cost band of each service. It has also adopted flexible financial devices – termed 'endowments' (*doti* in Italian) – covering the cost of the active policy, on the one hand, and supplementing income support, on the other hand (Di Lieto & Rizza, 2010). In this regional system, the anti-crisis measure for unemployed workers (the so-called *cassa integrazione guadagni in deroga*, CIGD) was flanked by a specific endowment scheme (*dote ammortizzatori sociali*, DAS) introduced by the Region in July 2009. It is a measure that, following activation policies already implemented in other European countries, aims at influencing individual actions by connecting social rights to conditions: rights and benefits begin if obligations are fulfilled, and the recipients are obliged to participate in work activities (Jessen & Tufte, 2014).[5]

In all the PEOs studied[6] it was usual to hear various references to some of the main principles that characterised the NPM and the modern activation policies. In particular, various front-line officers highlighted that the proactive role of unemployed workers is crucial. Moreover, they often repeated that the main role of PEOs is to support them in the activation process. For instance, Mino – front-line officer at the Milan PEO – explained:

> PEO rarely provides brokerage services at work, but the user has actively to seek a new job. When I have completed all the paperwork to give to the user the official status of unemployed I automatically register the user's name in the database of the Regional Job Exchange. But being in this database does not mean that an employer will contact the user. Nor will we contact him or her.
>
> (Mino, front-line officer, PEO of Milan)

Usually front-line officers suggested that unemployed people should explore the orientation areas of PEOs, which had been recently renovated in the employment offices that we studied. These are the areas in which we observed the first difficulties in translating into practices some principles that make up the active labour policies. Indeed, during the fieldwork we met many disoriented users in these areas. In many cases, they were disadvantaged workers, in terms of age (over 50), skills and levels of education. Front-line officers confirmed that the most common profile of workers that they met were low-educated, low-skilled and over 40–50 years old. For many of them even basic actions, such as consulting job offers on specialised websites or submitting their application online, may be difficult to accomplish autonomously. For this reason, in some PEOs, operators set up appointments with users to provide them with customised assistance. But, according to the front-line officers, they were not able to meet the needs of all users because their number had increased considerably in recent years while the number of operators had not grown accordingly.

In the PEOs studied, principles and practices that seemed to be strictly linked to modern activation policies cohabited with practices that were instead typical of the 'old' public employment office. One of the aspects that recalls older models of public job placement is the composition of users who, depending on the days and hours of the day, crowded the PEOs. During the days spent in the waiting rooms of the PEOs, we met various 'regulars' or 'habitués', that is, people who attended PEOs with a certain frequency and, for various reasons (age, insufficient skills, long previous spells of unemployment), had little chance of finding a job. It was not uncommon for some PEO waiting rooms to become meeting places for certain users. Once they reached the counter, the talk with the officer often ended in a few minutes. Nevertheless, presenting himself or herself at the PEO counter assumed for this type of user the features of a ritual that they performed almost weekly. Perhaps for these people, the PEOs were still important places not so much for what happened at the counter, but rather for hours that they spent in the waiting rooms. These moments were spent in a very crowded room where the 'regulars' could talk with other people who, in some respects, were experiencing similar difficulties and establishing human contacts (Ambrosini et al., 2014).

Moreover, notwithstanding some important changes, the Italian public employment offices seem to still maintain certain features that for many years have made them perceived more as places for obtaining economic relief than for finding a job. This perception still seems alive, as various statements made by the users confirmed:

> The time I spend here is wasted time. I need the statement to have the health ticket exemption, but to look for work I have to contact others.
> (Miranda, unemployed, Brazilian)

> My experience tells me that here they only offer low-level jobs, jobs only for a specific kind of workers. I have been enrolled at the employment centre since 2003 and they have never called me for a job. Private employment agencies are more efficient.
> (Sandra, unemployed, Italian)

The PEOs studied seemed still to perform two functions jointly: the bureaucratic one of performing the paperwork certifying the status of unemployed and, at the same time, the function of service provider for work reintegration. With regard to the latter point, the fieldwork showed that the attitudes of front-line officers could be important, influencing the 'first steps' that users usually do in the PEOs. We noted that, especially when the waiting room was not overly crowded, many front-line officers showed a particular propensity to listen to users, even when conversation moved from work experiences to various life fragments in which the work experiences were mixed with personal and social aspects in a tangle that often seemed inextricable. In particular, we observed that, in various cases, PEO front-line officers (at least the more 'willing' of them) used some of their working time to find information not strictly related to job search, answering to the multiple needs expressed by the users who daily have to cope with the fragmentation of the services network that characterises the Italian welfare system (Catalano et al., 2016). This attitude seemed to be more important during the economic crisis since many front-line officers reported an increase in people who, besides being jobless, suffered from multiple hardships (tangible and intangible), which often involved the entire household (with an increasing anger and distress related to their situation).

In this regard, we observed particularly effective operator/user actions and relations at the foreign offices of various PEOs. In particular, at the PEO of Cinisello Balsamo, the not-Italian native operator's relational ability proved crucial both for understanding the needs expressed by the users and for helping them. He habitually assumed pro-user attitudes, trying to put the person at his/her ease, overcoming language barriers, which in many cases complicated the communication. Some practices adopted by the operator as well as his ability to build informal networks with other front-line officers working in other public services (for instance, in the welfare services area of the municipality) often made it possible to provide concrete answers to each case, however difficult.

In the same contexts, we also observed tensions between, on the one hand, the personalisation and tailored services that are among the key features of the recent activation policies, and on the other hand, the users' needs: indeed, the number of users has considerably increased since 2009, while the number of PEO front-line officers has remained almost constant. In particular, we noted certain practices that seemed similar to the strategies of standardisation and triaging of clients outlined in Brodkin's (2011) and Wright's (2003) studies. But in our case, forms of 'routine discretion' (Brodkin, 2011) seemed to be basically caused by organisational constraints (i.e. limited resources) instead of NPM pressures to hit targets and minimise costs through more standardised services. This was the case, for instance, of the registration procedures at the PEOs. In general, the registration procedures, and the consequent change from being unemployed to a PEO user, was an important occasion that might steer the subsequent activation process in different directions. Basically, the fieldwork showed that these first steps of activation could partially influence the number of services used. As provided by the law, the take-up procedure should consist of two meetings. These are considered essential for establishing the user's work availability and to check his/her state of unemployment. However, the observations made at the PEOs revealed that these protocols could be followed in considerably different ways and times. Indeed, some PEOs condensed the two meeting into one in order to reduce the waiting time; others replaced the second meeting with collective meetings. In this way, in many cases the waiting time was reduced (it is an important factor with the growth of the number of users) by sacrificing, at least in part, a more detailed collection of the initial information concerning the users.

The use of discretion under top-down and bottom-up pressures

During the empirical research we specifically focussed the attention on the operators/users relations needed to access both the basic services provided by PEOs and the more articulated services provided by the anti-crisis measure that combines passive and active labour policies: the 'exceptional' wages guarantee fund integrated with the specific endowment scheme (*cassa integrazione in deroga*, CIGD + *dote ammortizzatori sociali*, DAS).

In various cases, we observed that front-line officers offered forms of support to the users, which assumed features similar to psychological and relational support. For many front-line officers, these kinds of support given to users were perceived as a sort of compensation, albeit partial, for the fact that PEOs do not guarantee a high probability of re-employment. But, at the same time, the relational support was considered an important preliminary stage in activation of the unemployed person. In particular, counselling was useful for the mental assimilation of job loss. This particular form of support seemed to help those who had lost their jobs to deal with the 'loss' of subjective wellbeing connected with the experience of unemployment (Jahoda, 1982). This was most evident in the support and activation of users who benefitted from the CIGD + DAS scheme. In this case, it was possible to observe more clearly how mutual trust arose between the worker and the tutor (the PEO front-line officer handling the worker receiving the DAS). Technical support (provided through interviews with different purposes, and services like skills assessment and tutoring) interwove with psychological and relational forms of support, albeit supplied by people without specific skills in those fields. The latter is a critical point that various PEOs operators highlighted:

> We are not sufficiently trained to deal with those people who feel themselves very down. It is a feeling of impotence, more because of my need to provide psychological and emotional support, as well as services to work. People experience great despair and are difficult to handle. It would require psychology courses for us, the operators, to learn how to handle these situations.
> (Milena, receptionist and front-line officer, PEO of Cinisello Balsamo)

The pro-user attitude manifested by most PEOs operators was far from the stereotyped (and negative) image of the public employee. Moreover, the front-line officers that we met distinguished their work from the work of the employee of private employment agencies. The latter was in fact represented as a worker whose main task was to find, as soon as possible, a number of candidates for specific job profiles, indicated by their clients, that are mainly private firms. Some PEOs' operators stated in this regard:

> We meet lost people, who are ashamed to say that they have lost their jobs and need help. We cannot overlook them by looking at some employment solutions that we may not even have. I think our job is to listen first. I've found 50-year-old people who at a certain point of the conversation have started crying: how can I not give a little time to these people?.
> (Sveva, front-line officers, PEO of Lecco)

We collected various similar statements from operators working in different economic, social and organisational contexts. At the individual level, they also had distinct educational levels and professional experiences. Amid this diversity, however, these workers shared two features: they were between the ages of 28 and 35 and their employment relationship was regulated by fixed-term contracts. In fact, the reorganisation of the PEOs had led to a decrease in the average age of the staff employed. Younger workers, employed by public administrations with temporary employment contracts, had been allocated to front-office functions and the most innovative service management. Most of the PEOs' front-line officers and users seemed thus to have created a certain proximity, given the uncertainty about the future of work that, although with different shapes and intensities, was common to those who go to the PEOs to look for employment and who work in the same PEOs. At the same time, however, the use of staff with the prevalence of fixed-term contracts, aimed at covering roles that seemed crucial in order to increase the chances of providing effective services, has highlighted the presence of some major contradictions in the Italian PEOs: if, on the one hand, attempts were made to give a more modern structure, function and image to PEOs – mainly through the delivery of a broader range of services aimed at activating unemployed workers – on the other hand, these attempts seemed to clash with a shortage of resources (especially in terms of workforce) that limit their full implementation.

The fieldwork also showed other difficulties, specifically in the actions aimed at offering training courses that matched the needs of workers. These problems were often due to limited time available to organise personalised employment services and training plans or to match the user's training needs with the offer of training courses available in the period covered by the economic support provided by the 'exceptional' wages guarantee fund (CIGD). Consequently, the personalised action plans (*piani d'intervento personalizzato*, PIP) often included generic training courses that are not relevant to the employment needs of the beneficiaries. In this case, the personalisation promoted by the programmes thus seemed to be more procedural than substantive, as already Sabatinelli and Villa (2015) showed for the *dote* system as a whole.

Concluding remarks

Both case studies show the persistence of old logics combined with the new one. We saw an increasing importance of relational aspects due to both push and pull mechanisms. Not only can they reflect the embeddedness of managerial principles of 'customer care' or a preliminary step in the effective implementation of personalised welfare policies. But they can also be a defensive or compensatory mechanism in response to pressure from below. Moreover, in both cases front-line workers admitted they sometimes felt as if they were 'social workers'. Given the segmentation that characterises the Italian welfare services, it is not surprising that users try to express all their different needs beyond the specific service they are addressing. For this reason much of the work time of front-line officers in both services was spent listening to personal situations and requests that frequently they could not handle. Our empirical studies have thus highlighted a clear need of 'acceptance' expressed by the users, to which front-line officers try to answer especially using their soft skills. It remains unclear whether these 'acceptance' actions should be more interpreted as actions that offset the poor effectiveness of public services or as 'preparatory' actions for the implementation of personalised interventions. Further researches are needed on this issue.

As concerns the transformational process of welfare state organisations, in both cases we observed an anomalous process of 'managerialisation'. Much of the mainstream literature tends to describe the consequence of NPM in terms of homogenising forces over occupational and professional identities, thus underestimating the differences. As a matter of fact, NPM-influenced changes have not so far produced a radical shift in institutional and organisational practices, but rather an evolutionary, adaptive process. According to Skålén (2004, p. 251) 'NPM creates heterogeneous, conflicting and fluid organisational identities rather than the uniform and stable business identity it is supposed to'. It is thus important to consider both the organisational level and the institutional and societal level.

Moreover, some scholars underline the path dependencies within the administrative tradition of each country, questioning the revolutionary nature of occurring changes (Pollitt, 2000; Gruening, 2001; Lynn, 2001). The extent to which NPM principles have been disseminated or translated may vary not only among each national context but also among various services. In this perspective, the comparison of multiple cases belonging to different fields of public administration is intended to not gloss over specificities (Page, 2005). Future research should investigate whether this is a question of time, basically because the Italian welfare state is still in a phase of transition, or whether it is the consequence of 'cultural heritage', occupational and professional logics and the specific characteristics of the welfare system.

Similarly, in both case studies we are far from seeing an actual transition to the new logic of public governance or network governance. However, we observed emerging 'creative spaces' where bureaucratic boundaries are blurring, which are used by front-line workers who 'exploit emergent ambiguities in the rules of the game in order to respond to changing environments' (Lowndes, 2005 cited in Durose, 2011). This seems particularly fitting with ERAP case where front-line officers present themselves as 'citizen agent' (Maynard-Moody & Musheno, 2000), whose work is defined by the relationship with users and who have to act in a pragmatic way.

Notes

1 This chapter is the result of joint work. You can still attribute to both authors paragraphs 1, 2 and 5, Micol Bronzini is more responsible for paragraph 3, while Diego Coletto on 4.
2 In recent years, Italy is one of the European countries that invested least in PEOs: according to a recent study by ISFOL (2014) Italy has invested 0.03% of GDP in the PEOs, compared to EU average of 0.25%. Italy also ranks low in terms of persons employed at public employment offices: in fact, they amount to around 9,000, as opposed to 11,000 Spain, 115,000 Germany, and 49,000 in France.
3 The most recent labour market reform (the so-called Jobs Act) has further changed the patterns of active labour policies, introducing a structural measure that combines economic support with employment services and training courses. The first tests of the new measure started in the first months of 2017.
4 The shadowing involved front-line practitioners of the Users' Sector and their supervisor (line manager) who had almost daily interactions with users as well. We shadowed front-line workers for 18 opening days, and the line manager for one week. The fieldwork took place between February and May 2016.
5 The endowment system described in the text has been further modified and simplified by the Lombardy region with the introduction in 2015 of the so-called 'dote unica lavoro' (DUL), which provides various employment and training services for unemployed workers. This new endowment scheme is based on the same principles of quasi-market and horizontal subsidiarity model of the previous schemes.
6 This part of chapter refers to a study on the unemployment and the economic crisis in Lombardy, of which the main findings have been published in Ambrosini et al. (2014). The fieldwork was conducted at the PEOs of Cinisello Balsamo, Lecco, Milano and Varese. In these places covert observations were combined with overt observations of the everyday work of job centre staff. The attention focused on the registration and so-called 'uptake' of users by the PEO, employment services, and actions related to the management of two endowments schemes, the dote lavoro (DL) and the dote ammortizzatori sociali (DAS). Moreover, semi-structured and structured interviews were conducted with the managers of the job centres. Overall, the fieldwork took place in the period between November 2009 and November 2010: around ninety days were devoted to the observations and interviews.

References

Ambrosini, M., Coletto, D., Guglielmi, S. (2014): *Perdere e ritrovare il lavoro*. Bologna: Il Mulino.
Bach, S., Bordogna, L. (2017): *Public Service Management and Employment Relations in Europe. Emerging from the Crisis*. London: Routledge.
Baldwin, M. (1998): 'The Positive Use of Discretion in Social Work Practice: Developing Practice through Co-operative Inquiry', *Issues in Social Work Education*, 18: 42–48.
Barberis, E. (2010): 'Il ruolo degli operatori sociali dell'immigrazione nel welfare locale', *Autonomie locali e servizi sociali*, XXX(1): 45–60.
Berton, F., Richiardi, M., Sacchi, S. (2009): *Flex-insecurity*. Bologna: Il mulino.
Brodkin, E. (2011): 'Policy Work: Street-Level Organizations Under New Managerialism', *Journal of Public Administration Research and Theory*, 21(Supplement 2): 253–277.

Brodkin, E. (2012): 'Reflections on Street-Level Bureaucracy: Past, Present, and Future', *Public Administration Review*, 72(6): 940–949.
Catalano, S.L., Graziano, P.R., Bassoli, M. (2016): 'The Local Governance of Social Inclusion Policies in Italy: Working via Organ Pipes', in: Heidenreich, M., Rice, D. (eds.), Integrating Social and Employment Policies in Europe, 118–138, Cheltenham: Edward Edgar Publishing.
Colombo, A. (2008): 'The "Lombardy Model": Subsidiarity-informed Regional Governance', *Social Policy & Administration*, 42(2): 177–196.
Denhardt, R. B., Denhardt, J.V. (2000): 'The New Public Service: Serving Rather than Steering', *Public Administration Review*, 60(6): 549–559.
Di Lieto, G., Rizza, R. (2010): 'Ammortizzatori sociali in deroga: quali welfare regionali?', *Rivista delle politiche sociali*, 4: 283–305.
Diefenbach, T. (2009): 'New Public Management in Public Sector Organizations: The Dark Sides of Managerialistic "Enlightenment"', *Public Administration*, 87(4): 892–909.
Durose, C. (2011): 'Revisiting Lipsky: Front-Line Work in UK Local Governance', *Political Studies*, 59(4): 978–995.
Evans, T. (2011): 'Professionals, Managers and Discretion: Critiquing Street-Level Bureaucracy', British Journal of Social Work, 41(2): 368–386.
Evans, T. (2013): The moral economy of street-level service, paper presented at IPSA (RC 32) 2013 Conference, Dubrovnik, Croatia.
Evans, T., Harris, J. (2004): 'Street-level Bureaucracy, Social Work and the (Exaggerated) Death of Discretion', *British Journal of Social Work*, 34(6): 871–895.
Ferrazza, D. (2008): *Tra ente pubblico e terzo settore: analisi dei rapporti tra diversi attori del welfare mix attraverso la lente della discrezionalità degli operatori*, paper presented at 1st Annual Conference Espanet Italia 2008, Ancona.
Ferrazza, D. (2010): 'Street Level Evaluation: un approccio innovativo allo studio delle politiche sociali', *Rivista Trimestrale di Scienza dell'Amministrazione*, 1: 75–95.
Fuertes, V., Lindsay, C. (2015): 'Personalization and Street-Level Practice in Activation: The Case of the UK's Work Programme', *Public Administration*, 94(2): 526–541.
Gofen, A. (2014): 'Mind the Gap: Dimensions and Influence of Street-Level Divergence', *Journal of Public Administration Research and Theory*, 24(2): 473–493.
Gruening, G. (2001): 'Origin and Theoretical Basis of New Public Management', *International Public Management Journal*, 4(1): 1–25.
Haque, M.S. (1999): 'Ethical Tension in Public Governance: Critical Impacts on Theory-Building', *Administrative Theory & Praxis*, 21(4): 468–473.
Hasenfeld, Y. (1972): 'People Processing Organizations: An Exchange Approach', *American Sociological Review*, 37(3): 256–263.
Haynes, E. A., Licata, J.W. (1995): 'Creative Insubordination of School Principals and the Legitimacy of the Justifiable', *Journal of Educational Administration*, 33(4): 21–35.
Heidenreich, M., Aurich-Beerheide, P. (2014): 'European Worlds of Inclusive Activation: The Organisational Challenges of Coordinated Service Provision', *International Journal of Social Welfare*, 23(1): 6–22.
Hill, M., Hupe, P. (2009): Implementing Public Policy, 2nd ed., Thousand Oaks, CA: Sage.
Hutchinson, S.A. (1990): 'Responsible Subversion: A Study of Rule-Bending Among Nurses', *Research and Theory for Nursing Practice*, 4(1): 3–17.
ISFOL (2014): *Lo stato dei Servizi pubblici per l'impiego in Europa: tendenze, conferme e sorprese*, Occasional paper no. 13.

Jahoda, M. (1982): *Employment and Unemployment: A Social-Psychological Analysis*, Cambridge: Cambridge University Press.

Jessen, J., Tufte, P. (2014): 'Discretionary Decision-Making in a Changing Context of Activation Policies and Welfare Reforms', *Journal of Social Policy*, 43(2): 269–288.

Jørgensen, T.B. (1999): 'The Public Sector in a In-Between Time: Searching for New Public Values', *Public Administration*, 77(3): 565–584.

Kirkpatrick, I. (1999): 'The Worst of Hoth Worlds? Public Services without Markets or Bureaucracy', *Public Money and Management*, 19(4): 9–14.

Kirkpatrick, I., Ackroyd, S., Walker, R. (2005): *The New Managerialism and Public Service Professions. Change in Health, Social Services and Housing*, New York: Palgrave Macmillan.

Lipsky, M. (1980): *Street-level Bureaucracy*, New York: Russell Sage Foundation.

Lipsky, M. (2010): *Street-level Bureaucracy: Dilemmas of the Individual in Public Services*, New York: Russell Sage Foundation.

Lowndes, V. (2005): 'Something Old, Something New, Something Borrowed… How Institutions Change (and Stay the Same) in Local Governance', *Policy Studies*, 26(3/4): 291–309.

Loyens, K., Maesschalck, J. (2010): 'Toward a Theoretical Framework for Ethical Decision Making of Street-Level Bureaucracy: Existing Models Reconsidered', *Administration & Society*, 42(1): 66–100.

Lynn, L. (2001): 'The Myth of the Bureaucratic Paradigm: What Traditional Public Administration Really Stood For', *Public Administration Review*, 61(2): 144–160.

May, P., Winter, S. (2009): 'Politicians, Managers, and Street-Level Bureaucrats: Influences on Policy Implementation', *Journal of Public Administration Research and Theory*, 19(3): 453–476.

Maynard-Moody, S., Musheno, M. (2000): 'State Agent or Citizen Agent: Two Narratives of Discretion', *Journal of Public Administration Research and Theory*, 10(2): 329–358.

Maynard-Moody, S., Musheno, M. (2003): Cops, *Teachers*, Counselors: Stories from the Front Lines of Public Service, Ann Arbor: University of Michigan Press.

Newman, J. (2005): 'Bending Bureaucracy: Leadership and Multi-Level Governance', in: Du Gay, P. (ed.), *The Values of Bureaucracy*, 191–210, Oxford: Oxford University Press.

Page, S. (2005): 'What's New about the New Public Management? Administrative Change in the Human Services', *Public Administration Review*, 65(6): 713–727.

Pollitt, C. (2000): 'Is the Emperor In His Underwear?', *Public Management: An International Journal of Research and Theory*, 2(2): 181–200.

Rees, J., Whitworth, A., Carter, E. (2014): 'Support for All in the UK Work Programme? Differential Payments, Same Old Problem', *Social Policy & Administration*, 48(2): 221–239.

Sabatinelli, S., Villa, M. (2015): 'Happy Ever After in the Quasi-market Place? The Dowry Logic of Active Labour Policy in the Lombardy Region', *International Journal of Sociology and Social Policy*, 35(11/12): 812–827.

Saruis, T. (2013): 'La teoria della Street Level Bureaucracy: lo stato del dibattito', *Autonomie locali e servizi sociali*, 3: 541–551.

Skålén, P. (2004): 'New Public Management Reform and the Construction of Organizational Identities', *International Journal of Public Sector Management*, 17(3): 251–263.

Stake, R.E. (1995): *The Art of Case Study Research*, London: Sage Publications.

Taylor, I., Kelly, J. (2006): 'Professionals, Discretion and Public Sector Reform in the UK: Re-visiting Lipsky', *International Journal of Public Sector Management*, 19(7): 629–642.

Thomas, G. (2011): 'A Typology for the Case Study in Social Science Following a Review of Definition, Discourse, and Structure', *Qualitative Inquiry*, 17(6): 511–521.

Trivellato, B., Bassoli, M., Catalano, S. (2015): 'Can Quasi-market and Multi-level Governance Co-exist? Insights from the Case of Lombardy's Employment Services System', *Social Policy & Administration*, 51(5): 697–718.

Van Berkel, R., Van Der Aa, P. (2012): 'Activation Work: Policy Programme Administration or Professional Service Provision?', *Journal of Social Policy*, 41(3): 493–510.

Wright, S. (2003): 'The Street-level Implementation of Unemployment Policy', in: Millar, J. (ed.), *Understanding Social Security: Issues for Policy and Practice*, 235–253, Bristol: The Policy Press.

Yin, R. K. (1994): *Case Study Research: Design and Methods*, 2nd ed., Newbury Park, CA: Sage Publications.

Chapter 11

New managerialism as an organisational form of neoliberalism

Kathleen Lynch and Bernie Grummell

This chapter demonstrates why new managerialism is not a neutral management strategy but rather a political project, borne out of a radical change in the spirit of neoliberal capitalism (Boltanski & Chiapello, 2005). It shows how it operates as an ideological configuration of ideas and practices that is instituting new orthodoxies in the running of public education in Ireland, aligning it more closely with the organisational logic and practices of the private market system.

Although united by its ideological re-configuration towards market-place logic, managerialism is realized differently across countries; it is shaped by the historical antecedents and the specifics of nation-state politics. Drawing on three empirical studies[1] undertaken by the authors on the impact of managerialism across primary, secondary, further and higher education (Grummell, 2014; Lynch, Grummell & Devine, 2015; Lolich & Lynch, 2016) the chapter explores the cultural and political specifics of managerialism across the education sectors in Ireland. It also explores the resistance to market norms, the counter-hegemonic actions of educational mediators within the machinery of the state and across the community (Lynch, 1990; Fitzsimons, 2017a).

Globalisation, trade and marketing public services

To understand the role of new managerialism in reframing education policy and practice, it is important to locate it in the wider political economy of neoliberal capitalism. Neoliberalism is governed by the principle of the small cheap state, where welfare is a personal responsibility and the state operates as a regulatory body in the market system (Harvey, 2005, pp. 70–81). The role of the state is to facilitate the development of markets for entrepreneurial entities and citizens. As neoliberalism is at once an ideology and a form of politics and set of practices (Peck, 2010), the commercialisation of what were hitherto public services is but one part of the neoliberal project.

The changing relationship between the services, manufacturing and agricultural sectors in a globalised capitalist economy has contributed significantly to attempts to commercialise public services. The investment returns from manufacturing declined significantly in rich capitalist economies in recent decades, for a range of complex reasons, not least of which is the emergence of a large, non-unionised labour pool for manufacturing in South East Asia. Agriculture, already a relatively minor player in employment terms in Western and Northern economics, could not provide alternative forms of employment to manufacturing, especially in the existing context of heavily regulated agribusiness and international trade agreements for agricultural products. The focus shifted to trade in services, including trade in some or all of particular public services. The goal of transforming public services into marketable service was part of the ideology of the General Agreement on Trade and Services (GATS) agreement, (Robertson, Bonal & Dale, 2002; Tomasevski, 2005), and, more recently, of the as yet unratified Transatlantic Trade and Investment Partnership (TTIP) agreement. The rationale for making education a tradable service was articulated by Merrill Lynch in *The Book of Knowledge* in 1999; it was defined as a service that presents major new profit opportunities for investors (Moe, Bailey & Lau, 1999).

Multilateral agencies, including the Organisation for Economic Co-operation and Development (OECD) and the World Bank, and political institutions such as the European Union (EU), played a key role in promoting the marketisation of education and the related knowledge-economy ideology as they exercised increasing normative influence over national education policies from the 1990s (Dale, 2005; Figueroa, 2010; Lingard & Rawolle, 2011; Sellar & Lingard, 2013). The cultural shift was especially evident in higher education (Jessop, 2008). World Bank reports, *Constructing Knowledge Societies* 2002 and The *Challenge of Establishing World Class Universities*, 2009 consolidated the market-led view of higher education in particular. While the power of multilateral agencies often operates indirectly, as through the 'Open Method of Co-ordination' within the EU, or expert 'advice' from the World Bank or the OECD, such advice is often a thinly disguised 'surveillance' procedure promulgating a new market instrumentalism under the guise of 'independent' expertise (Henry et al., 2001). Control may be exercised as 'soft' power in education; it is real power nonetheless (Lo, 2011). The scope of scale of European Union (via structural funding and research frameworks) and OECD influence on Irish education policy is not always clear. However, the close alignment between Ireland's strong policy focus on creating a knowledge-based *economy* rather than a knowledge-based *society* over the past 20 years is living proof of that influence (Loxley, 2014; Fleming, Loxley & Finnegan, 2017).

Managerialism as a neoliberal project

A managerialist approach to governance provides a unique type of moral purpose and regulation to public service organisations: efficiency and effectiveness are prioritised at the expense of more broadly based moral and social values related to social rights, care, trust and equality. This has the ultimate impact of defining human relationships at work in transactional terms, as the means to an end, the end being high performance and productivity (Lynch, 2010) Managerialism reduces first-order social and moral values to second-order principles; trust, integrity and solidarity with others are subordinated to regulation, control and competition. When managerialist practices achieve hegemonic control within organisations, they parasitise and weaken those very values on which the organisation depends. While few would question the value of efficiency, in terms of maximising the use of available resources, the difficulty with managerialism is that it does not just prioritise efficiency, it suppresses other organisational values so that they become incidental to the running of the organization (Ball, 2012). The net effect of the devaluation of moral purposes, in and of themselves, is that public services, such as education, are increasingly defined as commodities to be delivered on the market to customers who can afford to buy them. They are no longer defined primarily as capacity-building public goods that are governed by rights protected by law at national and international levels.

While managerialism is implemented in different ways across cultural and economic contexts, within the public sector, one of its primary objectives is to inculcate market values and practices in systems and processes (Clarke, Gewirtz & McLaughlin, 2000, p. 7). It is operationalised through a narrative of strategic change, realised through the linguistic reframing of organisational goals in output and performance terms (Holborow, 2015). It literally changes how we speak about education: the nomenclature of the market is adopted with references to clients, customers and efficiencies, rather than citizenship and social rights[2]. Power is also exercised through a practical control technology that challenges established practices among professionals (Deem, 2004). The process of managerialism involves a dualistic reformulation of control through the decentralisation of authority to line managers combined with retention of power at central level. Given its market logic, more casualised contractual employment arrangements also tend to be a feature of new managerialism (Clarke & Newman, 1997; Chandler, Barry & Clark, 2002). Once operationalised in state bureaucracies, these changes have profound implications for the purpose and operation of the welfare state, including education, which this chapter explores with respect to Ireland.

Neoliberalism in Ireland

The long tradition of conservative nationalism and anti-intellectualism in the Irish socio-political sphere (Garvin, 2004) provided a fertile ground in which to breed neoliberal policies (Lee, 1989; Phelan, 2007). The country's deep indebtedness in the 1980s, in particular, led to neoliberalism being adopted through political pragmatism and opportunism. It was also strongly reinforced by the media elite thereby consolidating its position in public discourse (Phelan, 2007). By late 1987, there was acceptance of three core principles of neoliberalism, that: (1) public spending had to be cut back (2) tax cutting was the key to encouraging enterprise by individuals and companies and (3) wage costs had to be reduced and union power restricted through legislation (Allen, 2000, pp. 14–15). Accompanying this economic curbing of the welfare state was the incorporation of commercial values into public service provision. This involved offloading the cost of the welfare state from capital to labour through processes of marketisation, deregulation, and privatisation of what were once public services (Allen, 2007).

The neoliberal turn happened within a broader context of the global capitalist marketplace, as the Irish state sought to attract transnational investment through a low regulation and taxation regime (Allen, 2000). As Ireland's economic base shifted from agriculture and industry towards marketable services, education became a central strategy in the promotion of the image of the 'knowledge' economy. Ireland sold itself to foreign direct investors as a vibrant 'knowledge economy' (AIB, 2013).

New managerialism was initiated in the Strategic Management Initiative (SMI) (1994) and enacted in law through the Public Service Management Act (1997). The new managerial project was framed as one of 'modernisation', as politically neutral, promoting greater efficiencies, openness and better services (Murray, 2001). However, the goals of the SMI were distinctly political in terms of the values and mores incorporated into systems of public governance, regulation and accountability. The language of the market was encoded in the law and in policy with a strong emphasis on accountability; systems for performance appraisal and measurement of outputs was built into the framework of governance. The objective was to run the government like a business (Collins, 2007, p. 31).

Impact of neoliberal policies on education

Like most European countries, Ireland greatly increased access to upper secondary and higher education in the post-war era (although in Ireland's case it did not take place until the later 1960s). Justification for investing heavily in education was increasingly based on its market potential, its ability to develop skills leading to new products and markets in the 'knowledge economy'. The market-informed human capital approach to education was first articulated as a policy objective in Ireland in the highly influential *Investment in Education Report* (1966); the massive expansion of free secondary education in 1967 and the subsequent development of Technological Institutes of higher education (originally known as Regional Technical Colleges) were premised on human capital assumptions. As was true in many other countries in Europe, a knowledge-based imaginary (KBI) developed over time: it sought to valorise 'knowledge' as the key driver of economic growth, wealth generation, and job creation in the private, public, and 'third' sectors (Hazelkorn, 2011; Loxley, 2014; Jessop, 2016). While the cultural and personal value of education was formally endorsed, a new emphasis on entrepreneurship emerged in the first decade of the 21st century: *'the provision of the innovative and creative graduates equipped with the skills needed to perform successfully in a competitive environment and contribute to fostering an enterprise culture and the nurturing of entrepreneurs'* was proclaimed as a key part of the 'vision' for higher education (HEA, 2008, p. 12). The entrepreneurial focus of education was reiterated in 2011 in the *National Strategy for Higher Education to 2030* report (DES, 2011, p. 32). It called for the development of a 'smart economy', an objective first outlined in 2008: *The objective is to make Ireland an innovation and commercialization hub in Europe – a country that combines the features of an attractive home for innovative R&D-intensive multinationals while also being a highly-attractive incubation environment for the best entrepreneurs in Europe and beyond* (HEA, 2008, pp. 7–8). While this vocational and employment orientation had prevailed in Irish educational discourse since the 1970s, what was striking was that it became detached from the broader social development ethos of the public education system; the focus shifted to the creation of a labour market primed for a global knowledge economy.

Fostering the 'entrepreneurial imagination' that it believed would 'empower future workers' (DES, 2011, p. 37) required a new mode of governance in higher educational organizations in particular (ibid., pp. 88–95). New managerialism became the new norm, resting on the neoliberal assumption that the management of change can be best understood through the deployment of market logic and market mechanisms (Lynch, Grummell & Devine, 2015). Concerns about inequalities in access, participation and outcomes of education, that were central to debates about public education in the 1990s, were peripheralised in favour of analyses about the market value and relevance of education services: there were only three references to 'disadvantage' in the *National Strategy for Higher Education* (DES, 2011) while there were twenty-eight references to the relationship between business and higher education. It was made clear that securing the 'short' and 'longer-term prosperity' of Ireland was higher education's primary remit (DES, 2011, p. 29).

Sharp distinctions emerged too in the strategies for developing the so-called 'high-skilled' and 'low-skilled' knowledge workers required by a global knowledge economy (Brine, 2006). The neoliberal distinction between high-skilled knowledge workers, trained through higher education for R&D (Research & Development), and the low-skilled knowledge workers trained through the Future Education and Training sector, became central to the Irish government's employment and education strategies. The Irish promise was to provide high-skilled knowledge workers capable of R&D work for the global knowledge economy, as well as 'skill-upgrading' for lower-skilled workers servicing the other end of the knowledge economy (SOLAS, 2014, p. 5, 22). Running throughout this transformation of the welfare state was a discourse of flexibility and employability of a mobile and transferable workforce primed to respond to the needs of a global marketplace and supported by national business-support agencies (such as Enterprise Ireland).

The move to make education into a handmaiden of the market has had profound implications for the purposes of education in terms of what is taught (and not taught), who is taught and what types of subjectivities are developed in schools and colleges (Olssen & Peters, 2005; Lolich, 2011). To encourage second-level students to take higher-level mathematics, bonus 'points' (extra marks) are given to students who take the subject at the higher level in the final year national examination at second-level (the Leaving Certificate); no other subject is prioritised in this way. There is a fetishizing of the marketable capabilities of mathematics that is deeply problematic educationally (Kirwan & Hall, 2016).

While recognising the merit and value of Science, Technology, Engineering and Mathematics (STEM), the degree to which they have been prioritised in the research field in Ireland is striking. The *Report of the Research Prioritisation Steering Group* (by the Department of Enterprise, Jobs and Innovation in 2012) did not reference any arts, humanities and social science research field among its 14 priority areas. The unintended consequence of this emphasis on STEM is that the knowledges, pedagogies and learning styles of these disciplines are prioritised at the expense of the arts, humanities and social sciences; rational-critical, calculative mathematical logics are prioritised over ways of knowing the world through indigenous, plebian, peasant or experiential knowledge (de Sousa Santos, 2014).

However, there is also quiet resistance to the smart economy narrative: a survey in the Dublin region of 4,245 higher education students found that many challenged the prioritization of the 'smart economy' and entrepreneurial framing of higher education While most students' primary reason for attending higher education was to realize their career ambitions through getting *'a well-paid job', 'a job I like', and/or being 'educated'*, their ambitions were not confined to career alone (Lolich & Lynch, 2017). When asked for their personal reasons for choosing to study in a particular field, the three most important factors, in order of priority, were *'Becoming an expert in my field', 'Helping others who are in difficulty', and 'Raising a family'. 'Being well-off financially'* or *'Having a successful business of my own'* were lower priorities (Lolich, 2015). Students had *'an affective imaginary'* as well as a market imaginary; post-college employment was valued not only in itself, but also as a way of securing their relational (care) futures and doing socially valuable work. While students recognise the employment realities of a global labour market, they align their moral and affective (care) priorities with their labour market goals (Lolich & Lynch, 2017).

Teachers and new managerialism

One of the objects of new managerial reforms is to curb the power of professionals in public welfare sectors through the enactment of performance indicators and the availability of surveillance mechanisms (Farrell & Morris, 2003).

Accountability was one of the key principles informing policy development in the Education White Paper in 1995 and Department of Education and Skills (DES) policy since then. Management complicity was vital for delivering the new managerial project, with the role of the senior manager or leader being reconstructed since the early 1990s in a new managerialist form (Gleeson & Shain, 2003; Houtsonen et al., 2010). The concept of the school leader as a chief executive officer (CEO) gained considerable ground in the 1990s and 2000s. The Universities Act (1997) gave chief executive powers to university presidents. Both primary and second-level principals formed their own management networks (the IPPN, Irish Primary Principals' Network and the NAPD, National Association of Principals and Deputy Principals). School leadership became an area of training and development in its own right, often following a technicist and executive focus that narrows the scope of professionals delivering education. Principals felt under pressure to conform to new managerialist principles, so that accounting for your achievements in a school became a project in itself.

Most of the primary and second-level principals we interviewed for *New Managerialism in Education* felt that their work was increasingly subjected to greater regulation and accounting than previously. They claimed there was 'too much bureaucracy', in terms of monitoring and accounting for achievements and standards, work that was distracting from the core work of the school, which was attending to the educational needs of children. The feeling that schools were increasingly accountable, not just to the Department of Education, statutory bodies, parents and children, but also to the media, was notable (Lynch, Grummell & Devine, 2015). The impact of reforms arising from the financial crisis has also affected the status of teachers. Since 2008 there is a growing casualisation of the teachers in both second-level schools (Mooney-Simmie, 2014) and in higher education (Courtois & O'Keefe, 2015; Cush, 2016): approximately 35% of second-level teachers were employed on a part-time and/or fixed-term basis while 9% of primary teachers are employed on a part-time and/or fixed-term basis after the financial crisis (Ward, 2014, p. 3). Two thirds of newly qualified second-level teachers were also on temporary or part-time contracts even when the crisis was over (ASTI, 2017), while 45% of lecturers in universities and 25% of core lecturing staff in the Institutes of Technology were temporary and/or part-time (Cush, 2016). These figures represent major changes from 20 years ago, when almost all primary and secondary teachers were on permanent contracts, and far fewer lecturing posts were temporary and/part-time.

The licensing of several for-profit second-level and higher education colleges in Ireland over the last 20 years has also been a significant development in Irish education; as labour market conditions in these colleges is generally not governed by trade union agreements, staff pay and general working conditions are generally very inferior to those in the public sector. While most of these colleges are small, Dublin Business School (DBS) is comparable in size to a number of the

Institutes of Technology while Hibernia College is the largest single provider of primary teachers in Ireland, as well as an increasingly important provider of second-level teachers. These trends exemplify the extent to which education is now seen as a business and a marketable product that can be traded nationally and internationally, a concept that was unthinkable a generation ago. While Ireland has always had an education market (Tormey, 2007) due to the constitutional rights of parents to send a child to the school of their choice for religious reasons, a culture of market competition has developed between schools in the last 20 years that is unprecedented; it is driven primarily by parental desires for class advantage rather than religious beliefs (Lynch & Lodge, 2002). New managerialism is both a product and facilitator of this new market trend.

Challenges to new managerialism in Irish schools: the role of educational mediators

Government control over education is subject to two major limitations, one being practical and the other organic (Dale, 1982, p. 139). First, the scale of the educational bureaucracy makes it practically impossible for central government to exercise complete control over all aspects of education. Second, each State apparatus, including education, has its own unique history. The balance of powers that exist within the educational site are historically and culturally conditioned, and the way these play out varies across nation states depending on the relative status and power of those who manage, oversee and administer the services at local level (Lynch, 1990).

While regional Education and Training Boards (replacing the original the vocational education committees in 2013), school management bodies, and national parents' organisations, exercise power over education policy-making in Ireland, there is compelling evidence that the most powerful mediators of primary and secondary school services are the teacher unions and the Churches, especially the Catholic Church. Thus, despite pressures towards marketisation, there are nation-state-specific social conditions that have militated institutionally and culturally against new managerialism.

The governance structure for primary and second-level schools in Ireland is set down in a number of Education Acts, the most significant of which is the Education Act (1998). This act gives educational partners, (namely the owners and managers of schools, parent representatives and teacher unions), authority to exercise influence in the governance of several areas of education, including school design and planning, and curriculum development through the NCCA (the National Council for Curriculum and Assessment). Teachers and teacher unions are also strongly represented in Teaching Council, the body that governs the education and professional development of teachers under the Teaching Council Act 2001–2016. The teacher unions are by far the most numerous and influential group on these bodies as they have the resources and professional staff to assign to various positions (Coolahan, 1981; Cunningham, 2009).

Irish teachers are highly unionised with almost all school teachers being union members. As their consultative relationship with the state and other statutory policy-making groups is embedded in law, unions are party to national wage negotiations and policy developments in the education field. They have been active in resisting new managerial reforms. While the power of the teacher unions to drive the education agenda was tested in the wake of the financial crisis of 2008, and the collapse of the social partnership arrangement between government and mediator groups, teacher unions remain very powerful. They have held several strikes to resist curriculum and assessment changes and to challenge cutbacks during austerity; they have also mobilised parents at times to support them on this. Additionally, teachers hold extensive political and social capital and are very active within political parties. The Prime Minister (Taoiseach) from 2011 to 2017 was a former school teacher, as was the Minister for Finance.

> The teachers' unions collectively, between them, had become the most powerful group in Congress… They had that solid institutional political clout, insofar as they permeated every parish in Ireland, every political party in Ireland, every cultural, sporting and recreational body.
> (Mulvey[3] in Cunningham, 2009, p. 217)

Religious bodies and boards, most of which are Catholic, control the management of the majority of schools nationally (Coolahan, Hussey & Kilfeather, 2012). In the context of an intense debate about introducing league tables and performance indicators for schools in 2009, the Catholic Church actively promoted a holistic vision of education beyond narrow academic goals or market demands stating that "a Catholic conception of education…[is]…primarily moral and spiritual, concerned with principled behaviour and focused upon community and public good outcomes…" Bishop Leo O'Reilly, keynote address to the CPSMA (Catholic Primary Schools' Managers' Association, April 24th Dublin 2009). While not mobilising against new managerialism *per se*, and indeed endorsing certain 'reforms', the Churches, especially the Catholic Church, has silently resisted others, not least by not opposing or challenging teachers' resistance to league tables and performativity measures.

Primary schools (especially) and to a lesser degree second-level schools, are small by international standards; there are over 3,000 primary schools and 740 second-level schools in a country of 4.5 million. Their size alone militates against a managerial model. The active role that many teachers and schools play in Irish social life also militates institutionally against new managerialism: the principal is a teacher in many small primary schools and in some smaller second-level schools. The manager and worker divide that is assumed within the new managerial frame does not apply: the management and delivery of education are not always discrete functions. Teachers, as deliverers of education, are not a distant professional elite; they are deeply embedded within local communities especially outside of major cities. They are also highly organised both inside and outside formal party politics; they work through trade unions, local community associations (including sporting bodies such as the Gaelic Athletic Association (GAA) which has clubs in most large villages and towns), and through the churches and community politics.

The power that the teacher unions exercise over education historically is far from unproblematic. While primary schools did change radically and become more child-centred in the 1970s, a trend that has largely persisted over time, second-level education has been largely subject-centred, didactic and far from innovative in terms of curriculum change. Protecting sectoral interests plays a very significant role in forestalling change in both curriculum and assessment in Ireland (Gleeson, 2010; Harvey, 2015).

How performativity was mediated in Irish education

Performance indicators, such as school league tables, were not formally introduced in Irish schools for a number of reasons. While standardised tests are administered at primary school, these are only disclosed to parents, teachers and the school, and remain private. The first public examination (the Junior Certificate) is undertaken when students are in their mid-teens, at the end of compulsory education at age 16. These school results (and those of the final year examination, the Leaving Certificate) could be made public but are not due to teacher resistance, but with the tacit support of parents, and the religious and other administrative bodies that own and govern second-level schools. A system of Whole School Evaluation (WSE) was introduced instead; school evaluations take place on a partnership basis between the school, the management body, parents and the inspectorate of the Department of Education and Skills (McNamara & O'Hara, 2012). These reports are made public; however, the work of individual teachers is not assessed in the reports. Since WSE was introduced, teachers have successfully resisted operating a system of in-school teacher assessment of their own student's work (for public examination) although this issue is still under negotiation at the time of writing.

While the government adopted the rhetoric of new managerialism, both rhetorically and in practice, by devising performance indicators, measures of accountability and strategic plans, (High Level Goals) for schools, Gleeson and O'Donnabháin's (2009) research on their implementation suggests that the reforms are less honoured in practice than in theory. A culture of 'contrived compliance' operates amongst teachers in terms of engaging with self-evaluation (Harvey, 2015). Most of the focus has remained on policy implementation at a general school level (Gleeson & O'Donnabháin, 2009).

However, a focus on performativity is becoming evident in other ways across Irish education. Standardised testing of individual students occurs at three stages (early, middle and end) of primary schooling and, while this data is only disclosed to parents and the school, this operates as an indirect form of regulation. As the performance of Irish students is compared with those in other countries in PISA and TIMSS tests, these also operate as a form of control and regulation (MacRuairc, 2012). Moreover, both the policy emphasis and the language-of-analysis have changed and are becoming more market-led, most notably at second level (Mooney Simmie, 2012, 2014). Although school-level examination results are not published as league tables, newspapers have created a type of second-level league-table system by using Freedom of Information requests to identify the percentage of children from different schools who go to higher education (Lynch, Grummell & Devine, 2015). This practice has been strongly critiqued, but has persisted as it has parental support, especially, among middle class parents, who have the resources and time to choose schools (Lynch & Lodge, 2002).

More widely, the power of the media to promote neoliberal values continues both outside (Phelan, 2007) and inside education (Lynch, Grummell & Devine, 2015, pp. 205–224), a trend that is not unique to Ireland (Blackmore & Thorpe, 2003). Although the media are not usually identified as major players in education policy-making, they are increasingly powerful in setting public agendas that school managers must heed in a media-driven age. In an increasingly competitive and diverse society, the reputational status of a school becomes increasingly significant (Lynch & Lodge, 2002; Devine, Grummell & Lynch, 2011). Principals become ever more conscious of how 'their' school is positioned in the competitive stakes. This is allied with the apparent objectivity of rankings systems, which 'become naturalised, normalised and validated, through familiarity and ubiquitous citation, particularly through recitation as 'facts' in the media' (Lynch, 2013, p. 8).

Higher education accommodating new managerialism

The situation in higher education, especially in the universities, is quite different to the primary and second-level school sectors. The government-initiated OECD review of higher education in 2004 (OECD, 2004) was a watershed in Irish higher education. The report strongly critiqued the lack of investment in higher education research in the sciences and technological areas in particular, emphasising the key role of higher education in developing a 'skilled work force for the economy'. There was almost no reference in the report to the developmental role of the universities or higher education in enhancing the civil, political, social or cultural institutions of society, either locally or globally. The National Strategy for Higher Education (DES, 2011) set out the framework for the future development of higher education in Ireland to 2030. It was even more heavily laced with the new managerial language of efficiency, flexibility and accountability; a whole section of the report is devoted to *Efficiency and Productivity*. The report highlights the role of higher education in rebuilding 'an innovative, knowledge-based economy'…having graduates who will be 'the productive engine of a vibrant and prosperous economy' (DES, 2011, p. 1). Reviewing the work of academic staff 'continuously...in all institutions as part of a robust performance management framework' is seen as central to the realisation of the new goals (ibid., p. 2). It also proposed to curtail university autonomy by ensuring that 'institutional strategies will be defined and aligned with national priorities' (ibid., p. 4). The Report also supported the idea of 'up-front fees and [an] income-contingent loan scheme', and '...greater productivity and commercial activity' (ibid., p. 5) to help fund higher education into the future (DES, 2011). While the debate about the future role of higher education continues, and there is strong resistance to the introduction of student loans *in lieu* of grants in particular, what is noticeable is the redefinition of higher education's purpose. It is defined by government increasingly as a public investment that should be more commercially-driven and market relevant.

Performance appraisal and ranking play a much more significant role in Irish higher education than at school level. Bibliometric databases, such as the H Index, Scopus, Google Scholar Citations, the Science and Social Science Citation Indices, catalogue and rank individual publications and citations and also contribute to subject ranking within and between universities. New modes of ranking universities as corporate entities has also been developed, such as Uni-Rank, the Academic Ranking of World Universities (ARWU), the Times Higher Education World University (THE) rankings and that of Quacquarelli Symonds (QS), a number of which are commercially controlled (Lynch, 2013, p. 6). The apparent objectivity of such ranking systems disguises the highly selective nature of their measurement procedures: they are heavily reliant on data provided by Thompson Reuters and Elsevier, companies that own many journals used in rankings, the majority of which are in English. Moreover, none of the prestigious rankings grade colleges in terms of their accessibility, inclusiveness or the quality of student experiences.

While there has been some resistance to the increased marketisation of higher education in Ireland, the power of the unions in the higher education sectors, especially in the seven Universities, is not comparable to that of their colleagues at primary and second-level. This occurs not only because there are a range of unions representing different staff, but also because union density among academics is much lower than that among teachers. In addition, many junior academics are on temporary and/or part-time contracts (Cush, 2016), and are not unionised, while many general services in higher education have been outsourced to private providers over the past 20 years. The highly individualistic culture that has always pervaded higher education is another factor that militates against collective action; in an age of individualised academic capitalism, many academics see themselves as sole traders, or even potential 'stars' who can, if successful, have very profitable academic careers (Slaughter & Leslie, 1997). All of these factors reduce the scope and influence of unions at the higher education levels, especially in the universities. However, it is important to note that the Teachers' Union of Ireland (TUI), which represents academic staff in the higher education

Institutes of Technology (and also represents many teachers at second-level), has been more active in resisting managerialist changes in the third-level sector than have unions in the universities. It held strategic strikes and lobbied successfully against legislative changes that would have undermined the autonomy of academics in the Institutes prior to national elections in 2016.

Overall, however, higher education colleges are being pressurised to change and be more business-oriented; there is a strong emphasis on productivity and targets with funding from government increasingly dependent on meeting specified benchmarks. The values of the commercial sector are increasingly encoded in the heart of the higher education systems and processes, often without reflection (Lynch, 2006), marking a profound shift in values away from the ideal of education as a public service.

Further education: susceptibility to new managerialism

The further education sector in Ireland is highly susceptible to the influences of new managerialism (Murray, Grummell & Ryan, 2014). As it has never had a clearly defined role or institutional framework, further education's position, between and on the borders of second and higher education, locates it at the margins. It is characterised by a diverse student cohort, most of whose families would have little or no further or higher education; the workforce is heavily casualised, and it has a complex funding and organizational structure, all of which increases its vulnerability to control and regulation.

Further education developed a new policy focus arising from the neoliberal demand for a flexible, employable and mobile workforce in the post-austerity period. The establishment of SOLAS (Seirbhísí Oideachais Leanúnaigh agus Scileanna, the Irish national education and training body) in 2013 led to the adoption of more explicit employability and performativity discourses. These were influenced by EU strategies such as the *Strategic Framework for European Cooperation in Education and Training* and *EUROPE 2020 A strategy for smart, sustainable and inclusive growth* (Holford & Špolar, 2012). In the Irish case, this greater alignment of education and training agendas, which had always characterised further education, was now incentivised by new statutory changes in labour market activation strategies, the increased conditionality of welfare, new public procurement processes for education providers, and the expanded reach of the accreditation processes of Quality and Qualifications Ireland (Fitzsimons, 2017b). An increased focus on market-oriented further education is aligned with the decimation of community development and community education support frameworks that are non-market led. There have been severe cuts in funding to community development programmes, family resource centres, special education needs programmes, disability and other support services (Fitzsimons, 2017a).

The further education sector has been particularly targeted by neoliberal discourses of performativity aimed at upgrading the employability of low-skilled and marginalized sectors of the population (Brine, 2006). The training agenda within further education and training (FET) moved from vocational education to employability and enhanced labour activation (Gleeson, Davies & Wheeler, 2005). The policy shift is evident in the discourses of the new statutory agencies of SOLAS and INTREO (Employment and Income Support Agency) (Hardiman, 2012). Both agencies emphasise employability and labour activation – a readiness to work rather than actually becoming employed. Measureable evidence of employability is stated as a priority in the *Further Education and Training Strategy 2014–2019* which focuses on

> Skills as a resource for economic growth; Skills as drivers of employment growth; Skills as drivers of productivity increase; Skills and 'smartening' of the economy; Skills as drivers of productivity increase, Skills and 'smartening' of the economy, Skills as a driver of social inclusion and social mobility; and Skills as an insulator from unemployment.
> (SOLAS, 2014, p. 4–5)

The focus on employability in further education was accompanied by continuous reforms in the accreditation system. Established under European quality assurance frameworks, QQI developed a national qualifications framework for learning awards across further and higher education. It focusses on hierarchical learning outcomes that the learner can visibly display for verification and accreditation purposes. This emphasises learning as individual achievement, output and performance that is dependent on the subjective interpretation and self-regulation of the learner, educator and assessor (Fitzsimons, 2017b).

The formalising of educational outcomes through qualifications structures places enormous pressures on students and staff who struggle to capture the complexity of their learning into measurable performance-related categories (O'Neill, Fitzsimons & O'Reilly, 2014; Fitzsimons, 2017b). The non-traditional background of many students and the diverse access routes provided by further and adult education struggles to fit into the performativity radar of formal learning outcomes of FET and QQI (Quality and Qualifications Ireland). As Allias argues, this emphasis on the end product disguises the learning context and processes, leading to a market-driven procurement process awarded to those who can deliver on prescribed measureable outcomes at the lowest cost (2014, p. 69).

Conclusion: the local contexts of the neoliberal project

While neoliberalism was initially sold as a simple modernisation project, the political nature of its purpose became increasingly visible over time. The focus on the human capital value of education persisted but it was married to a new education project focused on educating students for a market economy. This radically shifted the purpose of education in a welfare state from broader developmental and social goals towards more single-minded, market-driven objectives of employability in a knowledge economy. The development of an entrepreneurial and actuarial self-became the new mantra in an age of individualised modernity, not only globally (Peters, 2005) but also in Ireland (Inglis, 2008). Market logics increasingly began to dictate educational discourses and practices through a new managerial code. However, this process was nuanced by the varied contexts of Irish education as we explored in this chapter. The experiences of the school sectors have been very different to that of further and adult education setting, and each of these has differed from the higher education sector, revealing the complexity of new managerialism in the specific location and context of different welfare states.

While neoliberal policies have been challenged in the delivery of primary and second-level education, due to the power exercised by the Catholic Church and the teacher unions in particular, there has been an incorporation of market logic into further and higher education, and there have been demands for changes in educational management and organisation at primary and second-level. In the latter case, school principals are under surveillance from media and parents (especially at second level) to produce academic results through strong examination performances and to comply with new modes of school evaluation. While teacher unions and the churches can and do resist such demands, they cannot pre-empt them.

Higher education has provided a more fertile ground for new managerialism, given the globalised competitiveness of the higher education sector itself (Hazelkorn, 2011). Individualised citation counts, rankings, and the commercialisation of research funding, impel a more competitive and individualised culture that facilitates the internalization of new managerial norms (Lynch, Grummell & Devine, 2015). The adult and further education sectors also proved highly susceptible to the impact of new managerialism due to the lower status of the sector, the ongoing casualisation of its staff and expanding performativity and new professionalism requirements instituted in law and practice.

While culturally-specific conditions meant that there was and still is resistance to new managerialism in education, especially at primary and second level, and also by students at third-level, albeit not mobilised politically in the students' case[4], new managerial reforms inevitably get under your skin; there is no way of escaping, even for those who are not committed to the new managerial project. The call to be market-led rather than education-led has profound implications for the educators and learners who deliver and receive education. The new managerial focus is the product not the person, both in terms of what is attained and what is counted and countable. A culture of carelessness is created, one that is most evident in higher education (Lynch, 2010) and further education (Murray, Grummell & Ryan, 2014). Increasingly, it permeates all levels of education policy and management (Lynch, Grummell & Devine, 2015), with different education sectors varying in their degree of susceptibility or accommodation (in the case of further and higher education respectively) or resistance (in the case of primary and second-level schooling).

Notes

1 This this paper is based on three empirical studies: the first is a study of the procedures and criteria for appointing twenty three senior managers (school principals, heads of colleges and top-ranked posts in universities across primary (N = 8) secondary (N = 8) and further and higher education (N = 7). Those appointed to the posts and those who played the key role in the appointments (usually the chair of the board of assessors) were interviewed; 52 in-depth interviews with managers & assessors were undertaken (Lynch, Grummell and Devine, *New Managerialism in Education,* 2012, 2015, 2nd ed.) The second study, led by Kathleen Lynch, is an investigation of the relationship between working, learning and caring life in higher education: 102 interviews with staff — academic, management, professional, general service -across ten higher education institutions. (http://irc-equality.ie/) The third study was undertaken by Luciana Lolich under the supervision of Kathleen Lynch; it was a study of students' perspective (N=4265) on the market (smart economy)-focused changes enacted in higher education following the OECD (2004) Report recommending a more market-led approach (Lolich & Lynch, 2016, 2017).

2 There were 1,583 references to 'customers' on the Website of the Irish Revenue Commissioners (National Tax and Customs Authority) accessed May 10, 2017 www.revenue.ie/en/index.html

Department of Social Protection — over 2,000 references to 'customers' on the website accessed May 10, 2017 www.welfare.ie/en/Pages/home.aspx

The Department of Education has a Customer charter accessed May 10, 2017 www.education.ie/en/The-Department/Customer-Service/Customer-Charter/Service-Standards.html/

3 Kieran Mulvey served as Chief Executive of the Labour Relations Commission for over 20 years.

4 Students did run (...) a successful campaign in 2017 against the introduction of student loans, albeit one that was supported by a variety of other powerful groups.

References

Allen, K. (2000): *The Celtic Tiger: The Myth of Social Partnership in Ireland*, Manchester: Manchester University Press.
Allen, K. (2007): *The Corporate Takeover of Ireland*, Dublin: Irish Academic Press.
Allias, S. (2014): *Selling Out Education: National Qualifications Frameworks and the Neglect of Knowledge*, Rotterdam: Sense.
AIB (Allied Irish Bank) (2013): *Why Choose Ireland*, Dublin: AIB.
ASTI (Association of Secondary Teachers, Ireland) (2017): *ASTI Survey on Recently Qualified Teachers*, April 2017. www.asti.ie/news/latest-news/news-article/article/two-thirds-of-recently-qualified-second-level-teachers-in-precarious-employment-asti-red-c-survey/. www.asti.ie/fileadmin/user_upload/Documents/Education/Survey_of_Recently_Qualified_Teachers_ASTI__REDC_-_April_2017.pdf.
Ball, S. J. (2012): 'Performativity, Commodification and Commitment: An I-spy Guide to the Neoliberal University', *British Journal of Educational Studies*, 60(1): 17–28.
Blackmore, J., Thorpe, S. (2003). 'Media/ting Change: The Print Media's Role in Mediating Education Policy in a Period of Radical Reform in Victoria, Australia', *Journal of Education Policy*, 18(6): 577–595.
Boltanski, L., Chiapello, E. (2005): *The New Spirit of Capitalism*, London: Verso.

Brine, J. (2006): 'Lifelong Learning and the Knowledge Economy: Those that Know and Those that Do Not – the Discourse of the European Union', *British Educational Research Journal*, 32(5): 649–665.

Chandler, J., Barry, J., Clark, H. (2002): 'Stressing Academe: The Wear and Tear of the New Public Management', *Human Relations*, 55: 1051–1069.

Clarke, J., Newman, J. (1997): *The Managerial State*, London: Sage.

Clarke, J., Gewirtz, S., McLaughlin, E. (2000): *New Managerialism New Welfare?* London: Sage.

Collins, N. (2007): 'The Public Service and Regulatory Reform', in: Collins, N., Cradden, T., Butler, P. (eds.), *Modernising Irish Government*, 115–36, Dublin: Gill & Macmillan:

Coolahan, J. (1981): *Irish Education: History and Structure*, Dublin: Institute of Public Administration.

Coolahan, J., Hussey, C., Kilfeather, F. (2012): *The Forum on Patronage and Pluralism in the Primary Sector. Report of the Forum's Advisory Group*. Dublin: Department of Education and Skills.

Courtois, A., O'Keefe, T. (2015): 'Precarity in the Ivory Cage: Neoliberalism and Casualisation of Work in the Irish Higher Education Sector', *Journal for Critical Education Policy Studies*, 13(1): 43–66.

Cunningham, J. (2009): *Unlikely Radicals: Irish Post Primary Teachers and the ASTI, 1909–2009*, Cork: Cork University Press.

Cush, M. (2016): *Report to the Minister for Education and Skills of the Chairperson of the Expert Group on Fixed-term and Part-time Employment in Lecturing in Third Level Education*, Dublin: Department of Education and Skills.

Dale, R. (1982): 'Education and the Capitalist State: Contributions and Contradictions', in: Apple, M. W. (ed.), *Cultural and Economic Reproduction in Education*, 127–61, London: Routledge & Kegan Paul.

Dale, R. (2005): 'Globalisation, Knowledge Economy and Comparative Education', *Comparative Education*, 41(1): 1–17.

de Sousa Santos, B. (2014): *Epistemologies of the South: Justice against Epistemicide*, Boulder, CO: Paradigm.

Deem, R. (2004): 'The Knowledge Worker, the Manager-academic and the Contemporary UK University: New and Old Forms of Public Management?' *Financial Accountability & Management*, 20(2): 107–128.

DES (Department of Education and Skills) (2011): *National Strategy for Higher Education to 2030* (Hunt Report), Dublin: Department of Education and Skills.

Devine, D., Grummell, B., Lynch, K. (2011) 'Crafting the Elastic Self? Gender and Identities in Senior Appointments in Irish Education', *Gender, Work and Organization*, 18(6): 631–649.

Farrell, C. M., Morris, J. (2003): 'The Neo-Bureaucratic State: Professionals, Managers and Professional Managers in Schools' General Practices and Social Work', *Organisation - Interdisciplinary Journal of Organisation theory and Society*, 10(1): 129–146.

Figueroa, F. (2010): 'The Bologna Process as a Hegemonic Tool of Normative Power Europe (NPE): The Case of Chilean and Mexican Higher Education', *Globalisation, Societies & Education*, 8(2): 247–256.

Fitzsimons, C. (2017a): *Community Education and Neoliberalism: Philosophies, Practices and Policies in Ireland*, Switzerland: Palgrave Macmillan.

Fitzsimons, C. (2017b): 'Rhetoric and Reality: The Irish Experience of Quality Assurance', *Adult Learner*, Dublin: AONTAS. www.aontas.com/assets/resources/Adult-Learner-Journal/14218_Aontas_Adult_Learner_2017_WEB.pdf.

Fleming, T., Loxley, A., Finnegan, F. (2017): *Access and Participation in Irish Higher Education*. Basingstoke: Palgrave Macmillan.

Garvin, T. (2004): *Preventing the Future: Why Was Ireland So Poor for So Long?* Dublin: Gill and Macmillan.

Gleeson, J. (2010): *Curriculum in Context: Partnership, Power and Praxis in Ireland*, Bern: Peter Lang.

Gleeson, D., Davies, J., Wheeler, E. (2005): 'On the Making and Taking of Professionalism in the Further Education Workplace', *British Journal of Sociology of Education*, 26(4): 445–460.

Gleeson, J., O'Donnabháin, D. (2009): 'Strategic Planning and Accountability in Irish Education', *Irish Educational Studies*, 28(1): 27–46.

Gleeson, D., Shain, F. (2003): 'Managing Ambiguity in Further Education', in: Bennett, W., Crawford, M., Cartwright, M. (eds.), *Effective Educational Leadership*, 229–47, London: Sage: Grummell, B. (2014): 'FET: Responding to Community Needs or Shaping Communities to Suit a Global Marketplace in Crisis', in: Murray, M., Grummell, B., Ryan, A. (eds.), *Further Education and Training in Ireland: History, Politics and Practice*, 122–135, Maynooth: MACE.

Grummell, B., Lynch, K. (2016): 'New Managerialism as a Political Project in Irish Education', in: Murphy, M. P., Dukelow, F. (eds.), *The Irish Welfare state in the 21st Century: Challenges and Changes*, 215–235, Basingstoke: Palgrav.

Hardiman, F. (2012): *Finding a Voice: The Experience of Mature Students in a College of Further Education*. Unpublished EdD Thesis, Maynooth: National University of Ireland. http://eprints.maynoothuniversity.ie/3908/1/F._Hardiman_Thesis.pdf. Accessed 1 July 2015

Harvey, D. (2005): *A Brief History of Neoliberalism*, Oxford: Oxford University Press.

Harvey, G. (2015): *The Evolving Model of School Self-Evaluation in Ireland: How a Person's Perception of Purpose and Power Determines Practice*. Unpublished EdD thesis, Maynooth: Maynooth University.

Hazelkorn, E. (2011): *Rankings and the Reshaping of Higher Education: The Battle for World Class Excellence*, Basingstoke: Palgrave Macmillan.

Henry, M., Lingard, B., Rizvi, F., Taylor, S. (2001): *The OECD: Globalisation and Education Policy*, Amsterdam: Pergamon.

HEA (Higher Education Authority) (2008): *Strategic Plan 2008–2010*, Dublin: Higher Education Authority.

Holborow, M. (2015): *Language and Neoliberalism*, New York: Routledge.

Holford, J., Mohorčič Špolar, V. A. (2012): 'Neoliberal and Inclusive Themes in European Lifelong Learning Policy', in: Riddell, S. (ed.), *Lifelong Learning in Europe: Equity and Efficiency in the Balance*, 39–62, Chicago, IL: University of Chicago Press.

Houtsonen, J., Czaplicka, M., Lindblad, S., Sohlberg, P., Sugrue, C. (2010): 'Finnish, Irish and Swedish Teachers' Perceptions of Current Changes Welfare State Restructuring in Education and Its National Refractions', *Current Sociology*, 58(4): 597–622.

Inglis, T. (2008): *Global Ireland: Same Difference*, New York: Routledge.

Jessop, B. (2008): 'A Cultural Political Economy of Competitiveness and Its Implications for Higher Education', in: Jessop, B., Fairclough, N., Wodak, R. (eds.), *Education and the Knowledge-Based Economy in Europe*, 11–39, Rotterdam: Sense.

Jessop, B. (2016): 'Putting Higher Education in Its Place in (East Asian) Political Economy', *Comparative Education*, 52(1): 8–25.

Kirwan, L., Hall, K. (2016): 'The Mathematics Problem: The Construction of a Market-led Education Discourse in the Republic of Ireland', *Critical Studies in Education*, 57(3): 376–393.

Lee, J. J. (1989): *Ireland, 1912–1985: Politics and Society*, Cambridge: Cambridge University Press.

Lingard, B., Rawolle, S. (2011): 'New Scalar Politics: Implications for Education Policy', *Comparative Education*, 47(4): 489–502.

Lo, W. Y. W. (2011): 'Soft Power, University Rankings and Knowledge Production: Distinctions between Hegemony and Self-determination in Higher Education', *Comparative Education*, 47(2): 209–222.

Lolich, L. (2011): 'And the Market Created the Student to Its Image and Likening: Neo-liberal Governmentality and Its Effects on Higher Education in Ireland', *Irish Educational Studies*, 30(2): 271–284.

Lolich, L. (2015): *What Matters to Students in the Enterprise University: Students' subjectivisties in a Smart Economy*, University College Dublin, School of Social Justice PhD thesis (unpublished).

Lolich, L., Lynch, K. (2016): 'The Affective Imaginary: Students as Affective Consumers of Risk', *Higher Education Research and Development*, 35(1): 17–30.

Lolich, L., Lynch, K. (2017): 'Aligning the Market and Affective Self: Care and Student Resistance to Entrepreneurial Subjectivities', *Gender and Education*, 29(1): 115–131.

Loxley, A. (2014): 'From Seaweed & Peat to Pills and Very Small Things; Knowledge Production and Higher Education in the Irish Context', in: Loxley, A., Seery, A., Walsh, J. (eds.), *Higher Education in Ireland: Practices, Policies and Possibilities*, 55–85, Basingstoke: Palgrave Macmillan.

Lynch, K. (1990): 'Reproduction: The Role of Cultural Factors and Educational Mediators', *British Journal of Sociology of Education*, 11(1): 3–20.

Lynch, K. (2006): 'Neo-liberalism and Marketisation: The Implications for Higher Education', *European Educational Research Journal*, 5(1): 1–12.

Lynch, K. (2010): 'Carelessness: A Hidden Doxa of Higher Education', *Arts & Humanities in Higher Education*, 9(1): 54–67.

Lynch, K. (2013): 'New Managerialism, Neoliberalism and Ranking', *Ethics in Science and Environmental Politics*, 13(2): 1–13.

Lynch, K., Lodge, A. (2002): *Equality and Power in Schools: Redistribution, Recognition and Representation*, London: Routledge.

Lynch, K., Grummell, B., Devine, D. (2015): *New Managerialism in Education: Commercialization, Carelessness and Gender*, 2nd ed., London: Palgrave Macmillan.

MacRuairc, G. (2012): *Standardized Testing in Ireland*, (invited keynote) Proceedings of the INTO Education Conference, Athlone, March 2012. www.into.ie/ROI/NewsEvents/Conferences/EducationConsultativeConference/EducationConsultativeConference2011/.

McNamara, G., O'Hara, J. (2012): 'From Looking at Our Schools (LAOS) to Whole School Evaluation - Management, Leadership and Learning (WSE-MLL): The Evolution of Inspection in Irish Schools Over the Past Decade', *Educational Assessment, Evaluation and Accountability*, 24(2): 79–97.

Moe, M. T., Bailey, K., Lau, R. (1999): *The Book of Knowledge: Investing in the Education and Training Industry*, New York: Merrill Lynch.

Mooney Simmie, G. (2012): 'The Pied Piper of Neo Liberalism Calls the Tune in the Republic of Ireland: Ananalysis of Education Policy Text from 2000–2012', *Journal for Critical Education and Policy Studies*, 10(2): 485–514.

Mooney Simmie, G. (2014): 'The Neo-liberal Turn in Understanding Teachers' and School Leaders' Work Practices in Curriculum Innovation and Change: A Critical Discourse Analysis of a Newly proposed Reform Policy in Lower Secondary Education in the Republic of Ireland', *Citizenship, Social and Economics' Education*, 13(3): 185–198.

Murray, J. (2001): Reflections on the SMI. Working Paper 1, Institute for Policy Studies, Trinity College Dublin.

Murray, M., Grummell, B., Ryan, A. (eds.) (2014): *Further Education and Training in Ireland: History, Politics and Practice*, Maynooth: MACE.

OECD (2004): *Review of National Policies for Education: Review of Higher Education in Ireland*, OECD: Paris.

O'Neill, J., Fitzsimons, C., O'Reilly, N. (2014): 'Practitioner Reflections on FET', in: Murray, M., Grummell, B., Ryan, A. (eds.), *Further Education and Training in Ireland: History, Politics and Practice*, 147–168, Maynooth: MACE.

Olssen, M., Peters, M. A. (2005): 'Neoliberalism, Higher Education and the Knowledge Economy: From the Free Market to Knowledge Capitalism', *Journal of Education Policy*, 20(3): 313–345.

Peck, J. (2010): *Constructions of Neoliberal Reason*, Oxford: Oxford University Press.

Peters, M. (2005): 'The New Prudentialism in Education: Actuarial Rationality and the Entrepreneurial Self', *Educational Theory*, 55(2): 123–137.

Phelan, S. (2007): 'The Discourses of Neoliberal Hegemony: The Case of the Irish Republic', *Critical Discourse Studies*, 4(1): 29–48.

Robertson, S. L., Bonal, X., Dale, R. (2002): 'GATS and the Education Service Industry: The Politics of Scale and Global Reterritorialisation', *Comparative Education Review*, 46(4): 472–496.

Sellar, S., Lingard, B. (2013): 'The OECD and Global Governance in Education', *Journal of Education Policy*, 28(5), 710–725.

Slaughter S., Leslie L. (1997): Politics, *Policies and the Entrepreneurial University*, Baltimore, MD: John Hopkins University Press.

SOLAS (2014): *Further Education and Training Strategy 2014–2019*, Dublin: Department of Education and Skills. http://solas.ie/docs/FETStrategy2014-2019.pdf. Accessed 15 June 2015.

Tomasevski, K. (2005): 'Globalising What: Education as a Human Right or as a Traded Service?', *Indiana Journal of Global Legal Studies*, 12(1): 1–78.

Tormey, R. (2007): 'Education and Poverty in Combat Poverty Agency', in Cousins, M. (ed.), *Welfare Policy and Poverty*, 169–200, Dublin: IPA and Combat Poverty.

Ward, P. (2014): *Report to the Minister for Education and Skills of the Chairperson of The Expert Group on Fixed-Term and Part-Time Employment in Primary and Second Level Education in Ireland*, Dublin: Department of Education and Skills.

Chapter 12

Framing work injury/sickness in a changing welfare state – naming and blaming

Antoinette Hetzler

> My views were completely disregarded and I was forced, despite my protests, to accept my work situation.
>
> (F teacher, 0480)

> I was ordered to work with this student and I told the principal that I could not do it. I told him many times that I did not feel well. He said there was nothing to do. He told me that if I could not do the job, I should quit. They needed two people to help this student but one after the other took sick leave or quit. So I had to take care of him by myself.
>
> (F teacher assistant 0495)

This chapter looks at how 569 primary school employees in Sweden, women and men between 2012 and 2015, framed their illness as caused by work in their accounts reported to the Swedish Work Environment Authorities (SWEA).[1] The analysis of the accounts throws a new light on work in the public sector.

The promise of new public management (NPN) to modernise and make the public sector more efficient (Hood, 1991) was the accepted recipe for running Swedish schools during the 1990's, but failed to deliver. Analysis of the accounts of illness by school employees as caused by work environment reveals a dark side to new public management. The accounts suggest that the very tools designed to obtain standardisation and control while de-centralising schools to local municipalities led to workers fleeing their workplaces because of illness and/or exiting when they lost the sense of a professional identity.

To understand the context of the framing of accounts presented in work sickness cases, I present a brief introduction into the current organisation of Swedish primary schools. After specifying the context of school as a workplace, I turn to an analysis of the accounts. The subjective interpretations given in the accounts depict both naming who or what at the work-place is seen as responsible for the experienced illness and blaming processes at work in the school environment. A particular focus of importance in the analysis is uncovering a process of de-professionalising the identity of a school employee as a grade school teacher.

I argue that the effect of organising the administration of one of the major responsibilities of the nation-state, public compulsory education, when done according to principles closely aligned with NPM show how NPM can increase control over school employees and how this in turn can result in employees use of NPM instruments to control the behavior of each other. Accepting a definition of professionalism, as the ability to control one's own work, (Freidson, 2001), the chapter looks at the accounts as living descriptions of the lack and loss of professional autonomy. The chapter summaries the analysis of different accounts with a discussion of processes at the core of NPM and how they change the organisation of work in a way that affects de-professionalization of teachers as employees. I suggest that managerial tools designed to increase efficiency and transparency can be used to weed out undesirable workers and to create uncertainty within a previously assumed, as taken-for-granted, moral authority of professional public sector educational workers. The conclusion ties together how mechanisms of self-control are used to socialise employees to demands of the workplace while creating a basis for how employees learn to control colleagues.

Background. Schools in Sweden

Schools, as a special area of the public sector in Sweden, have gone through extensive organisational changes during a short period of time. De-centralisation of schools from the national state to municipalities in 1989 changed employment status for schoolteachers. They were no longer employees of the state but employees of the municipality. The municipality also was given the legal responsibility for running public schools.

In 1991, private independent schools were accepted and encouraged in Sweden as an equal valued school form guided by the same national laws as public schools and accorded the same amount of public financing per student as that allotted public schools. Arguments for introducing independent private schools on an equal basis with public schools was grounded in the idea that competition between schools would increase when private schools were free and parents could choose which school, public or private, was best for their children, as schools competed in attracting and maintaining students. Competition was thought of as a win-win situation. Proliferation of different types of schools would spread innovation throughout the educational system. Parents would be free to choose a school for their children without worry about costs. These two structural school changes – both the employment relations of teachers together with the transfer of school administration from a central to a local municipality and the inclusion of independent private schools as an equal value school form with free choice for parents to select a school – resulted in mass exits of qualified teaching personal from municipal schools, protests and an intense national school debate.[2] Both these school reforms were influenced by the current popularity of NPM principles.

De-centralisation of administration within the public sector was strongly touted as a technique that would allow management by expertise with preference given to local knowledge on how best to run local schools. In Sweden, the ruling Social Democratic party had throughout the 1980s prepared analysis on the importance of governing through open frame laws which argued for flexibility and for leaving details to local experts. In 1991, with a change in government to a center-right alliance, other NPM principles were also included in governing of compulsory education. This included introducing competition within the public sector by the public financing of private schools within the de-centralised school system. When the Social Democratic party returned to power in 1994, they kept the independent school system financed through the public sector. Twelve years later, in 2006, a central-alliance government regained majority power in parliament in part as a result of a campaign on the negative effects of de-centralisation of schools and the loss of national control over an equal school system.

De-centralisation of schools was equated with a de-regulation of schools.

The new government moved swiftly in 2006 to institute a national School Inspectorate as a powerful new government agency independent of the Swedish National Agency for Education, a new Education Act effective 2011, a program to strength career paths for teachers, and a new national curriculum for the compulsory school, as well as imposing more rigorous and earlier grading of students nationally.

Stricter enforcement of the new national 2010 Education Act by the School Inspectorate included demands on local schools for more documentation of processes within school. The demand on outputs produced by the schools was now both in total alignment with NPM principles and simultaneously increased the national control over Swedish schools. Schools, according to law, were obligated to give each student the support that they individually needed to obtain an equal education. Guaranteeing students rights involved comprehensive documentation not only of what was being done by teachers and school administrators ensuring students rights to an equal and safe education but also action-plans for each individual student. Documentation for dealing with degrading behavior at school was required at each individual school with obligations to review the plans and change them when and if necessary on a continual basis. Complaints against schools were publically available as were yearly school results in terms of grades.

The de-centralisation of schools to municipalities, the introduction of private schools publicly financed and stricter demands for more and better documentation of school output were a severe blow to the public education system in Sweden. Yet, these changes showed that despite different national political majority governments from 1991 to today, there was political unity of use of political arguments for improving schools grounded on basic NPM management principles. Cries to re-nationalise schools, proposed by one center-right political party, were not taken seriously by other political parties as members of the center-right coalition. However, in, 2016 and 2017, the center-left parties currently in power and led by the Social Democrat party are campaigning for law changes capping the amount of profit that owners of private for profit schools can realize.

The idea of something being wrong with Swedish schools undoubtedly has remained a strong election issue since the 1990s. However, the political debate shifted focus from issues of school bullying in the 1990s, to lack of national regulation in the early years of 2000 and after 2010 to problems of integration, segregation and provision of an equal educational outcome for all students. But in 2013, when the OECD PISA reported a rapid decline in Sweden's school results compared to results in 2003 and to the rankings of other countries, a somewhat earlier worried Swedish population became aware that there was "trouble at school".

As a national policy discussion ensued in Sweden about what to do to regain some sort of steady improvement in students' results, a micro level of everyday life at school started to emerge, portraying a school system in disarray. Parents were reporting disturbing events at school to the School Inspectorate. Teachers were leaving schools for other jobs. Recruiting new teachers was problematic. Teachers were increasingly reporting illnesses as caused by the social-psychological organisation of work.

It was obvious to me, while transcribing accounts of both injuries and illness among school employees, that the accounts uncovered what I term micro mechanisms accompanying changes in school policy. The micro mechanisms mirrored what happens when gradual structural organisational changes – de-centralisation of a national school system, introducing private but publically funded schools, increasing regulation and national control over a school system – became unbearable for school employees.

The development of law, politics and regulation produced, on the one hand, a cognitive culture affecting imagery for families and, on the other hand, an assumed script provided to school personal. Families encouraged by the image of a child as "owner" of a sack having a "bag" of school money to be given upon his/her admittance to the school of choice increased both expectations of students and families and demands on schools for delivering better support and better learning outcomes. The cognitive culture portrayed to teachers was a type of "script" outlining both the possible risk of fewer resources if students started leaving their schools, and increased administration and increased teacher responsibility while losing professional authority. The break in cognitive culture between parents, students and teachers was dysfunctional (Hetzler, 2012). The hypotheses below are derived from the analysis of the forms of dysfunction as they affect the everyday life of teachers.

My hypotheses are:

> The use of national regulation to regain control of a de-centralised school system by increasing required documentation of output of work exerts more control over school employees that leads to inward disturbances of the work place.

As control measures coupled with increased competition between schools and within schools become endogenous as a part of school culture, employees use of control mechanisms are directed against each other as a sorting mechanism, resulting in weakening the professional identity of a co-employee and increasing exit alternatives for employees

Method

Swedish law requires employers to report all work injuries or work illnesses to the Swedish Work Environment Authority (SWEA) and to the Swedish National Social Insurance Agency. All the employee needs to do is inform his employer about what has happened. Examples of work sicknesses can be a feeling of psychological distress because of a work conflict or stress at work.[3]

Methodologically, I work with a phenomenological understanding of the written documents as an intentional act (Ricoeur, 1976, 1978). Those writing about what happened assume a receiver of their account. They are answering a specific question. In the case of work-induced illness, the writer is asked, "What caused your illness/impaired your health." The question asks for an explanation of what caused illness. I was looking for examples of explanations that included stating a consequence of what happened because of the cause specified.

The accounts are treated as embodied experiences. By reading the documents, I hoped to capture meaning and common features of an experience or event. The accounts also can be seen as relating processes in an event. The methodology I used is that through reading all case accounts, I capture repeated patterns of what is revealed as links in what happened by the person experiencing the event. As such, I treat the gathered accounts as an instance of "causal reconstruction" of what underlies changing patterns of employment occurring at a macro level.

Renate Mayntz (2004) writes about "causal reconstruction" as a way to overcome an explanatory deficit when accounting for macro level changes. Thus, recognising causal mechanisms in micro processes, she aims at finding generalizations involving processes as a necessary tie-in between micro and macro phenomenon.

Finding the bridge between micro and macro processes is also a concern of new institutionalism. In this work, the emphasis is on the fact that studies of meaningful aspects of institutionalisation draw attention towards peculiarities of institutionalisation. As Tammar Zilber (2008) points out, "the specific contents of institutional structure and practices affect institutionalization and are embedded within larger meaning systems (p. 154)."

The accounts I studied revealed a group of employees that were predominantly, but not only, high-skilled teachers, subjected to psychosocial and organisational pressures of work. In many of the accounts, employees defined a situation that I termed "strategic violence". I define strategic violence as affecting the professional identity of the employee, taking place over a longer period of time and resulting in longer sick leaves or exiting the profession. Strategic violence was usually performed by colleagues at work and involved using aspects of the organisation of work.[4]

Violence at the workplace is often described in literature concerned with safety at the work place (DOL, 2015) as a result of encounters with external perpetrators, e.g. clients, students, customers or patients, who might threaten or attack the employee in everyday working situations. Violence *between* employees has not been recognized to the same extent and is usually defined as *relational violence*, e.g. bullying or sexual harassment, or *structural violence* that originates in the culture at the workplace, e.g. through demeaning language or performed tasks that put the employee at risk. I introduce the term *strategic violence* in this analysis to capture the dynamics involved in threat and violence by connecting the element of intention in behavior and the dynamics involved in movement between relations and organizational structure. Non-physical violence at the workplace is done by knowledge of how organisational structure can be used as a part of non-physical violence directed towards injuring an individual's sense of self and their work identity. There is a dynamic variation captured by the concept "strategic".

An analysis of a non-physical violent behavior makes it possible to depict how covert violent behavior evolves between different structural aspects of the organization of the work place.

I suggest that the written accounts describing the action producing an illness provide an empirical base over a sufficient number of cases and in a variety of situations and locations in a similar work organization, primary schools, to show processes that display mechanisms of work place aggression.

Table 12.1 Population percentages 2012–2015: Age, sick leave and gender

Population N = 569	2012% N = 118	2013% N = 122	2014% N = 153	2015% N = 176
Age				
< 34	11.0	11.5	17.6	16.3
35–44	23.7	22.1	20.9	31.0
45–54	29.7	32.8	37.9	28.7
55>	35.6	33.6	23.5	24.0
Sick leave				
0 days	33.9	32.0	24.8	26.7
1–3 days	1.7	6.6	7.2	2.3
4–14 days	30.5	22.1	47.1	27.8
14 days>	33.9	39.3	20.9	43.2
Gender				
Women	77.1	85.2	87.6	84.5
Men	22.9	14.8	12.4	15.5

Cases were transcribed by myself at the offices of the SWEA and later coded for 7 variables. These were year reported, time between the injury/illness and reporting, gender, age, length of sick leave (1–3 days; 4–14 days; over 14 days), years in the profession at the time of the reported injury/illness, employment category (teachers; before and/or after school pedagogues; child care taker; teacher assistant; other).

Cases of reported illness caused by work increased each year during the four-year period from 118 in 2012 to 176 in 2015. By comparing 2012 and 2015, we see that the tendency in the age of the group reporting work caused illness has moved from older workers (55>) to younger employees. Table 12.1 shows some characteristics of the population and how they have changed over the four-year period.

Analysis

Framing

Reviewing the accounts presented show that illness caused by work are framed as the starting of an event. The form that has to be filled-out structures the written accounts. The form asks for a description of what has happened. It should be mentioned that the account "giver" seldom lets the size of the space for recounting what has happened limit the report of the experienced account. Various techniques such as writing in a minimal hand style, or using atttachments were evident in more than 40% of the submitted cases.

The accounts often started with either framing an event as unexpected or as something that broke a pattern. I categorised events as framed as an *"unexpected change,"* an *"increased work burden,"* or *"the organization of work."* Examples of the three categories are given below:[5]

> It was the second day after the start of the school year and a colleague said she wanted a word with me privately. She accused me of treating her with disdain.
> (Unexpected change experienced by F, 1283)

> I have had an excessive work load for a long time. More and more new work tasks were piled on me without any taken away.
> (Increased work burden, F, 1406)

> Extensive cuts in our budget necessitated a reorganization with larger classes, fewer special pedagogues and other support personal.
> (Organization of work, experienced by F, 1439)

There is not a clear boundary between the categories framing an event. An event can start out as something unexpected that changes into more work or that develops into a broader organisational pattern. What does become obvious is that the writer of the account takes the reader from what can be perceived within a context of a private identity to what is going on in the work place and then to an understanding outside of a private identity to what was happening to her/his professional identity, an identity related to her profession as a teacher, and a reaction to what has been experienced.

This pattern – private identity, professional identity and reaction – can be illustrated by following the development of the written first account presented above. In the unexpected change in everyday working life by being accused of treating a colleague with disdain, the writer continues:

> She thinks that I do not treat people equally and that I am always trying to be best and that I think I am far better than her. She said that I align myself with certain people and that I create groups at work.
>
> (1283)

In this account, the allegations are extended to a criticism that the writer's personal characteristics affect the work place. The writer, in turn, points out that the same person has also accused other people in their workgroup and they feel bad because of the accusations. She also mentions that she has been told that "this colleague might have recorded the conversation". Responsibility is laid by the writer of the account on the accusing colleague for the following results:

> Because of this, I do not dare express my thoughts or my opinion for fear of being recorded. This colleague has called us in the work-team for racists and she has spread this to a new employee. I experience stomach pains when I am on my way to work and at work. I am irritable and have problems sleeping. I have also become afraid of conflicts and have become unsure in situations where I would otherwise be convinced of my viewpoint. That is I pull away instead of standing-up for myself.

The teacher that experienced a continual increase in her work load in the second account introduced above (1406) develops her account by focusing on what it means in her professional life as a teacher. In her case, she starts off directly with her professional identity and a reaction.

> I have been assigned extra hours of teaching in the classroom without giving me any more time for planning and preparing my lessons or time for work after the lessons, for example in correcting work handed-in or grading extra exams. I have been given a work schedule without 100% possibilities to take my legal right to pauses in work or for lunch. I have long work passes with out possibility to go to a lavatory. And there is no possibility for access to necessary continual education so that I can perform all of my work duties (1406).

The reaction experienced by the writer was a 14-day sick leave.

The third case (1439), which frames the event as a necessary re-organisation of the work place, goes directly into how the re-organisation due to budget cuts affects her professional identity.

> A burden has been laid on me as a subject teacher[6] to take responsibility for producing individual course schedules for those students taking my courses and to also plan the individual progress plans for each student and gather necessary study material for each of them to achieve their individual goals. If I do not do this in a satisfactory manner, I meet complaints from worried parents that their child is not getting the necessary help he/she needs to pass the course. Demands are made on teachers with reduced resources to fill higher demands, which is frustrating. The new school law has increased our legal obligations. We have also more students without Swedish as their native language and some of them are illiterate. In addition to all this, I also have my own class of 28 students and that is a safety risk. With all these things to do, I have not any help at all in how to prioritize my work tasks. I am under extreme pressure and I, and my colleagues, have written to our union representatives as well to our school security ombudsman (1439).

The above reaction to the above teacher's situation was a longer sick leave.

Naming

If a frame sets the boundaries, although vague, for what has happened and describes the event within a given context, *naming* those involved sets us into understanding who the writer believes is responsible or at least involved in the event. In the examples given above, the first case (1283) names a particular colleague as initiating the event. But in this account the writer also mentions other colleagues who were also victimized by the same person. The second case, names no one but gives a process of additional work that transgresses boundaries of what should be, according to law, a reasonable job. The third event names no one but describes the event as affecting more than one's own professional identity. The third case actually invokes what might be called a collective professional identity that names appeals to a union and a safety inspector.

Thus, naming someone in the accounts I read can differ from one person spreading ill will among many, to a process seen as unreasonable and against laws designed to protect workers, to a general breakdown in a system where work demands far exceed capacities. To understand what kind of "naming" is most prevalent in the read accounts, I looked at all accounts to come closer to who or what was being named. In a school context, it is apparent that besides the school employee there are students, parents, colleagues and management. In some cases, there are combinations. In this analysis, I examined who or what is named in the written account as involved in the work illness. When many are involved but no one is dominant, I excluded the case. If both colleagues and management (principals) are named together, I used a category of "both".

Dividing students and parents as one category and colleagues, management and "both" as another category captures the differences in the account moving from the personal exterior to an interior environment. I use the concepts *"exterior"* and *"interior"* in relationship to their legal connection to the school environment. Students and parents are considered as part of the *"exterior"* environment. They are connected to the school because of the legal service, compulsory education, provided by the school. The other category, *"interior"*, refers to those employed at the school, service providers. The category "both" is in the majority of cases used in the submitted accounts to mean a lack of support by both colleagues and management.[7] Table 12.2 shows us that there is a difference between accounts written in 2012 and those submitted in 2015. More accounts named students and parents in 2012. But accounts gradually shifted in the following years. By 2015 we could see that accounts involving students and family members are about the same. But accounts naming colleagues and administrators have increased for recognising that both are involved in the incident. Thus, there is a bit of a shift from naming exogenous factors to endogenous factors within schools. Most interesting, however, is that the account writer in 2015 more often grouped behavior from both colleagues and administration as acting together.

Naming is important. Disorderly students or complaining parents can contribute to a dysfunctional work environment. But as "outsiders" to those employed within the school, students and parents can be met by a united "insider" reaction. The "insider" reaction can be that both the students and/or the parents are seen as "not reasonable" and their complaints disregarded. A collective action by a school towards both students and parents can also be a collective and progressive action that finds solutions to conflict beyond what an individual can accomplish.

Table 12.2 Naming others as involved in the process. Percentages for the year 2012 and 2015

Named as Involved N = 271	2012% N = 109	2015% N = 162
Students	16.5	24.7
Parents	14.7	10.5
Colleague	31.2	26.5
Principal	27.5	20.4
Both Colleague and Principal	10.1	17.9

For the individual teacher, it is important when naming students or parents in their written account, how colleagues and the school react. Although our material only incorporates four years of written accounts, it is obvious that what is usually considered as irritable to school organisation, naming disorderly students and/or complaining parents, has gradually shifted towards naming colleagues and management as being involved in work illnesses. Thus, what might have been seen as a standard account or story in schools – uncontrollable students and unreasonable parents – has shifted to stories of interior causes generated within the structure of schools.

Blaming: blaming students and parents

An illness or event caused by a student is usually reported as an "accident" because a child fifteen or under is not considered legally responsible under Swedish law for his/her actions. Occasionally, a student is indirectly blamed in a written account of illness. The written account that names the student finds "blame" somewhere else, usually, within the organisation of the school.

> One does not get any explicit support in front of students and their parents, which undermines a teachers authority to do her/his job. This leaves it open for students to do more or less what they want. One day this culminated in pure harassment against me and ended in a deep depression with anxiety.
>
> (F, 0049)

Or, as in the case below, claiming that the boy does not belong in a classroom.

> A 12 year-old boy has threaten to kill me and has harassed me and others as well as his classmates. My job has been to stop him before he injures someone. The difficulties with stopping his impulsive dangerous behavior, the vast amount of aggression he continually displays and his acting-out behavior can with difficulty be handled within a classroom, even if we offer all of our competency, which we have done. There are many that are suffering and just now it is me.
>
> (Special pedagogue, F, 0122)

Although it is easier in the accounts to lay blame when parents are involved in an unexpected incident, even here management or lack of management from school is blamed.

> A very angry parent comes to school and is threatening and aggressive against me and a colleague. Being understaffed, and not knowing what procedures to follow when a colleague is on sick leave and with no good

plan on what to do in threatening and violent situations, has led to a frustrated parent coming to school behaving aggressively and threatening.

(F, 0045)

The parent in case 0045 is not responsible. In fact, responsibility is entirely given to management for not having the right procedures in place.

However, it does happen that a teacher can put blame on the parents, as we see in the following account where a male teacher blames a group of parents for an acute crisis reaction. He does this without blaming school management.

There was a conflict situation with a group of parents. The parents were extremely critical of me. They used comments against my person, many exaggerated descriptions of my behavior and even threats against me. I suffered an acute crisis reaction with depression, anxiety, loss of weight, problems sleeping and headaches and was on sick leave for an extended period of time.

(M 0010)

In the above case 0010, the teacher is not treated at all within his professional identity; instead, the parents "used comment against my person", or a private identity that causes an "acute reaction".

Blaming colleagues and principals

If naming involves those within the school organisation, criticism becomes more than something related to an individual identity; it becomes something that points blame to the organisation of work and is directed towards the employees professional identity. It is at this level of reading of the accounts of work illness that it is possible to see a clear connection to the organization of work according to principles of NPM. The written accounts are not *blaming* a person but are pointing to a process as responsible. The written account of work injury is being depicted as a consequence of changes in and/or demands made by management of work at schools either by invoking action or by neglecting to take action.

As I have mentioned above, I am working with hypotheses that management and the workplace are changed by changes in macro policy decisions. Changes affect the entire organisation and influence behavior between colleagues by being able to be used as part of an *exclusion* behavior between colleagues and/or by a behavior of *sorting* out employees by management. Thus, colleagues are involved in a process and the reaction affects the professional identity of an individual. This process is an endogenous process within the work organisation and involves strategic violence.

A typical case of being *excluded* by colleagues was reported in a long appendix attached to a reported illness in case 0389 below from a teacher that had been at a school for a number of years and noticed a gradual change over a few years after the appointment of a new principal. She describes it as if the school "culture" had changed:

> The school is run by a few very strong informal leaders and I found myself after a couple of years "out in the cold." I was treated as if I was "air." In our personal room, no one would talk to me and I began to be more and more isolated. If I tried to start a conversation, they would just turn away from me. And if I said something, they pretended that they did not hear me. Decisions at school were taken in the corridors and not at meetings. The possibility to participate did not exist. It became an untenable situation where I was excluded from coordinating my work with other class teachers. I found myself excluded from newly started projects that were originally my idea.
>
> (F, 0389)

She summarises her account by stating, "I was ignored. I did not exist. I was invisible. Nobody said 'hello' or talked to me, I did not exist. I did not get any work-related information and did not get information about students nor was I involved in projects involving students. Now, I am only working 60% and after a day at school I drive home and sleep an hour or two so that I can do something else. I have difficulty finding any joy in life".

A typical case of *sorting-out* is reported in a 5-page appendix in the submitted account of work caused illness. A teacher submits the case 0014. The teacher has competency as a special pedagogue. There are many difficulties at the school and continual changes as old colleagues leave the workplace and many temporary employees come and go. Many of the new and temporary employees are working together with her, taking care of students with special needs. A new school administrator is appointed, parents of the children with special needs are upset and the teacher tries to convey difficulties at the school to the new principal. Some of the main points addressed in the written account are the following:

> I was being attacked with lies, gossip and rumors. B called many meetings because I was being accused of an action against a student. I knew nothing about this. B said I had to go to a psychologist. My judgment was questioned. I was subjected to supervision of my work. I was given unreasonable work directives and my earlier work duties were taken from me. I was not able to work in a classroom because B did not trust that I had the capacity. My job was reduced from 60% to 40%. I was not given any work related information and when I thereby missed a meeting, the principal told me that it could be considered "refusal to work." I was

assigned a minimal work space and told that 'if I was not satisfied, I should quit.' B had told other teachers that they are not to work with me and has also sent a letter to parents telling them he has no confidence in me. When the parents unified, I was called into B's office where he said that if I were behind the parents' unification, I would be fired. After all of this, I was placed at home with pay for a few months.

(F, special pedagogue 0014)

The *sorting-out* process used by the new principal against the teacher can be considered an extreme case. In fact, written accounts where an employee can be considered an "insider" as well as a competent pedagogue, as was the case in the aforementioned 0014 account, is not easily resolved by an administrator wishing to be rid of a teacher. In the aforementioned account, the teacher was unable to get any information about what action she was accused of or how she was to defend herself. By invoking a cause for mistrust of the teacher resulting from something serious outside of the workplace, the administrator could justify separating the teacher from her work. Insisting that the teacher see a psychologist and ordering that her work be supervised are examples that the administrator used to get colleagues at the workplace to question the professionalism of the teacher. It is also a strong signal to the teacher that she should also doubt her competency. However, it is when the administrator goes outside of the internal environment and tries to engage the parents to the children with special needs that the administrator loses control of the situation. The parents ignore the administrator, side with the teacher and unify their opposition instead. The teacher is accused by the administrator of manipulating the parents and banished from the school.

What is unusual about case 0014 is that the teacher had strong resources, never doubted her professionalism and knew that she had support of both colleagues and parents. A situation, which was frequent, however, is the situation of the teacher in case 0389. The teacher felt herself as "invisible" and finally the situation as "untenable". Both cases are directed towards injuring the professional identity of a teacher, damaging the professional self-esteem of an individual resulting in isolation or voluntary leaving the work place.

Discussion

The accounts shown above end in one way or another in blaming bad management at schools as responsible for producing illness. But actually, it took almost 20 years for Sweden to understand that although they de-centralised its national school system and introduced competition with private schools, its central management tool, the independent Swedish National Agency for Education (SNAE) did not function to guarantee the goals of the Education Act. In fact, the SNAE, charged with seeing that there was universal implementation of the Educational Act, waved a "white flag" in their relationship with municipalities and private schools. Supervision of schools was haphazard. Both public municipal schools and privately own schools governed schools as they saw fit. Creating a separate School Inspectorate in 2006 with possibilities to take legal action against municipalities and private schools that were lax in following national education rules and procedures made documentation mandatory.

In addition, the NPM influences in introduction of competition and school choice was minimal for a number of years. The number of students choosing private schools got off to a slow start but a rapid increase started in Sweden at about 2007 and has continued with a concentration and expansion of large for profit school concerns.[8] Today about 14% of students in compulsory nine-year education in Sweden are in independent schools. Between 2008 and 2016 municipal schools in Sweden decreased by 13%.

It is possible to say that both increased requirements for documentation of output results and budget cuts for schools losing students because of competition from both private schools and better functioning municipal schools are exogenous pressures. These pressures increased local management problems and lead to further reliance on gaining efficiency by promoting even more documentation of outcomes.

Thus, we see clearly in the accounts of work-produced illness that increased demands for documentation led to greater possibility to increase control over school employees. Teachers are not only required to produce documentation, but they are also seen as responsible for failed learning processes. Parents tend to pull their children out of a school they see as "failing" or if their child is not getting better grades, which in turn leads to decreased revenue for schools.

Another method used in schools that can be misused and increase excluding or sorting-out school employees is the fragmentation of teachers' autonomy by breaking up the process of teaching into more distinct and smaller units. By introducing fragmentation into more distinct and smaller units it makes it easier to point out what might be seen as weaknesses in the outcome procedures. Focus is turned inwards in a situation of uncertainty. In such a situation, employees use control mechanisms against each other. It becomes easier to use endogenous processes of sorting out and exclusion in a collective identification as what is seen as "the weak link in the chain."

The number of cases within the written accounts that describe exclusion or "sorting out" resulting in an individual loss of self-esteem about his/her professional competency give witness to the fact that exclusion is not an isolated account.

When a principal is sorting-out an individual worker it is seldom that the person to be sorted-out is supported by the workgroup. It is interesting to note that between 2012 and 2015, the cases increasing the most were those where both colleagues and the principal were involved (See Table 12.2 above). Both *excluding* and *sorting-out* use the very tools available within the workplace to perform a non-physical act of violence attacking the professional identity of a teacher. Is what I term "strategic violence" intentional? One might argue that a process is not intentional; only the individual acts that further the process can be intentional. But the end process is known, and if one cannot say an individual act within the process was intentional, then an acceptance of the process by withdrawing support can be seen as participation – even if unwittingly – in the process of exclusion.

Conclusion

There are two processes existing simultaneously within Swedish schools. One is the process of changing the type of management at schools. The other is the reaction to a changing type of management by employees providing services in schools. Employees, when experiencing an illness they see as caused by their work, are providing written accounts of what is happening because of, or reactions to, macro level changes in how they should provide public services. This chapter looked at the work process of providing public service of obligatory compulsory education to those with rights to these services and to those demanding good services.

In the material used, the accounts recount how employees wound up sick and in many cases lost confidence in their professional identity. I use this result of losing confidence in their professional identity as representing the result of an act of strategic violence. Strategic violence is a process that exists at work. It is the link between the process of changing the social organization and management culture of schools and the illness experienced as caused by work. The accounts describe processes of exclusion and of being "sorted out" and how it affects a sense of professionalism.

I have attempted to use these accounts as eye views of everyday life from school employees in Sweden, an advanced welfare state. The accounts of employees are not simple diary notations of life at school. They are documents recorded as written accounts accusing the schoolwork environment of inflicting illness upon employees while they are doing their job.

Thus, I have not presented normal accounts of daily life at school. Instead, I have used the accounts that might well be a tip of an iceberg. The accounts I have presented come about as exceptions to everyday life. They have come from those that have accepted that their illness is work produced.

Fevre et al. (2012) mean that the reason illness caused by work has not become a public issue is because such concepts as "bullying" traditionally used in the literature to describe psycho-social organisationally caused illness did not lead to any attempt by researchers to generalize from the individual experience (p. 23). Concepts to describe incidents were such concepts that personalised the incident and thereby could only be helped by finding individual solutions. Incidents, according to Feyre et al. were thought of as private troubles and stayed private instead of treated as public issues.

The concept I used to describe the behavior is "strategic violence". It was necessary to discover a new concept that was embedded in the processes of organisational change in the public sector and clearly described in written accounts of work injuries by school employees. The accounts tell a public story. The concept enables us to look at accounts that make visible a process that is endogenous to the work place and clearly puts blame as lying within this process.

The stories take us into the professional identity as teacher, which is far more than a role that is played during working hours but is a part of a professional identity existing alongside a private identity, defining everyday life when work and private life are intertwined. The stories tell of how experiences of being excluded or an object to a "sorting out" process are experienced first as harm to a private identity. But as the story unravels, as we read the account, we see the individual in many cases talking about harm to a professional identity and a sense of loss.

What is important in the accounts in this chapter are that the written accounts are producing a new type of story. They are not stories of aggressive parents or unruly students even though those stories exist and are well known. Those stories made up the myth about schools. The accounts I read include some of these old stories but also stories that are new and are stories that are becoming a public issue. These stories have become a part of a larger picture of school culture and the consequence can be seen when people shy away from entering a profession that is no longer appealing.

In my examination of how new public management principles fragments the autonomy of school employees and creates a de-professionalism of their identity through the use of an endogenous process that I call strategic violence, I also became aware of the power of the written accounts.

As Paul Ricoeur argues, the written account is an intentional act. I as a reader am an interpreter and a translator. Every interpretation relocates what is read within knowledge of what is an available horizon of understanding. Thus, I am, by using concepts such as "interior" and "exterior" environments and by "excluding" or "sorting-out" behavior, changing what I read in the accounts to a conceptual rationalizing interpretation of my interaction with the accounts (1978, p. 303). The accounts create the possibility to show how another story develops about what is happening to work in the public sector.

These stories, outside of an interpretation of how new public management has influenced daily behavior at work, have become part of the culture of the Swedish public service workplace. And whether they are heard or read, these stories are passed on to others working within similar work places. The stories are strong stories and convey a solid picture of changing professionalism and changing work places. A collective and silent response is apparent as fewer chose to enter public sector professions and more workers in public sector professions withdraw through illness or exit.

Notes

1 This chapter is based on 569 cases. They are (100%) of the cases reported by law, of a work-related illness to the SWEA between 2012 and 2015. The 569 cases are a part of a larger population of 1808 cases gathered during the same time period but, which also included cases where injury caused at primary schools, was seen as an accident and usually caused by a student. Support for this research was provided by The Swedish Foundation for Humanities and SocialScience (P13–1197:1).
2 Throughout the 1990s, 6% of male teachers and 5.5% of women teachers left the teaching profession. Younger teachers leave the profession at higher rates with teachers under the age of 29 leaving at rates of above 10% throughout the period between 1990 and 1999. Today, one in every six persons who has been educated as a teacher does not work as a teacher. www.scb.se/statistik/_publikationer/UF0521_2001A01_BR_A40BR0103.pdft teachers leave the profession at higher rates with teachers under the age of 29 leaving at rates of above 10% throughout the period between 1990 and 1999. Today, one in every six persons who has been educated as a teacher does not work as a teacher. www.scb.se/statistik/_publikationer/UF0521_2001A01_BR_A40BR0103.pdft.
3 A Swedish employer must even report an event that could bring about an injury or illness, that is, incidents that could lead to an injury or illness even if they did not in the particular reported case result in an injury or illness.
4 Although bullying and harassment at work has been researched, the research looks at the events at an individual and descriptive level and follows the patterns of understanding adult bullying as extension of a phenomenon of bullying developed to explain the behavior of children. See the discussion in the conclusion of the chapter.
5 Each account presented is followed by the gender of the writer of the account and a number that has been assigned the account in the study. When I return to an account in the text the number of the case is presented again in parentheses. The accounts are modified to protect the anonymity of the account writer. Accounts presented are selected because they are representative of many individual cases that describe the cause of illness at word in a similar manner.
6 I use the expression "subject" teacher to describe it as being either in languages, social or natural sciences. The writer was not explicit which area was actual in her case.
7 In some cases, "both" can also include reference to parents, but this is in few cases.
8 There are presently 6 large active school conglomerates in Sweden.

References

Accounting, Organizations and Society, 20(2–3): 93–109.
assessment', in: Pereyra, M. A., Kotthoff, H.-G., Cowen, R. (eds.), *Pisa Under Examination*, 47–59, Rotterdam: Sense.
DOL. (2015): United States Department of Labor, DOL Workplace Violence Program, www.dol.gov/oasam/hrc/policies/dol-workplace-violence-program.htm
Fevre, R., Lewis, D., Robinson, R., Jones, T. (2012): *Trouble at Work*, New York: Bloomsbury Academic.
Freidson, E. (2001): *Professionalism, the Third Logic: On the Practice of Knowledge*, Chicago: University of Chicago Press.
Hetzler, A. (2012): *Why Law Fails*, Presented at the International Conference on Law and Society, 12th Annual Meeting, June 2012, Honolulu.

Hood, C. (1991): 'A public management for all seasons?', *Public Administration*, 69(1): 3–19.
Mayntz, R. (2004): 'Mechanisms in the analysis of social macro-phenomena', *Philosophy of the Social Sciences*, 34(2): 237–259.
Ricœur, P. (1976): *Interpretation Theory: Discourse and the Surplus of Meaning*, Fort Worth: Texas Christian University Press.
Ricoeur, P. (1978): *The Rule of Metaphor: Multi-disciplinary Studies of the Creation of Meaning in Language* (R. Czerny, Trans.), Toronto: University of Toronto Press.
Zilber, T. (2008): 'The work of meanings in institutional processes and thinking', in: Greenwood, R., Oliver, C., Suddaby, R. (eds.), *The SAGE Handbook of Organizational Institutionalism*, 150–169, London: SAGE Publications.

Chapter 13

Comply or defy? Managing the inclusion of disabled people in the Netherlands

Lieske van der Torre and Menno Fenger

Introduction

Sheltered employment is a policy instrument for the employment of disabled people (see for example: OECD, 2003). It is a provision for disabled people who do not succeed in finding a job on the labor market themselves (see for example: OECD, 2008; Visier, 1998). These jobs are provided by sheltered work companies (sw-companies). European examples of these types of organizations are the 'centros especiales de empleo' in Spain, 'Samhall' in Sweden or the 'ateliers protégés' and 'centres d'aide par le travail' in France. Work activities may include on-site assemblage activities, the maintenance and cleaning of public parks and streets or washing and ironing laundry from hotels and bungalow parks. In the Netherlands, sheltered work is offered by local or regional sheltered work companies. Together, sw-companies in the Netherlands employ over 100.000 people, which make them one of the biggest employers for disabled people in the Netherlands (van Santen, van Oploo & Engelen, 2013).

In the Netherlands, ever since the introduction of the Sheltered Work Act (SWA) in 1969, sheltered work was considered an open, inclusive and accessible way for disabled people to participate in society. Employment in sheltered work places in the Netherlands shows all formal characteristics of regular employment like a labor contract, a collective labour agreement, a trade union and regular payment. Since 1995 the idea of sheltered work as the preferred solution for labour market inclusion of disabled people has become increasingly contested (see, for example: Fenger et al., 2011, 2013) and employment of disabled people at *regular* employers became the (only) social goal.

Especially triggered by the very low number of people bridging the gap between sheltered work and the regular labour market, an intensive debate and consecutive reform measures have radically changed the contents and the management of the policy domain (ibid.; see also: van de Vrie, 2008). In this chapter, we highlight two important changes of the SWA: first, the changing ideas about the social character of sheltered employment. In this chapter, we will call this the 'ideational change'. Sheltered work is increasingly being considered as contributing to the *exclusion*, rather than the *inclusion*, of disabled people (see, for example: Fenger et al., 2011, 2013). On the one hand, because contacts and interactions with non-disabled are limited, on the other hand because the safe and protective environment may also form a barrier for disabled people to accept a job with a regular employer. With this regard, sheltered work may function as a protective cage for disabled people. Therefore, an important policy change in Dutch sheltered work policies has been to increase the focus on working *outside* the sw-company, at a regular employer (ibid.). This means sw-companies have to execute a social strategy focusing on employing as many disabled people as possible at regular employers. Second, we will focus on the *managerial change* to increase the responsibility of municipalities for the implementation of the SWA. In 2008, the Dutch cabinet moved the SW-budget from the 'governing bodies' to *individual* municipalities which creates a financial incentive for individual municipalities to increasingly interfere in employment policies of disabled people and increasingly take up the role of a 'principal' towards sw-companies. This was necessary because in practice sw-companies were often the actual policy makers and this creates the danger that business goals overrule social goals. In the perception of the national government, increasing the responsibility of individual municipalities for the execution of the SWA would contribute to increasing the number of disabled people employed at regular employers (van de Vrie, 2008).

These changes of the SWA are designed by the Dutch *national* government and imply that municipalities and the sw-companies would act according to these *ideational* and *managerial* changes. In this paper, we analyse whether this assumption is true. Do municipalities indeed comply with these shifting values, goals and roles? Do sw-companies (mainly) execute the social strategy to employ disabled people at regular employers instead? Do municipalities become a 'principal' that sets out the social strategy of its sw-company? This chapter focuses on the impact of the policy changes of the SWA on the roles and strategies of sheltered work companies. In doing so, it presents a valuable overview of the way in which *ideational* and *managerial* changes about appropriate work for disabled people are reflected in the management and strategy of sheltered work companies. It shows how and why the ideational and managerial changes in national policy find their way in the social strategies of Dutch sw-companies and that these changes are implemented in different ways and with different outcomes in strategy.

This chapter is structured as follows. In the next section, we provide the necessary background information about the context of sheltered employment in the Netherlands. Following that, we present a detailed description of the main *ideational* and *managerial* changes in sheltered work policy in the Netherlands since 1998. Then we introduce the ideas of the inclusion movement and NPM and use them to formulate expectations about the impact of the ideational and managerial changes on the strategies and relations with its municipality of sw-companies. After that the methodology and results of the case studies are discussed. Finally, we draw conclusions about the impact of the reform of sheltered work policy on the social strategies of Dutch sw-companies and the role of the municipalities in defining the sw-companies' social strategies.

Implementation of the Sheltered Work Act

Sheltered work in the Netherlands was regulated in the Sheltered Work Act, which dates from 1969.[1] This regulation aims at offering adapted jobs to those disabled people who do not succeed in finding a regular job themselves.

In the Netherlands, municipalities are responsible for the implementation of the Sheltered Work Act. They are free to choose their own 'implementation modality' (van de Vrie, 2008). Table 13.1 shows a global overview of the possible implementation modalities. The implementation modality affects the relationship between the municipality and the sw-company. In most cases, municipalities put the execution of the SWA in hands of sw-companies, but they can also decide to give other organizations the assignment of offering jobs to their disabled people. These other organizations can, for example, be private reintegration companies or employment agencies. In this chapter, we will only focus on sw-companies.

Sheltered employment in practice

In the Netherlands, there are around 90 sheltered work companies. Their main task is to provide jobs to persons that have to work under adapted circumstances because of their psychological, mental or physical disability (VNG, 2006). The jobs offered by sw-companies can be *internal* or *external* jobs. Internal jobs are jobs in the sheltered environment of the sw-company itself. In that case, the employees contribute to the production activities of the sw-company and the services it delivers. The type of jobs that sw-companies offer to their employees differs (Simons, 2009). Examples of products fabricated within sw-companies are wooden toys, chairs and posters. Examples of services delivered by sw-companies are the packing of products, laundry washing, greening and cleaning. External jobs are at regular employers e.g. guided jobs or secondment. In that case, people work in a regular company like a supermarket, posting company or garage. In the Netherlands, the different types of jobs are often presented as a 'workladder' where sheltered work is the lowest step and supported employment the highest (see Figure 13.1). The ultimate goal according to this 'workladder' is a regular job for disabled people.

Table 13.1 Four implementation modalities of the SWA for municipalities

Implementation modality	Explanation
1 A municipal service (e.g. similar to a social service)	Greatest mode of local control: from the municipality there is a direct responsibility and steering on the activities and the implementation of the SWA
2 A joined arrangement	Activities in the field of sheltered employment are part of the arrangement and will be legally executed in the public organization Tasks and powers are transferred to the 'cooperative authority'. The board of the 'cooperative authority' controls the activities. The sw-companies fulfil the actual tasks. The sw-workers are employed by the 'cooperative authority' (except those that work in supported jobs). In general, the executive committee is formed by the aldermen and the board mainly by council members
3 A joined arrangement with a privatized company	This model is similar to the previous one. An important difference is that the sw-company is privatised. It is a separate, private entity with its own legal capacity. Often there is a contractual relationship between the 'cooperative authority' and the sw-company. Sw-workers are employed by the 'cooperative authority' and seconded at the sw-company. The cooperating municipalities in the 'cooperative authority' have the administrative responsibility and bear the financial risks
4 A purchasing model	Activities are purchased from another municipality, 'cooperative authority' or individual reintegration company based on an agreement

Source: van de Vrie (2008) (translated).

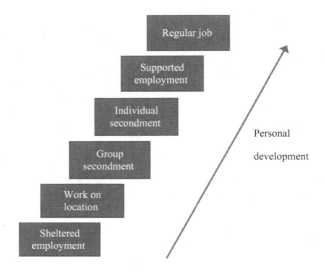

Figure 13.1 The 'work ladder' for disabled people.

Ideational and managerial changes in the Dutch Sheltered Work Act

After the short introduction to the Dutch sheltered employment sector we now turn to a more detailed description of the main *ideational* and *managerial* changes in the Dutch Sheltered Work Act. In the last 20 years, the SWA has greatly changed. Since 1995, the SWA has been increasingly criticized and adapted, especially due to its 'excluding character' and increasing costs (Fenger et al., 2011). In 1998, there was a great revision of the SWA. And in 2005 and 2008, the SWA was modernised in two phases. Since 2010 there are plans to merge the SWA in a new regulation with other regulations for people with a distance to the labour market. In 2015, this led to the implementation of the Participation Act. Core of the new regulation is the merging of the SWA with other regulations aimed at the labor market integration of vulnerable groups on the labour market, large budget cuts and a greater focus on non-sheltered work for disabled people. In the Participation Act, there were also plans for the introduction of a quota for employers, but these plans were cancelled (van der Aa, 2015). In this chapter we only look at the changes that relate to the Sheltered Work Act specifically and not to the Participation Act.

In understanding the impact of the SWA's changes it is important to realize that the changes of the SWA were, on the one hand, *ideational* changes and, on the other hand, *managerial* changes. In the next section, these two types of changes are discussed in more detail.

Ideational changes: 'from the inside to the outside'

The revisions of the SWA led to an increased focus on working at a regular employer as the ultimate goal for disabled people. The aim was to let as many disabled people work 'outside' the sw-company and let them participate 'normally' in society. Since 1995, the idea of sheltered work as the preferred solution for the labour market inclusion of disabled people was being increasingly contested (Fenger et al., 2011, 2013; see also: OECD, 2003, 2008). An illustration is the statement of prime minister Rutte that in sheltered employment people are excluded from society and put in 'boxes in the meadow with a bow around it' and that this is 'asocial' (Binnenlands Bestuur, 2011, p. 1)

New instruments were introduced in the SWA to contribute to the employment of disabled people at regular employers, like the introduction of supported employment as a new work modality (1998), wage subsidies and the no-risk policy (2005–2008). Supported employment differs from the other work types as the employee is employed by a regular employer instead of the sw-company. The sw-company still provides the essential guidance of the person with disabilities at the job. In the case of wage subsidies, the employee works for the statutory minimum wage (or the lowest scale of the collective labor agreement) and the employer receives subsidy from the government. The no-risk polis concerns the facility that the government pays the employees wage when he or she gets ill. This reduces the (perceived) risk of hiring disabled people. These instruments should stimulate employers to employ persons with disabilities.

Managerial changes: increase the responsibility of municipalities

The main managerial change in the revisions of the SWA in the past 20 years concerned the measures to increase the responsibility of municipalities for the implementation of the SWA (Fenger et al., 2011). Municipalities *themselves* had to develop a 'vision' on the employment of disabled people. Until then, many municipalities were inclined to leave policy decisions regarding the SWA to the sw-companies (Eerste Kamer, 2007; see also: van der Torre, 2016). The Raad voor Werk en Inkomen (2006, p. 5) also mentioned that municipalities were at such great distance of the execution of the SWA by sw-companies that de facto sw-companies were the actual policymaker regarding the implementation of the SWA.

The managerial change to stimulate municipalities to better supervise and steer on the sw-companies started in 1998 with the revision of the SWA. With this revision the administrative responsibilities for the SWA moved from the Minister of Social Affairs and Employment to the municipalities (Fenger et al., 2011). Also, the role of the formal employer of the persons making use of the SWA transferred from the national government to the local government and the financing system changed in a way that the municipalities got more discretion over the received subsidies. Previously, the national government had a detailed interference in how municipalities spent the SWA-subsidies and greatly looked at the *costs* made (TK, 1995–1996, 24, 787, nr. 3, p. 8). Now they changed to a new 'budgeting philosophy' to link the SWA-subsidy to a certain amount of jobs that has to be realized for people with disabilities (performance steering). According to the national government, this change in budgeting philosophy, which was now formalised in regulation, made it no longer necessary to have detailed interference of national government in the costs of municipalities regarding the execution of the SWA.

With the modernisation of the SWA in 2008 one of the main goals was to further strengthen the responsibility of the municipalities for the implementation of the SWA (VNG, 2006). An evaluation report in 2001 showed that the amendment of the law in 1998 had not led to the desired level of steering of municipalities regarding the execution of the SWA (ibid.). An explanation was that many municipal administrators just think 'it all goes well'. Several measures were initiated to stimulate the direction and control of municipalities over the SWA. First, the government subsidies went directly to the *individual* municipalities (Fenger et al., 2011). Before that time, the 'governing bodies' executing the SWA received the subsidies from the central government. In practice, most municipalities chose for a 'joined arrangement' in which multiple municipalities participate and that's concerned with the actual execution of the SWA. This could put restrictions on the possibilities of the individual municipalities to execute the SWA in their desired way (TK, 2005–2006, 30 673, nr. 3). In addition, the cabinet's argumentation for transferring the subsidies directly to the individual municipalities was:

> The Cabinet considers that the allocation of the SWA-budget to individual municipalities is necessary to enable municipalities to better understand the responsibility they already have for the SWA, so that the purpose of the SWA can be better are reached. [...] With the budget in hand, with a place for this in the municipal budget and in the municipal accounts, the board of Mayor and Aldermen can, in consultation with the city council, be directed more on both the policy and implementation of the SWA. In short, the municipality pays, so determines.
> (Eerste Kamer, 2007)

Second, municipalities had to account for *themselves* to the national government, and not the joined arrangement, for the results of the SWA in their own municipality (VNG, 2006). Third, individual municipalities had to manage the waiting lists for the SWA by themselves and give insight in these lists.

Social inclusion and New Public Management

In the previous section, we discussed two main changes of the SWA: (1) the *ideational* change to 'include more people in society' and (2) the *managerial* change to increase municipalities' responsibility for the implementation of the SWA. These policy changes do not stand alone but can be viewed in the context of broader international changes in social policies, specifically the trends of 'social inclusion' and 'New Public Management'. This section discusses this broader context.

Inclusion of disabled people

The increased emphasis in the SWA on the employment of disabled people can be linked to ideas of the social inclusion movement (see also: van der Torre & Fenger, 2014). Since the 1970s, the social inclusion of disabled people increasingly emerged as a societal and political issue in many countries (see, for example, Barnes & Mercer, 2005; Oliver & Barnes, 2010). Employment for disabled people was viewed as an important element to their social inclusion (see, for example, Barnes & Mercer, 2005). This is closely linked to the idea that citizenship is pre-eminently associated with paid work (Barnes & Mercer, 2005; Grint, 1998).

Municipalities as 'principal'

In the history of sheltered work in the Netherlands, many sw-companies until then had invested primarily in creating on-site production facilities where disabled could work in a sheltered environment. National policy-makers doubted the ability and willingness of sw-companies to adapt to a more inclusive strategy due to their business interests. Therefore, a managerial change accompanied the ideational change. The key of the managerial change was the creation of a principal-agent relation between municipalities and sw-companies. In a principal-agent relationship, the principal decides about the *why* and *what*, and the agent decides about the *how*. Only when the principal has defined a comprehensive policy proposal with clear goals and targets, does the agent – who agrees to do the job in exchange for compensation – enter the stage (Kettl, 2000; see also: White, 1985). The agent is exchangeable, which opens the floor for tendering and competition. Therefore, the attempts to redefine the relations between municipalities and sw-companies into a principal-agent model, is at the heart of the NPM-framework according to Dunveavy and Hood (1994; see also Pollitt, 2003). This principal-agent relation would contribute to increasing the implementation of a more inclusive strategy and therefore the goals of the SWA will be better met.

Theoretical expectations

Previously we discussed that the Dutch cabinet had changed the SWA in such a way that there are incentives for municipalities to increase their active involvement in the implementation of the SWA. These changes also had an economic logic. These incentives were strongly based on the *economic logic*: who pays decides. Municipalities were handed the SWA-subsidies for the employment of disabled people. In terms of the principal-agent theory it will be likely that municipalities take up the role of a '*principal*' who formulates what job needs to be done, searches an agency to execute this job and will account for the results (ibid.). In a classical principal-agent relationship, the principle decides about the 'why' and 'what', and the agent about the 'how'. Municipalities will steer more on the implementation of the SWA and look more critically at the results. According to the cabinet, this would increase the role of municipalities (the principal) and decrease the role of sw-companies (the agent) in formulating the local goals regarding the SWA. The Cabinet assumed this to result in increased employment of disabled people at regular employers.

The focus of this chapter is on the impact of the ideational and managerial policy changes of the SWA on the role and strategies of sw-companies. However, almost 50 years of implementation in public administration research has taught us that policies and ideas designed at the national level seldom are implemented unmodified in local contexts. Of course, this idea has been eloquently worded by Pressman and Wildavsky (1973) in their subtitle: "How Great Expectations in Washington Are Dashed in Oakland; Or, Why It's Amazing that Federal Programs Work at All", and thereafter illustrated in many different classical cases (see, for instance, Bardach, 1977; Mazmanian & Sabatier, 1989 and for a more extensive overview Hill & Hupe, 2014). If we assume full compliance with the ideational and managerial changes in the implementation stage, we might expect two changes in the strategies and positions of sw-companies. First, the main goal of Dutch sw-companies is the employment of disabled people at regular employers. This would mean that the ideational change of the SWA to increase the employment of disabled people at regular employers is completely implemented. Second, municipalities take up the role of 'principals' that define the 'jobs' the sw-companies have to execute. This implies that in order to comply with this change towards a principal-agent relation, municipalities should be in the lead in defining the mission, goals and strategy of sheltered work policy. If sw-companies are in the lead, we conclude that there is no compliance to this element of the reforms of the SWA (see Table 13.2).

Building upon the implementation literature, it is much likelier that we will observe modified implementation, or no implementation conform these changes at all. Therefore, we will identify in eight cases to what extent they have complied or defied the ideational and managerial changes from the national level, and why. Before proceeding to the results of this analysis, we will outline the methodology we used for this analysis.

Methodology

Eight case studies on the strategic practices of Dutch sw-companies were conducted in the period from September 2012 until July 2013. The unit of analysis was a sw-company. The case study data were gathered through more than 100 interviews with different stakeholders of the sw-company (staff, managers and clients), the local governments (the alderman, councilors and policy makers) and private organisations that made use of the services of Dutch sw-companies and/or buy their goods. Additionally, policy documents from sw-companies and municipalities were analysed, like the annual reports, websites and policy plans. For the analysis all interviews were transcribed and coded.

To determine the impact of the ideational and managerial policy changes of the SWA on the roles and strategies of sw-companies we look in this chapter at:

- To what extent and why do sw-companies adopt the employment of disabled people at regular employers as their main strategy? (implementation of the ideational change)
- To what extent and why is the strategy of the sw-company determined by the municipality as a 'principal'? (implementation of the managerial change)

Table 13.2 shows how we defined compliance and defiance of the ideational and managerial change.

In next two sections the results of the case studies are discussed.

Table 13.2 Explanation of compliance and defiance

	Comply	Defy
Implementation of the inclusion strategy (ideational change)	Social strategy: Relatively great emphasis on employing disabled people at regular employers	Social strategy: Relatively great emphasis on providing sheltered employment to people with disabilities *or* relatively great emphasis on developing the employee skills of people with disabilities
Municipality as principal (managerial change)	Social strategy is a result of the demands of the municipality	Social strategy is (mainly) a result of the vision of the managing director e.g. based on arguments regarding the resource environment *or* the organizational identity

The impact of ideational change: the implementation of the 'inclusion strategy'

The case studies showed that in 2012–2013 not all sw-companies have adopted the inclusive strategy aimed at employing disabled people at regular employers. Based on the cases studies three types of social strategies can be distinguished at sw-companies. The first strategy is to *provide work to disabled people at the sw-company*. This strategy puts no or very little pressure on sw-companies to find (eventually) work at a regular employer. Therefore, most disabled people work in sheltered work facilities. Organisations with this strategy can be labeled as a 'traditional sw-company' or 'production factory'. Sw-company 1 shows a clear example of this strategy. This sw-company was by the respondents called a 'traditional sheltered work company' for which it is important to be a 'firm' and a 'full-fledged partner in the market'. About the institutional norm to strongly focus on employing disabled people at regular employers the managing director stated

> [...] we [let] people free in where they want to work. [...] If they want to work at the sw-company, that's fine. If they want to work at a regular employer, we will support that kindly. There is no pressure from the sw-company to go anywhere

The second strategy is *a strong focus on the development of the skills of disabled people*. When their skills are developed enough work at a regular employer will be found. This organisation can be labeled as a 'human development organization'. Sw-company 2 is a clear example of this strategy. The manager of sw-company formulated their social strategy as: "[Their] course is therefore aimed at making as many people as possible ready for the labor market. Within the [internal] companies, clients are given the opportunity to develop themselves". The third strategy is *a strong focus on finding a job at a regular employer* and a very limited role for sheltered work. This strategy fits with the desired changes in the SWA. The sw-company is in that case a 'secondment organization' or 'reintegration organization' that can be viewed as a supplier of employees for employers. sw-company 3 had a clear example of this strategy. The following citation illustrates this clearly: "What we have said now: make sheltered work as little as possible, as much as possible development and work outside [the sw-company] [...]. With the starting point: nobody should work inside [the sw-company]".

During the case studies there were also two sw-companies transforming their sw-company from a traditional sw-company with a great focus on sheltered employment into an organization focused on supporting disabled people to find a job at a regular employer. Sw-company 4 described their transformation as 'from *employer* to *service provider*'. The sw-company was no longer mainly focused on employing disabled people themselves in their own sheltered facilities but was now concerned with delivering regular employers suitable employees.

In line with the different social strategies, the study also showed great differences in the results regarding the employment of disabled people at regular employers. For example, the Public Overview Results showed that the percentage of the total number of sw-employees who are seconded at a regular employer varies between 2% and 49% in the second half of 2012.[2]

Arguments of sw-companies to comply or defy the inclusion strategy

Sw-companies thus have different strategies regarding how to employ disabled people and different results in employing disabled people at regular employers. In this chapter, we are not only interested in *what* strategies sw-companies adopt, but we are also interested in *why* they chose their strategies. In order to better understand the different impacts of the *ideational change of the SWA* we discuss in this section the arguments of sw-companies to adopt or defy the ambition to employ as much disabled people at regular employers.

The case studies showed that the sw-companies implemented the inclusion strategy following different arguments. Five lines of reasoning can be distinguished. Some sw-companies combine different lines of reasoning for adopting or defying the inclusion strategy. The first line of reasoning is to adopt the inclusion strategy as a *financial* instrument for better financial results. Two sw-companies believed that the employment of disabled people at regular employers was financially a better strategy than to invest in sheltered employment. A manager of sw-company 5, for example, said

> In fact, we actually said [...] in 2005 or so, we're going to focus more on secondment. That was because we saw 'inside' was too expensive. So we said when we had to get more people out [at a regular employer]

Second, adopting an inclusion strategy was seen as an *ideational* instrument to increase the social inclusion of disabled people. Especially in sw-company 3 there was a strong *belief* in that working at a regular employer is better than working in sheltered employment. A third line of reasoning is to adopt the inclusion strategy to meet *national* policy goals. Two sw-companies had that line of reasoning. An illustrative citation is, for example: "The aim is, thinking of the intention of the [SWA], to offer [disabled people] as much employment in the regular labor market as possible, and if this fails to offer work at [sw-company 6]". The fourth argument to *adopt* the inclusion strategy is that sw-companies adopt this strategy to meet *local* political demands (case 2, 7 and 8). This is in accordance with the desired managerial change of the SWA as was discussed in previous paragraph.

Finally, we discuss the line of reasoning to defy the inclusion strategy. Sw-companies only partly adopt or defy the inclusion strategy because it is according to the managing director an *unrealistic policy demand* due to (local) labor market characteristics (case 1 and 6). In case 1, the managing director was convinced that market parties are not interested in employing disabled people: "we don't believe in that". Therefore, their main focus was still on providing sheltered employment for disabled people. The managing director of sw-company 6 mainly uses their specific labor market conditions as argument to only partly adopt the inclusion strategy. In the annual report of 2013 can for example be read: "Given the labor market [in municipality 6], with many small companies with fewer than five employees and many companies with a strong seasonal character, working within the manufacturing company of [sw-company 6] is often inevitable. Especially for people with a slightly greater distance to the labor market or in need of highly structured work, [sw-company 6] can offer structured serial production". Interesting is also that this managing director opposes the claim that focussing on the secondment of disabled people at regular employers is financially more interesting than having focussed on sheltered employment (the first line of reasoning).

The impact of managerial change: the municipality as principal?

Although the SWA aimed at increasing the responsibility of the municipalities in the local implementation of the SWA, we observed in five of the eight cases that the municipality doesn't take the leading role in choosing the strategy for its sw-company. In those cases, the municipality wasn't the 'principal' who beforehand already knows what job needs to be done by the sw-company. In the period 2012–2013, in practice many municipalities still heavily depend on the managing director of the sw-company for setting the goals of its sw-company. For example, sw-company E sets even its own targets. The municipal governor used the following explanation for 'non principal'-attitude: "Because [sw-company E] is a forward-thinking organization and especially its management is really looking at where do we stand within 3 years and where do we stand within 5 years". Other reasons for the 'non-principal'-attitude of municipalities that were mentioned in the case studies are: municipalities think of the managing director as the *'expert'* who is better capable of setting the strategy for the sw-company (case 6), municipalities were *not interested enough* in the strategies of the sw-company (as long as their financial result was positive) (case 1) or the municipalities *lacked the knowledge* (case 8).

In addition, it is relevant mentioning that in the three cases in which the municipality can be called the 'principal' this was in two cases strongly the result of the managing director of the sw-company who profiles the sw-company as a 'public organization' that needs guidance from the municipality. This made that the managing director actively invested in getting strategic guidance from the municipality. Only for case 4 counts that the municipalities initiated and steered the implementation of the inclusion strategy at the sw-company. The municipalities in this case hired a managing director that could implement the inclusion strategy as they had formulated.

Discussion and Conclusions

In this chapter we have argued that sheltered work policy in the Netherlands in the last decade has been characterised by two important changes: 1) the *ideational* change to focus on the employment of disabled people at regular employers and less on the provision of sheltered employment and 2) the *managerial* change to increase municipalities' responsibility for the implementation of the SWA. This chapter has explored to what extent *local* sw-companies have adapted their strategies and positions in compliance with these changes.

Our first conclusion is that, despite the limited expectations from the implementation literature, in the cases we have analysed we do observe a fair level of compliance. Three cases have implemented both the ideational and managerial changes in their strategies and positions, whereas another three cases have implemented the ideational, but not the managerial change. But there were also two sw-companies that have defied the trend towards work for disabled at regular employers by continuing work for disabled at the *sw-company*. What's interesting from a public management perspective here is that in three cases the ideational change has been implemented without implementing the managerial change of constructing a principal-agent relation between municipalities and sw-companies. The municipalities in these cases still heavily relied on the management of the sw-companies to formulate the future strategy of the organisation. But even though the managerial change was intended to support the ideational change by forcing municipalities to create incentives for sw-companies, the goals of more regular work for disabled were pursued by the sw-companies in these cases. Not because *they had to*, but *because they wanted to*. These cases highlight the power of the ideational reform. In Table 13.3, we have summarised the different forms of compliance that we have observed in our analysis.

When explaining the level of compliance to the goals as formulated by the national government different lines of reasoning have to be distinguished. *Compliance* to the ideational change was in some cases driven by the changes in

Table 13.3 Impact of the ideational changes and managerial changes

	Managerial change	
	Principal – agent	Agent-directed
Ideational change		
Comply	Full compliance (3 cases)	Ideational compliance (3 cases)
Defy	Managerial compliance	Full non-compliance (2 cases)

the SWA but in many cases the ideational change was actually driven by other arguments like finances and individual beliefs. Managing directors chose to *defy* the ideational change because in their opinion an alternative strategy fitted better to their local labor market situation and was more in accordance with their own beliefs about the desires of employers. *Compliance* to the managerial change wasn't only the result of municipalities increasing their responsibility for the SWA themselves but also of managing directors labeling their sw-company as a *public* organization that needs a clear task from its municipality to execute and therefore actively invested in stimulating their municipalities to formulate this task. So again, the installation of a principal-agent relation between municipality and sw-company did not occur because the municipalities *had* to do this, but because both partners *wanted to* do this. Non-compliance to the managerial change often wasn't the result of resistance from the sw-company due to their decreased strategic freedom but of the municipality still not picking up the role of a principal that formulates a clear job that needs to be done. The great reliance of municipalities on sw-companies for formulating the strategy of its sw-company is related to a lack of expertise, knowledge and interest at municipalities concerning implementing the SWA.

In conclusion, we may say that the impact of the managerial reform has been rather limited in our cases. If we see compliance with the national policy goals, this is often not because of a proper implementation of the ideational and managerial reforms, but because municipalities and sw-companies in local contexts more or less independently and coincidentally decide that a strategy aimed at regular work fits best in their situation, irrespective of the managerial relations between sw-companies and municipalities. So compliance or defiance is not the result of deliberate response to national policy changes, but of local decision-making by actors that had, and still have, a large amount of autonomy.

Notes

1 Since 1 January 2015 the SWA is 'closed'. Disabled people who need support to find a job can since then make use of the 'Participation Act'. Disabled people who had a permanent contract in the SWA before 31 December 2014 can still make use of the facilities of the SWA and be employed by the Act until their pension (Rijksoverheid, 2015). In this book chapter we will only focus on the SWA.
2 The average percentage in the Netherlands was 29%.

References

Aa, P. van der, Benda, L., van Berkel, R., Fenger, M., Qaran, W., (2015): *In-depth Analysis of Policy Innovations Country Report the Netherlands*, Rotterdam: INSPIRES.

Bardach, E. (1977): The Implementation Game: What Happens After a Bill Becomes a Law, Cambridge, MA: MIT Press.

Barnes, C., Mercer, G. (2005): 'Disability, work and welfare: Challenging the social exclusion of disabled people', *Work, Employment and Society* 19(3): 527–545.

Binnenlands Bestuur. (2011): *Cedris: 'bezuinigingen staan ambities in de weg'*. [www.binnenlandsbestuur.nl/sociaal/nieuws/cedris-bezuinigingen-staan-ambities-in-de-weg.832494.lynkx], 11 July 2017.

Dunveavy, P., Hood, C. (1994): 'From Old Public Administration to New Public Management', Public Money and Management, 14(3): 9–16.

Eerste Kamer. (2007): Wijziging van de Wet sociale werkvoorziening in verband met een betere realisering van de met die wet beoogde doelen. Memorie van antwoord, Kamerstuk 30673 nr. D. [https://zoek.officielebekendmakingen.nl/dossier/30673/kst-20072008-30673-D?resultIndex=6&sorttype=1&sortorder=4]

Fenger, M., Steen, M. van der, Groeneveld, S. M., Torre, E. J. van der, Wal, M. de, Frissen, P., Bekkers, V. J. J. M. (2011): Sociaal Beleid en Legitimiteit [Social Policy and Legitimacy], Nijmegen: VOC Uitgevers.

Fenger, M., Steen, M. van der, Torre, L. van der. (2013): The Responsiveness of Social Policies in Europe. The Netherlands in Comparative Perspective, Bristol: Policy Press.

Grint, K. (1998): The Sociology of Work, Cambridge: Polity Press.

Hill, M., Hupe, P. (2014): Implementing Public Policy. An Introduction to the Study of Operational Governance, London: Sage.

Kettl, D. (2000): 'Public administration at the millennium: The state of the field', Journal of Public Administration Research and Theory: J-PART, 10(1): 7–34.

Mazmanian, D., Sabatier, P. (1989): *Implementation and Public Policy*, Lanham: University Press of America.

Oliver, M., Barnes, C. (2010): 'Disability studies, disabled people and the struggle for inclusion', British Journal of Sociology of Education, 31(5): 547–650.

Organisation for Economic Co-operation and Development (OECD). (2003): Transforming Disability into Ability. Policies to Promote Work and Income Security for Disabled People, Paris: OECD.

Organisation for Economic Co-operation and Development (OECD). (2008): Sickness, Disability and Work: Breaking the Barriers. Vol. 3: Denmark, Finland and The Netherlands, Paris: OECD.

Pollitt, C. (2003): 'Public management reform: Reliable knowledge and international experience', OECD Journal on Budgeting, 3(3): 121–136.

Pressman, J., Wildavsky, A. (1973): Implementation, Berkeley, CA: University of California Press.

Raad voor Werk en Inkomen. (2006): Buitenkans. Aanbevelingen om meer Wsw'ers in een reguliere werkomgeving te brengen, Den Haag: Raad voor Werk en Inkomen.

Rijksoverheid. (2015): *Sociale Werkvoorziening*. [www.rijksoverheid.nl/onderwerpen/werken-met-arbeidsbeperking/sociale-werkvoorziening-vanaf-2015], 12 July 2017.

Santen, P. van, Oploo, M., Engelen, M. (2013): Wsw statistiek 2012, Zoetermeer: Research voor beleid.

Simons, E. (2009): Hoe werkt een SW-bedrijf?, *OSB Today*, June 2009.

Torre, L. van der, Fenger, M. (2014): 'Policy innovations for including disabled people in the labour market: A study of innovative practices of Dutch sheltered work companies', International Social Security Review, 67(2): 67–84.

Torre, L. van der. (2016): Sociale werkvoorziening tussen overheid, markt en samenleving. Een studie naar de achtergronden, praktijken en resultaten van de strategieën van hybride organisaties, Delft: Eburon.

Visier, L. (1998): 'Sheltered employment for persons with disabilities', International Labour Review, 137(3): 347–365.
VNG. (2006): De WSW in beweging. Een uitgave van de Vereniging van Nederlandse Gemeenten in het kader van de modernisering van de Wet Sociale Werkvoorziening, VNG: Den Haag.
Vrie, N. van de (2008): Modernisering van de Wet sociale werkvoorziening, Deventer: Kluwer.
White, H. (1985): 'Agency as control', in: Pratt, J., Zeckhauser, R. (eds.), Principals and Agents: The Structure of Business, 187–212, Boston: Harvard Business School Press.

Index

Accountability 59, 76, 92, **96**, 109, 186, 209–213
Accounting 35, 58–63, 68–69, 108, 209, 227
Activation 55–63, 98–99, 148–150, 183–185, 193–196, 215–216
Activation policies 55–56, 94, 98, 184–185, 192–195
Actor perspective 83, 88

Blame avoidance 40
Bureaucracy 27, 36, 59–63, 96–97, 108–109, 150–151, 183, 210

Casualised 205, 215
Choice 55, 93, 99, 104, 184, 224–226
Collective mobilization 165
Commercial 206, 214–215
Commodity 28, 152–159
Competitive 110, 114, 128, 155, 207, 213
Consumer 28, 97, 118, 188
Culture; Cognitive 226; Corporate 116, 156; Organisational 166; Professional 48–49

De-professionalism 239
Disability insurance 148
Discipline 28, 57, 59–63
Discretionary power 85–86, 94
Discursive modernisation 159
Dutch social policies; Dutch sheltered work policies 243; Dutch sheltered work act 246; social policies 249

Economics of convention 149
Education **17–18**, 79, 98, *116, 120–121*, 118–120, 130, 166, 193, 203

Employability 38, 46, 68, 104, 158, 207, 215–216
Employer orientation 151, 158
Employment policies 243

France 35–38, 242

Gendered labour struggles 164
Germany 37, 54, 62, 130–132
Governance 75–76, 82–86, 93, 97, 100, 150, 204–207, 210
Government 13–16, 36–37, 49, 57–59, 93–98, 108, 183–191, 206, 225, 243–247

Health professions 74
Healthcare reforms 131

Ideology 59, 168, 203–204
Individualised 22, 59, 64, 187, 214, 217
Inequalities 80, 166, 207
Information and communication technologies (ICTs) 13, *25, 29–30, 96, 102*
Integration 19–22, *25*, 60–63, 84, 147, 226, 246
Ireland 203
Italy 183–185

League Tables 109, 114, 211–213

Management 13, *25*, 35, 65, 74, 92, 107, **113**, 157, 173–176, 185–197, 203, 225
Managerialism 13–15, 31, 55, 74–77, 107, 166, 177–179, 187, 203–205
Market imagery 148–149, 159–160

Medical technocracies 75–77
Midwives 164
Moral entrepreneur 152
Multi-professional teamwork 81–87

Neo-institutionalism 51, 88
Neoliberal capitalism 203
Netherlands, The 242
New institutionalism 227
New Managerialism 203
New Public Management (NPM) 14–16, 35–36, 55, 100, 109, 128, 150, 166, 182, 239, 248–249

Occupational integration 147–158
Operator/user relationship 188
Organisation 42–47, 54, 74, 95–98, 108–114, 131–136, 148–149, 166, 186–191, 204–205, 251–252
Organisation studies 75, 129
orientation framework 133–141

Performance 15, 21, 35, 205–217, 59, 68–69, 76, 82–82, 92, **96**
Performativity 211–217
Placement professional 54
Policy implementation 182, 212
Political 15, 35–37, 45–51, 93–**101**, 107, 128, 148–152, 166
Politicisation of caring 164
Portugal 74–78
Principal agent 249–256
Professional identity 167, 223
Professional knowledge base 174–179
Professionalism 15, 23–*30*, 74–75, 83–88, 99–102, 164, 184, 217, 244, 236–239
Professions theory 74–75, 81–86
Proletarianisation 165–175

Public employment service 51, 54, 151, 185
Public institutions 54, 166

Ranking 47, 213–214, 226
Rationalisation 16, *25*, *29*, *30*, 43, 186
Resistance 23, 49, 165–168, 191, 208–214

Self-managing teams 21
Shared lifeworld perspective 18
Sheltered employment 154, 244, **245**, *246*, **251**
Sheltered work company 252
Social inclusion 114, 152, 159, 216, 248–235
Social worker 82, 94–102, 132–138, 141, 151, 165, 191–192
Strategic violence 227–238
Street-level bureaucracy 109, 183
Subjectification 56–63, 129
Surveillance 20–21, 204–208, 217
Sweden 164, 224, 242
Switzerland 147

Top-down and bottom-up pressures 183, 195
Trade unions 212

Unions 111, 123, 171–177, 210–215

Values 36, 45, 58–59, 77, 95, 123, 130–139, 159, 167–170, 184–187, 204–215, 243

Welfare bureaucracy 96, 150
Welfare professional work 165
Work illness 227–234